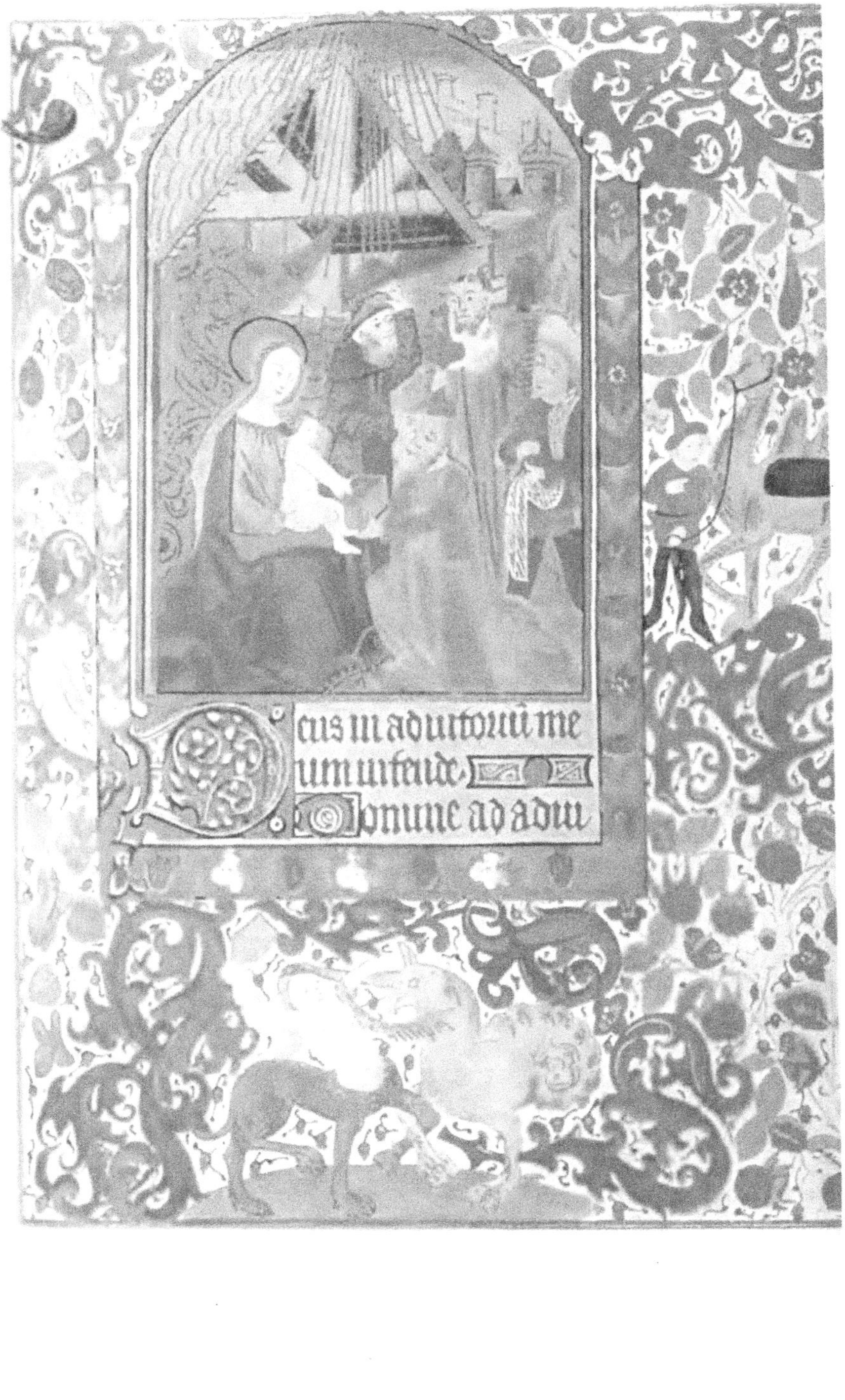
eus in adiutoriu me
um intende
omine ad adiu

THE DELPHIAN COURSE

A SYSTEMATIC PLAN OF EDUCATION, EMBRACING THE WORLD'S PROGRESS AND DEVELOPMENT OF THE LIBERAL ARTS

COUNCIL OF REVIEW

Very Rev. J. K. Brennan	Missouri
Cecil Guthrie, M.A.	University of Minnesota
Chas. H. Caffin	New York
James A. Craig, M.A., B.D., Ph.D.	University of Michigan
Mrs. Sarah Platt Decker	Colorado
Alcée Fortier, D.Lt.	Tulane University
Roswell Field	Chicago
Bruce C. Kingsley	Royal College of Organists, England
R. D. Luckenbill, A.B., Ph.D.	University of Chicago
Kenneth McKenzie, Ph.D.	Yale University
Frank B. Marsh, Ph.D.	University of Texas
Dr. Hamilton Wright Mabie	New York
W. A. Merrill, Ph.D., L.H.D.	University of California
T. M. Parrott, Ph.D.	Princeton University
Grant Showerman, Ph.D.	University of Wisconsin
H. C. Tolman, Ph.D., D.D.	Vanderbilt University
L. E. Wing, M.A.	Michigan

VOL. I

THE DELPHIAN SOCIETY

Land of Pyramids, Babylonia and Her Neighbors
Delphian Reading Course
Part One
Plus Study Guide

Copyright ● 2017 by Libraries of Hope, Inc. All rights reserved. No part of this publication may be reproduced, stored in a retrieval system, or transmitted in any form or by any means, electronic, mechanical, photocopying, recording or otherwise, without prior written permission of the publisher. International rights and foreign translations available only through permission of the publisher.
Compiled from:

The Delphian Course, by The Delphian Society, Chicago: The Delphian Society, (1913).

Study Guide, by The Delphian Society, Chicago; The Delphian Society, (1911).

Cover image: The Finding of Moses, by Sir Lawrence Alma-Tadema, (1904). From Wikimedia Commons, the free media repository

Libraries of Hope, Inc.
Appomattox, Virginia 24522

Website www.librariesofhope.com
Email support@librariesofhope.com

Printed in the United States of America.

Original Copyright

COPYRIGHT 1913
BY
THE DELPHIAN SOCIETY
CHICAGO
REVISED 1916
REVISED 1919
REVISED 1922

TABLE OF CONTENTS
PART I.

PAGE

The Delphian Movement...VI
Prehistoric Man; Customs and Occupations. Dawn of Civilization...XII

EGYPT.

Prefatory Chapter... 13

CHAPTER I.
Its Antiquity; Story of Joseph, Physical Geography, Prehistoric Egypt 20

CHAPTER II.
Sources of Egyptian History; Herodotus' Account of Egypt......... 31

CHAPTER III.
Pyramid Age; Early Egyptian Kings; Construction of Pyramids..... 37

CHAPTER IV.
Age of Darkness; Middle Empire; Reigns of Amenemhet I. and III.; Description of Labyrinth 43

CHAPTER V.
Egypt under the Shepherd Kings; Beginning of the New Empire; Conquests of Thutmose I... 51

CHAPTER VI.
First Egyptian Queen; Temple of Hatshepsut; Expedition to Punt 57

CHAPTER VII.
Military Kings; Hymn of Victory; Worship of the Solar Disk; Temple of Karnak 64

CHAPTER VIII.
Nineteenth Dynasty; Egypt under Ramses the Great; Twentieth Dynasty; Priest Rule; Ethiopian Kings 72

CHAPTER IX.
Social Life in Egypt; Houses, Dress, Family Life.................... 85

CHAPTER X.
Sports and Recreations.. 96

CHAPTER XI.
Agriculture and Cattle Raising; Arts and Crafts; Egyptian Markets; Military Affairs 100

I

TABLE OF CONTENTS—PART I.

Chapter XII.
Schools and Education; Egyptian Literature 112

Chapter XIII.
Religion of Ancient Egypt; Hymn to the Nile; Egyptian Temples and Ceremonies 119

Chapter XIV.
Art and Decoration 133

Chapter XV.
Tombs and Burial Customs 138

Chapter XVI.
Excavations in Egypt; Discoveries of W. M. Flinders Petrie 144

Descriptions of Egypt.

Description of the Nile 153
Feast of Neith 155
Karnak 159
Memphis 161
Hymn to the God Ra 163

Egyptian Literature.

An Old Kingdom Book of Proverbs 164
The Voyage of the Soul 168
The Adventures of the Exile Sanehat 171
The Song of the Harper 179

Present Day Egypt.

Alexandria 181
Cairo 182
Egyptian Museum 185
Suez Canal 187

BABYLONIA AND ASSYRIA.

Prefatory Chapter 193

Chapter I.
Early Civilization of Asia; Recovery of Forgotten Cities 201

Chapter II.
Sources of Babylonian and Assyrian History; Physical Geography ... 211

Chapter III.
Prehistoric Chaldea; Charms and Talismans; Semitic Invasion 218

Chapter IV.
City-States Before the Rise of Babylon; Hymn to the Moon-God 227

Chapter V.
Dominance of Babylon 232

TABLE OF CONTENTS—PART I.

Chapter VI.
Beginnings of Assyrian Empire; Conquest of Asshurnatsirpal........ 237

Chapter VII.
Assyria a Powerful Empire; Hebrew Account of the War with Assyria 245

Chapter VIII.
Last Years of Assyrian Dominance................................. 256

Chapter IX.
Chaldean Empire in Babylonia..................................... 264

Chapter X.
Social Life in Mesopotamia. The Babylonian and Assyrian Compared; Their Houses and Family Life................................ 270

Chapter XI.
Morality of the Ancient Babylonians............................... 276

Chapter XII.
Literature and Learning; Deluge Story............................. 283

Chapter XIII.
Clothing Worn by Assyrians and Babylonians; Their Food......... 293

Chapter XIV.
Architecture and Decoration....................................... 300

Chapter XV.
Religious Customs   307

Chapter XVI.
The Laboring Classes; Professions................................. 317

Chapter XVII.
The Medes   328

Chapter XVIII.
Condition of Persia Before the Age of Cyrus; Cyrus the Great and the Persian Empire 332

Chapter XIX.
War with Greece   340

Chapter XX.
Manners and Customs of the Persians; Their Religion............. 346

Chapter XXI.
Contributions of Babylonia, Assyria and Persia to Modern Civilization 357

TABLE OF CONTENTS—PART I.

Assyrian Literature.

	PAGE
Chaldean Account of the Deluge	361
Descent of Ishtar to Hades	367
Gyges and Assurbanipal	371a
Purity	371c
Zoroaster's Prayer	371d

THE HEBREWS AND THEIR NEIGHBORS.

Chapter I.
Syria 372

Chapter II.
The Land of Phoenicia; Reign of Hiram; Invasion of Asshurbanipal 378

Chapter III.
Phoenician Colonies and Commerce 390

Chapter IV.
Occupations and Industries; Literature and Learning; Religion 399

Chapter V.
Physical Geography of Palestine; Climate and Productivity 408

Chapter VI.
Effects of Geographical Conditions upon the Hebrews 418

Chapter VII.
Sources of Hebrew History 426

Chapter VIII.
Condition of the Hebrews Prior to Their Occupation of Canaan 434

Chapter IX.
Era of the Judges 441

Chapter X.
Morality of the Early Hebrews 448

Chapter XI.
Causes Leading to the Establishment of the Kingdom. David's Lament; His Reign. Solomon Rules; King Solomon and the Bees 453

Chapter XII.
After the Division of the Kingdom; End of Israel 469
Description of Illustrations 483

STUDY GUIDE 485

FULL PAGE ILLUSTRATIONS

PART I.

	PAGE
ILLUMINATED MISSAL	Frontispiece
DISTANT VIEW OF THE PYRAMIDS	44
NEAR VIEW OF PYRAMIDS AND SPHINX	68
TOURISTS SCALING THE GREAT PYRAMID	92
COLUMN AND PYLON OF KARNAK	124
BEAUTIFUL ISLAND OF PHILÆ	148
WINDOWS OF A HAREM	172
SHIP OF THE DESERT (Photogravure)	192
WINGED LION	236
MUSICIANS AND ATTENDANTS IN THE GARDEN OF ASSHURBANIPAL	284
SWORD-MAKER OF DAMASCUS	348
THE RIVER JORDAN	392
JAPPA HARBOR	432
ROSES OF SHARON	464
MAP OF ANCIENT EGYPT	VI

THE DELPHIAN MOVEMENT

TWO THOUSAND years before the sight of a new world burst upon the view of the Genoese mariner, there existed in north-central Greece a sanctuary famous in three continents. Located in mountainous Phocis, in a natural amphitheater, overhung by frowning rocks and reached only through mysterious caves, was the Oracle of Delphi. Here in remote times Apollo was believed to reveal his wishes to men through the medium of a priestess, speaking under the influence of vaporous breath which rose from a yawning fissure. Her utterances were not always coherent and were interpreted to those seeking guidance by Apollo's priests.

As its fame spread, the number of visitors to Delphi increased. More priests were needed to counsel and advise. Although the first blind faith in earlier deities lessened, the prestige of Delphi was nevertheless preserved. Apollo's priests became better versed in the affairs of Greece and the surrounding countries; their assistants became familiar with all vital issues, and thus intelligent replies were given to unceasing inquiries. In time the Greek divinities were almost forgotten and Christianity became the state religion, yet the Oracle of Delphi continued to draw men unto it until the fifth Christian century.

Ancient writers have left us abundant accounts of journeyings made thither by potentates and kings, and have described at length the rich offerings left by them in gratitude. The humble were seldom mentioned by early writers and it remained for the last few years to bring to light little leaden tablets—valueless from the standpoint of plunderers, earth-covered and revealed only by the excavator's spade—silent testimonials of appeals made to the oracle by the common people.

Perhaps at first thought we find the influence which the Delphian oracle exerted for more than a thousand years throughout Greece unaccountable, but upon reflection we perceive that it held its power because it was the best answer that epoch could give to man's eternal need for greater wisdom than his individual experience can provide. It may fittingly be compared to the influence of the Church in the Middle Ages. To it were referred alike questions of international policy, and the private affairs of humble citizens.

There is no doubt but that implicit faith directed the first visitors to Delphi, and beyond question this faith to some extent survived. The peasant accepted *literally* the presence of deity, but there have been in all ages the discerning who have distinguished between the symbol and that symbolized, and certainly the keen, alert Greeks did not remain blind adherents of antiquated conceptions. The wisdom of the Delphian priests was revered and their judgments accepted much in the same way as were those of the seers who taught the children of Israel at the city gates, so that the Oracle of Delphi still remained potent—a name with which to conjure—long after the belief that the deity himself was present had given place to another.

Today, the number who ask "Whence cometh wisdom, and where is the place of understanding?" is more than all who ever sought the offices of the priestess on her tripod. We have learned that not gaseous exhalations, but a thorough understanding of the past, will reveal the secrets of the future, and that these "oracles" are best interpreted by thoughtful groups, instead of by one frenzied prophetess. The name Delphian was chosen for this national educational movement because we too are seekers for wisdom, and we would not lose the spell of the storied past, as we renew the age-old quest.

Each new decade brings new needs, and the conditions of fifty years ago were wholly different from those confronting us today. Ours is an age characterized by intensity, strenuous effort and tireless exertion. Leisure seems to have disappeared from our national life and to be remembered only when reviewing pleasant stories of other times. Educators complain that we are neglecting the wisdom of the past—that the enduring thoughts of men as preserved to us in their writings have ceased to be familiar. The thoughtful deplore the loss of culture, courtesy and old-time chivalry. Frequently the critics fail to look beneath the surface for reasons leading to the very evident result. The truth is that in no previous age have the hearts of people been more sensitive to injustice, more united for fair dealing between man and man, more eager for the best the world can offer. It is only that the cultural methods which served in the past are unsuited to our machine-driven civilization. Of course time will adjust this, but we who are living in the transition period must meet modern conditions with modern methods.

At present people accumulate fine libraries and rarely read them; for their shelves they seek the best—for their diversion the lightest and most transient literature. Few are there who do not dream of a happy time when it shall be their delight to browse among their books and find companionship in them. Still the years fly by relentlessly and many who are not mere theorists are sounding a warning: This time so fondly anticipated will never come to many of the present generation; seize today; snatch a brief moment for the consideration of enduring thoughts; do not merely provide for the temporal wants and leave the soul famishing. Dr. Eliot, late president of Harvard, in repeated lectures and addresses has voiced this crying need.

"From the total training during childhood there should result in the child a taste for interesting and improving reading, which should direct and inspire its subsequent intellectual life. That schooling which results in this taste for good reading, however unsystematic or eccentric the schooling may have been, has achieved a main end of elementary education; and that schooling which does not result in implanting this permanent taste has failed. Guided and animated by this impulse to acquire knowledge, and exercise his imagination through reading, the individual will continue to educate himself all through life. Without that deep-rooted impulsion he will soon cease to draw on the accumulated wisdom of the past and the new resources of the present, and, as he grows older, he will live in a mental atmosphere which is always growing thinner and emptier. Do we not all know many people who seem to live in a mental vacuum—to whom, indeed, we have great difficulty in attributing immortality, because they apparently have so little life except that of the body? *Fifteen minutes a day of good reading would have given any one of this multitude a really human life.*"[1]

To meet this condition, which prevails throughout the length and breadth of our land, to stimulate a deeper interest, quicken a latent appreciation and facilitate the use of brief periods of freedom for self-improvement, the Delphian Society was organized and the Delphian plan of education mapped out.

Believing that only a comprehensive course could meet the requirements of the day and prove acceptable to a large number of people, the Delphian Society has included those subjects which are now offered in the curriculums of our leading colleges and universities—history, literature, philosophy, poetry, fiction, drama, art, ethics, music. Mathematics, being in its higher forms essential to few, has been omitted; languages, requiring the aid of a teacher, and such sciences as make laboratories necessary, are not included. None of these subjects possesses purely cultural qualities. Technical information has no place whatever in such a scheme. The branches of human interest which remain are those of vital importance to everyone.

Not only is the list of subjects widely inclusive, but the method of treatment has been carefully considered. Finding the beginnings of most modern activities in antiquity, the Delphian Course presents the gradual unfoldment of each subject from earliest times to our own. The distance between an imitation of the hunt, as found among the diversions of primitive people, and a modern play is great, and yet no complete idea of the latter can be acquired without some conception of dramatic origins. The crude picture drawn upon the sooty hide which formed a hut in early times and the crowning masterpiece of a Raphael present extremes, and yet he who would follow the gradual growth of painting realizes that each has its place in the progress of art. Only in comparatively recent times has the value of each link which forms the long chain of development been understood. No amount of heterogeneous reading can compare with the

[1] Eliot: Educational Reform.

systematic tracing of one subject from its early manifestations to its present forms.

Correlation of topics presents wonderful possibilities. If we become interested, for example, in society as portrayed in the earliest English novels, how much more shall we then appreciate the canvases of Hogarth, which depict the same social conditions. If the age of idealism in literature be under consideration, the productions of contemporaneous artists grow to have for us a new significance.

It is a mistake to imagine that relaxation and diversion are obtainable only from reading matter of the day. Oscar Kuhms calls attention to the fact that "to spend hours over illustrated magazines, Sunday newspapers, and the majority of popular novels, has very little to do with the art of reading in its larger sense." To a far greater extent than is generally imagined, the inordinate reading of magazines accounts for the host of superficial readers of our generation. To see how temporary is their interest one needs only to examine journals three or four years old.

The pleasures of travel may be greatly enhanced by definite knowledge of countries visited—their recorded past, the manner of life of those who dwelt within them and those now populating them; ruins, old temples, surviving art, make slight appeal to those wholly unfamiliar with the ages that produced them. The enjoyment of a play is more poignant for the one who has in mind the changes which plays and playhouses have witnessed. There is something impressive in the thought that for ages audiences have been thus held spellbound. Four centuries before the Christian era imposing dramas and keenly satirical comedies were given before larger assemblies than modern theatres could accommodate. Only in modern times has a curtain separated the players and spectators. Formerly the favored sat upon the stage itself; in the Elizabethan playhouse the majority stood throughout an entire performance. Sentences in Shakespeare's plays are meaningless without taking these facts into account. Some extended acquaintance with pictures would put an end to comments made not infrequently by critics that the spectacle of groups of people today in attendance upon an art exhibit supplies an astonishing sight. The majority—

so it has been stated—find a number in their catalogues, search frantically about for a picture so designated, and when they discover it, sigh with satisfaction and begin the search for another—"for all the world as though they were indulging in a simple hunting game!" Why Raphael painted so many Madonnas, why Watteau seems to have known only the gay and carefree—these are simple questions which many might find perplexing to explain adequately.

The traveler whose time in a foreign land is limited does not seek the commonplace and unattractive; he does not try to compass all a city might have to show in the brief period he can spend there; rather, he obtains the guidance of those more familiar with the locality, and gives his attention to the best it has to offer. So if our time for reading and self-improvement must be brief, we shall find small satisfaction in wasting it blindly searching for what may satisfy. Educators are usually less pressed by insidious cares and more free to give their devotion to favorite subjects.

Finally, let us remember that we are not reading chiefly for information. We read to develop our insight into the mystery of life; to gain an individual viewpoint; to establish our standards of conduct and modify our standard of judgment. Reading which is mere diversion can never bestow this power. It is for this reason the Delphian plan concentrates upon the knowledge whose value has been proved by time. This is the information which will provide the true perspective for the drama, the art, the literature and the history of our time. From the vantage point of familiarity with it, we can discern more clearly the merits of what is new, and best of all, we shall make the pleasing discovery that through ceasing to read only for diversion, all of our reading has become more diverting.

The Delphian chapter programs have been planned to bring about individual development through group activity. Through the group are gained, poise, practice in self-expression, and the broadened outlook of differing viewpoints. The ideal of the society is that each Delphian chapter shall be a means for broadening and deepening the interests of every member in all things which build up the community, in higher education, personal improvement and social progress.

PRIMITIVE DRAWING OF MAN.

PREHISTORIC MAN

THE word *prehistoric* means, literally, *before history begins,* and by prehistoric man we mean those human beings who lived upon the earth before records were kept. History, properly so called, does not begin until civilization is reached. The roaming of savage people over land in search of food has little or no importance for the student of history, although knowledge of a people in its savage state may throw some light upon its future development. While prehistoric ages are the concern of the archaeologist rather than the historian, we shall find that historic ages owe a great debt to prehistoric ages, and with this aspect of the matter the historian has deep interest.

The science of geology teaches us that the earth has not always possessed its present familiar appearance. On the contrary, countless years were consumed in molding it to its present shape, and even yet it is undergoing constant change. It is supposed that in the beginning all was a chaotic heap of Matter. In the words of a familiar story: "The earth was without form and void, and darkness was upon the face of the deep."

Whether the first cause of motion was direct Divine will or the working out of purely scientific law is not our province to determine here. Speaking in terms of geological record, the whole chaotic mass grew rounder and rounder, flattening slightly at the poles, or the ends of the axis. Gradually the surface of the mass cooled, and cooling, formed the earth's crust. Because it did not cool evenly, but shrunk to fit the still molten mass, this surface or crust was left with deep crevasses and higher ridges. This marked irregularity was further increased by mighty upheavals caused by pressure of heat from within. Thus were many of the mountains formed.

This process, so slightly indicated here, extended over a vast period of time. It is supposed that later, for a protracted period, rain fell. When the age of rain had passed, the deep depressions in the earth's surface were left filled with water—our present oceans and some of the seas. It would be impossible for us to review rapidly all the stages through which the earth passed in its making. Suffice it to say that conditions upon it were not always favorable to life as we know it. In course of long geological ages —perhaps millions and millions of years—forests of trees, plants, shrubs and flowers sprang up and covered the bare earth. Last of all, probably, *man* appeared. How all these things came about no one understands, but it is generally accepted that they occurred in an order similar to that just given. It would be useless for us to inquire into all the reasons that have led to these conclusions, but the most important one has been *evidences within the earth itself*.

Men who work deep down in mines know that as they descend lower and lower, the temperature rises, until there is a noticeable difference between the temperature at the entrance of a mine and at its lowest point. Moreover, not infrequently volcanoes pour forth streaming lava, smoke and fire accompanying the eruption. While such evidences lead to the conclusion that the temperature of its interior is very high, still there are many reasons for believing that the earth is a solid mass. From the examination of the various earth strata, their composition and the evidences each bears of the conditions under which it was formed, we learn of periods of rain, heat and cold prevailing. All these facts belong to the realm of geology however, and concern us here only as they have concerned the progress of mankind. These same earth layers or strata which preserve eloquent testimony regarding the earth's development, contain also remains of prehistoric men—men who lived in the far away time before records were made and of which the rocks alone give testimony.

Of the beginnings of the human race we know little. Many scientists, notably Darwin and his followers, have sought to show that man evolved from some lower animal life, in a way similar to that in which we find some plant or flower perfected from inferior origin. Whether the theory of man's evolution from some lower animal will ever be shown to be true the future alone can tell, even though the scholarly world today has generally accepted the evolutionary view of life and the world.

Buried within the earth along river-beds, around cliffs, in mounds and many other places, have been found remains of primitive man. While the beginnings of the human race, as has been said, are utterly unknown, the earliest stage of which we have knowledge has been called the Paleolithic Age,—the age of the River-drift Man.

Whether we accept the theory of man's evolution from the lower animal kingdom or not, we must admit that the earliest Paleolithic people of whom we have knowledge differed but little from the wild beasts. They lived in caves along rivers,—natural retreats where wild animals might have taken refuge. They lived on berries, roots, fish and such small game as they could kill by blows. They did not cook their food, but devoured raw meat much as did the wild beasts. They did not even bury their dead. From the stones accessible to them they selected their weapons, chipping them roughly. The crude weapons of this period have given it the name of the Rough Stone Age.

The Paleolithic man, or man of the Rough Stone age, did not try to tame the beasts he encountered. He stood in great fear of those with whose strength he was not able to combat. He feared especially strange beings like himself, and with his family dwelt apart from others so far as possible. He did not plant nor gather stores for the future; thus when food failed in his vicinity, he was obliged to roam on until he came upon a fresh supply of acorns, berries, roots and small animals. Any cave served for his dwelling. He protected himself from cold by a covering made from the skin of the beast he had slain. He had few belongings and these were scarcely valued, being easily replaced.

It is not difficult to see why the man of the Rough Stone Age preferred to live by the side of some river. In early times, before paths were worn through the forests, travel was easiest along the river bed. Food was more abundant here, for fish inhabited the streams and thither also animals came to drink, and in the reeds by the river's side, birds and wild fowl breeded. Morever, man was a timid creature and feared to venture far inland.

From all this we see that man in his primitive state gave

little promise of his future development. For how long a time he continued in this stage, we cannot estimate. Yet we find a decided improvement in the latter part of this Paleolithic Age, for fire and its uses became known. This brought about a wonderful change.

The man of the Paleolithic or Rough Stone Age was followed by the man of the Neolithic Age—the cliff dweller. He exchanged a home by the river for one higher up ; secure in some elevated cliff, the Neolithic man lived, away from molesting beasts. Again, the stone weapons were greatly improved. No longer were they rough ; on the contrary, they were now polished smooth. Ingenious from the beginning, man found that sharp edges of stone were more useful than blunt ones, that smooth handles were more convenient than irregular stones with no handles at all. For this reason, this period has been called the Smooth Stone Age. Other improvements no less momentous had been wrought. Food was now cooked, and as a result, man grew a little less ferocious. He had less fear of the wild beasts than before, and domesticated some of them. No longer was he wholly dependent upon such food as nature provided, for he had learned how to sow grain and gather it. He had learned how to fashion bowls and other receptacles of clay. He now buried his dead with weapons and other useful articles, proving that he believed that the dead still had need of such things. We must not, however, suppose that he believed in immortality, for the evidence shows that his conception of a hereafter was very vague. In most cases the care for and fear of the dead ceased a few years after their burial. Before the close of this period men had journeyed far from abject savagery.

Finally we come to the Metal—sometimes called the Bronze—Age. The discovery of metal proved the greatest boon, for now it was possible to make sharp tools and weapons. Hitherto the mere cutting down of a tree had taken a prodigious time. With a bronze ax, it could be quickly accomplished. Progress made rapid strides after this invaluable discovery. Nor this alone. Having learned to domesticate the beasts, men passed from a purely hunting into a pastoral stage. Sowing and reaping made it desirable and it became convenient to have a fixed habitation. Instead of dwelling apart, it proved safest to settle in hamlets or villages. In other words, man had become *civilized*, and with the dawn of civilization we find the dawn of history.

From this cursory view of the three important stages in prehistoric times, it is possible to derive mistaken notions. For example, there was never a time when stone was the only material available to man. Wood, ivory and shell were probably always known and frequently procurable. Neither is it to be supposed that each of these periods broke off abruptly or that they extended over all lands simultaneously. Quite on the contrary, stages in human development are never abrupt, and changes come about unnoticed. In nature results are slowly attained and there are no sharp distinctions between them. The three divisions of Rough and Smooth Stone and Metal Ages refer to conditions of progress—not to periods of time. The Egyptians had passed through all three stages before the dawn of history; the American Indians were in the Smooth Stone Age when Columbus discovered America; and in Central Australia there are tribes today just emerging from the Smooth Stone period. The rapidity with which a tribe passes from one to another of these stages depends upon the natural conditions of the country, contact with outside peoples and many other factors.

When written records enable us to weigh the true and the false, to sift out fact from fiction and legend from verified event, several nations had come into possession of a very fair degree of civilization. They had settled homes in towns and villages, recognized some form of government, understood the uses of fire, planted crops and garnered them, spun, wove and made pottery; they had attained considerable skill in the working of metals, had domestic animals and cultivated plants; they possessed a spoken, and sometimes a written, language and had attained no little skill in decorative art. A rich legacy was this for historic ages. Surely there is interest for the historian in this remote time that lies clouded still by much uncertainty. Let us consider some of these more important attainments and try to see how naturally men grew to master them and how in obscure ages the human race travelled so far on the high road to progress.

Discovery of Fire.

We have already noted that there was a time when fire was unknown. How then could the Paleolithic man, thrown wholly upon his own observation and resources, come upon this discovery, which was to work such changes for the future? Only from his observance of natural phenomena. When storms swept over desert and plain, vivid lightning flashed, and occasionally some tree was struck by the bolt and flamed up, greatly to the astonishment and alarm of the unknowing mind. At other times, volcanic eruptions occurred, and dry leaves and forests caught on fire from flying cinders. In the natural course of events, men soon found that the warmth of burning wood was agreeable, that fire at night allowed them to keep watch over possible invaders—whether man or wild beasts—and that the interior of a tree's trunk could be more easily removed by burning than by laborious scraping out with stone implements. After man had tasted roast flesh, a desire for cooked food was probably developed. Such a valued possession as fire proved, needed to be carefully tended, and when it was exhausted, human ingenuity set to work to create it anew. It is not unlikely that sparks occasionally struck out from flint when it was being chipped into shape for a weapon or implement. Necessity and desire have always worked wonders, and primitive man learned shortly to produce the vital spark, both by friction and by drilling.

The art of fire-making once mastered, many innovations were consequent upon it. Some fixed habitation was necessary if the coals were to be kept covered from day to day, and from meal to meal. Cooked foods gradually took the place of raw ones; in cold weather the family grew to gather around the fire, where meals were prepared and warmth was to be found. When the family, clan or tribe removed to a new home, coals were carried to kindle the fire upon the new hearth. When men journeyed abroad in the night, they carried torches to guide them; when they labored at home, fire grew indispensable for baking their clay pottery, smelting their ore, and manifold purposes.

While fire became one of man's aids, it wrought a decided change in the position of woman. Before its discovery, man and woman had probably gone side by side, sharing alike dangers and hardships. With its acquisition, some one was required to stay to watch lest it go out, and thus was developed the fireside and the home. "The fire has made the home. We have heard much in these later days about woman's position. We are assured that she has not all her rights. Now, there can be little doubt that the primitive woman had all her rights. It is probable that she was as free as her husband to kill the wild beasts, catch fish, fight her savage neighbors, eat the raw meat which she tore by main strength from the carcass of the lately slain beast. The beginning of woman's slavery was the discovery of the fire. The value of fire known and the need of feeding it recognized, it became necessary that someone should stay by it to tend it. Notwithstanding the fact that woman had all her rights and was free to come and go as she would, it was still true that, on account of children and certain physical peculiarities, the woman was more naturally the one who would remain behind to care for the feeding of the flame. Before that, men and women wandered from place to place, thoughtless of the night. After that, a place was fixed to which man returned after the day's hunt. It was the beginning of the home."[1]

The House.

The man of the Paleolithic Age crept into any cave that offered shelter from the storm and molesting beasts. Such caves were plentiful along the river's bank. Here today, elsewhere tomorrow, little heed was given to the particular shelter in which he took refuge. With the possession of fire, a fixed home became desirable. Even so, caves still remain the homes of men for a long period of time.

The Neolithic man sought an abode farther away from the main highway—the river. In cliffs towering above the river bed—sometimes away from streams altogether, he scooped out a cave similar to the ones occupied by his ancestors. Thus in many countries remains are found of a race of cliff-dwellers. In ancient Greece, for example, have been found evidences of people living thus, and Indians in Mexico and Arizona three thousand years later were discovered in similar dwellings.

With a settled life, and cultivation of the soil, man frequently was forced to provide a home for himself. The material from which he made it depended upon the resources of the locality. In Egypt and Babylonia, sun-baked

---
[1] Starr: Some First Steps in Human Progress, p. 28.

mud huts afforded the simplest, least expensive structures, both in point of time and labor. Among pastoral tribes, tents formed of animal skins sewed together were easiest to provide. This was the usual shelter also of the American Indians and other hunting tribes. The Laplander found cakes of ice suited for his home, while man in the tropics quickly constructed a shelter from the huge palm leaves, available on every hand.

"Of all places for studying construction of huts, Africa is the very best. There one may see samples of everything that can be thought of in the way of circular houses; built of straw, sticks, leaves, matting ; of one room or of many ; large or small ; crude or wonderfully artistic and carefully made. They may be permanent constructions to be occupied for years or temporary shelter for a single night ; they may consist of frameworks made of light poles over which are thrown mats or sheets of various materials and which after using can be taken apart, packed away, and transported."[2]

From lightly built, temporary dwellings, it was but a short step to the more substantial, more enduring ones. Stone houses, dwellings made of timber and of brick, as the country afforded, replaced the earlier homes, and when written records bring the full light of knowledge upon the life of nations, in the matters of constructing dwelling places, several peoples had become proficient.

Food.

It would be difficult to discover any plant or animal life which had not served at some period for food. Primitive man knew nothing about harmful plants, and only by long experience did he learn to avoid such as worked him woe. No insect or animal is so repulsive but that it has been appropriated by the food-hunter in some age and country, and things today which we would refuse in time of distress were used as a matter of course by earlier people.

Nature supplied acorns, berries, roots, fruits, fish and plenty of game. All these articles were at first eaten in their native state. When fire became well known, cooked foods grew in favor. It is supposed that these were at first roasted. To suspend meat over a fire or make a large opening in the ground

[2] Starr; Some First Steps in Human Progress, p. 151.

cover the floor with stones, heat these very hot, then remove the fire and bake the food, these are the most primitive—as well, perhaps, as the most satisfactory—ways known to us. Boiling was probably a later method, and this was not done as we boil food today. Rather, stones were heated very hot and tossed into kettles of water. In this way the water was brought to a boiling point and the food cooked.

Cultivated Plants.

Before men learned to cultivate plants and to domesticate animals, subsistence was always an uncertain matter. They roamed about in one vicinity until nature could no longer supply their needs, then left the exhausted land to recover itself while new territory afforded means for satisfying hunger. After fire became such a potent factor, as we have seen, a fixed abode was desirable. It fell to the lot of women to stay and tend the hearth. Shut off from the long expeditions undertaken by men, they soon learned to make as much as possible of the space around about their homes. Sticks were sometimes placed around plants or bushes to protect them from the careless step until their fruits matured. Occasionally plants were dug up and replanted nearer the hut. The garden and grain field were but natural results of this spirit of husbanding the stores provided by mother earth.

While women were the first to domesticate plants in the simple way just indicated, not much came of it until men adopted the idea and carried it further. With sharp sticks they scratched the soil and with the help of animals they trod in the seeds. Irrigation was sometimes needed—as in Egypt—to insure good crops. Thus from slight beginnings developed the agriculture of the world. With reasonable labor and painstaking, the tiller of the soil could be sure of a living for himself and his family, and before historic records illumine the life of several nations, farming was well understood. Indeed it is safe to say that until very recent times methods followed by tillers of the soil in quite a number of countries advanced very little upon those of the prehistoric man.

It is interesting to trace the history of present day foods, grains, vegetables and fruits, with the attempt to ascertain where each was native. All have been greatly improved by cultivation and not alone our varieties, but even distinct fruits and plants have resulted from man's propagation. Often the original species have been vastly improved. For example, the potato was a native of Chili. Found there in the sixteenth century of our era, it was described as "watery, insipid, but with no bad taste when cooked." It is supposed that it was taken from some Spanish ship to Virginia, and in the latter part of the same century carried to Europe. Its cultivation has spread over many countries, and from a small, watery tuber it has been brought to large size, mealiness and taste agreeable to the palate. Even today it flourishes in its wild state in Chili and Peru.

The cabbage was once a weed, growing on rocks by the seashore. By man's care it has been developed to the vegetable widely used today; moreover, its blossom has been exaggerated until a wholly new vegetable in the form of the cauliflower is the result.

"When we visit a vegetable garden or see fresh, attractive fruits offered in market or inspect the wonders shown upon the tables of county fairs and agricultural shows, we seldom realize how truly they are all the work of man.

"One of the most wonderful illustrations of what man can do in changing nature is seen in the case of the peach. Some time, long ago, perhaps in Western Asia, grew a wild tree which bore fruits, at the center of which were the hardest of hard pits, containing the bitterest of kernels; over this hard stone was a thin layer of flesh—bitter, stringy, with almost no juice, and which, as it ripened, separated, exposing to view the contained seed; such was nature's gift. Man taking it found that it contained two parts which might by proper treatment be made of use for food—the thin external pulp and the bitter inner pit. He has improved both. Today we eat the luscious peaches with their thick, soft, richly-flavored juicy flesh—they are *one* product of man's patient ingenuity. Or we take the soft shelled almond with its sweet kernel; it is the old pit improved and changed by man: in the almond, as it is raised at present, we care nothing for the pulp and it has almost vanished. The peach and almond are the same in nature; the differences they now betray are due to man."[2]

[2]Starr: Some First Steps in Human Progress, p. 80.

Many of the grains were known and grown by prehistoric man. Millet, wheat and barley were known in earliest recorded times in Egypt; these grains were also cultivated before historic times. Oats and rye were early plant products. Corn was native to America and unknown to the antiquity of the Old World. Several of our vegetables, such as the radish, carrot, turnip, beet and onion, were early grown for food. The lemon, orange, fig and olive were all native to Asia. Many flowers are mentioned by early writers and they too were unquestionably carefully tended in remote times. It is a subject for pleasant investigation to find out where flowers, cultivated in some countries, grow wild in others.

Domestication of Animals.

Desiring to provide food for time of want, primitive man learned to keep a wounded animal instead of at once killing it. Quite naturally it might come about that such a creature would grow less wild and become a pet. To secure a supply of meat without exertion, enclosures were probably thrown around herds of goats, deer or sheep. Ingenious man soon seized upon these half tamed beasts to help him in his work. Their use being proven, he would not rest until he had tamed them to his hand. The dog was the first dumb friend of men, accompanying them upon the hunt and aiding in bringing game to bay. The oldest friend, the dog, has also proven the most faithful of the animal kingdom. When history dawned, the dog, cow, sheep, goat, donkey, and pig were already domesticated. The horse was less commonly known in remote times. All these animals were originally small and not to be compared with their present day descendants.

Dress in Prehistoric Times.

Among primitive people dress is invariably a simple matter. In warm countries little clothing is needed, and even in colder lands, ornaments are valued above mere protection from the elements. It has been well established that love of decoration has been a powerful factor with primitive tribes, and that to this passion the habit of wearing clothing can largely be traced. Skins of wild beasts were often used by early men as protection from the cold, but it will be remembered that the

Indians found by early discoverers in America were very scantily clad, although furs were available on every hand. Yet the Indian, who braved the winter's blast unclad, was eager to barter his all for glass beads, scarlet cloth, or little trinkets with which he could ornament himself. The habits of different tribes and peoples have differed considerably ; some have adopted clothing earlier than others ; some still go unclad. Generally speaking, we may note that during the hunting stage, if men have worn clothing except for ornamentation, it has been the skins of animals ; as spinning and weaving have become known, coarse, home-made stuffs have come into use. In Egypt, linens were early woven; in northern countries, woolen stuffs were made. Feathers, furs, fabrics woven of grasses or reeds, leaves, shells, teeth, tusks and metal ornaments have held varying favor for decorative purposes.

Art.

At first thought it seems surprising that art can be ultimately traced back to the self-ornamentation of the savage ; yet this is probably true. The earliest people of whom we know loved to paint their bodies ; the American Indians made ready for feast or war by painting their bodies in startling colors, and the tribes lowest today in the social scale—tribes of Central Australia—have a similar practice. Dark skinned tribes have frequently painted themselves with white ; fair skinned tribes with dark colors. The use of colors among primitive peoples is an interesting study, and it is significant to note that red has always been a favorite.

"Red—and particularly yellowish red—is the favorite color of the primitive as it is the favorite color of nearly all peoples. We need only observe our children to satisfy ourselves how little taste on this point has changed. In every box of water colors the saucer that contains the cinnabar red is the first one emptied ; and 'if a child expresses a particular liking for a color, it is nearly always a bright dazzling red. Even adults, notwithstanding the modern impoverishment and blunting of the color sense, still, as a rule, feel the charm of red.' It may be questioned whether the strong effect of red is called out by the direct impression of the color, or by certain associations. Many animals have a feeling for red similar to that of man. Every child knows that the sight of a red cloth drives oxen and turkeys into the most passionate excitement. As to the primitive peoples, one circumstance is here significant above all others. Red is the color of blood, and men see it, as a rule, precisely when their emotional excitement is greatest—in the heat of the chase and of the battle. In the second place, all the ideas that are associated with the use of the red color come strongly into play—recollections of the excitement of the dance and combat. Notwithstanding all these considerations, painting with red would hardly have been so generally diffused in the lowest stages of civilization if the red coloring material had not been everywhere so easily and so abundantly procurable. Probably the first red with which the primitive man painted himself was nothing else than the blood of the wild beast or the enemy he had slain. At present most of the decoration is done with a red ochre, which is very abundant nearly everywhere, and is commonly obtained through exchange by those tribes in whose territory it is wanting."[4]

The difficulty found in this means of decoration is that it is not lasting. However skillfully the savage covers himself with solid coloring or design, a short time only and his labor is effaced. To overcome this trouble, tattooing was devised. By this means the color was placed beneath the skin and thus not subject to change. Very elaborate patterns were sometimes worked out and the man so ornamented was far more attractive in the eyes of his fellowmen.

Next to the personal adornment of primitive peoples comes the decoration of their weapons and implements and the patterns in their handicrafts, such as basketry and mattings. Generally speaking those are in imitation of nature, and more, imitation of human and animal forms. Heretofore it has not been unusual to dismiss these as merely geometrical designs. Surely they were never such in the mind of the ancient worker. He copied things that he saw around him—copied them awkwardly no doubt, but nevertheless certainly. Some of these patterns we can recognize; others defy us. For example, the waving line has been interpreted to represent the course of the serpent;

[4] The Beginnings of Art, Grosse, p. 61.

the herring bone pattern originated as a copy of the feather. Sometimes the patterns copy the skin markings of some animal or serpent; sometimes they imitate the scales of a fish. Very seldom have these early artists attempted to copy plants or flowers. Sometimes the bone knife bears an excellent drawing of a bird or fish; occasionally the whole object has been given the form of some living creature, as, for example, bone needle cases have come to us which have the form of fish or birds. Shields, knives, bows and arrows, and weapons of whatever sort often bore some picture, more or less decorative. Such a picture upon an arrow enabled the savage to identify as his game some animal that died some distance from where it was wounded. Clubs and throw-sticks remain whereupon is scratched the picture of some familiar animal—a kangaroo, a snake, or a fish. But the pictures painted by primeval man were not limited to those which adorned their weapons and implements. The *hide* pictures, or pictures painted or scratched upon hides are very interesting. Generally the hide used for this purpose was a portion of the hut. During times when inclement weather forced the early tribesman to remain inside for shelter, it may be, merely for diversion he occupied himself by scratching some picture upon the soot-covered skin that formed his hut. A tooth or bit of flint furnished him with a tool. Or again, a piece of charcoal, snatched from the hearth, furnished him means of picturing some scene upon a fresh skin. Figures of men and animals, drawn in outline, make up the picture. Now a battle, now a hunting scene may be delineated. The Eskimo brings into his picture some of the round snow huts, with the animals which he hunts—bears, walruses, and the like. In detail and accuracy of outline the tribes still in the hunting stage greatly excel those which have developed into a settled farming people. Nor is this difficult to understand. The success of the hunter depends in no small degree upon his ability to follow the faint foot-prints of the game. He must be susceptible to many indications wholly unseen by the casual eye. The keen vision of the uncivilized hunter is well recognized. When he no longer needs this wonderful sight to accomplish his daily tasks, it disappears. For this reason we find a fidelity to nature in the pictures of the early hunting peoples which is missed in the productions of more highly developed peoples.

Finally we may gather these conclusions from the facts known of primitive art—or of art among primitive peoples. While no great masterpieces remain as models for future generations, it is among prehistoric men that art had its beginnings. Nor is it possible to sweep aside the art of this remote period, relegating it to the realm of the curious alone. Recent scholarly investigators in this field have reached far different conclusions, finding here the indications of man's artistic possibilities and the promise for the future.

"The agreement between the artistic works of the rudest and of the most cultivated peoples is not only in breadth but also in depth. Strange and inartistic as the primitive forms of art sometimes appear at the first sight, as soon as we examine them more closely, we find that they are formed according to the same laws as govern the highest creations of art.

The emotions represented in primitive art are narrow and rude, its materials are scanty, its forms are poor and coarse, but in its essential motives, means, and aims, the art of the earliest times is at one with the art of all times."[5]

Religion of Prehistoric Men.

It is naturally very difficult to trace the religious belief of the people of earliest times. Of their art, their dress, their food, their dwelling places, we may conjecture with some degree of accuracy because of the evidences they have left behind. But how shall we gain any worth-while knowledge of their ideas when they had no means of communicating them in indelible forms? We must judge of primitive man's thoughts by what he did. In the earliest times man did not bury his dead, but by the Smooth Stone Age there is such advance in this respect that it is probable the Neolithic man received his first glimmerings from his Paleolithic brother. He buried his dead with weapons and implements which he imagined would be as useful in the next world as they had proven during the earthly life.

It is impossible to state clearly without better evidence just what his imagination pictured for his dead friend or relative. The living man was dimly conscious of a Great Spirit, whose voice and temper were discernible to him in nature. To this Great Spirit he committed his dead friend.

[5] The Beginnings of Art, Grosse, p. 307.

It could not be said the living man had anything approaching a conscious faith in the unseen; he dimly felt a duality of existence. His friend had entered into this other part. It is not improbable that dreams helped to awaken in man this sense of dual existence. That "inner voice" which has forever prompted man seemed to tell him of another self. This "other self" very naturally seemed to tell him of an existence outside himself, and to this "outside spirit" he gave elementary veneration through the forces of nature this spirit appeared to employ.

The early man who had developed a religious sense, worshipped two different kinds of forces; the forces of nature, and his ancestors. The savage bowed down to the stick that tripped him in the forest. He could not understand how such a small object could possess power to throw him and since it apparently did possess it, he worshipped it. The sun brought light and warmth. By its presence man was benefited. Therefore, primeval man worshipped the sun.

Ancestor worship was inspired by quite different motives. If it were true that the dead lived on, then it must be possible for them to work one's weal or woe. If the dead were cared for and ministered unto, they would be appeased and would have no desire to bring trouble or misfortune upon the survivor.

The taboo held an important place in early religious beliefs and practices. A taboo is a prohibition laid upon some object or some performance, with the superstitious idea that injury will follow if the object be used or the performance done. Some of the tribes of Central Australia, today in the Smooth Stone stage of development, hold the idea that the meat of the emu may be eaten only by the elders of the tribe. For women, therefore, there is a taboo on this meat, and its use by them would be regarded as a great sacrilege. The early Hebrews had a similar taboo, recorded in the earliest set of commandments preserved by them. It was " Thou shalt not seethe the kid in its mother's milk." This does not mean one of many foolish meanings worked into it, but rather that the early Hebrews for some reason had placed this taboo on kid cooked in milk. The use of beans was similarly tabooed by Pythagoras and forbidden to his followers. A study of the taboo is interesting indeed.

The *totem* was important to the primitive man. A totem is an animal or species of animal from which a social circle derives its origin. One clan owed its being to a black hawk, another to an eagle, and so on. No one of a clan would kill its totem, or in other words, there was a taboo placed upon the totem. Of course this taboo affected only the one clan.

Early religion consisted for the most part in certain observances—not so much in formulated beliefs. To be sure, the primeval man believed that harm would overtake him if he failed to perform certain ceremonies, but it was the performance or the refraining from the performance that was important.

Among the earliest people associated into tribes there were distinct moral requirements. There were some people who were not to be killed, except upon due provocation, while to kill those of other tribes brought great glory. Again, it was not right to lie to those of one's own tribe, but to others one might lie at all times. "An eye for an eye, and a tooth for a tooth," was the primitive way of viewing injury, and yet when history sheds its light upon certain nations of antiquity, some of them had already come into the transition state, where damages might be given if satisfactory to the injured. The Babylonians afford an excellent example of this condition.

Conclusion.

Each individual passes through many of the stages through which the race has come. A child may pass in a week or a month through a stage covering centuries in the development of the race, but nevertheless he experiences it clearly for the time being. The savage personified everything around him. If he struck himself against a tree, he was angry with the tree that had hurt him, and he tried to hurt the tree in revenge. The child today falls against a chair and hits the chair that hurt him. Now just as the child by such experiences, scarcely noted by others, realized far less by himself, comes into the clear vision of manhood, so by similar experiences the whole race has come to its present development. We are too prone to smile at the conceptions of the primitive world, and, grown wise with the flight of centuries, cast aside the beliefs of early ages when men adjusted themselves to life. Let us reflect then upon the attainments of prehistoric man and attempt to fathom how great a debt historic peoples owe him. In view of his achievements, we must grant that by his efforts civilization was greatly aided. The stepping stones on which he rose from abject savagery to higher things stand out sharply in spite of absence of records and scant remains. The rough pioneering had been done, in a great measure, and not alone the rudiments of civilization but evidences of culture were plainly visible at the dawn of history, properly so-called.

ABORIGINAL ROCK-CARVINGS.

EGYPTIAN AFTERGLOW.

" 'Tis sunset hour on Egypt's arid plains,
    Each mighty pyramid, with purpling crest,
    Looms dark against the glory in the west.
Swiftly the heaven's beauty dies and wanes,
    Till sudden darkness its rich splendor stains.
      Then slowly, dawn-like, on the shadows rest
      Faint crimsons, violets, tint to tint soft pressed;
They brighten, glow, then fade and darkness reigns."

P. F. CAMP.

EGYPT

PREFATORY CHAPTER

THERE never was a time when men were so intensely interested in origins and development as they are today. Our biologists are studying life in all its forms, from the single cell to the highest mammal. Our psychologists are studying mind—what consciousness is; how attention, habit, memory are formed. Our physicists, not content with studying gravitation, heat, light, electricity, etc., are inquiring into the very nature of matter itself, and, together with the astronomers and geologists, are telling us not only how the earth, but also how the universe came to be. Our anthropologists, ethnologists and sociologists are just as actively and patiently inquiring into the origins of customs, institutions, law, religion, society. The historian is no longer content to rehearse a story because it is interesting; he insists upon getting at the original documents, at the facts in the case, not at theories. The savage, when asked why he observes a certain custom or performs some ceremony whose meaning he does not know, replies that his ancestors did the same. To inquire beyond this seems to him more than useless. Until the beginning of our modern scientific age the answer to similar questions among ourselves—as it still is among the Chinese, would have been, "it is written," "thus saith the Lord," "Aristotle, Plato or St. Augustine thought so and so about the matter." But today all is different. We are no longer content to know what is written, or what somebody thinks about a subject, we insist upon demonstrating or having some one demonstrate for us, the proposition put forward. We want the "facts." Our whole system of education encourages pupils to perform experiments and thus verify the statements they may find in their text-books on chemistry, physics and other subjects.

It is the inductive method which gives the pupil the facts and encourages him to draw his own conclusions.

But what has Egypt to offer the modern man? Does it interest any but specialists and archaeologists? Apparently it does, for every year sees an increase of tourists in the Nile valley. It is true many go there because of the ideal climate or because it has become the fashion to do so. But if we look at the matter more closely, do we not see other, deeper reasons? Is it not true that many go because in their youth they had read about the pyramids and the wonderful temples of Egypt, and because now when they have the opportunity they desire to see these for themselves? The architect, the engineer, the contractor, all are interested in these masses of masonry. Again, when we are beginning to reclaim the desert areas in our western states, Egypt with its system of irrigation, older than history, arouses a new interest. The fact is that in spite of our practical nature, as some would put it, or rather, as we prefer to have it, because of our intensely practical nature, we are beginning to feel the necessity of inquiring into the activities of other peoples, be they past or present, not only because such inquiry will satisfy our curiosity or enliven our dull moments, but because of the lasting benefit we derive from it. We insist upon knowing the people who have achieved, who have accomplished things, and surely the pyramids alone would demonstrate that the ancient Egyptians belonged to this class.

Man attained to civilization for the first time in the Nile valley. We study the natives of Australia and Africa for social origins. It is here we can gather most information about the primitive forms of marriage and the growth of the family; about the beginnings of dress and ornament; about primitive warfare, magic, religion and early forms of tribal government. Just as we pay special attention to the development of the mind of the child in the study of psychology, so we feel that the best way to study the complex features of our civilization is to observe the simpler life of the savage. But the child becomes a man while the savage has not yet developed a civilization before our eyes. The growth of the race is slow. It is only when we are able to observe a race through a period of thousands of years that it is possible to see it grow from infancy to manhood. We can follow our own ancestors from the time they had advanced little beyond the stage of savagery, but it is to be observed that they did not *develop* but *borrowed* their civilization. Of the beginnings of the Greeks and Romans, whose civilization our ancestors took over, we know but little, but in the case of the Egyptians matters are different. We are able, by means of archaeological, monumental and inscriptional remains to follow them as they developed in the Nile valley, unassisted by any outside civilization—for none existed, the world's first great civilized state.

"It may appear paradoxical to affirm that it is in arid districts, where agriculture is most arduous, that agriculture began; yet the affirmation is not to be gainsaid but rather supported by history, and is established beyond reasonable doubt by the evidence of desert organisms and organizations."[1] This lesson drawn from the life of the Papago Indians might just as well have been drawn from Egyptian life. Egypt is practically rainless, but the soil of the Nile valley, ever renewed by the silt deposited by the yearly inundation, yields enormous returns provided only man uses his energy and ingenuity. Long before our written records begin the Egyptians had developed an extensive system of irrigation. Thus by arduous toil, organized and watched over by the growing state, Egypt developed an enormous agricultural wealth—the foundation upon which her civilization was built. With Egypt it was not a question of the "conservation" but of the development of her natural resources. The Egyptian was forced to keep up a continuous struggle with nature and as a result he was always practical. Egypt has been called the mother of the mechanical arts. It is not surprising that the imaginative Greeks, when they became acquainted with the material civilization of Egypt, her pyramids and temples, her system of irrigation, her craftsmanship, conceived an exaggerated opinion of the wisdom of the Egyptians. Even today we hear surmises of "lost arts" which were used in the construction of the pyramids. But we know better. The pyramids were built by the brawn of tens of thousands of serfs, without the use, it would seem, of even a pulley; not even the roller seems to have been known. On the other hand, we have only to visit the museums here and abroad—especially

[1] W. J. McGee, "The Beginning of Agriculture," American Anthropologist, 8, 375.

the one in Cairo, to realize the marvellous skill the Egyptian workman acquired in the carving of wood, ivory and stone, and in the working of metals. Our architects are studying the products of the greatest geniuses Egyptian culture produced, and our students of design may learn many a lesson from the workmanship of her artisans.

Not long since it was not unusual to see ridicule heaped upon the theories of the "high-brows" by our farmers, manufacturers and other "practical" men. Probably our system of education *was* at fault. Nevertheless, these same farmers, manufacturers and other practical men are beginning to realize the importance of the researches and investigations of the specialists. We cannot hope to compete with the industries of the Germans which rest upon a scientific basis, as long as ours are conducted by "rule-of-thumb" methods. There is no better opportunity offered anywhere for observing the limitations of an exclusively practical system of education than the study of Egyptian learning.

The Egyptian regarded learning as a means to an end, and that end was never the increase of the sum of human knowledge or the advancement of humankind, but always freedom from manual labor. Next to a few folk songs, preserved in the decorations of Fifth Dynasty tombs—by mere accident, for a scribe would never have thought of preserving them, the oldest literature of the Egyptians which has come down to us consists of the precepts of Kagemni and Ptah-hotep.[1] This wisdom of the viziers of the Pharaohs of the Fourth and Fifth Dynasties, is similar to that of the books of instruction from all periods of Egyptian history, and consists largely of rules of conduct. The sole object of an education was to obtain a position as scribe or secretary of higher or lower rank in the government service, and this could only be done by gaining and keeping the favor of the Pharaoh or of one of his officials. These scribes never weary of telling of the superiority of their calling over that of the man who must labor with his hands, who is like a heavily laden ass driven by the scribes. Of course we too recognize the gulf fixed between the educated and the unlettered, but we try to bridge it. It is not probable that many of the laboring classes knew more than the barest elements of reading and

[1] See page 164.

writing. The Egyptian script was exceedingly cumbrous, and probably few would have seen any use in mastering it, even if they had had the time, unless they intended to enter upon a scribal career. Of course many such careers were open, for the elaborate bureaucratic system of administration demanded the services of a host of secretaries and overseers. In time these constituted a distinct middle class, largely recruited, we may be sure, from the laboring class below. The Egyptian was always ready to recognize and reward ability, no matter where it was found. Now a word about the limitations of such a view of education. As already indicated, the object of an education was to gain a government position. In Egypt, as elsewhere, the chief end of government, in the eyes of the officials at least, was the collection of revenues. Taxes were in kind and as a result the work of the scribe consisted in finding out the amount of the harvest and deducting the king's share. The extensive mining and building operations conducted by the Pharaohs required the services of hundreds of scribes and overseers to superintend the work and distribute the rations of the armies of workmen employed in these projects. In this work the scribe developed a remarkable facility with figures. But he never advanced beyond concrete examples. Multiplication and division in our sense of the terms were unknown to him, their places were taken by addition and subtraction. For example: to multiply seven by nine, the Egyptian scribe would proceed, $1 \cdot 7 \quad 7$, $2 \cdot 7 = 14$, $2 \cdot 14 = 28$, $2 \cdot 28 = 56$, etc. That is he always doubled the last figure. It was nothing but addition. He wrote his results as follows:

1	7
2	14
4	28
8	56
16	112

and then found which of the numbers of the first column added together would give the sum 9. These were 8 and 1. He then added the corresponding numbers in the second column and got the result, $56 + 7 = 63$. So $50 \div 7$ would have looked like this: $50 - 28 = 22$; $22 - 14 = 8$; $8 - 7 = 1$. The result was $(4 + 2 + 1)$ sevens with 1 as remainder. The

Egyptian scribe could not handle fractions other than those with one as numerator. Two-thirds was the only exception. The Egyptian knew that the area of a rectangle was to be found by multiplying the two adjacent sides together, and that the area of a right angled triangle was equal to half the area of a rectangle whose base and altitude were equal respectively to the sides adjacent to the right angle. When his problem was to find the area of an isosceles triangle he applied the same rule, that is, multiplied the base by one of the sides and divided by two. Here theory might have helped him, had he been able to develop it. He never reached the conception of base and altitude. His rule for finding the area of a circle is worth mentioning. He took the diameter, subtracted one-ninth of it therefrom, and squared the result. In a word, he had not come far from the correct value of π. But the Egyptian always dealt with concrete examples, he never was able to generalize and carry his mathematics into the theoretical. As a result he never attained scientific accuracy. Not that he did not set himself difficult problems. Indeed many of them are so complicated that they required an immense amount of reckoning, by his methods, to solve. Without giving his solution, let me add one more of his problems: "A man owns 7 cats; each cat eats 7 mice daily; each mouse eats 7 ears of grain; each ear contains 7 grains; each grain gives a sevenfold return in the harvest. What is the sum of the cats, mice, ears and grains?"

The Egyptians observed the stars. They had names for all of the principal constellations; knew the circumpolar stars from those which at times disappeared below the horizon, but they never seem to have noticed the difference between fixed stars and planets. They invented a calendar with a year of 365 days as early as 4241 B.C. This was based upon the heliacal rising of Sirius (Sothis) coincident with the beginning of the inundation. But they never discovered, or if they did, never bothered about the fact that their year was one-fourth of a day too short. They were deeply interested in medicine, and their recipes prescribe everything that can be swallowed. Many of these were borrowed by the Greeks and from them have come down into the folk-medicine of modern Europe. No doubt many of their remedies were helpful, but magic always played the most important rôle in their medicine, as it does among all primitive peoples and as it did in our own until the beginning of our modern scientific age.

The progress made by the Egyptians in the development of a purer conception of religion will be discussed at length in the body of this volume, especially on pages 131 and following. The Egyptians were not far from monotheism.

But the Egyptian culture must be studied as a whole. Time was when the study of the civilization of Egypt, Babylonia and Assyria, together with that of the Hebrews, was regarded as a sort of introduction to the study of history, which began with the Greeks and Romans. Much was said of the immovable East. It was supposed that progress was exceedingly slow there as compared with that in the West. But our wider knowledge of the history and life of these peoples shows how false this conception was. We can trace Egyptian civilization from its beginnings in the palaeolithic and neolithic ages; see it develop from many petty states into an absolute monarchy; follow it as it emerges after a period of anarchy into a Feudal Age, and as it rises after two centuries of foreign oppression into a mighty empire pushing its southern frontier away into Nubia and its northern one to the Euphrates. Meanwhile we are not neglecting to study the economic and intellectual forces at work. Society has been developing steadily. A monotheistic religion has been growing up. But Egypt has reached her zenith and the age of decline sets in. In time she falls before foreign invasion, because she has used up her vitality. Her civilization is not to be studied as a preliminary to anything else, but as the achievement of a gifted race. Of course we are to compare her progress with that of other peoples, to see the faults of, but also to appreciate the good in, her culture.

THE SPIRAL DECORATION OF SCARABS.

EGYPT.

CHAPTER I.

Its Antiquity.

AMONG Old Testament stories familiar throughout the Christian World, a general favorite with boys and girls from their earliest years is the story of Joseph—a seventeen year old lad, the son of his father's later life, and most loved of all his children. In Genesis we may read how his brothers became jealous of Joseph because of Jacob's care for him, and their anger increased when the boy related a dream wherein he had seen himself exalted to high position while his family and all the world did honor to him.

His people led a pastoral life, and when the dry season came, the older brothers went away with the flocks in search of fresh pastures. Soon the father grew anxious to hear from them, and sent Joseph to locate them and then return to tell him how they fared. After some searching, Joseph drew near the flocks and was seen afar by his brothers. They were now many miles from home, and what they might do was not likely to reach the ears of those who knew them. So they plotted to kill Joseph and ascribe the deed to some wild beast. Reuben, more compassionate, urged that they should not have this awful crime upon their hands, but suggested instead that they cast him into a pit, from which plight, we are told, Reuben intended to deliver him. The others yielded to his plea, and Joseph was cast into the pit. Shortly after, a caravan came in sight, passing on its way to Egypt. At once a surer way of disposing of Joseph suggested itself—they would sell him as a slave and free themselves from further responsibility in the matter. The company of merchantmen drew nearer, journeying with their spices and their wares. To them Joseph was sold, and with them he "went down into Egypt."

His varying fortune for the next few years is briefly told. Now we see him a trusted servant, given responsibility and acquitting himself with credit ; then upon false accusation, he is cast into prison, but even here he wins the confidence of his jailer. Here too, he establishes a fame for the interpretation of dreams, which ability is soon noised abroad. So widely did it become known that when the king's counsellors were unable to explain his repeated vision, from prison walls Joseph was summoned to reveal its hidden meaning. He thereupon foretold the seven years of plenty and the seven years of famine through which the land of Egypt would soon pass. The king, impressed with his wisdom and sincerity, chose him steward of the realm.

All know the outcome of the tale—how Joseph soon became second in importance to the king himself, trusted, depended upon and loved ; how he bought up the heavy yield of grain throughout the realm for seven years and hoarded it in "store cities," until he ceased to chronicle the amount, so vast it was. Then when the years of famine came, he sold again to those who would buy, and when their money was exhausted, he took their flocks, their lands and their slaves as security—yes, even the service of citizens was pledged to the king in exchange for food.

It was during these tedious years of want that Joseph learned of his family, when the same brothers who had done him so much injury came into Egypt to buy grain, and through his generosity they were united once more, and at his invitation brought their families to dwell near him. The king commanded that they be well provided for and they prospered and increased in number.

Years passed and Jacob died, and at last Joseph himself. Then we are told there came to the throne a king " who knew not Joseph. " He looked with dismay upon a foreign people growing up within his country, whose traditions, customs, and religious beliefs were wholly unlike those of his own nation. Then followed the years of oppression when he sought to exterminate the race with relentless work and cruel persecution. Within recent years. one of the "store cities," supposed by some scholars to have been built by the Hebrews during this period of their life in Egypt, has been unearthed—verifying the account of their bondage as preserved to us in the book of Genesis.

It is difficult for us to realize the vast antiquity of Egypt. When Joseph as a seventeen year old boy came with that band of merchantmen into its borders more years had passed over its civilization than have passed since Homer told his stories of gods and heroes to the Hellenes who gathered around to hear him. The three great pyramids had stood in their majestic calm under more moons than have risen and set since Christ was born in Bethlehem of Judea ; and the Sphinx had watched, for how many years men cannot tell. When we come to the land of Egypt, we are appalled by its age. America was discovered about five hundred years ago ; England has been inhabited for more than twenty hundred years, but Egypt counts its history back for thousands of years and loses itself in tradition and legendary periods preceding these. The story of Joseph, told in Genesis, the book of earliest Biblical tradition, records an incident early in the history of the Hebrews, but the Egyptians had already been governed by many ruling dynasties and had known the oppression of invading kings whom they had at last driven from the throne. They had built colossal structures which were to perpetuate the memories of their mighty kings as well as to provide their everlasting tombs, and these stand today the marvel of all who gaze upon their vast proportions. They had developed a complex religious system, and had reached some perfection in decorative art. Egypt had long been the granary of the civilized world and consequently of great importance from an economic standpoint. The Nile, that wonderful river which caused Herodotus to exclaim : " Egypt is the gift of the Nile ! "—a sentiment quoted ever since by all who have written about the country or the river—had cut down its river bed and had already built up a rich soil in the valley by its deposits, left by the overflow of countless seasons.

We look today upon the cathedrals of Europe, standing as they have since the Norman conquest, even, in some instances antedating it, and we exclaim that the builders of these impressive edifices built for ages to come. Yet in Egypt the pyramids have stood for almost five thousand years, and it is safe to say that they will proclaim to many millenniums more, the wealth and power of the Pharaohs who raised them for their everlasting abodes. Hundreds of years dwindle in the contemplation of thousands, and these are ever before the student of Egyptian history.

Physical Geography of Egypt.

Egypt is located in the northeastern corner of Africa. To the east lies the Isthmus of Suez—the pathway to Asia, and the Red Sea—separated by a range of mountains from the Valley of the Nile. To the south lies Nubia, and to the west stretches away for hundreds of weary miles the Sahara, the old bed of an extinct ocean.

Egypt is by no means the country it is sometimes represented to be on geographical maps. That Egypt someone has called a "geographical fiction." On the contrary, it has always consisted simply of the Nile valley and delta. It is about one-half as large again as the state of Massachusetts, containing approximately 12,000 square miles.

The Nile is unlike any river of our land. It takes its rise in a chain of lakes near the Equator. These lakes lie in a heavy rain belt and at a certain season the rainfall is so constant that the river is greatly swollen. It is joined by tributaries which in turn are overflowing with the melting snows of mountains wherein they take their rise, and altogether the main river continues so to increase that it overflows its channel and spreads out into the valley on either side.

In America we know how disastrous spring floods frequently become, but here the overflow is violent, tearing down bridges and embankments, bringing injury rather than benefit to the land. In Egypt the rise of the Nile is gradual; dwellings are built on elevations of land or on the outskirts of the valley.

Without the yearly inundation there would be no food to maintain the dense population of the country.

During the period of high water the Nile is heavily loaded with mud. When the river recedes, this fertile silt is left upon the surface of the land. This, and this alone, has made the land of Egypt different from the deserts on either side of it. And now we see how truly Herodotus spoke when he exclaimed that Egypt is the gift of the Nile. Containing about the same number of miles as our state of Maryland, for numberless years this little country has been the granary for surrounding lands. Thus may we judge of its remarkable fertility.

Much of the loam which the river has brought down has been spread over the valley, but a considerable amount has been emptied each year at the mouth of the stream, forming in course of time a *delta*,—so called by the Greeks from its resemblance to their letter *delta*. Because of its long threading valley and this delta, Egypt has sometimes been likened to a lily ; the delta representing the flower and the valley the stem.

After flowing four thousand miles, the waters of the Nile find their way at last to the Mediterranean Sea, and towards this sea the land gradually slopes. Passing southward through Egypt from the Mediterranean, one journeys more than a hundred miles through the delta. This great plain has been formed entirely of the mud washed down by the mighty river. Each year for countless ages it has been extended at least eight feet farther into the sea, and thus its area continues to increase. This portion of the country, or this delta, is frequently referred to as Lower Egypt.

Continuing south, one enters the valley. This narrow strip of fertile land measures about six hundred miles from the apex, or southern extremity of the delta, to the first cataract. The bed of the Nile is very irregular in its upper course and falls over ten cataracts in its downward flow before the southern boundary of Upper Egypt is reached. In width the valley varies from one to ten miles. This portion of the country is known as Upper Egypt.

Imagine, if you can, a river flowing through a valley skirted on either side by deserts whose boundaries are so abruptly marked that one may stand with one foot in the fertile, life-producing valley, and with the other in the shifting sands of desert waste. On the east lies the Arabian desert, while the many colored peaks of a lofty mountain range form a well nigh impassable barrier between it and the Red Sea, save where famous mountain passes lead to the waters beyond.

Nubian mountains, to the south, supplied most of the gold

and precious ore used by the ancient Egyptians, and were held in greatest dread by those taken in captivity, for the work within them was relentless and none ever returned when once sent to join the hopeless, heartsick throng of laborers employed by the king to develop the mines.

The Sahara west of the valley is not a flat region, but is made up of shifting sands, hills and rocks of limestone. It is plain that the Valley of the Nile was once a part of this desert, but the river, with its tremendous volume, set to work to cut down its bed. The channel, so worn down, is the present valley. "Egypt is the temporarily uncovered bed of the Nile, which it reclaims and recovers during a portion of each year, when Egypt disappears from view, save where human labor has by mounds and embankments formed artificial islands that raise their heads above the waste of waters, for the most part crowned with buildings."[1]

It is plain, as we note the nature of the land through which the great river flows, that no rich soil would be accumulated from the banks it washes in its downward course. We must look to the high tablelands where the two large tributaries, the Blue Nile and the Atbara, have their beginnings, to find the mountain loam that has given the valley a fertile soil, thirty feet in depth, and has built up the grain-producing delta, one hundred miles in length and more in breadth. Again and again we are forced to remember that Egypt is indeed the gift of the Nile.

YEARLY RISE OF THE NILE.

This brings us back once more to the subject of the inundations. Early in June the Nile begins to rise below the first cataract. In July it has become swollen throughout its course.

The highest water mark is reached about September fifteenth. By the first of November the river begins to recede and is at low water again by the last of January, although it continues to diminish until the following June.

Nilometers are used to register the river's rise. These are wells in which the water can fluctuate freely, with a stone column in the center marked as a scale. The *ell* is the unit

[1] Rawlinson; Ancient Egypt, p. 6.

of measure, being equal to about twenty-one and one-third inches. At low water the river registers about seven ells. If during the inundation sixteen ells are reached, all Egypt is supplied with water and fine crops are assured throughout the land.

NILOMETERS.

From earliest times the rise of the Nile was closely watched, and nilometers, which were under the special protection of the State, constructed. Today these water gauges are under the inspection of government officials. Taxes have always been apportioned according to the amount of the inundation, and it has been to the interest of the government, naturally, that these be as heavy as possible. For this reason it has often been claimed, both in ancient and modern times, that the official report of the high water mark greatly exceeded the actual rise.

There is no rainfall in the valley and little in the delta, so whatever moisture Egypt receives must come from the Nile. The entire valley is not of equal elevation but becomes higher as it spreads out on either side, and so a vast system of irrigation must be maintained to make good crops possible. Large sums have been expended in the construction of dams, embankments and canals to contain the water after the river recedes, allowing the amount thus retained to be drawn off as it is needed. From canals it is drawn off into trenches for still higher land, and artificial means of various kinds have always been employed to lift the water from one level to another. It is estimated that tens of thousands of men and boys are constantly engaged in this elevation of water from one level to another, in order that farms throughout the valley may receive the necessary moisture and fertility. As rapidly as one crop is harvested, the soil is made ready for another, so that as many as five crops are frequently harvested in a year on a given acreage.

INFLUENCE OF TOPOGRAPHY.

With a sea on the north, mountains on the east, cataracts to the south and a desert on the west, what would be the natural effect upon the inhabitants of physical conditions such as these prevailing in the land of Egypt? They determined that the Egyptians would be left to develop their civilization unmolested for the most part by outside influences. Such physical features account for the fact that for hundreds of years that was a land, not of war, but of peace. Think for a moment what natural boundaries have meant to nations of Europe. England's isolation has been largely due to her stormy channel, while the independence of the Swiss is accounted for by their inaccessible mountain home. Austria, on the other hand, has known the disastrous effects of repeated invasions, while Poland has lost her identity and has been appropriated by her neighbors because of unfortunate situation and the lack of natural defenses.

Not only did the topography of the land surface determine the political fortunes of the ancient Egyptians in a large degree; it materially influenced the very temperament of the people. Many civilizations have developed in lands broken by hills and valleys, plains and plateaus, dotted with lakes, skirted by forests, bays, inlets and a thousand irregularities of nature. Few trees grow in Egypt and few wild flowers are found. Each spot that might have become a tangled thicket was early appropriated by the practical tiller of the soil. The valley has always supported too dense a population to permit of wilds and abandoned corners, and only that remains uncultivated which has proved too marshy for grain production. Possessing no timber suitable for ship-building, the Nile dwellers did not become sailors. Their communication from one part of the country to the other was established by means of small boats or donkey paths. Rain was scanty and mud huts sufficed to shelter the people. While constant attention was required to maintain an extensive system of irrigation, the soil was so fertile and the climate so favorable that two, three and even more crops per year were possible. Nature worked with—not against—man. "A serene temper, and a reliance in nature were fostered. A submissiveness was developed which allowed the king to turn all into a fighting people, or into a body of forced laborers." The absence of nearly all that inspires, that stimulates the energy and quickens the imagination may largely account for the placid temperament of the ancient Egyptians. Passing their lives in a land of slightly varying processes, they could imagine nothing more satisfactory for a hereafter than a shadowy land wherein they might till the soil as of yore, only water should always reach the needs of the remotest, and perplexities removed, each should complete his yearly circuit through eternity.

Prehistoric Egypt.

Long before northern Africa acquired its present land surface, made up so largely of deserts, it is believed that the portion which we call Egypt was a fertile country, visited by frequent rains. It is possible that the Nile did not exist; at least, it had not eroded its present channel, and the fertility of the soil was due to causes other than yearly inundations. This, we must remember, was many geological ages ago and cannot be computed in years at all. Remains of rude flint implements are scattered over the heights of the desert plateau to the west of the Nile valley. The people who used these lived in settlements, traces of many of which have been found; but of their relation to the later inhabitants of Egypt we know nothing. They belong to the field of archaeology rather than to history.

Climatic changes took place in Africa. Gradually the country assumed its present surface of desert and valley. It is supposed that Libyan tribes came from northwestern Africa and settled in Egypt; these were joined later by Asiatic hordes who crossed the Isthmus of Suez in search of better pastures for their flocks, or because of some shifting of the tribes in their rear. This inference, based upon the Semitic elements in the grammar and vocabulary of the language of the earliest Egyptian inscriptions, has been raised almost beyond doubt by the latest researches. From the mingling of these Asiatic tribes with others already established in western Africa, sprang, so it is believed, the early Egyptians. The Egyptians, however, like the ancient Greeks, regarded themselves as autochthonous.

Roughly speaking, prehistoric events in Egypt include all those preceding the year 4000 B.C., and our knowledge of them has been gathered from the disclosures of excavated tombs. While a discussion of the Egyptian religion will be taken up later on, some slight knowledge of it is necessary at the start.

The Egyptian of both early and later periods believed firmly in a future life, but he believed further that the future welfare of the soul depended wholly upon the preservation of the body. This belief led him to study how best to preserve the dead body, and to bring embalming to such an art that tombs opened today, after the flight of five thousand years, reveal bodies in complete states of preservation. Again, it was believed that the same needs would be felt in the future life as had been experienced during the earthly career. For this reason, foods, vessels of pottery, weapons, and even toilet preparations for personal adornment, were enclosed in the tomb. From a study of the contents of these ancient tombs most that is at present known of the ancient Egyptian has been ascertained.

When many implements furnished with ivory handles are found in these tombs, together with occasional pictures of elephants scratched on bone and bits of pottery, even those of us who are neither antiquarians nor historians might infer that the elephant was contemporaneous with the prehistoric Egyptian. Pictures of boats, of animals and men, decorating pieces of pottery, throw light upon this early civilization.

From all remains recovered in tombs antedating the year 4000 B. C. the following conclusions have been reached : these primitive people reached considerable skill in the making of pottery and stone receptacles. From copper they made knives and implements ; they built very fair river boats, wove coarse fabrics, although skins of wild animals usually constituted their clothing : they hunted and fished and were to some extent an agricultural people. At this remote time Egypt was not the one united country it later became. It was composed of nomes, or districts, of which the late lists give 22 for Upper and 20 for Lower Egypt. Their number probably varied considerably during the course of Egyptian history. In early times each nome probably had been the home of an independent tribe, having its own chief and its own religious customs. Gradually, however, powerful chieftains conquered other nomes, until just before our written records begin, the two more or less compact kingdoms of Upper and Lower Egypt were established.

Throughout Egyptian history each locality held to its peculiar religious beliefs, and although there was always a state religion and a state god, dearer to the hearts of men were the deities of their own vicinity; and it is possible to trace several religions in the one composite system of later years.

By 4300 B. C. the men of the Delta had divided the year into 365 days, and again into twelve months of thirty days each, with five extra days for sacred festival. For six thousand years, then, the calendar which we use has experienced little change. Take it all in all, the Egyptians of this age had traveled far from the state of savagery.

UPPER EGYPT. LOWER EGYPT, UPPER AND LOWER EGYPT.
ROYAL CROWNS.

CLEOPATRA.

CHAPTER II.

Sources of Egyptian History.

The study of prehistoric man is largely a matter of conjecture and has little interest for any save the archaeologist and antiquarian. There is yet so much uncertainty regarding historic periods in Egypt that the general reader must leave prehistoric ages to others. Reaching authentic ages, in addition to the remains discovered within old tombs, we are aided by written records, and these fall into three classes : facts regarding Egypt as recounted in the Old Testament ; writings of the Greeks ; inscriptions of the ancient Egyptians themselves. The light thrown upon the subject by old Hebrew writers is slight. They chronicled the history of their own people and mentioned other nations only when in some way the Hebrews came into contact with them. Hebrew traditions, customs, and religion differing wholly from those of Egypt, at best there would have been but little understanding between them. Biblical comment upon Egyptian life is slight. In connection with the story of Joseph we find that some facts concerning the land unwittingly creep into the narrative. Modern discovery has verified such facts as are recounted, and buried and forgotten cities have been sought and located from mere mention of them in some Old Testament passage. Thus the Bible is rightly included with the sources of Egyptian history.

So far as treatment of Egypt by Greek writers is concerned, we can stop for only the most important. Best known are the works of Herodotus, who lived about five hundred years before the Christian era. He was the first to bring forward the historical style of writing and for this reason he has been called the Father of History.

Herodotus journeyed to Egypt and abode there some little time. He did not understand the language of the country and depended largely upon priests who spoke Greek for his information. He apparently believed all they told him, and likewise accepted the tales with which his guides entertained him, incorporating all their marvelous stories into his writings. Consequently much that is found in his works cannot be credited. Whatever he himself saw and understood he recounted with simplicity and truth, as recent discoveries have proved. It is easy today to point out the failings of Herodotus and to wonder that he was so ready to credit all he heard, but judged by the age in which he lived, his writings may be the better understood. We are told that portions of his works were read by him at the Olympian Games, and that those who listened received his stories with enthusiasm. To the imaginative Greeks no report was too fanciful to find credence. They delighted in the unusual and strange, and they made up the audiences for which Herodotus wrote. It is not surprising, then, that the Father of History brought back to his countrymen the unique stories he heard concerning the Egyptians—a people whose life and customs were thought by foreigners until long years after, to be deeply shrouded in mystery.

More valuable has proved the work of Manetho, an Egyptian priest who wrote in Greek. He is said to have made a complete list of Egyptian kings from records preserved in the temples. This list has been lost and only portions quoted from time to time by later writers have come down to us. These fragments have been of much service to students of Egyptology. It was Manetho who divided the history of his country into three periods: the Old Empire, Middle Empire, and New Empire. He also treated the past by dynasties rather than years. These general divisions have been retained by all subsequent historians. Those who are not specialists in Egyptology are apt to be confused by the widely divergent systems of chronology found in the different histories of Egypt, or they reach the conclusion that all is uncertainty in this field. This is not the place to enter into a discussion of this difficult technical problem. Suffice it to say that in the opinion of the best scholars, Eduard Meyer, the great historian of the Ancient Orient, has said the last word on this subject. Contrary opinions notwithstanding, the accession of Menes and the beginning of the dynasties cannot be placed before 3400 B.C., nor can the beginning of the twelfth dynasty have been earlier than 2000 B.C.*

Coming lastly to monumental inscriptions, we approach the

difficulties of the Egyptian language. Let us try to understand why it proved so difficult for scholars who read Hebrew, Greek and Latin, together with some older tongues, to comprehend the language of the Nile dwellers.

In prehistoric times the Egyptians understood one another but it was long before they had any means of expressing their thoughts in writing. It may have occurred to them finally that the pictures which they drew for decorative purposes might be used to convey messages, and thus they began to express simple meanings, using pictures rather than symbols. Sometimes to make doubly sure the meaning of several pictures, they added another which combined the meaning of all into one. These added pictures have been called determinitives, and the pictures used to convey meanings in this way are known as hieroglyphics. There was something very attractive and decorative about this method of writing by thus picturing out stories, and it was used extensively in tombs and temples. It became too elaborate, however, for daily use, and gradually only the *main outlines* of the original pictures were used to represent the idea or word. This system of writing was more practical for constant, everyday needs than the more ornamental hieroglyphics. It is known as the hieratic writing. Finally, late in the history of Egypt, these hieratics were very much abbreviated, mere dots and lines being substituted. This cursory system is known as *demotic* writing. It was adopted by the people generally, and might perhaps be compared to modern shorthand. To make the whole more complicated still, all three methods were used for different purposes contemporaneously.

Hundreds of years passed; the language of the ancient Egyptians was forgotten and so, indeed, were the people themselves. In modern times the learning of ancient peoples was revived and their writings eagerly read. Quite naturally students wished to know something of the earliest civilizations, particularly of the civilization of the Nile valley. Here they were confronted by what seemed baffling indeed. Three forms of writing used contemporaneously, even interchangeably, defied all effort to decipher them. Attempts were made to explain certain inscriptions, but these explanations were found later to have been far astray. In 1799, one of Napoleon's soldiers, while excavating in the mouth of the Rosetta, came upon a stone which bore a royal decree written in three ways : in hieroglyphics, in demotic and in Greek. This supplied a key at last, and scholars set themselves to the task of deciphering ancient Egyptian writings. Other inscriptions written in two or more languages were found and verified the conclusions reached earlier in the translation of the Rosetta Stone.

In recent years a large number of inscriptions from tombs and temples have been read and many rolls of papyrus have been translated. This has enabled historians to read back, step by step, into far away ages, and to carry the thread of Egyptian civilization to its beginnings. Maspero, Eduard Meyer, Breasted, Petrie and other painstaking students of Egyptology have given their lives to the task of unraveling the past, both by deciphering inscriptions and unearthing forgotten cities. From the tireless efforts of men like these, tombs hidden for centuries have been recovered, temples and colonnades laid bare of drifting sands, inscriptions transcribed and translated, and volumes of scholarly material written for the special student, while at the same time the general reader may find much of interest concerning the life of a remarkable people whose works have borne testimony through the ages.

Herodotus.

The following lines are taken from the pages of Herodotus wherein he relates what he saw and heard when he visited Egypt nearly twenty-five hundred years ago.

"There is no country in all the whole world that hath in it more marvelous things or greater works of buildings and the like than hath the land of Egypt. And as the heavens in this land are such as other men know not—for in the upper parts there falls not rain but once in a thousand years or more, and in the lower parts not often—and the river is different from all other rivers in the earth, seeing that it overflows in the summer and is at its least in the winter, so also do the manners of the Egyptians differ from the manners of all other men. For among them the women buy and sell in the market but the men sit at home and spin. And even in this matter of spinning they do not as others, for others push the shuttle in the loom from below upward, but these men push it from above downward. Also the men carry burdens on their heads, but the women carry them on their shoulders. And the women pray to none, neither god or goddess, but the men pray to all. And there is no duty laid on a son to succor father or mother, if it be not his pleasure to do it, but on a daughter there is laid, whether she will or no.

"In the matter of mourning for the dead, these folks have a strange custom, for they let grow the hair upon the head and chin when they mourn, but are shaven at other times. And whereas other men hold themselves better than the beasts, the Egyptians have these in great honor, keeping them in their houses, aye, and worshipping them. Nor do they eat the food of other men, holding it a shame to be fed on wheat and barley which others use, and eating the grain of millet only ; and the dough that is made of it this they knead, trampling it with their feet ; but mud and like things they are wont to take up with their hands.

"Now as to the beasts and the honor in which the Egyptians hold them, there are many strange things to be told. The crocodile some of the Egyptians hold to be sacred, but not all. And in every city where they hold it, as in Thebes and in the cities round the lake Moeris, they keep one crocodile to which they do special honor. This they train to be tame to the hand, and they put earrings of glass and gold into his ears, and bracelets on his forefeet, and give it a portion of food day by day, and make offerings to it, and when it dies they embalm it and bury it in the sacred sepulchres. But the people that dwell in the city of Elphantine count them not to be sacred at all, but slay and eat them.

"The cat the Egyptians hold in great honor. Of this beast there is a very marvelous thing to be told. When it chanceth that a house is burning a strange madness cometh upon the cats, for they are very desirous to leap into the fire. And the Egyptians set guards round the place if by any means they may keep the cats from their purpose; nor do they care to quench the fire, if so be that they may do this ; but the cats nevertheless, making their way through them, or leaping over them, have their will and so perish. Over this the Egyptians make great lamentation. If a cat die in the course of nature, all that are in that house shave their eyebrows only, but all dwellers in a house where a dog dies shave their heads and whole bodies. The cats, when they are dead, they carry away for burial to the city of Bubastis, but the dogs they bury each in the city where he dies, only in the holy sepulchres.

"For food the Egyptians have bread made of millet as has been said before. They have wine made of barley, for the vine groweth not in their land. Of birds they eat doves and pigeons, and such small kinds as there are in the country.

" Such of the Egyptians as dwell in the marshes of the river have also for food the seed of the water-lilies, which grow abundantly when the river overfloweth the plains. This seed is like to the seed of a poppy, and they make of it loaves which they bake with fire, having first dried it in the sun. Also the root of this water-lily (which they call the lotus) may be eaten, being round, and of the bigness of an apple. Other lilies there are growing in the river, like to roses, which have a fruit very like to a wasp's comb, and in it many seeds of the bigness of an olive, which the men eat both green and dry. Also these marsh folk gather the reeds, and use the upper part for other things, as for the making of paper and the like, but the lower part, as much as a cubit's length from the ground they eat.

"All the Egyptians worship not the same gods, but Isis and Osiris they all worship and this Osiris is the same as he whom the Greeks call Bacchus or Dionysus, and his feast is in all things like to that which the Greeks keep to their God, only that there is no acting of plays. As for Isis the Greeks call her Demeter, that is to say, being interpreted, Mother Earth.

"Let so much then be said about the Egyptians and their customs and manner of life, and the gods whom they worship."

EGYPTIAN NUMERATION.

CHAPTER III.

The Pyramid Age.

Menes was the king who succeeded in accomplishing the unification of Egypt. We are told by Manetho that he was at first chief or governor of the eighth nome of Upper Egypt, whose capital city was Thinis, and being ambitious, subdued the surrounding nomes, until at last all Egypt was brought under his control. No doubt earlier chieftains had begun the work of conquest and left the completion to Menes, whose personality and executive strength were sufficient to efface the reigns of his predecessors.

Having brought the Delta under his control and crowned himself with the white crown of Upper and the red crown of Lower Egypt, Menes realized that a capital for such a straggling kingdom as his would best be centrally located. He therefore fixed upon a site just south of the apex of the delta and built the city of Memphis. Quite possibly there was a settlement here before this time.

It happened that the Nile flowed close to the western hills in this locality. The king knew well that his capital would be safer and the more easily protected were the river between it and possible Asiatic invaders on the east. So he undertook what has ever since been regarded as a bold feat of engineering; he built a high embankment across the Nile and compelled the stream to seek a new course farther east. Filling in the old channel, he built a wall around the new city, caused a temple to be at once erected to Ptah, the ancient deity of the locality, and shortly a town grew up around it. Thus we see the beginnings of the Old Empire, so called by Manetho and subsequent historians. For convenience scholars sometimes group Dynasties I. and II. and Dynasties III. to VI. together, The first period (3400-2980 B.C.) is called the Thinite age because the rulers of these two dynasties came from Thinis. The name Old Kingdom is then limited to Dynasties III. to VI. (2980-2475 B.C.)

It would be useless for us to attempt to become familiar

with all these early kings—some fifty in number—with reigns varying from one to many years. Should we succeed in collecting the meager facts known of each we would have little to repay us for our trouble. It is more to the purpose that we know something about the period as a whole—its general characteristics and attainments.

During this period hieroglyphic writing became widely used, having been but rarely known before the age of Menes. A line of forts was built along the Isthmus of Suez to stay invaders from Asia. Tribes on the south were brought into subjection and pledged service to Egypt in time of war. Stone quarries and mines were developed and granite ranges sought and found. In the sixth dynasty one man-of-war sufficed to accompany the transports sent to bring granite for the kings' tombs from the southland—a fact recorded with pride by the pharaohs, since it gave proof of their far reaching might.

From earliest times the Egyptian kings were builders, particularly of tombs, which during the Old Empire took the form of pyramids. Of far greater importance than the earthly abode was thought to be the tomb—the dwelling place for eternal years, consequently tombs and temples received the attention of Egypt's kings in early as well as later times.

In 1897 the tomb of Menes was discovered. It was a brick-lined pit containing an inner chamber of wood. Around the mummy of the pharaoh had been placed the bodies of different members of his household. Similar to this were royal tombs until the Third dynasty, when stone was first used. To the kings of the Fourth dynasty belong the famous pyramids, unsurpassed by any subsequently built, and still today the wonder of the world.

The Egyptians always located their cemeteries toward the west. Into the west the sun sank at night, and by the same way the soul started upon its long journey to the realm of Osiris, god of the future world. The irregularity of the Nile usually made it possible for the city of the living to grow up on its eastern bank, while across the stream, on the west shore, lay the City of the Dead. To the west of Memphis lay its cemetery or Necropolis, and while this remained the capital of Egypt, the pyramid-shaped tomb remained in favor. Sometimes the pyramid tombs were small; sometimes they were large. More than sixty have been found, and large numbers have doubtless disappeared for all time. Three, however, were made so prodigious in size as to cast into obscurity all the rest, and these have come to be called the "three Pyramids of Gizeh," quite as though they were sole examples of their kind. Khufu was builder of the largest; this is generally called "the Great Pyramid." His son Khafre built the one next in size, known as the "Second Pyramid," while the third, much smaller than these, was built by Menkure. Were we indifferent to the political development of Egypt, we would still wish to learn about these mammoth structures which are scaled each season by wondering tourists, and have excited the admiration and awe of travelers since the time of Herodotus.

It is difficult to realize the vast size of these piles, and we can do so only by comparing them to things with which we are familiar. The base of the largest pyramid covers thirteen acres of ground, solid masonry; it was originally 482 feet high. Since it is almost one solid mass of stone, it is not difficult to credit the statement of Herodotus that it took 100,000 men twenty years to build it, an additional ten years being necessary to quarry the stone and bring it to the chosen site.

"The tradition recorded by Herodotus as to the labor employed, is so entirely reasonable for the execution of such work, that we cannot hesitate to accept it. It is said that a hundred thousand men were levied for three months at a time (i. e. during the three months of the inundation, when ordinary labor is at a standstill); and on this scale the pyramid-building lasted twenty years."

How complete must have been the organization of a government which could promote such an extensive project as this! How entirely were the resources of the empire at the disposal of the king when free citizens could be impressed to satisfy the vanity of the proud pharaoh! To have supported 100,000 non-producing men must of itself have taxed the treasury. The rulers who built these majestic tombs wished to make their names immortal, as well as to preserve their bodies from harm and decay. This first they certainly accomplished, but in light of modern investigation, when each stone lifted into place has been estimated to have cost at least one human life, these proud pharaohs elicit less admiration and commendation than they doubtless thought to win.

Three kinds of stone were used in the construction of these pyramids. The inner part, or core, was formed of material plentiful near the building site. This was a spongy limestone that was not durable if exposed to the elements, but adequate when covered with other stone. The successive layers, put on in the form of steps, were of stone brought from across the river, having been quarried in the mountains on the east. It has been conjectured that a causeway was laid from the mountains to the side of the pyramid, and that blocks of stone were dragged by men this distance. Finally, the beautiful granite used for outer casing was found near the southern border of Egpyt, floated down the stream when the water was high, and having been polished like a mirror, was fitted over the rougher stone. 2,300,000 blocks, averaging two and one-half tons each, were used for the construction of the largest pyramid.

"If we had so much stone, what could one do with it?" is asked in The Boy Travelers in Egypt. And it is answered: "You could build a wall four feet high and two feet thick—a good wall for a farm or a garden—all the way from New York to Salt Lake City, and were New York in danger of an attack and desired to surround the whole of Manhattan Island—21 miles—with a wall forty feet high and twenty feet thick, here would be material to do it." Rawlinson tries to bring its size home to us by comparing it to structures with which we are familiar. He says: "In height it exceeds the capitol at Washington by nearly 200 feet, and its cubic contents would provide a city of 22,000 houses solidly built of stone having walls a foot thick, twenty feet frontage and thirty feet deep, thirty feet high, allowing one-third for dividing walls."

For several hundred years the Mohammedans have occupied Egypt and they have taken away quantities of stone from the lesser pyramids, from temples and other ancient structures of Memphis, to be used in their mosques and buildings in Cairo, near-by. The outer casing of the Great Pyramid, beautiful granite as hard as iron, was removed to build the large mosque of this comparatively modern city. The removal of this casing has left the under layers bare, and these, step-like in appearance, are annually scaled by tourists. With the help of Arab guides, one may ascend to the very top of the huge pile, gaining thence a splendid view of the surrounding country.

Even the pyramids left cased in granite are no longer smooth. The weathering of ages has roughened their sides and dulled their polish. They are of a tawny orange color and gleam by certain lights like gigantic piles of gold.

Within the pyramids were chambers for the remains of kings and their families and chambers for friends to gather for worship—for after his death, an Egyptian king was worshipped as a god. Even a spacious gallery was provided near the top of the Great Pyramid, in order that air might circulate freely and thus keep the tomb dry.

The ambitious, short-sighted Fourth dynasty kings exhausted the resources of their realm. During the Fifth and Sixth dynasties the pyramids became smaller. Even the long-suffering land of the Nile could no longer muster vast forces to provide huge abiding places for the pharaohs. Marvelous temples would still be erected, and wonderful feats of architecture accomplished, but the passion for tremendous tombs had in a measure spent itself.

"The essential feeling of all the earliest work is a rivalry with nature. In other times buildings have been placed either before a background of hills, so as to provide a natural setting to them, or crowning some natural height. But the Egyptian consented to no such tame co-operation with natural features. He selected a range of desert hills over a hundred feet high, and then subdued it entirely, making of it a mere pedestal for pyramids, which were more than thrice as high as the native hill on which they stood. There was no shrinking from a comparison with the work of nature; but, on the contrary, an artificial hill was formed which shrunk its natural basis by comparison, until it seemed a mere platform for the work of man.

"This same grandeur of idea is seen in the vast masses used in construction. Man did not then regard his work as a piling together of stones, but as the erection of masses that rivalled those of nature. If a cell or chamber was required, each side was formed of one single stone. If a building was set up, it was an artificial hill in which chambers were carved out after it was piled together.

"The sculptor's work, and the painter's, show the same sentiment. They did not make a work of art to please the taste as such ; but they rivalled nature as closely as possible. The form, the expression, the colouring, the glittering transparent eye, the grave smile, all are copied as if to make an artificial man. The painter mixed his half-tints and his delicate shades, and dappled over the animals, or figured the feathers of birds, in a manner never attempted in the later ages. The embalmer built up the semblance of the man in resins and cloth over his shrunken corpse, to make him as nearly as possible what he was when alive.

"In each direction man then set himself to supplement, to imitate, to rival or to exceed, the works of nature. Art, as the gratification of an artificial taste and standard, was scarcely in existence ; but the simplicity, the vastness, the perfection, and the beauty of the earliest works place them on a different level to all the workers of art and man's device in later ages. They are unique in their splendid power, which no self-conscious civilization has ever rivalled, nor can hope to rival ; and in their enduring greatness they may last till all the feebler works of man have perished."[1]

[1] Petrie; History of Egypt, Vol. I, p. 66.

CHAPTER IV.

THE AGE OF DARKNESS.

With the close of the Sixth dynasty, records practically cease, and few indeed are the facts established regarding those kings whom Manetho included in his Seventh and Eighth dynasties.

From earliest times each nome had been the seat of some noble family—the descendants of chieftains, possibly, or perhaps the recipients of royal land grants. Certain it is that each nome had its noble family of wide estate, from whose number the governor was usually chosen, as was also the high priest of the local temple. By the end of the Sixth dynasty, the claimants to the throne were not strong enough to hold together the land they aspired to rule; they maintained their capital at Memphis, but neither the Delta or Upper Egypt recognized their sway. On the contrary, each prince in his own nome tried to increase his individual strength at the expense of the general government. Asiatic invaders seem to have strengthened themselves in the Delta, while to the south Theban princes came into prominence.

During the period which Manetho accorded to the Ninth and Tenth dynasties, a prince often bought the favor and assistance of as many nobles as he was able, and with his united forces established himself in his own vicinity.

The vast resources which had been so completely at the command of the Fourth dynasty kings were now divided among many petty nobles, each seeking to aggrandize himself. Naturally, no costly tombs could be constructed to perpetuate the memories of these who now aspired to Egypt's throne; the tombs which had to satisfy were less enduring, and this no doubt explains why so few remains of the period have come to light in recent years. The thread of history is almost lost during the age of darkness which included the Seventh, Eighth, Ninth and Tenth dynasties. Shut off from the disclosures of tombs, Egyptologists have turned to the mines and quarries. All kings of importance have there left traces of their operations, but the mines contain no tablets, no decrees, no records of quarrying undertaken in these years, save here and there an inscription indicating that some noble carried on work within them on his own behalf.

It is probable that the land passed through a most trying experience in the time intervening between the Old and the beginning of the Middle Empire, when neither property, possessions, nor life itself were safe throughout the land, but anarchy, strife and turmoil were everywhere rife. The kings maintained their capital at Heracleopolis, but they were in continual struggle with the princes of Thebes. How great had been the confusion we may judge when one of the Tenth dynasty rulers takes pride in recording the fact that order had characterized his reign. " Every official was at his post, there was no fighting, nor any shooting an arrow. The child was not smitten beside his mother, nor the citizen beside his wife. There was no evil-doer nor any one doing violence against his house. When night came, he who slept on the road gave me praise, for he was like a man in his house ; the fear of my soldiers was his protection."[1]

THE MIDDLE EMPIRE.[2]

Order and prosperity returned to Egypt after years of darkness and confusion. Thebes superseded Memphis as the center of political life. Great material development characterized the beginning of what Manetho designated as the Middle Empire. Before taking up the work of the early Theban kings, let us learn something of the locality wherein they dwelt.

Memphis, as has been shown, was located conveniently to both Upper and Lower Egypt, while the Nile protected the city from sudden Asiatic attacks. What then were the points of advantage for Thebes, lying 400 miles farther south ?

" Here the usually narrow valley of the Nile opens into a sort of plain or basin.

" The mountains on either side of the river recede, as though by common consent, and leave between themselves and the

---

[1] Trans. by Breasted, Hist. Egypt, 149. The approximate dates of this period are: Dynasties VII. and VIII. *Ca.* 2475-2445 B. C.; Dynasties XI. and X. *Ca.* 2475-2160 B. C.
[2] Dynasties XI. and XII.. 2160-1788 B. C.

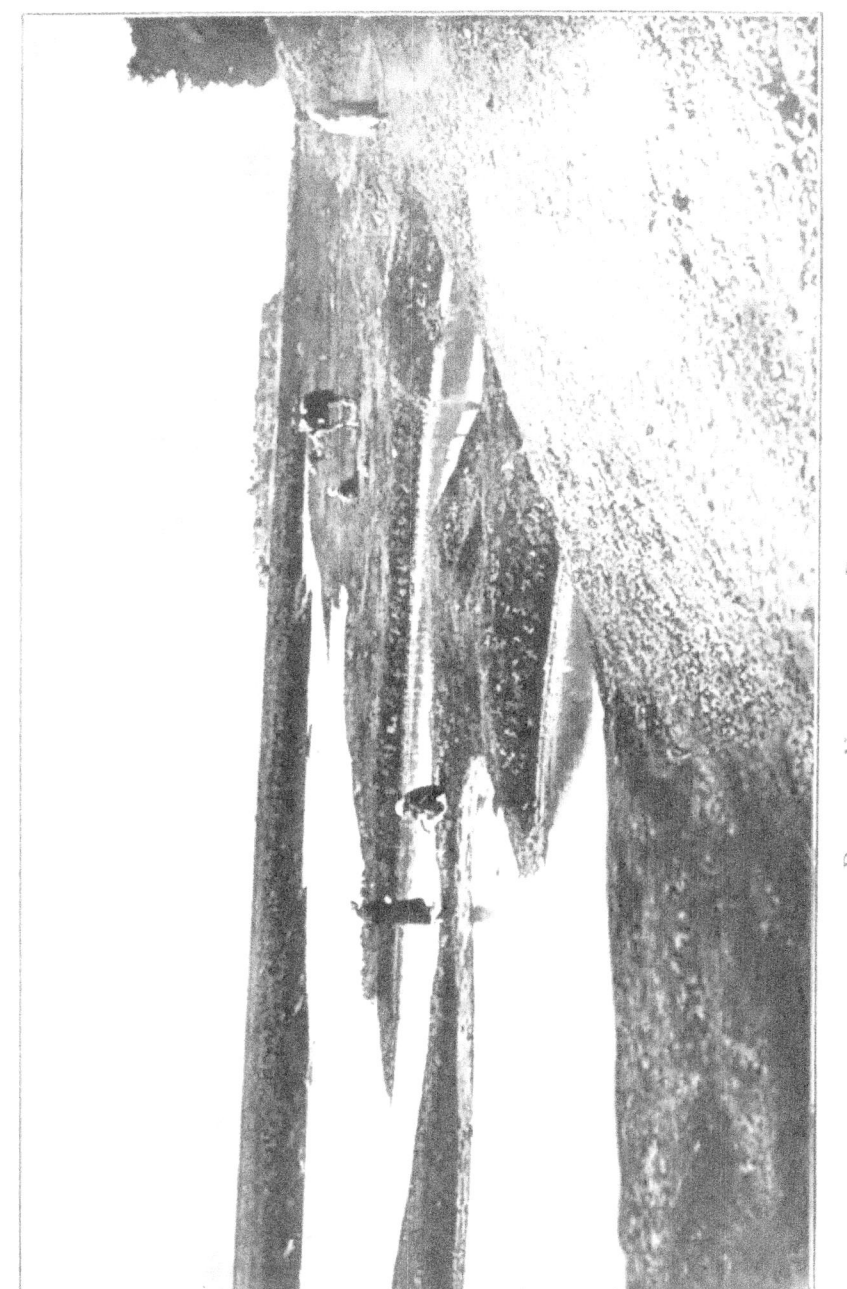

DISTANT VIEW OF THE PYRAMIDS

river's bank a broad amphitheater, which in each case is a rich green plain—a soil of the most productive character—dotted with doom and date palms, sometimes growing single, sometimes collected into clumps or groves. On the western side the Libyan range gathers itself up into a single considerable peak, which has an elevation of 1,200 feet. On the east the desert-wall maintains its usual level character, but is pierced by valleys conducting to the coast of the Red Sea. The situation was one favorable for commerce. On the one side was the nearest route through the sandy desert to the Lesser Oasis, which commanded the trade of the African interior; on the other the way led through the valley of Hammamat, rich with valuable and rare stones, to a district abounding in mines of gold, silver and lead, and thence to the Red Sea coast, from which, even in very early times, there was communication with the opposite coast of Arabia, the region of gums and spices."[2]

Such being the location of Thebes, we shall see that it grew until in time it became the mightiest city of the ancient world.

With the establishment of the Eleventh dynasty (*Ca.* 2160-2000 B.C.), the work of reuniting and re-establishing a centralized government began. The Delta had to be reclaimed from invaders who had gained the upper hand while the land was divided against itself. Unity being at last secured, rulers were free to launch out upon other enterprises. One of the later kings had a deep well provided for those who served in the quarries; another sent an expedition of 3,000 men to bring back stone for his tomb. These men were also instructed to go beyond the quarries—to Punt, which must have lain on the Somali coast of East Africa, and bring back products of that region. The expedition set out under the leadership of a nobleman whose report has fortunately come down to us. It states that his men built stations and made wells along their route, to the lasting benefit of those who might journey thence. Part of the detachment was left to quarry stone, while the rest proceeded to Punt and procured spices, gums, precious woods, and rare animals. After noting their safe return, the prince adds: "Never was brought down the like thereof for the king's court; never was done the like of this by any king's

[2] Rawlinson, Ancient Egypt, 95.

I—5

confidant sent out since the time of the god. I did this for the majesty of my lord because he so much loved me."[3]

The Twelfth dynasty (2000-1788 B.C.) brought forth some of Egypt's ablest kings. Their creative ability was perhaps not excelled by subsequent pharaohs. Amenemhet I. (2000-1970 B.C.) proved himself strong enough to curb the power of the feudal princes. These hereditary nobles had probably received gifts of land from earlier kings in recognition of loyal service. The estates passed from father to son, and while the central government had been weak, the princes became more and more aggressive. They fortified themselves, each in his nome, retained large retinues of officials, servants, militia and realized vast incomes from extensive tracts of arable land. It was neither possible nor prudent to remodel the entire system, but Amenemhet I undertook to modify it. Whenever one of these landed princes died, the king himself chose from the heirs the one who should succeed him. Naturally, he selected one whose loyalty to himself and to the government was unquestioned. Again, the boundaries of the nomes had never been officially determined, and during the years of confusion, strong nobles had infringed upon the possessions of weaker ones. The king made a tour through the country, heard all complaints of such encroachments, and decided the limits of all disputed boundaries. This did much to restrict the strength of ambitious princes.

His son, coming to the throne, subdued the Nubians on the south and extended the empire to the second cataract; but it was left for Sesostris III. to make this conquest sure, and then to post his decree along the river.

"This is the southern frontier; fixed in the eighth year of the reign of his majesty. Usurtasen [Sesostris], ever living. Let it not be permitted to any negro to pass this boundary northward, either on foot or by boat; nor any sort of cattle, oxen, goats, or sheep belonging to the negroes. Except when any negro comes to trade in the land of Aken, or on any business, let him be well treated. But without allowing boats of the negroes to pass Heh northward forever."[4]

[3] Trans. by Breasted, Ancient Records, I, §433.
[4] Petrie, Hist. of Egypt, Vol. I, 181.

In gratitude to the king for thus securing to them safety by repulsing the negroes, the Egyptians sang extravagant hymns to Sostostris. Some of these have been rendered into English, and are regarded as excellent specimens of Egyptian poetry. The following is one of these songs:

"Twice joyful are the gods,
   Thou hast established their offerings.
Twice joyful are thy princes,
   Thou hast formed their boundaries.
Twice joyful are thy ancestors before thee,
   Thou hast increased their portions.
Twice joyful is Egypt at thy strong arm,
   Thou hast guarded the ancient order.
Twice joyful are the aged with thy administration,
   Thou hast widened their possessions.
Twice joyful are the two regions with thy valor,
   Thou hast caused them to flourish.
Twice joyful are thy young men of support,
   Thou hast caused them to flourish.
Twice joyful are thy veterans,
   Thou hast caused them to be vigorous.
Twice joyful are the two lands in thy might,
   Thou hast guarded their walls.
Twice joyful be thou, O Horus! widening thy boundary,
   Mayest thou renew an eternity of life."[3]

Amenemhet III.

The greatest name of the Twelfth dynasty is that of Amenemhet III. (1849-1801 B.C.). He directed his attention to internal improvements. Realizing the dire effects upon Egypt when the Nile failed to supply sufficient water or when too much water was forthcoming, he studied various ways of controlling the river. Once or twice in a century the rainfall, always heavy in the Abyssinian highlands, is yet greater; the river rises rapidly to unexpected heights and works general havoc. Or sometimes the supply may be less than usual. Having watched the stream with anxious eyes for many a week, the people

[3] Petrie, Hist. of Egypt, Vol. I, 182.

behold it recede, although only the adjacent plains have been refreshed and upper portions of the valley lie parched and lifeless, while famine stares Egypt in the face.

Amenemhet III. believed that a vast reservoir might regulate the supply, receiving the water when it was at high flood and giving it out once more when the stream was low. He looked about for a natural depression and found it to the west of Memphis, beyond a narrow range of hills. Canals were made leading into this basin and Lake Moeris was the result. Some hundreds of square miles were gained by this new means of irrigation and the tract thus made arable, became royal domain. The district is known as the Fayoum. Near its entrance Amenemhet III. built his pyramid. It differed from earlier tombs in that the chamber destined to receive his mummy was reached by passages even more secret and winding than ordinary. False doors were placed here and there to mislead any who might attempt to molest the body.

Under his direction, a wonderful building was constructed. It was called the Labyrinth. Being about 800 feet wide and 1,000 feet long, it contained 1,500 rooms above the ground and as many more below it. There were many courts with numerous doors leading from them and Strabo, a Greek geographer, who saw it long after Amenemhet had taken his journey to the realm of Osiris, said that the ceilings and sides of the rooms were made from single stones ! It is believed that the king planned this structure to serve as a great capitol for his kingdom, and that there were suites of halls for every nome, with chapels for their gods. A vast number of chambers would naturally be required for this, and probably there was no thought of making the building baffling or bewildering, as the name labyrinth now signifies. This was counted among the wonders of the ancient world, but, like the city built around it, disappeared ages ago. Herodotus has left us a description of the huge building, written to inform his countrymen of a structure more remarkable than anything they could boast. When he saw it, almost five hundred years before the time of Christ, it was still in perfect condition.

"I visited the place," he says, "and found it to surpass description ; for if all the walls and other great works of the Greeks could be put together into one, they would not equal this Labyrinth. The pyramids likewise surpass description, and are severally equal to a number of the greatest works of the Greeks ; but the Labyrinth surpasses the pyramids. It has twelve courts, all of them roofed, with gates exactly opposite one another, six looking to the north, and six to the south. A single wall surrounds the whole building. It contains two different sorts of chambers, half of them under ground, and half above ground, the latter built upon the former ; the whole number is three thousand, of each kind fifteen hundred. The upper chambers I myself passed through and saw, and what I say of them is from my own observation ; of the underground chambers I can only speak from report, for the keepers of the building could not be induced to show them ; since they contain, they said, the sepulchres of the kings who built the labyrinth, and also those of the sacred crocodiles. Thus it is from hearsay only that I can speak of them ; but the upper chambers I saw with my own eyes, and found them to excel all other human productions ; for the passages through the houses and the varied windings of the paths across the courts, excited in me infinite admiration, as I passed from these colonnades into fresh houses, and again from these into courts unseen before. The roof was, throughout, of stone, like the walls ; and the walls were carved all over with figures ; every court was surrounded with a colonnade, which was built of white stone, exquisitely fitted together. At the corner of the Labyrinth stands a pyramid, forty fathoms high, with large figures engraved upon it, which is entered by a subterranean passage."

In comparison with the Old Empire kings, those of the Middle Empire seem to us much more modern in spirit. Instead of merging the whole population into instruments to work out the pharaoh's fancy, instead of squandering the riches of the land and the lives of subjects to provide mammoth tombs which should eternalize the ruler's memory and flame forth his power and greatness unto succeeding generations, the farsighted Twelfth dynasty kings devoted their time and resources to the improvement of their kingdom. Wells were dug ; roads constructed ; public buildings erected ; fortifications strengthened ; frontiers extended. The attention of the monarch was directed to the commercial prosperity of the realm, to the agricultural conditions and their improvement—in short, the best years of the Middle Empire were years of material gain for the Nile dwellers, wherein men developed the arts of peace, and the valley testified to wise administration. Through a second period of depression a nation was to look back upon the age of its material progress with longing eyes, and still better, to retain even under adverse conditions standards of government and life which would later be recovered. After the death of the great king, called Amenemhet the Good by his grateful subjects, none appeared able to adequately fill his place, and his glorious reign was overshadowed by a second period of darkness.

CHAPTER V.

The Shepherd Kings.[1]

The Thirteenth dynasty kings were not sufficiently strong to hold intact the kingdom which passed into their hands. Soon again the feudal princes of nome and city were contending with one another for additional power. The Fourteenth dynasty rulers had their capital in Xois, a Delta city. Both dynasties lasted but a brief time, filled with unrest and contention. We can imagine into what state Egypt fell when a negro of Nubia, of a race despised by the Egyptians, set himself up as their king. Several princes ruled at the same time in various portions of the realm. Sources of information for these chaotic years are scanty; no monuments have come down to us, the inference being that the resources and energies of the land were required for more immediate needs than the erection of costly tombs for rulers of disputed right.

The whole country must have suffered greatly. The system of irrigation set in order by Amenemhet III. required both national supervision and national funds for its maintenance. As neither could have been forthcoming, the food production must have been materially diminished. Engaged in civil war, Egypt soon fell a prey to foreign invaders.

For hundreds of years it had been not unusual for Syrian bands to ask permission to settle within Egyptian borders. In the tomb of a provincial governor of Upper Egypt has been found a painting which portrays a company of seventeen Bedouins bringing presents to the nobleman and asking that they be allowed to locate in his dominion. In Genesis we read concerning Abram: " And Abram journeyed, going still toward the south. And there was a famine in the land of Canaan; and Abram went down into Egypt to sojourn there; for the famine was grievous in the land." Since Abram was rich in cattle and in gold, he undoubtedly brought many of his family and followers to dwell with him in the land of plenty. Similar incidents were common. If the rainfall was short in Canaan, in the territory of the Hittites or even in Arabia, Egypt was

[1] Dynasties XIII to XVIII, including the Hyksos, 1788-1580 B. C.

ever regarded as a last resort. The Nile never failed to supply water for the flocks; here, too, it was customary to store grain in royal store-cities, in order that in time of need Egypt could sell advantageously to her neighbors. In a pastoral age, such favorable conditions as these were highly prized.

The Pharaohs diligently fortified their frontiers, and it must not be supposed that in times of peace foreigners were allowed to come at will into the land. There were, on the contrary, officers stationed along the boundaries to apprehend any who wished to enter, to receive their requests and forward them to the governor of the nome. Until he was heard from, strangers were detained on the border. It seems to have been usual, however, to admit such petitioners unless it was thought that they might become a menace to the state. It naturally came about, therefore, that the tribes on the east looked with envious eyes upon the rich valley of the Nile, and when Egypt was disrupted, her resources and soldiers no longer at the command of one ruler but divided among several contending nobles—each of whom valued his personal interests above those of his country—while anarchy and disorder infested the coveted land, an overwhelming host of Semitic hordes poured into the Delta, spreading thence into the valley. Before them Egypt was helpless.

Asia and Egypt as well were inhabited in early times by many wandering or nomadic tribes. A tribe dwelt in one locality while pasturage was good, and when it was exhausted, would move on to new fields. Sometimes the tribe in possession of one district would learn that other tribes were drawing near, and in an age when strangers were considered enemies, this would furnish sufficient pretext for starting out on the march again. Periods of unrest sometimes swept over vast areas; in such a time as this, perhaps, Asiatic tribes poured into Egypt. In her pitiable plight, the country lay an easy prey to such invaders, who Manetho tells us numbered a quarter of a million. It is said that they took possession without a battle. Just who they were or where they came from is not known. We now know that the Hittites invaded Babylonia during the reign of Samsu-ditana, the last king of the First Dynasty of Babylon, and that this was the indirect cause of the fall of this dynasty (about 1750 B.C.). Scholars are beginning to suspect that the invasion of Egypt at this time was either led by the Hittites or due to Hittite pressure back of the tribes in Syria-Palestine. Their kings were called Hyksos, and from a doubtful etymology of this name they are still styled the "Shepherd kings."

The invading conquerors put many of the Egyptians to death, taking their wives and children into slavery. Worshipping gods of their own, they hated the gods of the Egyptians and destroyed many temples and monuments. Generally speaking, they remained in the Delta and the Fayoum, the Theban princes ruling in the south as their vassals.

Gradually these fierce Asiatics took on the civilization of the land they had invaded. They donned Egyptian dress, spoke and wrote as the Egyptians, and built temples much like theirs. The country rallied from its recent disaster and life became not unlike that of earlier times.

In time the Theban nobles increased in power ; the Hyksos —or their descendants in the Delta—grew alarmed lest the native princes might become powerful enough to force them from the throne they had usurped. Determined to check any threatening strength on the part of the Egyptains, the foreigners tried to bring about open conflict, sure themselves of victory. At first the Theban princes sought to avert war, but the demands of the Hyksos grew heavier. There was a folk-story to the effect that the usurping king in the Delta sent word to the Theban prince that the noise of the sacred hippopotami in the pools and canals allowed him rest neither by night or day, and must be disposed of. However simple this appears, it may easily signify that the final break came because of religious difficulties.

Roused at last, the Egyptians determined to drive the invaders from their land. This occurred during the Seventeenth dynasty—for Manetho continues his list of Egyptian kings throughout the period of foreign rule. The Asiatics were driven north, and the first pharaoh of the Eighteenth Dynasty, King Ahmose (1580-1350 B.C.), gathered a vast army and forced them beyond his borders. Five years were consumed in accomplishing this, and in the end many of the foreigners were reduced to slavery.

Summing up the results of the invasion of the Hyksos, we may note that Egypt learned much during her period of oppression. Before the invasion, her fighting had been confined to the defense of her frontiers. Asiatic and African, and the tribes with which she had waged war had been her inferiors. In the Asiatic tribes she had at last met a people more skillful in military affairs than she. They used horses and chariots, and their mode of warfare was superior to the clumsy, undisciplined efforts of the Nile-dwellers. It was by adopting their methods that Egypt finally succeeded in expelling them from the land. Hereafter we find the horse and chariot used extensively in Egyptian wars.

Another important result was the elimination of the feudal lords. They had opposed both the Hyksos and the successful king Ahmose, and fighting for personal interests alone, had most of them perished in the conflict. The vast areas which had been their portion reverted to the crown and became royal domain.

It has been thought that Joseph served under one of the foreign kings, and that the conditions spoken of at the close of his career—when all Egypt was subdued and at the command of the Pharaoah—coincide with the situation shortly after the feudal lords had disappeared as a political factor. All this is, however, doubtful.

In marked contrast with the gloom of long years under foreign oppression shines the splendor of the New Empire.

The Beginning of the New Empire.[1]

The wide differences which we have noted concerning dates accepted by various Egyptologists disappear as we approach the Christian era, and there is general agreement that the sixteenth century before Christ saw the dawn of the New Empire which had its beginning when the independence of Egypt was established and Hyksos rule thrown off. Petrie calls this the most glorious page in Egyptian history.

Ahmose had much to do before the safety of the government was assured. While he pursued the Hyksos into Asia, crippling their allies, the Ethiopians infringed upon his southern border. Three different expeditions had to be sent against them before they were reduced to submission. Then only did the king find opportunity to direct his attention to the domestic concerns of the kingdom. Thebes, the capital, was given first consideration in the matter of building and adornment. The foundations for the famous temple of Karnak, of which we shall hear more at length, were begun.

---

[1] Dynasties XVIII to XX, 1580-1090 B.C.

Ahmose's son succeeded him, but aside from putting down an uprising of the troublesome Ethiopians, little of importance attached to his administration.

It was left for Ahmose's grandson, Thutmose[1] I., to give Egypt the position she was to occupy among the nations for many years. Thutmose I. was instinctively a soldier. Coming to the throne when a mere boy, the Ethiopians made war directly, thinking they could easily overcome so inexperienced a king. Thutmose at once gave indication of his capacity by marching immediately into their territory and defeating them with tremendous slaughter. To prevent further annoyance from these people the king divided their country into districts and over each he placed an Egyptian official. Thus the land of Kush became an Egyptian province.

Having now a well organized army, Thutmose pressed into Asia—for the experience of Ahmose had shown that rich plunder there awaited the victor. Some tribes yielded voluntarily to Egypt; others were forced to yield.

Although the king penetrated some distance east of the Euphrates, these districts were not permanently won for Egypt. On the contrary, we shall find that subsequent pharaohs did over and over again what this king attempted, and for this reason: each time a nation was conquered, Thutmose withdrew his soldiers from it, imposing tribute and asking hostages. So long as the tribute was forthcoming, the tribe was left undisturbed. This gave wide opportunity for the conquered peoples to unite among themselves and make attempts to shake off control whenever a new ruler succeeded to the throne of Egypt. This proved eventually a most extravagant policy for Thutmose to have followed.

Henceforth Egypt had to take her place as a military power, and with her every new aspiring nation had to reckon. When we recall the peaceful Egyptians of early times, secluded in their quiet valley, disliking foreigners and having as little intercourse with them as possible, we realize what a change had been wrought in them by their contact with the Hyksos during the years of their oppression.

Egypt's future was largely marked out by Thutmose I., as later reigns demonstrated. Perhaps his greatness has not been wholly appreciated. "The greatness of Thutmose[1] I. has

[1] Usually written Thothmes. The form Thutmose is, however, nearer the original.

scarcely been sufficiently recognized by historians. It may be true that he did not effect much ; but he broke ground in a new direction ; he set an example which led on to grand results. To him it was due that Egypt ceased to be the isolated, unaggressive power that she had remained for perhaps ten centuries, that she came boldly to the front and aspired to bring Asia into subjection. Henceforth she exercised a potent influence beyond her borders—an influence which affected, more or less, all the western Asiatic powers. She had forced her way into the comity of the great nations. Henceforth whether it was for good or for evil, she had to take her place among them, to reckon with them, as they reckoned with her, to be a factor in the problem which the ages had to work out—what should be the general march of events, and what states and nations should most affect the destiny of the world."[1]

[1] Rawlinson, Ancient Egypt, 168.

his death. Nor would Hatshepsut have her temple like those around her. Rather, a site was chosen out of Thebes, where the hills rose to quite an elevation. A series of four terraces, each having its beautiful colonnade, led to the temple itself, which was hewn out of the rocky hill.

The young queen wished to build such a temple as she fancied might have been sacred to Amon—the ancient deity of Thebes—in his own land of Punt, on the East African coast. It was a myth of the Egyptians that long before they existed, the gods abode in the land of Punt, called by them the Holyland, or God's land. Tradition held that in this land the myrrh tree was sacred to Amon, and so one day Queen Hatshepsut announced to her ministers that the god Amon had revealed to her his desire that here in Thebes, before the new temple, his favorite myrrh tree should grow.

Now myrrh incense for offerings had been procured from merchantmen who brought their spices into Egypt, and the tree itself grew only in Punt, which lay to the furthermost corner of the ancient world. However, the queen was determined to satisfy the god—and incidentally, perhaps, her own fancy. So, nothing daunted, her subjects set to work to construct a fleet suitable for the journey necessary for procuring the incense-bearing tree.

It is supposed that some canal connected the river with the Red Sea; whether or not this was the case, the ships were built at Thebes, and there is no record of their having been carried over land to the port. They were fitted out with both sails and oars, so that the expedition might not be hindered by calm weather. Beside the oarsmen and the crew, soldiers accompanied the fleet to give protection should it be needed.

After many days the ships came at last to the Holy Land, or Punt. Messengers were dispatched to the native king with presents from Queen Hatshepsut and a request that he acknowledge the sovereignty of Egypt, and allow her subjects to bring back products from his land—especially the coveted incense-tree. The king was delighted with the gifts and made up a procession to go down to the shore and meet the Egyptians. He had a funny little dwarf wife, belonging, it is supposed, to one of the dwarf tribes of interior Africa. She on her donkey, her three children, the king and several of his chiefs, proceeded to the shore to greet the strangers. They were led to the native houses—curious round huts built on piles and entered only by ladders, while palm and incense trees sheltered their occupants from the hot rays of the tropical sun. The travelers were treated royally throughout their sojourn in the land of Punt, and were allowed to exchange the products they had brought from the valley of the Nile for the native products—such as ebony, ivory, incense, leopard skins, metals, and the much desired myrrh trees.

At length the Egyptians were ready to set sail for the home land, and now some of the natives, the dwarf queen, some of the chief men and others decided to return with them and see the queen of great renown; so with these for passengers, the ships cleared port.

Upon arrival, their return was the occasion for a gala-day at the capital. The state troops were out on parade, the veterans of the expedition formed in procession with the thirty-one myrrh trees which had been carefully packed and shielded under awning from the sun's rays; the strange animals from Punt—dogs, baboons, monkeys, a tame leopard with his keeper, natives who gave their war dance, the dwarf queen of Punt, who with her chief men brought gifts to Hatshepsut—all these made up a great spectacle sufficiently absorbing to the throngs who filled the streets of Thebes. All went to the temple where Queen Hatshepsut made offerings to Amon, and then the myrrh trees were planted before his temple. It would be interesting to know how many of these thirty-one trees withstood the radical change, but probably trees which had occasioned such a national outlay had no choice but to flourish.

Queen Hatshepsut felt a natural pride in the result of her expedition which had the effect of establishing lasting trade between the two countries, to the benefit of both. She did not wish it to be forgotten, and so had the whole story depicted on the walls of her temple by artists who probably accompanied the fleet. There some of the pictures may still be seen. The first portrays the embarking of the Egyptian fleet. An inscription before it reads: "These are the ships which the wind brought along with it. The voyage on the sea, the attainment of the longed-for aim in the Holy Land, the happy arrival of the Egyptian soldiers in the land of Punt, according to the arrangement of Amon, King of the gods, Lord of the terrestrial thrones in Thebes, in order to bring to him the treasures of the whole land in such quantities as will satisfy him. This was done by the Queen of Egypt, the daughter of the Sun, never has anything similar been done in the times of a former king in this country."[1]

The second scene shows the reception in Punt ; the third, the traffic ; the fourth picture, the loading of ships for the return. Men are seen bringing trees and other products of Punt on board This inscription reads: "The loading of the ships of transport with a great quantity of the magnificent products of Arabia,[2] with all kinds of precious woods of the Holy Land, with heaps of incense, resin, with verdant incense trees, with ebony, with pure ivory, with gold, and silver from the land of Amon, with tesep-wood and the cassia bark, incense, hounds, skins of leopards, apes, monkeys, with women and children. Never has a coming been made like this by any king since the creation of the world."

The fifth is the "Return to Thebes." The accompanying inscription: "Excursion completed satisfactorily, happy arrival at Thebes to the joy of the Egyptian soldiers. The princes of Punt after arrival in this country, bringing with them costly things of the Arabian[2] land, such as never had yet been brought by any Egyptian king, for the Supreme Majesty of the god Amon-Ra, Lord of the terrestrial thrones."

The sixth scene represents the presentation of the tribute of Punt to the Queen, while princes of that land kneeling before her ask for peace.

> "Homage to thy countenance,
> O Queen of Egypt, Sun,
> Beaming like the sun-disk
> After your mistress, who is
> Arabia's[2] mistress."

In the seventh painting the Queen offers gifts to Amon; the eighth shows the weighing of the incense; the ninth, the formal announcement of the successful expedition before

---

[1] These inscriptions are translated in Records of the Past, ed. by Sayce, Vol. X
[2] The translation is to be corrected to Punt.

Amon, and the tenth and last, the formal announcement of the happy issue before the Egyptian court.

Other paintings which adorn the walls of this temple, depicting the birth of the Queen and the guardianship exercised over her by the goddess Hathor, while less famous are quite as indelible and interesting from a social standpoint.

This temple in its architectural conception was a departure from Egyptian models. It impresses us with its fine proportion and the skillful use of the colonnade.

It has not long been accessible to visitors, having been uncovered only in the last few years.

Other building enterprises were undertaken by Queen Hatshepsut, notably the erection of two obelisks of polished granite in honor of Amon.

Possessing some tributary territory in Asia and Punt and maintaining a policy of peace, the national revenue was much increased. The proud queen left a record of her kingdom's prosperity chronicled in stone : " My southern boundary is as far as Punt ; my eastern boundary as far as the marshes of Asia, and the Asiatics are in my grasp ; my western boundary is as far as the mountain of Manu (or the sunset) ; my fame is among the Sand dwellers altogether. The myrrh of Punt has been brought to me, all the luxurious marvels of this country were brought to my palace in one collection. They have brought me the choicest products, of cedar, of juniper, and of meru-wood ; all the goodly sweet woods of God's-land. I brought the tribute of Libya, consisting of ivory and seven hundred tusks which were there, numerous panther skins of five cubits along the back and four cubits wide."[1]

In addition to new structures, Queen Hatshepsut repaired temples fallen in decay. In one of these temples she caused to be written : " I have restored that which was in ruins, I have raised up that which was unfinished since the Asiatics were in the midst of the Northland, and the barbarians in the midst of them, overthrowing that which had been made while they ruled in ignorance of Ra."[2]

Thutmose III., a younger brother—a mere child at the death of his father—grew restless at being held so long from the

[1] Trans. by Breasted, History of Egypt, 280.
[2] Ibid.

throne by his ambitious sister. The sudden death of the queen again raised the question as to whether the sovereign had died as a result of court intrigue. Certain it is that Thutmose III. retaliated for the restraint the queen had exercised over him by commanding that her name be stricken from all the monuments she had erected, his own to be substituted. Fortunately his workmen followed his instructions so badly that it has been possible to read the original name in many cases, and thus possible to trace the career of the world's earliest recorded queen. Thus have later ages been able to realize how well Queen Hatshepsut met the requirements of her day, and to appreciate her courage in overcoming the prejudices which as a woman on the throne of the Pharaohs she is sure to have encountered.

QUEEN HATSHEPSUT.

CHAPTER VII.

Great Military Kings.

The accession of a new king was the signal for Asiatic nations, long held in tribute, to revolt from a servitude that had always been galling to their pride. Thutmose III. at once established his reputation as a king of prompt decision and strength by marching immediately into the revolting territories and defeating the league formed against him. During his reign of some fifty years he is reputed to have carried on nineteen campaigns. The wealth of Egypt was materially increased by these expeditions which were frequently marauding excursions rather than open-battle victories.

"Altogether Thothmes [Thutmose] III. is said to have carried off from the subject countries about 11,000 captives, 1,670 chariots, 3,639 horses, 4,491 of the larger cattle, more than 35,000 goats, silver to the amount of 3,940 pounds, and gold to the amount of 9,954 pounds. He also conveyed to Egypt from the conquered lands enormous quantities of corn and wines, together with incense, balsam, honey, ivory, ebony, and other rare woods, lapis lazuli, furniture, statues, vases, dishes, basins, tent-poles, bows, habergeons, fruit-trees, live birds, and monkeys! With a curiosity which was insatiable, he noted all that was strange or unusual in the lands which he visited, and sought to introduce the various novelties into his own proper country. Two unknown kinds of birds, and a variety of the goose, which he found in Mesopotamia, and transported from the valley of the Khabour to that of the Nile, are said to have been 'dearer to the king than anything else.' His artists had instructions to make careful studies of the different objects, and to represent them faithfully on his monuments. We see on these 'water-lilies as high as trees, plants of a growth like cactuses, all sort of trees and shrubs, leaves, flowers, and fruits, including melons and pomegranates; oxen and calves also figure, and among them a wonderful animal with three horns. There are likewise herons, sparrow-hawks, geese and doves.' All these appear gaily intermixed in the pictures, as suited the simple childlike conception of the artist. An inscription tells the intention of the monarch. 'Here,' it runs, 'are all sorts of plants and all sorts of flowers of the Holy Land, which the king discovered when he went to the land of Ruten to conquer it. Thus says the king—I swear by the sun, and I call to witness my father Amon, that all is plain truth; there is no trace of deception in that which I relate. What the splendid soil brings forth in the way of production I have portrayed in these pictures, with the intention of offering them to my father Amon, as a memorial for all times.' "[1]

Egypt had now become so powerful that many of the Phoenician cities voluntarily came under her protection, thinking in this way they could best secure safety for their extensive commerce on the seas. The Phoenicians were the middle-men for antiquity and desired above all to keep their triremes safe from sea pirates. Seeking the protection of the greatest world power, in this age they turned to Egypt.

A vast amount of Asiatic plunder found its way to the temples as offerings to the gods who were supposed to have made victory possible. This accumulation of wealth within the temples proved a most important factor in strengthening the priesthood—a power with which the future had to reckon.

A song of victory, composed in honor of Thutmose III., is preserved in the temple of Karnak. The god Amon is supposed to be speaking. We may be sure that it was not wholly the flattery of priests, written to appease the ruler, but that it embodied the general opinion as to the power bestowed by the god upon the king, who was his representative upon earth.

[1] Rawlinson, Ancient Egypt, 196.

Hymn of Victory.[2] *(Amon speaking.)*

I have come, causing thee to smite the princes of Zahi;
I have hurled them beneath thy feet among their highlands.
I have caused them to see thy majesty as lord of radiance,
So that thou hast shone in their faces like my image.

I have come, causing thee to smite the Asiatics,
Thou hast made captive the heads of the Asiatics of Retenu.
I have caused them to see thy majesty equipped with thy adornment
When thou takest the weapons of war in the chariot.

I have come, causing thee to smite the eastern land,
Thou hast trampled those who are in the districts of God's-Land.
I have caused them to see thy majesty like a circling star,
When it scatters its flame in fire, and gives forth its dew.

I have come, causing thee to smite the western land,
Keftyew and Cyprus are in terror.
I have caused them to see thy majesty as a young bull,
Firm of heart, ready-horned, irresistible.

I have come, causing thee to smite those who are in their marshes,
The lands of Mitanni tremble under fear of thee.
I have caused them to see thy majesty as a crocodile,
Lord of fear in the water, unapproachable.

I have come, causing thee to smite those who are in their isles;
Those who are in the midst of the Great Green (sea) hear thy roarings.
I have caused them to see thy majesty as an avenger,
Who rises upon the back of his slain victim. . . .

I have come, causing thee to smite the uttermost ends of the lands,
The circuit of the Great Circle (Okeanos) is included in thy grasp.
I have caused them to see thy majesty as a lord of wing (hawk),
Who seizeth upon that which he seeth, as much as he desires.

[2] Breasted, Ancient Records, II, §§ 658f.

I have come, causing thee to smite the Nubian Troglodytes,
As far as Shat (they) are in thy grasp.
I have caused them to see thy majesty as thy two brothers.[1]
I have united their two arms for thee in victory.

Thy two sisters,[2] I have set them as protection behind thee,
The arms of my majesty are above, warding off evil.
I have caused thee to reign, my beloved son,
Horus, Mighty Bull, Shining in Thebes, whom I have begotten in uprightness of heart.

Thutmose, living forever, who hast done for me all that my ka desired;
Thou hast erected my dwelling as an everlasting work,
Enlarging and extending it more than the past which has been.
Thou hast fêted the beauty of Amon-Re,
Thy monuments are greater than those of any king who has been.
When I commanded thee to do it, I was satisfied therewith;
I established thee upon the Horus-throne of millions of years.

Thutmose III. left his individuality strongly stamped upon the empire his military skill had welded together. Tribute poured into his coffers from all the petty nations throughout western Asia, from the tribes of the Sahara, and lands south of Egypt. He was reckoned without question the greatest military leader the country ever produced, and he was a tireless builder. The great temple of Amon in the city of Thebes was his pride and many other temples were built and restored by him. He was succeeded by his son, but no very important event claims our attention until the accession of his great grandson, Amenhotep IV.

The beautiful Queen Tiy was the mother of this monarch. There is no foundation for the oft repeated assertion that she was of foreign, probably Asiatic, origin. Maspero's belief that she was of Egyptian (perhaps obscure) origin is most probable. We may well believe that she exercised considerable power over her son, but we have no evidence for asserting that it was from her that he received the new religion which he attempted to force upon the country, as a result of which the whole land was thrown into a tumult.

[1] Horus and Set.
[2] Isis and Nephthys.

We have already seen that Egypt was originally composed of many little states, each independent of the rest and each having its own religious system and customs. As the many states were assimilated into one, a state religion resulted, into which the main elements of each local cult were combined. Although the people throughout the land worshipped the state god, the local gods were always more particularly endeared to the masses. Now had Amenhotep IV. desired to change the state god, the official deity, the people would have accepted the change readily, but when he attempted to sweep away the entire religious system of his realm and substitute an utterly new system, the masses could not understand such a radical change. They were enraged at what they considered an indignity put upon their gods and the gods of their fathers.

Realizing how impossible it would be to accomplish his reform in the ancient city of Thebes, the king determined to change his capital. Thebes had long been the religious as well as the political center, and the worship of Amon was fundamentally associated with the city. In order to set up the worship of one deity, Aton—the Solar Disk—in place of Amon, with the complex system of deities, Amenhotep IV. went north of Thebes and began the construction of a new capital[1] which was never completed. Its name signified "The Horizon of the Solar Disk." Within this new capital the new religion was to be firmly established and thence spread throughout the realm. Just what teachings this religion embodied is not now understood. While the sun was worshipped in a new form as Aton, this may have been merely symbolic of one God—one Spirit, felt to be one and alone. Acceptance of the Solar Disk religion necessitated an abandoning of all earlier deities, especially the powerful Amon, and his name was commanded to be stricken from all monuments throughout the land.

The result of this religious crusade was a total failure. Amenhotep IV. realized how great was the innovation he sought to make, but he underestimated the strength of the priests of Amon, the treasures of whose temple at Thebes were loaded with

---

[1] On the site of the modern Tell el-Amarna, about a hundred and sixty miles south of Cairo, on the east bank of the Nile. Here the famous Tell el-Amarna Letters were discovered in 1887.

GREAT PYRAMID, SPHINX AND TEMPLE OF ARMACHIS.

the spoil of Asia. This "reform" while in line with the theology, was utterly at variance with the popular religion of the day. Angered beyond measure by the injury to their faith, the people rose up against the new teaching. The old-time worship was reinstated, the former deities elevated to their former dignity, and the Eighteenth dynasty which had begun so auspiciously came to an end in confusion and disorder.

Karnak.

The temple of Karnak belongs to both the Eighteenth and Nineteenth dynasties. Thutmose III., Amenhotep II. and Amenhotep III. each added rooms to the great structure, although it was left for Seti I. to build the crowning Hall of Pillars. Three centuries witnessed its erection and many kings contributed to its greatness. Most famous of all Theban architecture, it is still mighty in its ruins.

Karnak is the name of one of the four districts into which the irregular Nile divided the city of Thebes. From this district, or ward, the great temple dedicated to Amon—ancient deity of Thebes—took its name.

In some ways, perhaps, the temples of Egypt corresponded to the temples of the Greeks, or even to modern churches, yet there were material differences. Indeed, the similarity is slight. Modern churches are supposedly places of worship; Greek temples were erected in honor of Greek gods and thither offerings were brought by a trusting people. Egyptian temples were built by rulers in honor of some god whose help and protection they believed had enabled them to put down their enemies and given their country its victories and prosperity. While a temple was erected especially in honor of some particular deity, as Karnak was dedicated to Amon, other deities might have shrines within it. While it did honor to the god whose protection had allowed the ruler to rise triumphantly above all obstacles, yet it was the glory of the king that the temple exalted—his pictures adorned the walls, his deeds were set forth in minute detail, his courage in war and relentless energy in times of peace,—these were carved in stone and written in hieroglyphics until it was difficult to find a section of wall, a column, a stone ceiling unadorned. Hymns of victory were inscribed in the temples ; songs of praise and fulsome flattery not infrequently were composed by the priests. Sometimes the god who presided over the temple seems to have been well nigh lost sight of, yet even so, honor was accorded him, since the king was his representative on earth. Because Karnak received the particular care of many kings, it is one of the most interesting temples to study, apart from its beauty, its stupendous size and proportions.

Lists of dimensions are seldom interesting, and yet, unless we compare the size of Egyptian structures to others known to us, we fail utterly to grasp the tremendous scale on which these people built. We have mentioned the avenue, more than a mile in length, guarded on either side with sphinxes, which connected this temple with one built by Queen Hatshepsut. This avenue led finally to a gateway, flanked on both sides by towers. Either of these towers were themselves spacious enough to have contained a temple. The temple court was enclosed by a wall 25 feet thick and varying from 60 to 100 feet in height. Vast wealth was stored in the temple, and this wall made it possible, in an age before gunpowder, to protect the place from sudden attacks—always possible contingencies. The temple itself was 1,180 feet long and 600 feet wide, and was composed of many rooms and halls built by various kings. We shall give attention to one alone—the famous Hall of Pillars.

Often has it been said that to describe this hall and do it justice exceeds the power of mortals. It is on such a vast scale that modern times have produced no structures with which to compare it.

The Hall of Pillars was originally 329 feet long and 170 feet in width. Through its center were placed two rows of columns, six in each row. Excluding pedestal and capital, these measured 60 feet in height and in circumference were so large that should six men stand with arms extended, fingers touching, they could scarcely encompass one. Seven rows of pillars, somewhat smaller, were placed on either side of these ; the ceiling was supported by all these columns and was formed of mammoth blocks of stone. Finally the entire interior was covered with sculptures, paintings, and hieroglyphics—all recounting the exploits of the king who built the hall. In a similar fashion the entire temple was ornamented.

King succeeded king and each burned with ambition to exceed the skill of his predecessor. Room after room was added to Karnak and the original plan greatly expanded. Seti I. however built on such a tremendous plan that none other eclipsed him, and the Hall of Pillars remains today a mighty monument to a mighty ruler.

AMMON-RA, THE GREAT GOD OF THEBES.

CHAPTER VIII.

The Nineteenth Dynasty.[1]

Before Seti I., founder of the Nineteenth dynasty, succeeded to the throne, peace and order had been once more restored to Egypt. One important change had crept into the military life of the country, which was to lead to trouble later on. Heretofore, Egypt had depended solely upon her national troops to protect her borders and maintain her position as first among the nations. Now her armies were increased by mercenaries—foreign soldiers hired to do her fighting for her. History has shown that uniformly when a people ceases to depend upon its own citizens for the main strength of its army, taking instead hired soldiers who fight simply for the love of fighting and for gain, serving one cause today and another tomorrow,—whenever a nation has adopted this policy of providing its armed forces, its years of strength are numbered. So it was in Egypt. Troops from Libya, from Nubia and Ethiopia made up her armies. During times of peace they returned to their kindred and gave glowing accounts of the vast wealth of the Nile valley. It came about naturally then, that African, as well as Asiatic, tribes looked with longing eyes upon the coveted country and stood ready at the first sign of internal weakness to revolt and share the spoils. Strong rulers of the Nineteenth dynasty held their possessions intact, and foreign nations bided the time when the first sign of weakness should be the signal for action.

The immediate successor of Thutmose III. had little trouble in keeping Syria in subjection. Taxes regularly reached Thebes. During the reigns of the Amenhoteps, III. and IV., the Hittites began pushing south from Asia Minor and organizing the revolt against Egypt. Upon ascending the throne Seti I. found it expedient to push into western Asia and quell a vigorous uprising. He was one of Egypt's most capable and farsighted kings, and being as well a fearless warrior, he carried all before him. He struck terror to the hearts of his enemies and returned home

[1] 1350-1205 B. C.

to find the Libyans threatening his western borders. After defeating their chiefs with great slaughter, Seti I. received a large number of their soldiers into his army as mercenaries. This did very well for the time, but before four hundred years had passed, their chiefs had become powerful enough to snatch the throne of Egypt from its rightful claimants.

Like most Egyptian rulers, Seti I. was a builder. From earliest years in Egypt, imposing structures had supplied surest means by which a monarch could leave evidences of his power. The position of chief architect to the king had been filled by princes, who held it as a post of honor. Often the king's sons planned temples for the king's construction, and not infrequently gave personal supervision to their erection.

During the last period of civil disorder, many public monuments and temples had fallen into decay. These Seti I. caused to be restored. He invariably adhered to the original ideas of the builder, adding but an inscription to show that by him they were restored. In this respect his course differed widely from that of many of the Egyptian kings, notably Ramses II., who boldly appropriated scores of temples and monuments, substituting his name for that of the original builder. Frequently his workmen did their task so badly that the first name has been deciphered. In other cases, the true builder of the temple is now uncertain.

It was this king who erected the Hall of Pillars, of which we have just learned. While temples were erected and restored throughout the land, much of his attention was directed to Thebes—the great and splendid city so long the capital of Egypt.

Thebes was built on the east side of the river. On this side dwelt the pharaohs, the wealthy, and the poor. Here too were the shops, the places of business and amusement. In fact, all the interests of living, pulsing Thebes were centered here. On this side also, in the district of Karnak, was the great temple of Amon. South of it rose the palace of the king; around this were mansions of the wealthy, while in the narrow streets reaching into the desert lived those of moderate and limited means. South of Karnak lay the district of Luxor, and along the river between these two districts stood the mud huts of the poor.

Crossing the Nile to the western bank, one came into radically different surroundings. Here lay the City of the Dead. This was quite unlike any cemetery of modern times. Here were temples, tombs of kings and queens, tombs of the wealthy and the prosperous citizens, and the symbolic lake of the dead. Here were the unpretentious tombs of the masses. Nor was this all. We have seen that the Egyptian felt it necessary to supply his dead with all the necessities of life, such as food, furniture, and ornaments. Here, then, were the shops where such things might be obtained. Here were the embalmers, the makers of linen used by them; here lived the priests who said prayers over each finger and toe of the deceased and made the body ready for its everlasting home. On the west bank of the river lay a city in itself very different from the living one across the water. Funeral processions constantly wended their way to this City of the Dead; wails and lamentations often mingled in the air with songs of the priests at their devotions. At sunset the gates admitting to this portion of Thebes were locked and guarded against bands of robbers who laid in wait for the riches enclosed in the tombs. The tombs reached out to the rocky range of hills on the west and were with difficulty protected.

Ancient Thebes extended some miles in each direction and covered considerable territory. Little today remains to mark its early splendor. The ruins at Karnak, the ancient mounds of Luxor, topped by a squalid Arab village, some tombs opened, some still hidden by the sands, are left. Much excavating has been done in this so-called "Valley of the Kings." Strabo and other early writers left some description of the original city, but aside from such records, little is left today to indicate the glories of that Thebes which was for hundreds of years the pride of Egyptian kings.

Ramses.

Seti I. was followed by his son, the famous Ramses II., or Ramses the Great. Recent historians claim that this king has been given undue prominence, and that he was outranked by several Egyptian monarchs, including his own father.

While this is probably true, it would seem that this pharaoh was as popular as any king who ruled in Egypt. He was young and handsome when he ascended the throne, and possessed a power of winning people to himself. That he was filled with self-pride, no one can deny. He attached his name, as we have seen, to every temple and monument where it was possible, and scattered statues of himself broadcast. Yet the only poem that suggests the epic in all Egyptian literature is the one known as " Pentuar's Poem," in which his bravery at the battle of Kadesh was sung.

Ramses had penetrated into Asia to bring the revolting tribes back to submission. During this particular battle, he became separated from his body guard and suddenly found himself facing 2,500 charioteers alone. His personal bravery on that occasion was splendid; his soldiers pressed on to him quickly, but his daring was seen by them and greatly admired. The poem of Pentuar was written to celebrate the king's courage in this crisis.

Pentuar's Poem.[1]

" Then the King stood forth, and, radiant with courage,
He looked like the Sun-god armed and eager for battle.
The noble steeds that bore him into the struggle—
'Victory to Thebes' was the name of one, and the other
Was called 'contented Nura'—were foaled in the stables
Of him we call 'the elect,' 'the beloved of Amon,'
'Lord of truth,' the chosen vicar of Ra.

Up sprang the king and threw himself on the foe,
The swaying ranks of the contemptible Cheta.
He stood alone—alone, and no man with him.
As thus the king stood forth all eyes were upon him,
And soon he was enmeshed by men and horses,
And by the enemy's chariots, two thousand five hundred,
The foe behind hemmed him in, and enclosed him.
Dense the array of the contemptible Cheta,
Dense the swarm of warriors out of Arad,
Dense the Mysian host, the Pisidian legions.

[1] Records of the Past, ed. Dr. Burch. The author is unknown, but the poem is known by the name of a scribe who once copied the production.

Every chariot carried three bold warriors,
All his foes, and all allied like brothers.

" 'Not a prince is with me, not a captain,
Not an archer, none to guide my horses !
Fled the riders ! fled my troops and horse—
By my side not one is now left standing.'
' Great father Amon, I have known thee well,
And can the father thus forget his son ?
Have I in any deed forgotten Thee ?
Have I done aught without Thy high behest,
Or moved or staid against Thy sovereign will ?
Great am I—mighty are the Egyptian kings—
But in the sight of Thy commanding might,
Small as the chieftain of a wandering tribe.
Immortal Lord, crush Thou this unclean people ;
Break Thou their necks, annihilate the heathen.
And I—have I not brought Thee many victims,
And filled Thy temple with the captive folk ?
And for Thy presence built a dwelling place
That shall endure for countless years to come ?
Thy garners overflow with gifts from me.

" 'I offer Thee the world to swell Thy glory,
And thirty thousand mighty steers have shed
Their smoking blood on fragrant cedar piles.
Tall gateways, flag-decked masts, I raised to Thee,
And obelisks from Abu I have brought,
And built Thee temples of eternal stone.
For Thee my ships have brought across the sea
The tribute of the nations. This I did—
When were such things done in former time ?
For dark the fate of him who would rebel
Against Thee ; though Thy sway is just and mild.
My father, Amon—as an earthly son
His earthly father—so I call on Thee.
Look down from heaven on me, beset by foes,
By heathen foes, the folk that know Thee not.
The nations have combined against Thy son ;
I stand alone—alone, and no man with me.

My foot and horse are fled, I called aloud
And no one heard—in vain I called to them.
And yet I say : the sheltering care of Amon
Is better succor than a million men,
Or than ten thousand knights, or than a thousand
Brothers and sons though gathered into one.
And yet I say : the bulwarks raised by men
However strong, compared to Thy great works
Are but vain shadows, and no human aid
Avails against the foe—but thy strong hand.
The counsel of Thy lips shall guide my way ;
I have obeyed whenever Thou hast ruled ;
I call on Thee—and, with my fame, Thy glory
Shall fill the world, from farthest east to west.'

"Yea, his cry rang forth even far as Hermonthis,
And Amon himself appeared at his call ; and gave him
His hand and shouted in triumph, saying to the pharaoh
'Help is at hand, O Rameses. I will uphold thee—
I thy father am he who now is thy succor,
Bearing thee in my hands. For stronger and readier
I than a hundred thousand mortal retainers ;
I am the Lord of victory loving valor.
I rejoice in the brave and give them good counsel,
And he whom I counsel certainly shall not miscarry.'

"Then like Menth, with his right he scattered the arrows,
And with his left he swung his deadly weapon,
Felling the foe—as his foes are felled by Baal.
The chariots were broken and the drivers scattered,
Then was the foe overthrown before his horses.
None found a hand to fight ; they could not shoot,
Nor dared they hurl the spear, but fled at his coming—
Headlong into the river."

Having quelled the disturbances incident to his accession—for a change of rulers was generally the occasion for tribes held in tribute to seek their freedom—Ramses was free to devote the remainder of his reign, some forty years, to internal improvements. New cities, embankments, fortresses, statues, obelisks and temples absorbed his untiring interest. He seems to have been especially fond of grotto temples,—those hewn out of rocky hills or mountain sides. Most beautiful of these was the temple of Abu Simbel, guarded by four famous statues of this king. They stand today much as they stood three thousand years ago. One who has gazed upon the unaltering expression of these sentinels says of them : " The artists who wrought the statues were daunted by no difficulties of scale. Giants themselves, they summoned these giants from out the solid rock and endowed them with superhuman strength and beauty. They sought no quarried blocks of syenite or granite for their work. They fashioned no models of clay. They took a mountain and fell upon it like Titans and hollowed and carved it as though it were a cherry stone ; and left it for the feebler men of after ages to marvel at forever. One great hall and fifteen spacious chambers they hewed out from the heart of it, then smoothed the rugged precipice toward the river, and cut four huge statues with their faces to the sunrise, two to the right and two to the left of the doorway, there to keep watch to the end of time.

" These tremendous warders sit sixty-six feet high, without the platform under their feet. They measure across the chest twenty-five feet and four inches. If they stood up, they would tower to a height of at least eighty-three feet, from the soles of their feet to the tops of their enormous double-crowns."[2]

To estimate the cost of all those tremendous undertakings in human life would be impossible. It is believed by some that Ramses II. was the pharaoh of the oppression of the Hebrews. However, during his administration they were well fed and while their tasks were hard, they were not harder than those of other workmen similarly employed. It was left for his son and successor to make their lot so grievous that a deliverer was raised up to lead them out of bondage.

Regard for human life, compassion for the lowly, and the spirit of humanity were qualities almost unknown in antiquity. The importance of the individual has only in modern times come to be acknowledged. At the period of which we are studying, there was no restraint upon the will of the sovereign.

---

[2] Edwards: A Thousand Miles Up the Nile, 262

To satisfy his ambition and to gratify his pride, hundreds of thousands of slaves, captives, and impressed citizens were continually sacrificed. Some were driven to the mines : others were harnessed to huge blocks of stone to draw them from the quarry mountain to the building site ; some were set to work in the brick fields, and over all were placed overseers to goad the workers on, giving little rest or respite.

Regarding the Hebrews, it must be remembered that before the Nineteenth dynasty, they prospered in the land of Egypt. A new king who "knew not Joseph" looked with disfavor upon these foreign people waxing strong within his borders. Feeling that they might become a menace to the country, he determined to exterminate them by dint of excessive work. One of the "store-cities" built by them under these circumstances has been unearthed. It was surrounded by a wall thirty feet thick, which enclosed about twelve acres. Besides a temple, the enclosure contained subterranean cellars built of sun-dried brick. The bricks themselves confirm the biblical version of the story. While some are mixed with straw, as was customary, others were mixed with leaves and reeds—indicating that straw was no longer supplied. Still others were made simply of sun-dried mud.

Ramses II. so covered the land with his works and monuments of his greatness, that his personality has stamped itself everywhere.

It caught the attention of early writers and has ever since impressed itself upon the traveller, so that this king has been exalted to a prominent place in Egyptian history. Best known of Egypt's kings, for that reason, possibly, he has been most popular.

At length Merneptah ruled in his father's stead. Few qualities did he possess to awaken admiration. When his armies were forced to face an invasion of African tribes, reinforced by mercenary troops, he remained in camp while his soldiers won victory for him. The god Ptah, so he explained, had commanded him to stay inside. This did not deter him from taking full credit for the successes. Upon his monuments were inscribed records similar to this: "These people were meditating to do evil to Egypt. They were as grasshoppers. Lo, I vanquished them; I slaughtered them, making a spoil of their **country**."

It is supposed that at this time Moses came to the relief of Israel, and asked permission for his people to withdraw a few days into the desert to offer sacrifices to their God. This was the occasion for the king both to deny the request and to double the tasks meted out to the brickmakers by withholding straw and requiring the same amount of work to be accomplished as before. Then, according to the Hebrew version, grievous plagues were sent upon Egypt, and only when the king's son, with the other first born, was stricken in the night, did the monarch concede to the entreaties of his own people and bid the Hebrews depart from his land. The story is familiar to all—how when he came to think of the six hundred thousand valued bonds-people of which he was now bereft, he dispatched the flower of Egyptian charioteers to prevent the Hebrews crossing the Red Sea and bring them back to do his bidding. To these despairing people to whom light seemed about to dawn, the fact that they were able to cross over while the Egyptian horses were ensnared and drowned, seemed a miracle enacted for their deliverance. It has since been noted that similar tidal action at this point has sometimes repeated itself. To the Hebrews, believing firmly in the inspired mission of Moses, it was regarded later as an example of how for the dutiful " all things work together for good."

Twentieth Dynasty.[1]

Ramses III. was the first important ruler of the Twentieth dynasty. He and his immediate successors were able to hold intact the vast empire won by earlier kings. We hear no more of aggressive wars for conquest. However, the time had come when Egypt did well when she maintained such territories as belonged to her.

Men of Crete, other islanders and sea-faring people, made common cause against the Asiatic shore early in this reign. Ramses watched their progress until they attacked the Egyptian province of Palestine. Not willing to lose this, the pharaoh marched against the plundering bands and utterly routed them, taking many captives. Three other campaigns were directed by this king, but they were carried on to defend Egyptian borders and hold together tributary provinces.

Like his father, Ramses III. was a builder. Like him, too,

[1] 1200-1090 B. C.

he appropriated earlier temples and monuments for his own fame and glory. He built a fleet on the Red Sea, continued the profitable commercial intercourse with Punt, and caused a large reservoir to be constructed in Palestine. Another thing he did, which all histories have been careful to chronicle: he ordered trees and shrubs to be systematically planted throughout the realm. In a land where for months together the sun pours its hot rays down on a defenseless people, he tried to bring rest and cooling shade where both were sorely needed.

We have often noted the growing power of the priesthood in Egypt, and have seen that a large amount of the booty and tribute which flowed into the country from Asia found its way to the temples. An inventory of the resources of the temples during this reign has come down to us in a statement prepared by Ramses III., known now as the Papyrus Harris. From this it appears that the temples owned 107,000 slaves—or 2 per cent of the entire population; they possessed 750,000 acres, or over 15 per cent of all the arable land in the valley. Some 500,000 head of cattle, over 80 vessels, 53 workshops and ship-yards, brought an annual income; and 169 towns in Egypt Kush and Syria were theirs. All this property in a land of less than 10,000 square miles and possibly 6,000,000 people, was exempt from taxation.

The lion's share of all this wealth fell to the temples sacred to Amon. The priests of Amon had charge of it, and as time went on, they came to be regarded as superior to other priestly orders and their High Priest became the head of all priest-hoods in the realm. Of all the temple estates, Amon owned two-thirds. In slaves, this god owned seven times as many as any other; of the cattle, more than four-fifths; of the ships, all but five; of the workshops, forty-six of the fifty-three were his. Regarding Amon's coffers, Ramses had inscribed: "I have filled its treasury with the products of the land of Egypt: gold, silver, every costly stone by the hundred thousand. Its granary was overflowing with barley and wheat; its lands, its herds, their multitudes were like the sands of the shore. I taxed for it the Southland as well as the Northland; Nubia and Syria came to it, bearing their impost."[a]

[a] Breasted: History of Egypt, 493; trans.

In showering all these princely gifts upon Amon, Ramses was but following the example set by his forefathers. The kings themselves held the priests somewhat in fear, believing that they had influence with the gods and could indirectly influence not only their earthly prosperity but their future welfare.

While this lavish wealth overflowed the coffers of the temples, we find the workmen in the service of the government, laboring in the City of the Dead—the Necropolis—having to resort to strikes, or in older phraseology, "having to lie at home," because their monthly rations were not forthcoming. The revenue of the government had, apparently, become the spoils for corrupt officials who sought to increase their personal incomes at the expense of the public treasury. Repeatedly starving laborers left their work and started with their families to leave Thebes, whereupon part of their rations would be given them and they would be urged to continue at their tasks! Nor was this all. Records have come down to us of bands of robbers who made a profession of rifling tombs of the dead. Worse still, cases for trial were frequently dismissed because officials themselves and priests of lesser position were sharing in the booty! Some of the Ramessides removed their ancestors from the original tombs and had all placed in a shaft where guards could keep watch over them. It was next to impossible to protect the wide-reaching City of the Dead, but it was worse than useless to attempt such a thing when those supposed to lend protection were themselves participating in the robberies.

After the death of Ramses III., his descendants to the number of ten succeeded him. Then the High Priest of Amon snatched the power from Ramses XIII., taking the title of king as well as the authority which he already held. For some time the kings had been practically subservient to him. For almost a hunderd and fifty years priests ruled in Egypt.[1] Under priestly rule the government was quite as corrupt as it had been previously. Discontent on the part of the workmen, bold robberies of tombs, were the order of the day. First Libyan, then Ethiopian chiefs gained possession of the throne. The country fell apart; the days of Egypt's glory were gone.

From this time forward her political power was at an end.

---
[1] Twenty-first Dynasty, 1090-945 B. C.

To be sure, Ethiopian kings took on Egyptian civilization—as a matter of fact, their country had long been Egyptianized. They tried to rule as pharaohs before them had done, worshipping Egyptian gods and keeping temples in repair. To the average citizen, life was no doubt much as it had been in former periods. But the old ideas were steadily falling away. The Assyrians invaded the country, and later, the Persians under Cambyses conquered it. Now and then a native prince would temporarily get control and repulse the Libyans and Ethiopians on the west and Asiatic peoples on the east. Such reactions and returns to the old order were short-lived, and like the sudden glow of dying embers, bespoke an approaching end.

Foreign people and foreign influences pushed into the valley. Especially did they come from Greece. We have seen that rapid change and quick assimilation were alien to the nature of the Egyptian. While the Greeks gained much by this contact, their coming served but to make briefer the remaining years of Egyptian life. Greek learning was taught and Greek religion spread into the valley. Finally with the conquest of Alexander in 331 B. C., the prevailing element in the land became Greek and so remained until Rome extended her sway over all the ancient world.

When we think that each succeeding invasion was the occasion for destruction; when plunder and fire vied with each other in despoiling the conquered land; when later the few temples which had withstood these experiences were robbed of their contents, and obelisks, monuments and statues were scattered among the nations of the earth, to satisfy personal gratification, we can no longer wonder that so little remains of that Egypt we have been studying.

After the period of the priest-kings, the history of Egypt belongs to the history of Assyria, Babylonia, Greece and Rome, and no longer concerns us in our attempt to become acquainted with the "earliest nations."

We feel some way that the end of Egypt's political power should have been more splendid than it was—more worthy of her former dignity and strength, and almost regret that the masses of her citizens had not met their final repulse in some desperate rally to drive invaders from their borders But the end had been long drawn out. Generations of alien rule had accustomed the people to accept this as a natural condition. Rawlinson puts it well: " As it was, Egypt sank ingloriously at the last—her art, her literature, her national spirit decayed and almost extinct—paying, by her early disappearance from among the nations of the earth, the penalty of her extraordinarily precocious greatness."[4]

Such being a brief survey of her political achievements, we turn now to the life and customs of her people.

[4] Rawlinson: Ancient Egypt, 402.

OSIRIS

SOCIAL LIFE IN EGYPT

CHAPTER IX.

Introductory.

THE social life of ancient peoples has for many greater interest than their political development. Before the days of Greece self-government was unknown, and the king embodied in himself the government. Upon his personal character, his foresight and statesmanship, the weal of the country depended. For this reason, as we trace the political fortunes of one nation and another in antiquity, we find that the story consists largely of the doings of the monarch. When kings were strong and ambitious, wide activities characterized their reigns; when they were weak, unprincipled and selfish, their periods were less brilliant. In any case, one feels how powerless were the masses—how utterly at the will of the sovereign. To be sure, even in antiquity, it ill behooved a ruler to disregard his subjects altogether, but conditions had to be extreme before they would assert themselves against him.

Apart from a nation's political life, however, there is always a greater life—the life of the people, regardless of their political relations. One never exists without the other, and one is influenced by the other; but the social body includes each and every one, whether of low or high estate, while the political body may include but a portion of a nation's people. Again, in spite of bad government, the selfishness of kings, even in spite of invasions of the enemy, the daily life of the great majority of early people varied but little. They procured food and clothing, cared for their children, worked at their various callings, as civilized beings have done in all ages. Certain peculiar customs are to be found among each nation, and it is these very peculiarities, probably, that relieves what might otherwise become a monotonous repetition.

We cannot too often recall that the recorded history of ancient Egypt extended over three thousand years. The manner of life, dress, customs, etc., changed considerably in that long period, and just as we divide the social life of England into various epochs—such as social conditions under Saxon kings, during Norman rule, in Elizabethan years, etc.—so, for any protracted investigation of social Egypt, we would find it necessary to make several divisions of the subject.

The greatest source of knowledge for Egyptian social life is of course the tombs. From their contents and from the pictures that adorn their walls much has been ascertained. To be sure, many details are yet lacking, and Egyptologists seek still for answers to unanswered queries. Many recovered remains have not yet been classified, and rolls of papyri lie still untranslated, so undoubtedly the future will make many contributions to what has already been worked out. Nevertheless, even now many aspects of the life of the old Nile-dwellers have been reconstructed with considerable degree of certainty. These recent conclusions have proven the ancient Egyptian to have been quite a different creature from what he was long supposed. Until late years it was believed that he was a solemn, serious individual, overwhelmed with an ever-present thought of death, for which many of his acts in life prepared him. This idea was mistaken. The religion of the ancient Egyptian led him into many curious ways, beyond a doubt, but he was withal a contented person who found some humor in life. The happenings of his earthly career were as potent to him as ours are to us. The study of history should do one thing for us at least: it should teach us to find strong similarities between the people we see around us today and those of whom we read and study in antiquity. The normal human being has in all ages been governed by certain controlling interests, passions and desires, has pulsed with the vigor of life and its manifold interests—as we do now and as the Egyptian did, five thousand years ago.

Houses.

In strong contrast with the solid, substantial tombs and temples were the private dwellings. No need was felt to make these enduring. Rather, they were constructed in such a way as to allow free circulation of air and to preserve coolness. The walls were thin, being made of stucco, mud brick, or wood. The outside of the house was decorated in gay colors, and was hung with brightly tinted carpets or mattings. Similar coverings adorned the inner walls.

Many pictures of ancient Egyptian houses have been found in tomb pictures. It is apparent that the well-to-do citizen desired seclusion for his home. An outer wall usually surrounded the house and out buildings. The general plan of houses for people of comfortable means was this: a gateway, often of cedar, gave entrance into a court. The gate was kept locked, save when the keeper opened it to allow visitors to enter or depart. Crossing the court—of varying size—one entered a vestibule, guarded by a porter. This vestibule led directly to the dining hall, the largest and most important room in the house. Sleeping apartments for the family were reached through a second vestibule and the kitchen, store-rooms, and servants' apartments, though joined on one side, were separated from the main portion of the house by an inner court. Often the houses were two stories in height. Generally a stairway led to the roof, which was used for many purposes when the heat of the sun was passed.

The wealthy required many buildings. One would be set aside for the women; another contained reception halls for distinguished guests; a third, store-rooms and supplies; and besides these there might be several stables and separate quarters for slaves and servants. Service was cheap and slaves plentiful, so people of even moderate means had numerous assistants.

The elaborate estate of the wealthy was exceeded by the magnificence of the pharaoh, who frequently constructed his own city, as it was called. Here the king might have plenty of land and surround himself with as many buildings as he chose, enclosing the whole by a wall. In bitter contrast to this royal splendor was the squalor of the poor, whose shelter was a tiny hut built of sun-dried mud.

For those whose incomes permitted, the garden was the favorite spot. This we would naturally expect in a country where out of door life is interrupted only in the middle of the day by the intense heat. In the garden, trees, shrubs, and many kinds of flowers were planted. Its size depended upon the prosperity of the owner. Sometimes the court, however tiny, provided all the garden plot he possessed; sometimes extensive grounds included flower-gardens, date orchards, and sycamore groves, while summer houses and artificial ponds were scattered over wide areas. Small wonder was it that the "pious Egyptian hoped his soul, as its supreme felicity, would return to sit under the trees he had planted, by the side of the ponds he had dug, there to enjoy the refreshing breeze from the north."

The Egyptians were passionately fond of flowers. They grew them in their gardens, filled their houses with the blossoms, used them lavishly at their feasts and carved them on their tombs and in their temples. They sought ever to increase their varieties, originally few, and we have seen that the kings often prized new specimens found in other lands above their tribute.

"Everywhere on the monuments we meet with flowers; bouquets of flowers are presented to the gods; the coffins are covered with wreaths of flowers; flowers form the decoration of the houses, and all the capitals of the pillars are painted in imitation of their colored petals. The Egyptian also loved shady trees. He not only prayed that the 'Nile should bestow every flowering plant in their season' upon his departed soul, but also that his soul might sit 'on the boughs of the trees that he had planted, and enjoy the cool air in the shade of his sycamore.' The arable fields, the shadeless woods of palms, the bare mud soil, scarcely provided the scenery which he most admired; he therefore tried to supply the want by landscape gardening. In the oldest periods there were parks and gardens; and the gentleman of ancient Egypt talked with pride of his shady trees, his sweet-smelling plants, and his cool tanks. All the sentiments with which we regard the woods and meadows of nature, the Egyptian felt towards his well kept garden; to him it was the dwelling place of love, and his trees were the confidants of lovers.

"On the 'festival day of the garden,' that is on the day when the garden was in full bloom, the wild fig-tree calls to the maiden to come into the shade of the fig leaves as a trysting place:

"The little Sycamore,
　Which she planted with her hand
　She begins to speak,
　And her (words are as) drops of honey.
　She is charming, her bower is green,
　Greener than the (papyrus).
　She is laden with fruit,
　Redder than the ruby,
　The color of her leaves is as glass,
　Her stem is as the color of the opal.
　It is cool in her shadow.
　She sends her letter by a little maiden,
　The daughter of her chief gardener
　She makes her haste to her beloved :
　Come and linger in the (garden)
　The servants who belong to thee
　Come with the dinner things ;
　They are bringing beer of every (kind),
　With all manner of bread,
　Flowers of yesterday and of today,
　And all kinds of refreshing fruit.
　Come, spend this festival day
　And tomorrow and the day after tomorrow
　Sitting in my shadow.
　Thy companion sits at thy right hand,
　Thou dost make him drink,
　And then thou dost follow what he says.
　I am of a silent nature
　And I do not tell what I see
　I do not chatter."[1]

Having attractive grounds as a setting, the houses of the wealthy Egyptians were also attractive indoors. The dining room was the important room of the house. Guests generally sat on stools when dining. When ladies gathered for a banquet, they frequently sat on costly rugs spread upon the floor. Servants or slaves served those assembled from a large table loaded with tempting viands.

The Egyptian seems no longer far away and mummy-like

[1] Erman: Life in Ancient Egypt, 193.

when we learn that he was fond of good things to eat. Roast goose was a favorite dish; bread and beer were constantly in demand, quite as they are in Germany today. In naming over the dishes he hoped to supply his departed, in a tomb we may read: five kinds of birds, sixteen kinds of bread and cake, six varieties of wine, and eleven different fruits. The bread, molded into fancy shapes, was made of barley and wheat. Grapes were generally grown, and fig trees too. Tame monkeys were trained to go into the high branches of the fig trees and throw down the fruit.

Many specimens of ancient household furniture have been found in Egyptian tombs, such as chairs, couches, tables and bedsteads. In the sleeping apartments, high couches were reached by steps. Wooden headrests took the place of pillows. These were used in order that the wigs and elaborate head dresses might not be disturbed while the wearers slept.

The student who would make an exhaustive study of the Egyptian house and its contents must go to the museums where discovered articles have been preserved, or at least to the detailed descriptions of these given by Maspero and other Egyptologists. We could not well leave a consideration of the subject however, without giving brief attention to the dwellings of the poor, who in every age and country have made up a large part of the population.

The fellah of today lives much as did the peasant of antiquity. His dwelling was a hut built of mud and roofed with palm leaves. While the poorest had but one room, those who were more industrious, perhaps, might have two or three. Once or twice in a century, rain would fall. Then these huts would dissolve and flow away. When the storm ceased, all the family would set to work, level off the spot and construct a new dwelling from sun-dried mud, which after being exposed to the heat of a few days, would be as good as ever. This leveling of huts, whether caused by storms, or because it was easier to build a new house than cleanse the old one, has elevated the land in many parts of Egypt. Frequently it is the case that peasants have dwelt so long on the sites of buried cities, that the explorer who today would reach the original settlement must tunnel down through many layers of sun-dried mud, once the dwellings of the poor.

Family Life.

It is frequently said that the test of a nation's civilization is the position accorded to woman. Applying this test to Egypt, her civilization would rank well with nations of modern times as well as with those contemporaneous with her. From the earliest times of which we have record, Egyptian women were the companions and trusted counsellors of their husbands. During the New Empire it was the boast of one of the Ramessides that any woman might go alone and unveiled as far in any direction as she wished, confident that she would not be accosted nor disturbed.

Two customs prevailed in ancient Egypt that are contrary to the moral standards of our day: one was the practice of a brother marrying his sister; the second, a husband having more than one wife. Early peoples did not regard these practices in the light of modern opinion. The Hebrews, for example, frequently took two or more wives, and the same habit obtained among the Babylonians and Assyrians. Among pastoral tribes of the present day this custom survives. In all cases, *one* woman was regarded as the legitimate wife, and her children were heirs to their father's estate, while children by his other wives might or might not be recognized by the father as his heirs, according to his pleasure. As a rule, only the well-to-do Egyptian could afford the luxury of two wives, so that polygamy was not common among the lower classes. There seems to have been little friction in the Egyptian household between the several wives. Stories have come down to us of women who cared enough for other wives of their husbands to name children for them. Certain marks of honor were the right of the first wife and were conceded as a matter of course.

The marriage of those close of kin was quite usual. The word *sister* in Egypt came to be used interchangeably for wife or sister. In this land it appears to have frequently resulted that a boy and girl, brought up in the same family, having similar ideas and interests, married and lived happily together in their married life.

Multifarious were the duties of a wife of the middle class. She cared for the family, spun and wove, sent the little ones to school and took them a lunch at mid-day. She drew water at the nearest pool, ground corn into meal and made the meal into cakes; she drove the cattle to pasture and collected the fuel. What did not this mother do? It is little wonder that from lack of care and nourishment, large numbers of children died before they became ten years of age. Those who lived were indeed the survival of the fittest, and aside from a disease of the eye—brought on by the glaring sand and burning sun— they were generally healthy and equal to any hardship. Marrying young, women were often grandmothers at thirty. Although they faded early, they did not suffer in their position in the family on that account. Great respect was shown them while they lived, and after their death they were worshipped— for the Egyptian always worshipped his ancestors. Believing that the soul lived on, it might work harm for the surviving relatives and friends unless appeased with marked consideration. This desire to escape possible harm by satisfying the departed appears to have been the strong motive inducing ancient peoples to worship the dead.

The children were left with the mother until almost four years of age. Dolls and other toys found buried in the tombs with little ones show that they, in those far away times, were quite like children who have lived since. When four, they were sent to an elementary school. If at ten the son had evinced any special ability that would justify educating him, he was put into a school maintained by the priests. Here he was trained for a scribe unless his early promise was borne out by rapid progress, in which case he was educated for the priesthood. If by the age of ten he had given no special evidence of ability, he was taught a trade.

The old idea that caste was strongly marked in Egypt is not only misleading but untrue. Class distinctions were closely drawn in Egypt, as they are today, even in America. The average child born in the slums of a city seldom comes to importance. The son of a day laborer rarely marries into the wealthy or so-called "old families." The reason for this is not so much that there is objection in America to the humblest born rising to any height, but that the opportunities for progress to one born into such surroundings are few. It was somewhat similar in Egypt. Chances for rapid advance were by no means as favorable then as now, but nevertheless, there are

TOURISTS SCALING THE GREAT PYRAMID.

many cases on record where men attained high official position in spite of great social disadvantages.

The affection of the Egyptians for their children was almost universal. Large families were desired, even by those in moderate circumstances. Indeed it was necessary that families be perpetuated, for thus alone would family tombs be kept up and respect be shown those who had departed. Among all people who worship ancestors, children are especially desired and to be bereft of them is the greatest hardship and affliction.

In spite of all that has been said of the respect paid to women, the happy domestic relations in Egypt and the affection for children, it is doubtful whether or not there was much home life as we today understand the phrase. The importance of the individual is a modern conception. The will of the king was paramount in Egypt and all citizens were first of all subservient to his wishes. Less security, less freedom in pursuing one's own course probably resulted in brief periods of family unity. Surely such must have been the result of early marriages which took children from their parents at a tender age.

Dress.

Suppose for a moment that some unforseen catastrophe should wipe out the inhabitants of England, and future generations attempted to reconstruct their history, from the age of King Arthur and his knights to the peaceful days of Edward the Seventh. After working out an outline of their political development, suppose it should be asked, But how did these people dress? Think of the variety of costumes that have been popular since the Round Table days! Who could describe them all? The task would be disheartening indeed. And yet, far more years sped over Egypt than England has yet known.

Living in a warm country, the Egyptian required simpler raiment than the Englishman. In early times a short, scant skirt was worn by both men and women—the children were generally not clothed at all. This skirt, which formed the foundation of all the later, more elaborate dress, changed in style from one age to another. Sometimes it was scantier than at other times and it varied in length. During the Sixth dynasty, either by means of pressing, or by some device, the front of the skirt was made to assume a stiff, triangular appearance. As pictured on the tombs, it looks like a three-cornered apron. In the Old Empire, the great lords threw a panther skin across their shoulders, when, as Erman expresses it, "they wished to appear in full dress."

In the Middle Empire people of high position wore two skirts, the under one short and of heavy linen; the outer skirt so sheer that the contour of the body was quite visible.

By the Eighteenth dynasty it had become customary to clothe the upper portion of the body. Even now the arms were left free. The king appeared occasionally in a mantle and the nobles also donned mantles for festival days.

Working people always clothed in the simplest fashion. All garments were frequently discarded in the field, as they impeded rapid movement. The supersensitive modesty of our day which cries out against a low bodice or lace hose, even raises objection at undraped marble statues, had no part in the thought of these simple-hearted, pure-minded people; yet they showed a fitting sense of decorum and dignity.

It was the men in Egypt who delighted in finery and showy costumes, while the dress of the women was plainer and remained almost wholly unaltered for centuries together. Their usual garment during the later periods was a close fitting gown reaching from under the arms to the ankles, and mistress and maid were dressed much alike. In the New Empire a cloak was added, but it and the gown beneath were of sheerest linen procurable. As time went on, garments of both men and women were elaborately embroidered.

The ancient Egyptian desired to preserve absolute cleanliness. Scenes characteristic of washing day have been pictured on many a tomb. The chief washer was assisted by others who beat the clothes, wrung them out, bleached and dried them. It was the desire to be clean which led these people to shave their heads and beards. Wigs of curled wool and others of long hair are constantly seen in the old pictures, although it sometimes appears that these covered heads already crowned by a natural growth. While they shaved off the beard as something unclean, the Egyptians still shared in the idea common to oriental peoples that a beard gives added dignity, hence the king and men of rank wore artificial beards on state occasions. Even Queen Hatshepsut assumed one when she wished to appear regal.

Sandals and foot gear were not popular at any time, although men of the higher classes wore them when they walked abroad. Men and women alike donned necklaces and bracelets, while women wore anklets also. Earrings were introduced by foreigners and rings seem to have been confined to seal rings. Walking sticks were carried as badges of honor and each style of stick indicated a degree of social rank.

The Egyptians painted their faces, rouged their lips, blackened their eyes, and oiled their hair and bodies. At a feast a slave would bring a ball soaked in oil for each guest, place it on his head, in order that the oil might gently percolate through the hair of the banqueter during the meal. The dead were provided with many kinds of oil, perfumes, and rouges for use of the double, or ka.

Probably many allowed their hair to grow long, for we find physicians taxed to their utmost to supply concoctions which would produce heavy growths of hair, strengthen it and prevent it from turning grey. All these remedies are found in old papyri:

To prevent the hair turning grey: "The blood of a black calf, cooked in oil—a salve."

Or this: "Two parts of bloods, horn of a black cow, warm it up for a salve."

When the hair fell out: "Take fat of the lion, of the hippopotamus, the crocodile, the cat, the snake, and the ibex."

To strengthen the hair: "Anoint it with the tooth of a donkey crushed in honey."

Or try this: "Boil the hoof of a donkey in oil together with a dog's foot, and some date kernels."

VIEW OF MANSION, FROM THE TOMB OF ANNA, EIGHTEENTH DYNASTY.

CHAPTER X.

Sports and Recreations.

The pastimes and diversions of any people fall easily in two divisions; those which are adapted to the open air, and those enjoyed indoors. The popular outdoor sports among the Egyptians were hunting, fishing and boating, while the banquet with its attendant dancing and music, helped them to pass those hours when Amon, god of the sun, concealed, reigned over all.

The wealthy Egyptian liked to take his wife or family in his light boat and wander at will among the reeds and marshy plants abounding in the little streams and lakes left still undrained. It was fine sport to flit in and out among the tall papyrus, rouse a flock of birds and bring some of them down with the boomerang. Fishes were plentiful in the streams, and the sportsman chose to get them with a two-pointed spear. If he became expert, he could spear two at once—one on either point. To be sure, the game dealers, requiring large numbers of fish and fowl, caught both in a net. Only the noble or the well-to-do had time to indulge in hunting and fishing for mere diversion. In the tomb pictures, gentlemen are shown seated in their gardens, on costly rugs, it may be, leisurely spearing fish in their own artificial ponds. This was too simple a process for any but the most indolent, and did not appeal to the true sportsman who loved the natural streams.

Great was the attraction of these marshy lakes. "Much of the country formerly covered by marshes and tropical forests was already arable land. At the same time old river beds remained; stretches of marsh and half-stagnant water, overgrown as of old with papyrus reeds, offered shelter to the hippopotamus, the crocodile and to numberless water-birds. This was the happy hunting ground of the great lords of ancient Egypt, the oft-mentioned 'backwaters,' the 'bird tanks of pleasure.' They played the same part in Egyptian life as the forest in German folk lore; the greatest delight perhaps that an Egyptian knew was to row in a light boat between the beautiful waving tufts of the papyrus reeds, to pick the lotus flowers, to start the wild birds and then knock them over with the throw-stick, to spear the great fish of the Nile and even the hippopotamus, with the harpoon. Pictures of all periods exist representing these expeditions, and we have but to glance at them in order to realize how much the Egyptians loved these wild districts, and how much poetry they found in them."[1]

Danger mingled with sport in capturing the larger game— the hippopotamus and crocodile. Pictures of crocodile hunts have not been found. Probably they were not painted, because in certain parts of Egypt these animals were held sacred to some god, and even those who did not share this belief might not have cared to record the killing of them in the tomb. No such feeling existed concerning the hippopotamus and he who was successful in securing one seldom failed to have the hunt pictured in his tomb. You will remember that in ancient Egypt, each person built his own tomb during his life time, and so decided for himself for what he was to be remembered.

The deserts and mountains on either side offered game to the hunter. Gazelles, antelopes, foxes, hares, and other small animals, such as rabbits, abounded. Did one crave greater adventure, he might follow the leopard and the lion. It was quite the custom for the wealthy man, who followed the chase for sport, to collect wild animals and add them to the menagerie usually found on the large estates. Here were elephants and baboons from Asia, giraffes from the upper Nile, lions, leopards, hyenas and gazelles from the deserts. Some became quite tame and were taught tricks. Lions were favorite pets, and kings often took them along on their campaigns. Monkeys were found in almost every household; and since hunting was so popular, various kinds of hounds were more numerous than other species of dogs.

In addition to the small canoe in which he hunted water birds, the nobleman usually had a large, square-sailed, double-masted boat in which he would take his family and friends for an evening sail down the river. His musicians would accompany him, and dispense sweet strains on their harps and lutes, in harmony with the quiet waters.

Feasting was popular alike with men and women. Music

[1] Erman: Life in Ancient Egypt, 235.

and dancing were invariably furnished as means of entertainment. Many pictures of the banquet remain. Sometimes ladies in elaborate toilettes are shown, partaking of all sorts of dainties, while dancing girls move gracefully before them, beating time to the music which accompanied them. Sometimes the dances were intricate; one of them pictured in a tomb seems to represent papyrus reeds, swaying in the wind. Others were yet more elaborate

Music was popular among all classes. Flutes, lutes and harps are shown in the tomb pictures. Singing often accompanies the harp. Among the superintendents of "all the most beautiful pleasures of the king" were superintendents of singing. Thus it seems royalty, at least, did not trust to inspiration for entertainment, but prudently had it arranged and rehearsed in advance. At Memphis there is said to have been a school where music was taught to girls.

Some games of chance were popular in Egypt. Checkers was known and a picture remains wherein Ramses II. is playing the game with his daughter.

It remains to speak of certain other customs of the feast. The ladies would come together to make their toilets, rouging their lips, blackening their eyes, offering one another their flowers to smell, and examining each other's jewelry.

"The serving boys and girls go round, offering ointment, wreaths, perfumes, and bowls of wine. They challenge the guests at the same time to 'celebrate the joyful day' by the enjoyment of the pleasure of the present moment; the singers also continually repeat the same as the refrain to their song. They sing to the guests as they quaff the wine:

'Celebrate the joyful day!
Let sweet odours and oils be placed for thy nostrils,
Wreaths of lotus flowers for the limbs
And for the bosom of thy sister, dwelling in thy heart
Sitting beside thee.
Let song and music be made before thee.
Cast behind thee all cares and mind thee of pleasure,
Till cometh the day when we drew towards the land
That loveth silence.'

or:

'Put myrrh on thy head, array thyself in fine linen,
 Anointing thyself with the true wonders of God.
 Adorn thyself with all the beauty thou canst.
 With a beaming face celebrate the joyful day and rest not therein
 For no one can take away his goods with him,
 Yea, no one returns again, who has gone hence.'"[2]

The men banqueted alone. Dancing and music diverted them during the feast. It was customary to pass the image of a mummy around at the feast, while words similar to these were repeated: "Look upon this and know, even as it is, so shalt thou be—for all must die." This in no way dampened the pleasures of the night; rather, each sought to enjoy to its fullest capacity the fleeting hours.

[2] Erman· Life in Ancient Egypt, 255.

FACADE OF A HOUSE TOWARD THE STREET.
SECOND THEBAN PERIOD.

CHAPTER XI.

Agriculture and Cattle Raising.

Owing to the inexhaustible fertility of the Nile valley, fine crops were always forthcoming on the land reached by the annual overflow. The rich mud deposited by the flood left the productive qualities of the soil restored, and it was never necessary to leave the fields lie fallow. However, the ground had not only to be merely reached by the river waters, but to be saturated, for rain seldom fell and whatever humidity was supplied the growing vegetation, came from the overflow. A system of irrigation brought the water in trenches as near each farm as possible. From these trenches, thousands of men and boys, employed throughout the country, lifted water in buckets to the higher land, that all the crops might receive sufficient moisture.

As soon as the river receded, all the valley was astir with busy people, getting the ground ready for the grain and other seed. Implements of the farm were crude indeed, and crude they are today. A high official in recent times had a quantity of agricultural implements, such as are used by the most progressive farmers in America, imported into Egypt and endeavored to encourage the peasants to use them. Not they. What had served the needs of seven thousand years in their valley was deemed sufficient for them, and after some time, the entire outfit had to be sold for old iron.

Pictures in tombs depict many scenes connected with grain production—from the plowing of the soil to the storing of the grain into granaries. From these pictures we are able to outline the daily life of the peasant.

Their plows were crude, wooden implements, which at best did little more than scratch over the soil. Coarse clods of earth had to be broken with a sort of wooden hoe. Then the farmer scattered seed over the mellow ground, driving flocks of sheep across the fields to tread it in. Aside from the matter of irrigation, the crops needed little attention until the time for harvest. Then the grain was cut by a sickle, loaded on to donkeys and taken to the threshing-floor, located near the village. Here in early times it was trodden out by donkeys, driven back and forth over it. Later oxen were in greater favor for threshing. The grain was freed from chaff by throwing it up into the air rapidly. The grain fell straight down, while the chaff was blown forward. Now it was ready for the "scribes of the granary," who measured it and supervised it while being stored safely away. Sometimes the boats of a nobleman would ply back and forth for weeks together, bringing his heavy yield of millet and barley to his granaries.

One word about the "corn" of Egypt. The Indian corn which we call corn today is a native American product, and was unknown to antiquity. Corn has been used as a common name for all grain. Wheat, barley and millet were the leading grains of Egypt.

Taxes were paid in kind—in produce; so naturally, large quantities of grain were poured yearly into the coffers of the government. This was stored against times of need which occasionally fell upon Egypt. It was in one of these years when a famine swept over the east that Joseph's brothers came down into the valley to buy grain from government granaries.

Little is known of the vegetables grown in antiquity. Probably many of those common today were raised. Melons were extensively grown; onions and cucumbers were probably known and the grape vine was extensively cultivated.

Cattle raising was carried to some perfection The Egyptians understood well the secrets of high breeding and produced especially fine specimens of cows and oxen. Being fond of all animals, they were partial to the ox, symbolic of great strength, and to the cow, sacred to Isis. As the lion, with its strength, has appealed to many people, so the ox was a favorite with the dwellers on the Nile.

The herders made up a class by themselves. In the summer they drove the cattle up north, into the marshes, where pasture was good. The average Egyptian looked upon these men with deepest disgust, for they let their hair grow, and wore beards. They lived in portable reed huts. Their lives were quite primitive and they had a general unkempt appearance. They dressed very little, and their efforts to copy the Egyptian skirt in their stiff matting, afforded the townsman much amusement. They spent their idle time weaving papyrus reeds into mats, and wove boats from the same useful plant.

When the fall came, they returned with their herds from the northern marshes. When they reached home, officials came to inspect the flocks. They noted the increase of the stock, all losses and other matters of interest to the owners. Records show that single proprietors sometimes owned as many as 1,300 cows, in addition to other cattle.

Large flocks of sheep were kept, and goats were plentiful. Few pictures of pigs are to be seen, and those only in the New Empire period. The pig was objected to on religious grounds, as unclean.

Their fondness for animals led the Egyptians to receive as many wild animals as possible into their flocks. These were fattened with the cattle. Mention is made of the ibex and antelope being especially valued when they had been fed for awhile with the herds.

Birds were apparently not extensively domesticated. This was not necessary, for the bird-catchers could find any number of ducks and geese in the marshes, fatten them for a time, and supply them without the trouble of raising them. The goose was the favorite bird. Roast goose was a favorite dish and was offered as a delicacy to the gods. Pictures even show geese kept as pets, in the place of dogs or monkeys.

While the whole civilization of Egypt was based on its agriculture and its cattle raising, the farmer and herder had no social standing. The tiller of the soil was regarded as an overworked creature who never became prosperous. The land was generally owned by great noblemen of wealth, who themselves received the profit.

"The following sad sketch of the lot of the harvestmen was written by the compiler of a didactic letter, of which many copies are extant, and implies not only a personal opinion, but the general view of this matter: 'The worm has taken half of the food, the hippopotamus the other half; there were many mice in the fields, the locusts have come down and the cattle have eaten, and the sparrows have stolen. Poor miserable agriculturist! What was left on the threshing floor thieves made away with. Then the scribe lands on the bank to receive the harvest, his followers carry sticks and the negroes carry palm rods. They say: 'Give up the corn '—and there is none there. Then they beat him as he lies stretched out and bound to the ground, they throw him into the canal and he sinks down, head under water. This is, of course, an exaggerated picture, which is purposely overdrawn by the writer, in order to emphasize the striking contrast that he draws in his eulogy of the profession of scribe; in its main features, however, it gives us a very true idea, for the lot of the ancient peasant very much resembled that of the modern fellah. The latter labours and toils without enjoying the results of his own work. He earns a scanty subsistence, and, notwithstanding all his industry, he gains no great renown amongst his countrymen of the towns: the best they can say of him is, that he is worthy to be compared with his own cattle."[1]

Artisans and Their Crafts.

Countries today can easily import such articles of manufacture as are not produced within their own boundaries. A single household may possess silk made in India, porcelain from China, curtains and laces from Belgium, cutlery from England, and some musical instruments made in Germany. All this was different in antiquity. Egypt long remained isolated. She developed a higher civilization than her neighbors, and what her people required had to be produced for the most part within her borders. It followed naturally that a wide variety of trades and crafts grew up in the limited valley of the Nile. To be sure, during her empire period many lands sent their choicest products as tribute, yet even then, Egyptians held first place in certain arts and crafts.

There was little native wood in the valley. When the conquests of Thutmose I. established relations with Syria, woods were imported to some extent. Mummies have been found encased in the rare cedars of Lebanon. Generally speaking, however, substitutes had to be found for timber. Light boats were made from reeds, and for the making of larger ones, boatmakers became expert in joining together small pieces of wood, thus forming large boards, strong enough to bear severe strains. For some purposes, cartonage was sub-

Erman: Life in Ancient Egypt, 415.

stituted. This was composed of several layers of coarse linen glued together. It was used extensively for the manufacture of coffins. In veneering rare woods upon less costly foundations, the Egyptians far surpassed any modern efforts. Wood carvers reached a high degree of skill in fashioning little statuettes and images from wood, also in carving, with exquisite detail, tiny wooden amulets and ornaments. Handles of knives sometimes display the dexterity of the wood carvers.

Even greater, perhaps, was their success in metal work. Bronze was commonly used for articles of every day use. Iron was known and was reserved more especially for weapons of warfare and for some kinds of knives. For a time, silver was more highly valued than gold, being more rare. Later it was found in greater quantities, and took rank with gold, or had even less value. Statues of the gods were made commonly in bronze, although many were fashioned from gold. The goldsmith was a person of good social standing. He made statues of the gods to adorn the temples and he cut and set jewels for royalty. The number of precious stones was quite extensive in Egypt. Diamonds, rubies and sapphires were seemingly unknown, but amethysts, emeralds, garnets, agates, jasper and lapis lazuli were available. The Egyptians, both men and women, were very fond of personal adornments, and jewelry was worn in profusion by the wealthy and to some extent by all. Amber, turquoise, coral and pearls were popular. Every man wore a seal ring—and this not merely as an ornament. Letters and documents were never signed in these ages—rather, one affixed his seal. The noble wore a costly ring; the citizen of humble position, one of slight value, but every one who expected to transact any business or carry on any correspondence wore a seal ring of some kind. Women, to the same extent, wore necklaces. Most elaborate ones have been discovered in the tombs of royalty; very simple ones adorned the necks of the humbler women, yet none was so poor as to lack a necklace altogether. Bracelets, anklets, hair combs and ornaments, amulets, chains, and scarabs were greatly in demand, and the goldsmiths of ancient Egypt attained great originality, skill and perfection in his art. So constant being the demand for inexpensive jewelry, remarkable skill was reached in imitating precious stones in glass.

Indeed, it is difficult for experts today to determine in some cases whether the stone be real or imitated.

In glass work, the Egyptians preferred colored glass to the clear. Whatever glass utensils remain are invariably colored. Blue was a favorite color. Thin layers of glass were used sometimes to decorate coffins. Blown glass was not made in early times, statements to the contrary notwithstanding. Pictures once supposed to represent glass blowers at work are now understood to depict one stage of metal working.

Pottery was never brought to any high mark by the Nile dwellers. Clay utensils were used for only the most ordinary purposes, and the jars, bowls, and vases which remain give evidence of poor material having been used in the first place, indifferent labor in the next place, poor fire and little skill in ornamentation. These indifferent results were satisfactory enough for the commonest uses and for anything more, something in metal appears to have been demanded.

Hunting being a favorite pastime, and cattle raising carried on to such a wide extent, Egypt became rich in skins. The skins of rarer animals were never shorn of the natural hair. This was dressed and used for coverings of couches and chairs—for shields and even garments. Skins of cattle were made into leather and worked up into sandals, straps and aprons for workmen. Pictures of boats are shown with leather sails, and leather was used for manifold purposes.

The extensive use of linen for clothing necessitated a large production of flax. Those who wove—mostly women, in spite of Herodotus to the contrary—attained a high skill and dexterity in their work. Linen was generally kept white, and was frequently made so thin and sheer that the outlines of the body were visible through it.

Of the condition and life of the average artisan, we know that he was allowed to hold no office under the government and had no political rights whatever. Every man was obliged by law to have some calling and to follow it, nor could he work at trades other than his own. This insured good work—always exacted by the Egyptians from their workmen who often received but meager food and no wages. Probably the highly prized work of the goldsmith was well paid. The Egyptians frequently paid for their goods in kind.

Large numbers of laborers belonged to the state or the temples, and they were provided only the bare necessities of life. Some of these men knew how to chisel the hard granite which almost defies the strong steel of today; others could decorate tombs with animated scenes which still today retain their original colors. All these men lived in wretched poverty, in little mud huts, and often had to besiege their overseers for bread. It appears to have been customary to give these workmen their monthly rations at the beginning of the month. Probably the supply was scanty at best, and the hungry laborers made heavy inroads upon it during the first few days. Ere twenty days had passed they were often entirely out of meal for bread, to say nothing of oil and other necessities. Only a threat to appeal to the king would at times bring the needed food. The workmen maintained that the officers withheld from them their dues, only to add it to their own personal stores—a claim that was no doubt well founded, and needs no better proof than the granting of more food to those who united and ceased to work until supplies were forthcoming.

MARKETS.

For an understanding of the old Egyptian market we can do no better than read the description worked out by Maspero from scenes still existing in the tombs:

"We . suddenly emerge into the full sunshine of a noisy little square, where a market is being held. Sheep, geese, goats, asses, large-horned oxen, scattered in unequal groups in the center, are awaiting a purchaser. Peasants, fishermen, small retail dealers, squat several deep in front of the houses, displaying before them, in great rush baskets or on low tables, loaves of pastry, fruit, vegetables, fish, meat raw or cooked, jewels, perfumes, stuffs, all the necessities and all the superfluities of Egyptian life.

"The customers stroll past and leisurely examine the quality of the commodities offered for sale; each carries something of his own manufacture in his hand—a new tool, some shoes, a mat, or a small box full of rings of copper, silver, even of gold, of the weight of an *outnou* (a little over two ounces), which he proposes to barter for the objects he requires. Two customers stop at the same moment in front of a fellah, who exhibits onions and wheat in front of a basket. Instead of money, the first holds two necklets of glass or of many colored earthenware, the second a round fan with a wooden handle, and one of those triangular ventilators which the cooks use to quicken the fire. 'Here is a beautiful necklet which will please you, this is what you want,' cries the former; whilst the latter urges, 'Here is a fan and a ventilator.' However, the fellah, quite overcome by this double attack, methodically proceeds to first seize a string of beads for closer examination. 'Let me see it, that I may fix a price.' The one asks too much, the other too little; from concession to concession they finally come to terms, and settle the number of onions or the weight of corn which the necklet or fan may be worth. Elsewhere it is a question of bartering a pair of sandals or a row of enamelled beads for some perfume. 'Here,' urges the buyer, 'is a very strong pair of shoes.' But the seller does not require shoes for the moment, so he offers one of his small pots in exchange for a row of beads. 'It is delicious when a few drops are poured out,' he explains, with a persuasive air. A woman thrusts under the nose of a kneeling individual two jars, probably containing some ointment of her own manufacture. 'Here,' she cries, 'it smells sweet enough to entice thee.' Behind this group two men are discussing the value of a packet of fish-hooks; a woman, box in hand, is a vendor of bracelets and necklets; another woman endeavors to obtain a reduction upon the price of a fish, which is being dressed before her.

"When it is a question of a large animal, or of objects of considerable value, the accounts become intricate. For instance, Ahmosou sells a bull for a mat, five measures of honey, eleven measures of oil, and seven objects of different kinds. Now, imagine the calculations which must have been made before he succeeded in establishing such a complicated balance. The mat was estimated at 25 outnou, the honey at 4. the oil at 10, and so on, the whole weighing 119 outnou, which is not too dear for a beast in good condition. This custom of payment by one of the usual metals is so convenient, and dispenses with so many calculations, that it has been adopted even for the minor transactions of daily life. The butcher, the baker, the corn-chandler, all the small tradesmen prefer exchange for metal, which is of small compass and does not spoil, to exchange for objects, often bulky in size, which is liable to deteriorate if kept too long in the house. A pair of ducks is worth a quarter of an outnou in copper; a fan, a quarter; a bronze razor is worth a whole outnou; a pickaxe, two; a goat, two; an ox-head, half an outnou in silver; a leather bottle of fine wine, three outnou of gold.

"Two or three commercial streets or bazaars open from the other side of the square, and the crowd hastens towards them when it leaves the market. Nearly their whole length is filled with stalls and shops, in which not only Egypt, but the majority of the oriental nations display their most varied productions. Beautifully ornamented stuffs from Syria, Phoenician or Hittite jewellery, scented woods and gums from Punt and the Holy Lands; lapis and embroideries from Babylon; coral, gold, iron, tin and amber from the far-distant countries beyond the seas, are found scattered pell-mell amongst the native fine linen, jewels, glass-work and furniture. The shop is usually independent from the rest of the house, and is let separately. It is a small, square room, often a simple shed, widely open in front, and closed every evening by means of wooden shutters, held in place by cross-bars with one or two mats, one or two low stools, some shelves fixed to the wall, which hold the goods; perhaps behind the shop are one or two carefully closed rooms where the most valuable objects are stored. Most of the tradesmen are also manufacturers. They have apprentices or workmen who work for them, and they join them during the intervals between their sales. Artisans of the same trade have usually a natural tendency to collect together, to dwell side by side in the same place—blacksmiths with blacksmiths, curriers with curriers, goldsmiths with goldsmiths, forming a small city in which objects of the same kind only are found."[2]

The Business of War.

It would be misleading to speak of the profession of war in Egypt, for the Egyptians were essentially unwarlike. In

---
[2] Maspero: Ancient Egypt. 18.

early times they lived in their isolated valley, and the nature of the country on either side of them was not such as to tempt them to reach out to conquer it. When Nubian and nomadic tribes stole their cattle and otherwise molested their outlying districts, it was a comparatively simple matter to repulse them and reduce their number. Such raids were not regular military campaigns—far from it. They were expeditions of plunder and pillage. "I have carried off their women and captured their men; for I marched to their well; I slew their oxen, cut down their corn and set fire to it." Thus did one pharaoh record his victory on a monument raised to commemorate it. War with tribes of this strength was not likely to elevate the military standard of Egypt.

Contact with the Hyksos during the Middle Empire taught the Nile dwellers more of warfare than they had previously known. By superior use of arms these Asiatics were able to take possession of the land, which they held until, from the struggling feudal nobles, a ruler came forth, strong enough to establish himself and collect an army. By adopting the method of battle practised by the enemy, the Hyksos were at last driven from the valley, and were pursued far beyond their former borders.

The New Empire saw a brief period of military successes, but they rested on a slight foundation. The Egyptians were naturally poor soldiers. A strong and fearless general was able to rouse them to action, and by meeting detached tribes, they were able to overcome them. Then with confidence born of success, they sometimes made a brilliant progress to the civilization of Mesopotamia. Asiatics had not yet learned the real nature of those to whom they offered tribute. When once it was learned, tribute was no longer forthcoming, or indeed, it was sometimes demanded by the Asiatics of Egypt.

Of the life of a private soldier, we know very little. During times of peace he was a tiller of the soil, or a common laborer. He thought no hardship greater than that which compelled him to enter the service of an army. He regarded war as the greatest evil and was disheartened by the slightest defeat. This was poor material to convert into effective soldiers and only when the Egyptian king received a large number of mercenaries into his ranks was his army particularly efficient.

Many times several thousand soldiers were dispatched to escort workmen sent to obtain granite for the king's tomb. It is probable that their duties were less military than civil, for they no doubt were set to cutting out the granite from the quarry and assisted in transporting it to the building site.

Of the equipment of the soldiers, it seems that in early times they carried simply a bow, wearing ostrich feathers on their heads as a token of victory. Later they carried shields and spears or battle axes. The order of battle in later times was to place chariots in the front and rear, with strong detachments of infantry between them. Ramses II. caused the whole story of his victory over the Hittite king at Kadesh to be painted in his temple. This is one of the best sources for military history during the New Empire. "We see how the soldiers of the 'first army of Amon' pitch their camp; the shields are placed side by side so as to construct a great four-cornered enclosure. One entrance only is left, and this is fortified with barricades and is defended by four divisions of infantry. In the middle of the camp a large square space indicates the position of the royal tent; the smaller tents of the officers surround it. The wide space between these tents and the outer enclosure serves as a camping-ground for the common soldiers and for the cattle, and here we see a series of life-like scenes, in the representation of which the Egyptian artist has evidently taken great delight. In one corner stands the rows of war-chariots; the horses are unharnessed and paw the ground contentedly, while they receive their food. Close by are posted the two-wheeled baggage cars; the oxen are looking round at the food, and do not appear to trouble themselves about the king's big tame lion, which has lain down near them wearied out. The most characteristic animal in the camp, however, is the donkey with his double panniers in which he has to carry the heavy sacks and jars of provisions. We meet with him here, there, and everywhere, in all manner of positions; for instance, he drops on his knee indignantly, as if he could carry his panniers no longer; he prances about when the soldiers want to lade him with the sacks; he lies down and brays, or he takes his ease rolling in the dust near his load. The boys, also, whose business it is to fasten up the donkeys to pegs, contribute to the general liveliness of the camp; in more than one place they have begun to quarrel about their work, and in their anger they beat each other with the pegs. Other boys belonging to the camp have to hang the baggage on posts, or to bring food for the soldiers, or to fetch the skins of water. These boys insist upon quarreling too; the skins are thrown down, and they use their fists freely.

"In contrast to these scenes of daily life in the camp, we have on the other hand a representation of the wild confusion of battle. Close to the bank of the Orontes is the royal chariot, in which the king stands drawn up to his full height; behind and on each side the chariots of the Cheta[1] surround him; while many more are crossing the stream. The Egyptian chariots are indeed in the rear of the king, but in order to come to his help they would have first to force a way through the chariots of the Cheta. In the meantime, the Pharaoh fights by himself, and pours down such a frightful rain of arrows on the enemy that they fly in wild confusion. Hit by the arrows, their horses take fright, dash the chariots to pieces, and throw out the warriors, or they get loose and breaking through their own ranks, spread confusion everywhere. The dead and the wounded Cheta fall one upon another; those who escape the arrows of the king throw themselves into the Orontes and try to swim across to Kadesh, which is seen on the opposite bank surrounded by walls and trenches.

"Whilst the Pharaoh thus slays the Cheta, the prince of the latter people stands watching the battle from the corner between Kadesh and the Orontes in the midst of a mighty square of 8,000 foot soldiers of the elite of his troops; 'he does not come out to fight, because he is afraid before his Majesty, since he has seen his Majesty.' When he sees that the battle is lost, he says in admiration: 'He is as Sutech the glorious, Ba'al lives in his body.'"[2]

[1] That is, the Hittite king.
[2] Erman: Life in Ancient Egypt, 529.

CHAPTER XII.

Praising Learning.[1]

I have seen violence, I have seen violence, give thy heart after letters.
I have seen one free from labors; consider there is not anything beyond letters.
Love letters as thy mother. I make its beauty go in thy face.
It is a greater possession than all besides.
He who has commenced to avail himself is from his infancy a counsellor.
He is sent to perform commissions.
He who does not go is in sack-cloth.
I have not seen a blacksmith on a commission, a founder who goes on an embassy.
I have seen the blacksmith at his work at the mouth of the furnace.
His fingers like things of crocodiles, he smells worse than the eggs of fishes.
Every carpenter carrying tools,—is he more at rest than the laborer?

I tell you the fisherman suffers more than any employment.
Consider, is he not toiling on the river? he is mixed with the crocodiles.
Should the clumps of papyrus diminish, then he is crying for help.
If he has not been told that a crocodile is not there, terrors blind him.
Consider, there is not an employment destitute of superior ones
Except the scribe, who is first, for he knows letters; he is greater than they.
Shouldst thou walk after great men, thou art to proceed with great knowledge.
Do not say proud words. Be sealed in thyself alone.

[1] From inscription on a tomb; trans. in "Dwellers on the Nile."

Schools and Education.

The Greek loved learning for itself alone. Not so the Egyptian. He, too, praised learning and considered no calling so worthy as that of the scribe. It was not because an education lifted one out of a sordid world to purer heights of knowledge, however, but rather, because the scribe was exempt from physical exertion, and if ambitious and persevering, might find all official doors open to him. A citizen wished his son to receive an education in order that he might occupy a position superior and less arduous than he could otherwise hope to fill. The lot of the laborer in Egypt was hard. Working constantly he could but provide himself and family with their scanty food and scanty clothing. At any time he might be pressed into public service and here he was fortunate if he received " one clean garment once a month," in addition to his monthly rations. Scribes were safe from physical toil. Quite naturally, it followed that a family would make every possible sacrifice that one of the children might be fitted for a life more safe and comfortable than the average. No higher ideal, no loftier motive seems to have actuated the parent than this: to qualify his son for an easy and lucrative position in life.

There were elementary schools in Egypt in an early age. These were open to all children, who probably paid a small fee to the teacher. Gradually also, there grew up around the temples schools for the training of boys for the priesthood. As the empire grew and tribute was asked and received from many tribes and countries, many scribes—copyists and accountants—were needed in the service of the government, and schools were opened in connection with the court to educate boys to meet this new demand.

Having spent a few years in the elementary school, the average boy was set to work to assist with the cattle, gather fuel, care for the ducks and geese about his home, and later was put to learn a trade—generally the trade of his father. However, if a boy showed special aptitude for learning or seemed more alert and clever than ordinary, he was sent to the school for scribes. Here the training was vigorous. The scribe would waken the youth, calling: "The books are already in the hands of thy companions, take hold of thy clothes and call for thy sandals!" Discipline was rigid indeed. An old adage held that a boy's ears are placed on his back—he hears if he is flogged.

You will remember how complex were the Egyptian styles of writing—both hieroglyphic and demotic. Consequently to be able to read and write was considered a great accomplishment. Having mastered the art of writing, the youth was set next to copying. Many of the old copy books still exist, for it was customary to place them in the tomb with the deceased. Three pages a day was the usual lesson. "By the age of ten or twelve," says Maspero, "the child was apprenticed to a scribe in some office, who would undertake to make him a *learned scribe*. The boy accompanied his master to the office or work-yard, and there passed entire months copying letters, circulars, legal documents, or accounts, which he did not at first understand, but which he faithfully remembered. The pupil copied and copied, the master inserted forgotten words, corrected the faults of spelling, and drew on the margin the signs or groups unskillfully traced. When the book was finished and the apprentice could write all the formulas from memory, the master entrusted him with the composition of a few letters, gradually increasing the number and adding new difficulties. As soon as he had fairly mastered the ordinary daily routine his education was ended, and an unimportant post was sought." [2]

The Egyptians never investigated a subject until they reduced it to a science. A certain knowledge of geometry was necessary to determine boundaries of land, so valuable along the river that very small areas were sometimes in dispute. A knowledge sufficient for this purpose the Egyptians possessed, but they never delved deeper into the matter and became proficient in it. They studied astronomy and made charts of portions of the heavens. They studied arithmetic, but never, for example, wrote a fraction with a numerator larger than 1; instead of writing $\frac{2}{3}$ or $\frac{5}{8}$ they wrote: $\frac{1}{3}, \frac{1}{3}; \frac{1}{2}, \frac{1}{8}$. It has taken much patience and some ingenuity to understand problems found already worked out in the copy books.

[2] Maspero: Ancient Egypt, 9.

The subject of medicine was deemed important, but the ancient Egyptians knew nothing about it, generally speaking. Magic, drugs, herbs and incantations were used together. Believing that the welfare of the soul depended upon the preservation of the body, students never had the opportunity of dissecting bodies, either animal or human. They had no idea of the vital organs, and when they were successful in relieving a patient, it was when, like some old herb woman, they had learned the properties of healing plants and had watched their effects in many cases until they became skillful in administering them. When one was ill, it was thought that an evil spirit had entered his body. By magic words this must be driven out before recovery could be hoped for. Magic greatly aided medicine, according to this view. Here is a formula for a magic mixture: "Take two grains of incense, two fumigations, two jars of cedar oil, two jars of tas, two jars of wine, two jars of spirits of wine. Apply it at the place of thy heart. Thou art protected against the accidents of life; thou art protected against a violent death; thou art protected against fire; thou are not ruined on earth, and thou escapest in heaven."

LITERATURE.

Egypt seems to have been lacking in any considerable number of literary works. Records were kept in the temples; treatises on religion, magic and medicine have been found. The Book of the Dead was familiar to the living and indispensable to the departed. Some folk lore, hymns of worship and of victory, and a few stories, more or less complete, remain. Vast numbers of papyri have undoubtedly perished, but reference would probably be made in existing manuscripts to great productions, and these are lacking. Giving all credit to what has been recovered and allowing for the destruction of time, the fact remains that in literature Egypt was not productive.

There are no literary remains antedating the Middle Empire; however, we have traces of folk songs and of myths which were earlier known. The old belief that the Egyptians had no secular literature was mistaken. Our greatest sources of knowledge regarding their literature have been the tombs and temples, and these were not places in which a people would have chosen to preserve its lighter literature.

It is probable that just as the workmen sing today, while they work along the Nile, so too they chanted in earliest time. Under the most trying conditions in Egypt, laborers sang as they worked. The scribes did not think it worthy of their dignity to chronicle folk songs. Probably little thought was ever given to them. Occasionally a few lines are quoted beneath some tomb pictures to make it more vivid.

"'The herdsman wading in the mud as he drives his sheep over the fields from which the flood has not yet entirely retreated, says to his flock: 'In the water walks your shepherd with the fishes; with the catfish talketh he; with the fish he changeth greeting.' Another song accompanied the work equivalent to threshing. The ancient Egyptians, like the Israelites, did not use flails, but after scattering the corn on the threshing-floor, they drove oxen over it to tread out the grain. Then was sung with variations: 'Thresh, oh ye oxen! Thresh for yourselves! Oh ye oxen thresh for yourselves! Thresh straw for your fodder, thresh grain for your master. Take ye no rest, cool is the air this day.'"[*]

Mythological tales grew out of an attempt to explain natural phenomena—the rising or setting sun, the struggle between light and darkness. All phenomena which attracted sufficient attention furnished material for myths. It has been observed for instance, that certain stars never set, whereas others after performing their courses sank below the horizon. The Egyptians expressed this by the myth of the Crocodile of the West, which fed upon the setting stars.

"The sunrise and sunset, alternation of day and night, the solar drama in all its details, furnished the subject of Egyption mythology. In other countries the sun-god rode in a chariot; in Egypt he rode in a boat. Hence the sky is considered an expanse of water, the Nile being the earthly representative. Seb is the earth, Nut the heaven. Osiris their son, is the sun and is wedded to Isis, the dawn. From their union sprang Horus, the Sun in his full strength. Set the destroyer, is another child of Seb and Nut. He is darkness

[*] Popular Literature of Ancient Egypt. Wiedermann.

and weds Nephthys, the Sunset. The contest between Seb and Osiris is the constant subject of mythological story."

Traces of these early folk songs and early myths survived in Egyptian literature. The literature of the Middle Empire shows an eager interest in travel. Of the few books that remain from this period several relate adventures in distant parts.

Most of the remaining literature belongs to the New Empire. Lyrical and didactic poems, stories, records and documents were then produced in considerable number. It would appear that the Egyptians never wrote a history of their country. Accounts, more or less in detail, cover several reigns, but nothing like a chronological treatise of their development was apparently undertaken. The New Empire knew far less of the Old Empire than we know today.

In the realm of religious writing, the Book of the Dead was most important. Its negative confession to be made before the judges of the dead would imply a high degree of morality, but the truth was that it came into being in an early stage when words were thought identical with the thing itself. We find all peoples passing through a period when great importance was given the spoken word. "I have not been idle; I have not been intoxicated; I have not told secrets; I have not told falsehoods; I have not defrauded; I have not slandered; I have not caused tears; I have given food to the hungry; drink to the thirsty, and clothes to the naked." That confession was probably formulated in this early period when such stress was given to the spoken word. Later, when people understood the difference between the name and the thing itself the confession remained the same, because all things pertaining to religion are last to change.

The *Precepts of Ptah-hotep*, prince of the Fifth dynasty, is one of the oldest known books in the world. It is now in the Bibliothèque Nationale at Paris and is made up of what would be equivalent to twenty printed pages of precepts written to admonish the young. The following indicate their nature:

"Be not arrogant because of that which thou knowest, no artist being in possession of the perfection to which he should aspire."

"If thou hast become great after having been little, harden

not thy heart; thou art only the steward of the good things of God."

"Let thy face be cheerful as long as thou livest; hast any one come out of the coffin after having once entered it?"

Before leaving this brief consideration of Egyptian writing, we should understand what supplied the writing material of Egypt. The papyrus reeds have frequently been mentioned with no explanation of their use. From this word papyrus has been derived our word *paper*.

The reeds grew thick along the sides of streams. Their stems were three cornered and about three inches wide at the base. By peeling off the outer tough green covering, a white pith was obtained. Splitting it and laying strips together, the edges lapping, and upon a surface so formed placing a second layer running the other way, sprinkling the whole with the muddy Nile water, and putting it all under a press made up the process of manufacturing a composition which could be cut into thin sheets. These afforded all the writing material known until the seventh century after Christ, when prepared skins, or parchment, were sometimes substituted.

EGYPTIAN SCRIBES

CHAPTER XIII.

Religion of Ancient Egypt.

The life of the ancient Egyptians was in a great measure controlled by their religious beliefs. In prehistoric times, as has already been explained, each nome, or province, was independent, and was the home of some tribe or tribes. Just as we find the American Indian worshipping the stick that was powerful enough to throw him in the forest, so these primitive people worshipped animals and trees. Each animate object was conceived as possessing a soul or spirit, and this spirit accounted for the qualities or characteristics of the object—were they good or ill. A lion possessed savage tendencies—hence they would worship him and propitiate his spirit, and their attitude was the same toward the crocodile, the ram, the elephant, and many other animals. The date-palm brought them great blessings—therefore they would worship the tree and insure a continuance of these blessings. As time went on, they grew to worship gods, and to the gods these trees and animals, worshipped earlier on their own account, were thought sacred.

Each village and town had its own local deity and special objects of worship, while the nome as a whole recognized gods of a more general character. In this way, each province of Upper Egypt—which was older in civilization than the Delta—and various portions of Lower Egypt, developed religions complete and independent of one another. After many hundred years, when all Egypt was united under one government and one king, the priests attempted to comprise these various beliefs into a common faith, to recognize the principal gods of all the nomes in the temples, and to evolve one religious system from the many local systems. This they never succeeded in fully accomplishing. They included in their lists some seventy deities, and harmonized some features of worship, but each locality clung to its ancient deity and several different religions can be traced throughout Egyptian history.

Like most primitive people, the Egyptians worshipped the sun. This god revealed himself in many forms, but chiefly as Horus, represented by a falcon, and Re or Ra, represented by the Scarabaeus.

Osiris ruled in the kingdom of the dead, and he was thought to be just and good. With his wife, Isis, and his son, Horus, he was worshipped throughout the land, while everywhere Set was regarded as the principle of Evil.

Qeb was the god of Earth and Nut, his wife, the queen of the heavens, which in this connection signifies the skies. Their children were Osiris, Isis, Set, and Nebthet (Nephthys). Mat was the goddess of truth and justice.

One finds similarities between some of these divinities and the divinities of the Greeks—as for example, Nut reminds one of Hera, and Set was feared as much as Pluto; but it is dangerous to make these comparisons, for the religious conceptions of the two nations were fundamentally different.

The Egyptians usually represented their deities with human bodies and the heads of the animal sacred to each. So, for example, Horus always has the head of a sparrow-hawk; Thot, that of an Ibis, and so on. The prominent feature of this religion was the veneration of animals. It was believed that sometimes the god-spirit took up his abode within certain animals, and for this reason certain animals were regarded as sacred and were therefore, objects of worship. Ptah was the god of Memphis. He, it was believed, took the form of the Apis-bull, hence this bull was regarded as sacred.

"The Apis bull dwelt in a temple of his own near the city, had his train of attendant priests, his meals of the choicest food, his grooms and currycombers who kept his coat clean and beautiful, his chamberlains who made up his bed, his cup-bearers who brought his water, and on certain days was led in a festive procession through the main streets of the town, so that the inhabitants might see him, and come forth from their dwellings and make obeisance. When he died he was carefully embalmed, and deposited, together with magnificent jewels and statuettes and vases, in a polished granite sarcophagus, cut out of a single block, and weighing between sixty and seventy tons. The cost of an Apis funeral amounted sometimes, as we are told, to as much as $100,000. Near Memphis the number of Apis bulls buried in this fashion was found to be sixty-four."[1]

In another locality the crocodile was the object of adoration, because, as in the case of the Apis bull, it was believed that some god dwelt within it.

"The crocodile was principally worshipped about Lake Moeris. A chosen number of these animals were kept in the temples, where they were given elegant apartments and treated to every luxury at public expense. Let us imagine a crocodile, fresh from a warm, sumptuous bath, anointed with the most precious ointments and perfumed with fragrant odors; its head and neck glittering with jeweled earrings and necklace, and its feet with bracelets wallowing on a rich and costly carpet to receive the worship of intelligent human beings! Its death was mourned as a public calamity; its body, wrapped in linen, was carried to the embalmers, attended by a train of people weeping and beating their breasts in grief; then having been expensively embalmed and bandaged in gaily colored mummy cloths, amid imposing ceremonies it was laid away in its rock sepulchre."

For these absurdities the Egyptians were ridiculed by other nations of their own times. Their adoration of animals led to most degrading excesses. The cat was considered sacred throughout the land, and punishment of death was meted out to persons injuring one.

WORSHIP OF THE NILE.

HYMN TO THE NILE.

Hail to thee O Nile!
Thou shewest thyself in this land
Coming in peace, giving life to Egypt;
O Ammon (thou) leadest night into day,
A leading that rejoices the heart!
Overflowing the gardens created by Ra.
Giving life to all animals;
Watering the lands without ceasing,

[1] See Mariette's Monuments of Upper Egypt.

The way of heaven descending,
Lover of food, bestower of corn,
Giving light to every home, O Ptah!

Bringer of food! Great Lord of provisions,
Creator of all good things!
Lord of terrors and of choicest joys!
All are combined in him.
He produceth grass for the oxen,
Providing victims for every god.
The choice incense is that which he supplies.
Lord in both regions,
He filleth the granaries, enricheth the storehouses,
He careth for the state of the poor.

Thou shinest in the city of the King;
Then the householders are satiated with good things,
The poor man laughs at the lotus.
All things are perfectly ordered.
Every kind of herb for thy children,
If food should fail,
All enjoyment is cast on the ground,
The land falls in weariness.

O inundation of Nile, offerings are made to thee:
Oxen are slain to thee:
Great festivals are kept for thee;
Fowls of the field are caught for thee,
Pure flowers are offered to thee.
Offerings are made to every god
As they are made unto the Nile.

Incense ascends unto heaven,
Oxen, bulls, fowls are burnt!
Nile makes for himself chasms in the South;
Unknown is his name in heaven,
He doth not manifest his forms,
Vain are all representations!

Shine forth, shine forth, O Nile, shine forth
Giving life to his oxen by the pastures,
Giving life to men by his oxen,
Shine forth in glory, O Nile!

More natural seems to us the worship of the Nile. There was a certain beauty which we today can still appreciate in the festivals celebrated each year on the banks of the rising water—which alone brought happiness and prosperity to all. Hapi was the god of the Nile and he was worshipped alike throughout Upper and Lower Egypt. Hymns were chanted to him, as it was believed he might be importuned to rise high enough to insure sufficient water, while if neglected, only a partial flood might occur. One of these hymns was something like this:

Hail to thee, Hapi
Who descendeth upon earth
And giveth life unto Egypt.
Thou who art hidden in the unknown
Whose waters spread upon the fields
Which the sun-god hath created;
And giveth life to all who are athirst.
Thou, the Creator of corn,
The Maker of barley——
Do thy waters cease to flow,
Then are all mankind in misery;
When thou wanest in heaven
The gods and all living things perish.

It would be useless for us to attempt to become familiar with all the Egyptian divinities. In the age when people conceived and worshipped them, the gods of a given locality were often unknown in a neighboring city, and the animals held to be sacred in one town might be eaten as food in another.

In addition to all their deities, ancestors were worshipped by the Egyptians, and an altar was erected to the departed in every home.

It was believed that the soul left the body after death in the form of a bird (ba), dwelled apart from the body, but would often return to it for nourishment and earthly comforts. In early days, therefore, food in great abundance was placed in the tomb, or the priests were paid to provide daily food for the deceased. Later it was felt that the ka—or that portion of the dead which required nourishment—was a mere shadow, a ghost, a phantom, and so pictures of things to eat would satisfy as well as the articles themselves. Carrying out this idea, the Egyptians pictured upon tomb walls all stages of growing grain, from the time the seed dropped upon the mellow soil until the ground flour was served in loaves for the feast; meat was shown, in all its forms: from the ox, feeding in the pasture, to the juicy roasts, made ready for the table. Such scenes as these adorned the interior chambers of the tomb; upon them, it was believed, the phantom-like ka might look and be appeased.

In a recently excavated tomb, liquid honey was discovered. Meats too, encased for at least 3,000 years, for the sustenance of the deceased, were here, while a lengthy menu covered a wall, stating the amount of food at the disposal of the departed. 5,006 geese, so it read, were at his command, but the number 5,006 was simply written beneath one pictured goose!

Beds, chairs, toilet articles, chariots, and countless other objects were left in the tomb of the well-to-do Egyptian, but were placed apart from the mummy, which was sealed up in a private apartment by itself, while a statue or image of the deceased was left near the belongings.

It was believed that at death the ba—or soul—went on a long journey to the land where Osiris reigned, and so great were the dangers of the way that many amulets and charms were laid by the departed to assist him in passing the obstacles of the road he must needs encounter. He who arrived at last at the land of Peace, where the joys of life abided without the sorrows of earth, came into the presence of Osiris. Here he made a negative confession, similar to the following: "Hail unto you, ye lords of Truth! hail to thee, great god, lord of Truth and Justice! I have not committed iniquity against men! I have not oppressed the poor! I have not laid labor upon any free man beyond that which he wrought for himself! I have not starved any man! I have not caused any to weep! There is no crime against me in this land of the Double Truth!"

DROMOS AND SECOND PYLON, TEMPLE OF KARNAK.

These and many more denials of sin were made and it sometimes happened that the confession was inscribed on one wall of a tomb while elsewhere were shown captives taken in war, slaves oppressed by labor, and other incidents in the earthly career of the departed which lead us to infer that the gods were supposed to be too mighty to take notice of most remarkable contradictions.

After the confession of the candidate for admission to the realm of Osiris, his good and evil deeds were weighed in a balance and if his virtues outweighed his failings, he was admitted to the land of the departed, a counterpart of his own Egypt.

A vast priesthood was required to preside over a religious system so complex as that of Egypt and the priests gained great influence over the people. The reason for this is apparent when we consider the prevailing ideas of the country. The body of the dead must be preserved, for upon its preservation depended the fate of the soul. To this end the body must be properly embalmed and entombed. The embalmers were under the control and supervision of the priests. Again, the soul of the departed must be assisted upon its perilous journey to Osiris by prayers said over each finger and each portion of the body. These prayers could be offered only by the priests themselves. Such a condition as this gave the priesthood of Egypt an opportunity to make itself supreme in the land, and this opportunity it was quick to seize upon.

Temples.

Many questions concerning Egyptian worship still remain unanswered. What part did the citizen take in the worship of his national gods? What effect did the worship of these gods have upon his life? We do not know—we cannot tell. It appears that his ancestral gods, worshipped at an altar in his own house, where of first importance. Some understanding of the temples and temple ceremonies cannot fail to throw light upon this old religion. Several of the old ruined temples may be seen today, standing like forest trees which have outlived their neighbors.

There is not in all Egypt a temple perfectly preserved; but by locating here an avenue of approach, there, a gateway, finding courts in other places, and halls and chapels, one comes at length to piece the whole together and to get some conception of the original entirety of the ancient temple.

In Greece the people built temples to their gods. In Egypt the king built them. Offerings were brought to the shrines of the Greek gods by every citizen in the land. In Egypt most of the gifts came from the king. To be sure there were special offerings made by all on feast days, but the king and the priests were alone responsible for the Egyptian temples; and while throngs accompanied processions thither on days of sacred festival, there is nothing to show that they had any part in the ceremonies.

The general plan of the temple was this: an avenue of approach—varying in length, and lined usually on either side by rows of sphinxes—led to a gateway, guarded by towers. In the Old Empire these towers served for defense, and seem later to have been preserved for decorative purposes. The gate admitted one to a court, open to the sky and outlined by pillars. In direct line with the gateway was the entrance to a large hall, supported by columns and lighted by small openings under the roof. Within this hall were celebrated the sacred festivals. At the end of the hall a small chapel was built which contained an image of the god of the temple. Sometimes two other chapels were placed, one on each side of this, and contained images of the god's wife and son, or his wife and daughter. The images sometimes represented the animal sacred to the god, or, again, would have a human body and merely the head of the sacred animal or bird. Later an image of the god himself was attempted. The tiny room or cell wherein these were kept was called the Holy of Holies. Before the door were inscribed these words: Four times must he purify himself who enters here.

Some temples were much more elaborate and complex than the simple one just described.

The doors of these chapels were always left sealed, and whenever they were opened, a clay seal was affixed. Having purified himself, the priest would fill the hall with the smoke of incense, break the seal, open the door and fall down, offering incense and kissing the ground before the image. Then a hymn of praise was probably sung.

Rise of the Nile.

"King and Father, gift and giver,
  God revealed in form of river,
  Issuing perfect and sublime,
  From the fountain-head of time;

"Whom eternal mystery shroudeth,
  Unapproached, untraced, unknown;
  Whom the Lord of heaven encloudeth
  With the curtains of his throne;

"From the throne of heaven descending,
  Glory, power, and goodness blending,
  Grant us, ere the daylight dies,
  Token of thy rapid rise."

Ha, it cometh! Furrowing, flashing,
  Red blood rushing o'er brown breast;
  Peaks and ridges, and dome dashing
  Foam on foam, crest on crest!

But the time of times for wonder
  Is when ruddy sun goes under;
  And the dust throws, half afraid,
  Silver shuttles of long shade.

Opens then a scene, the fairest
  Ever burst on human view;
  Once behold, and then comparest
  Nothing in the world thereto.

Every skiff a big ship seemeth,
  Every bush with tall wings clad;
  Every man his good brain deemeth
  The only brain that is not mad.

'Tis the signal Thebes hath waited,
  Libyan Thebes, the hundred-gated;
  Rouse and robe thee, River-priest
  For thy dedication feast!
  —Blackmore: Florilla.

Religious Ceremonies.

The Egyptian believed that his god had needs similar to those he himself experienced. Consequently each day the god needed to be clothed and fed. "The priest laid his hands on him (the image of the god), he took off the old rouge and his former clothes, all of course with the necessary formulae. He then dressed the god in the robe called the Nems, saying: 'Come white dress! come white dress! come white eye of Horus, which proceeds from the town of Nechebt. The gods dress themselves with thee in thy name *Dress,* and the gods adorn themselves with thee in thy name *Adornment.*' The priest then dressed the god in the *great dress,* rouged him, and presented him with his insignia: the sceptre, the staff of ruler, and the whip, the bracelets and anklets, as well as the two feathers which he wore on his head, because 'he has triumphed over his enemies, and is more splendid than gods or spirits.' The god required further a collarette and an amulet, two red, two green, and two white bands; when these had been presented to him the priest might then leave the chapel."[2]

Food and drink must needs be placed daily on his table. Lists of offerings made by the Ramesides have come down to us. One records offerings in the temple as follows: each were received 3,220 loaves of bread, 24 cakes, 144 jugs of beer, 32 geese, besides honey, flowers and incense. This food was probably used to feed the corps of assistants around the temple—the priests, servants and laborers. On feast days the people sent offerings. A large number of loaves of bread are recorded on certain days; these probably came from the poorer people. Again, an overwhelming number of cakes and jugs of wine would indicate offerings from the wealthy.

On feast days the king would himself perform part of the ceremonies, and as a king he would worship himself as a god. It sometimes seems as though the offerings and the ceremonies were made more to do honor to the king than to the god. When Ramses called for plans for a new grotto temple and heard the reports of his architects, an inscription tells us that he answered them after this fashion: "The

---
[2] Ancient Egypt, 274.

temple we have in mind already lies hidden by the gods in yonder mountain. You have but to clear away the waste material and your work is done. See to it, however, that the deities Ra and Isis and Ptah and I are all represented in becoming size on the facade as guardians—two on each side of the pylon. And mark you: see that no god has choice of position over the king; let the likeness and the form of them all be mine. Osiris must man the eight piers which support the roof, and we four be seated in the sanctuary, side by side."

Many buildings surrounded the temple, and the whole was enclosed by a wall. Various buildings were needed in order that all the functions of the temple could be performed. On one side was a court where the animals and birds intended for sacrifice were prepared. To the rear was a kitchen. The priests often received private revenues for providing food for the departed. This food as a rule was prepared in the kitchens of the temple. Dwellings for the priests, and the servants, store houses, granaries, the treasure house, gardens and an artificial lake lay within the temple wall. In the sacred lake the priests bathed, and in it they washed the vessels pertaining to the sanctuary.

The priestly duties were manifold. Certain priests poured out drink offerings; others recited from holy books; others kept the annals of the temples. Their incomes were paid in kind—like all other obligations of the time. So many loaves of bread, so many jugs of wine, beer and cakes made up their annual revenue.

While we may gain some feeble idea of these places of worship, built to do honor to the god—and to the king,— any description of them must necessarily be inadequate. "We may agree that neither the boldest imagination nor the most exact study, can enable us to form an adequate conception of the splendors of an Egyptian temple in its perfect state. The vast space it occupied; its lofty gateways; the long avenues of sphinxes; the glittering obelisks and the lifelike expressions of the monstrous statues, form a combination of the most imposing architectural grandeur. The æsthethic qualities of these structures cannot briefly be summed up. As we ponder them we shall be willing to acknowledge, for we shall discover, the exceptional constructive power of the ancient architects; we shall see how closely they followed Nature, and at times drew as well upon foreign art, though always preserving their own principles of form. There is always one grand imaginative vein running through all their work—which expresses the principal idea of their faith—*imperishability*.

"The ancient Egyptians copied no one. Their art sprang from their surroundings. What they have left continues to baffle us in many ways. We may understand perspective better than they did; we are their superiors in the use of light and shadow. We dare to build higher, and we are willing to trust thousands of lives to walls which would be wrecked if a single Egyptian column should fall against them; but we do not yet understand how they lifted their great masses to such lofty places, nor do we know where their architects studied art."[1]

Little has thus far been said of the sphinxes which ordinarily flanked the avenues leading up to these temples. These imaginary creatures were carved in stone, and having the body of a lion, had either the head of a ram or a human head. When the *Sphinx* is mentioned reference is usually made to the huge stone monument lying near the Great Pyramid. This was a natural rock, to which was given, more or less accurately, the external appearance of that mythological animal. The head was sculptured; the body was sculptured; the body was formed of the rock itself, filled out where necessary, by rather clumsy masonry of limestone. The total height of the Sphinx is 65 feet. The ear measures 6 feet 5 inches; the nose, 5 feet 10 inches; the mouth, 7 feet 8 inches. Its ponderous human face, grave in its eternal repose, rising in the midst of desert wastes, has been a great puzzle to people for thousands of years. It was probably hewn out of the rock as a symbol of the power of some Pharaoh of the Pyramid-age. The sphinxes which lined approaches to the temples were of course much smaller than this, and were carved merely for decorative purposes. An Egyptian god was given the image of the sphinx, and whether it was in honor of him, or merely

[1] Edward Wilson, Scribner, Oct. '88.

because the symbol was a favorite one, that so many of these mystic animals were used, is not known.

A final word regarding the faith which prompted the building of the Egyptian temples should perhaps be added. We hear much about the absurd and corrupt side of the Egyptian religion, but few have taken the trouble to acquaint themselves with its brighter side. Our ideas on the subject have been determined largely by the writings of the Greeks and Romans who knew only the last decadent period of Egyptian history. The decipherment of the hieroglyphs has enabled us to study the contemporary documents and inscriptions, and as a result the religious ideas developed by the Egyptians have not only aroused our deepest interest, but are commanding our admiration.

Like all other peoples in the same stage of culture, the primitive Egyptians feared and tried to render harmless, and perchance useful, the powers of nature, always mysterious because not understood. Thus arose the worship of natural phenomena, plants, animals and the dead. If we remember that among our own ignorant masses many of the religious ideas of our primitive forefathers survive in what we call superstition, we will not judge the common people of Egypt for holding fast to the beliefs of their ancestors, for it is true that they did so all through Egypt's long history. Hence the ridicule of the Greeks.

But there is another side to the picture. No people has ever developed a culture like that of the Egyptians without also reaching a purer conception of God. Way back in the Fifth dynasty we find the beginnings of a monotheistic tendency in the religion of Egypt. Indeed even earlier the priests of Heliopolis had taught the idea of the unity of the deity who manifested himself in the creative energy of the Sun. The Pharaohs of the Fifth dynasty took up the cult of Re (or Ra) as this god was called, raising mighty obelisks on the edge of the desert back of Memphis, before which stood altars of alabaster under the open sky: for this god could not be represented by any image and consequently needed no temple, no house of god.

As time went on this idea of the unity of the deity—largely, it is true, as a "mystery" understood only by the priests and other "initiated" ones, spread over the whole of Egypt. As a result the local deities, no matter what their origin, came to be regarded as manifestations of the one god Re, whose name was added to those of the local gods. We are all familiar with Amon of Thebes. This god, whose origin is very obscure, was of course a local deity, and when Thebes became the capital of the Empire, was raised to the kingship of all the gods. But it will be observed that to do this, the priests felt it necessary to identify him with Re and to speak of him henceforth not as Amon, but as Amon-Re.

But this was not a step forward. The priests of Re had taught that god is one and might be worshiped anywhere. It was not even necessary to have temples. When, however, such a local divinity as Amon of Thebes was identified with Re, as one of this god's manifestations, he received all the attributes of the one god, but at the same time remained god of Thebes and the priests never raised any theological objections when the Pharaohs erected the mighty temples of that city for the glory of their god and the perpetuation of their own deeds. Indeed the Pharaohs regarded themselves as his viceroys on earth. The attempted "reform" of Amen-hotep IV., which, as we saw, was so disastrous for his line, was largely an attempt to restore the purer worship of the Sun-god, not as Re but as Aton. But the priests of Amon-Re, who had already looked with disfavor, which they dared not express, upon the claims of the earlier Pharaohs of the Eighteenth dynasty—Amen-hotep III. during his lifetime had gone so far as to build a temple in which he worshipped his own *ka*, broke with Amen-hotep IV., were persecuted by him after he had removed to his new city, but in the end were able to overthrow the dynasty and place upon the throne kings who would recognize them as the intermediaries between god and man. In the end they themselves seized the throne—and it was not long before Egyptian history was at an end.

"God is the Eternal One. He is eternal and infinite; and endureth forever and ever. He hath endured for countless ages and He shall endure to all eternity.

"No man knoweth how to know Him. His name remaineth hidden. His name is a mystery unto His children. His names are innumerable; they are manifold and none knoweth their number."

—*Trans. from Brugsch; quoted in Budge, Egyption Religion.*

CHAPTER XIV.

Art and Decoration.

During the Old Empire certain rules regulating drawing were invented which were adhered to throughout the history of Egypt. The stiff, unnatural appearance of all Egyptian figures was due to strict observance of these rules, which became binding upon artists and prevented any perfection of art in the valley of the Nile.

Egyptian painting consisted of mere outline sketching. The human body was first entirely drawn; then clothing was added. The artists knew no more of anatomy than did the physicians. They did not even follow each his own ideas, but there was *one* established way of drawing the head, the arms, the limbs, and all felt obliged to hold to this conventional method. The extended arms show no elbows, the fingers no joints. An endeavor to draw the body in profile resulted in portions of it facing the spectator, other parts in profile, and still other sharing the characteristics of both positions. For many years the human figure, animals and birds could only extend the foot or arm—in case of a person— farthest away from the spectator, and each figure must be shown with the right side to the front. In course of time artists drew people of the lower classes with more freedom, but it would have been deemed disrespectful to have portrayed those of high rank in any but the conventional positions. Thus, in a picture of a noble being served by a slave, the latter might be drawn in a natural pose, while the noble still retained the stiff, grotesque position of early times. Again, the king was given colossal proportions, to indicate his power and strength, while children may be distinguished only by their tiny forms.

Side by side with this conventional school of art there developed a realistic school that exercised greater freedom with the human body. Tomb pictures remain wherein persons are shown with their backs to the spectator, and in many positions not permissible according to established rules. However, these paintings are invariably in the tombs of the lower classes. It would not have been deemed fitting that such freedom be used in decorating the tombs of nobles, or of persons of high social standing. Artists of this school seem to have been in disfavor in ancient Egypt. To be sure, in the matter of portraying scenes where captives, slaves or the humble people were gathered, artists of the conventional school drew these with considerable degree of freedom and ease. In the same picture the king, or noble, or high official was represented according to the established custom.

All Egyptian drawing of human figures, birds and animals is plain, and it is possible for any one today to read the stories of long series of tomb pictures—studying them out, one by one. However, when it came to representing a temple, a house, or a garden, the desire to show every portion of it resulted in some confusion. The artist was in doubt as to how to portray it all. "In treating such an important and complex object he wished if possible to show every part of it; he therefore did not draw the house from the front nor from the side, but made a picture of both sides together, and when the house had an upper story with three chambers, he put these three rooms close by also. He considered his duty accomplished when he had placed all the details before the spectator, but he did not care whether the spectator understood how these details fitted together.

"We have to face another difficulty in order to comprehend these pictures; the Egyptian artist has no sense of proportion between the different parts of the representation. If, for instance, the king is standing in one of the rooms of the building in question, our artist would, regardless of truth, draw that room ten times as large as all the others together, and even in one picture he frequently changes his standard of measurement."[1]

All pictures were painted, some only in outline, some entirely. The interiors of tombs were made to assume a gay appearance since tomb colors were always bright. Red, the color of the sun, and blue, the sky reflected in the Nile, were thought to be sacred.

Sculpture served two needs: it furnished statues of the

[1] Erman: Life in Ancient Egypt, 174.

dead for relatives to worship, and statues of the kings and gods, with the animals sacred to each, for the ornamentation of the temples. Thus the scope of the sculptor was limited in the beginning. Furthermore, the proportion, form, color and expression of every statue was fixed by laws prescribed by the priests. The aim of the artist was in every case to show absolute repose.

When we realize that many of the surviving monuments were chiseled from granite as hard as iron, upon which the artist could work with only a small metal chisel, we view them as monuments of the artist's untiring patience, as well as of kingly greatness and statues of the gods. These artists also knew how to make good use of poor material. In soft limestone their task was easier; scenes were frequently cut in this, covered with stucco and then painted. Inexpensive statues were often made in this way.

Art seems at first to have taken rapid strides in Egypt, but after reaching a certain point, it was prevented by established laws, enforced by the priesthood, from going farther. So it deteriorated. Unfortunately we know little of the artists who wrought these works and nothing of the training they received.

Decorative art, as developed by the dwellers on the Nile, has perhaps greater interest for the modern artist than their paintings or statuary. The modern conventional school of decorative art finds much to copy and adapt from patterns which survive in Egypt. In the first place, the hieroglyphics were in themselves decorative. They were often used as friezes, and never do we find them cut across figures, as was the case in Assyria. Among designs commonly called geometrical, but in the beginning the representation of something familiar, the zigzag line was popular. A double zigzag formed little squares, and by various arrangements, many combinations were possible. The scroll was also a favorite decoration. There was an old legend to the effect that the spiral represented the wanderings of the soul, but just what connection existed between the two—if indeed there had ever been one—was lost in distant ages.

Coils, hooks, links and endless scrolls were used, and the fret patterns were but modifications of the spiral. The checkered design was originally worked out by the shepherds and herdsmen who wove baskets and mats of rushes. The source of one of the earliest imitations was the feather, with its variety of forms. Only a few flowers were copied. The lotus, papyrus, daisy, convolvulus, vine and palm were the only ones used to any great extent. By far the most popular of these was the lotus. This water lily has been worshipped in many countries. The Egyptians did not regard it as a national flower—by no means. It was considered the emblem of immortality.

"The lotus is the symbol of 'life,' of resurrection. Bouquets of it were presented to guests at funerals. It was sometimes called the symbol of the Sun. 'The solar significance of the lotus is elementary and most important. A text reads: The Sun, which was from the beginning, rises like a hawk from the midst of its lotus bed. When the doors of its leaves open in sapphire-colored brilliancy, it has divided the night from the day.'

"A confessional chapter of the Book of the Dead closes with the words: I am a pure lotus, issue of the field of the Sun. The Egyptian idea of the resurrection and of a future life was connected with a worship of the creative and reproductive forces of nature, which were conceived and worshipped as solar in character and origin. It is the supposed passage of the sun at night through a lower world, during its return to the dawn of a following day which makes Osiris —the Sun at night—the God of the lower world and of the dead, hence himself represented as a mummy. As the God of the resurrection, his special and emphatic character, he represents the creative energy of the Sun-god. Hence, the lotus as attribute of Osiris is at once a symbol of the sun, of the resurrection, and of creative forces and power. Since the doctrine of a future life and a belief in a spirit world were ever present to the Egyptian mind, we cannot too strongly insist on the funeral symbolism of the lotus."[2]

This brief explanation of the lotus' significance given by one who has made a detailed study of this particular Egyptian symbol, helps us to understand its universal use. It was pictured with the gods, given as offerings to them, employed as

[2] Goodyear: Grammar of the Lotus.

capitals for columns, and had many significant uses. It has been suggested that the bright yellow ovary stigmas of this water-lily, with its rayed appearance, might have been thought a symbol of the sun. As time went on, the flower developed into a monstrosity, and became so conventionalized that it has been difficult in many cases to determine what the artist intended to represent.

The grape vine, with its fruit, was a popular decoration. Ceilings were often painted golden yellow, with vine leaves and bunches of grapes hanging down. In glazed work grapes, convolvulus and thistle were used. Golden stars on a blue-black background found favor as a ceiling decoration.

In prehistoric times, ideas of ornamentation were often gained in curious ways. Jars of pottery were sometimes tied with a string to support them while drying. The string naturally left an impression in the clay. This suggested the notion of twisting the string and so obtaining not only an impression but a pattern. From this very illustration we may realize how completely many origins of decoration have been lost in obscurity.

CEILING DECORATION.

CHAPTER XV.

Tombs and Burial Customs.

We have seen in a former chapter that the Egyptians believed one to be composed of three parts: his earthly body, his soul, or ba, and his ka, the ghostlike phantom that grew up with him in life and after death experienced the same needs that he had known while living. All three parts were essential to the existence of any one of them. On this account the Egyptians made every effort to perpetuate the body and to provide necessities for the ka, lest the soul should wither up and be no more. Granting the truth of these beliefs, all that the Nile dwellers did in consequence of a faith in them was logical and natural.

When an Egyptian was ill, a physician and one skilled in magic were summoned. They did what they could to restore him. When their efforts failed, they usually discovered that from his birth it had been decreed that he would meet with an early death, and in this ingenious way they maintained their influence unimpaired.

Upon the death of a relative, all the women of the house rushed into the street with disheveled hair, shouting loud lamentations. In this way their loss was made public. Then they returned and the body was sent to the embalmer.

Three methods of embalming were commonly employed. The most costly method involved seventy days and absorbed perhaps the total income of the year, unless the family was wealthy. The second was less costly and required less time; finally there was a comparatively inexpensive method which had to satisfy the poor.

The vital organs and those parts of the body hardest to preserve were removed. This was strictly necessary according to later Egyptian ideas, yet so dreadful did they regard any mutilation of the body that the men who performed this task were intensely hated and considered as unclean. They were not allowed to mingle with other classes, nor could one rise out of his class. When they had done their work, they were stoned away from the house.

The body was now put into a bath of chemicals to remain for many days. When at last it was taken out, it was filled with linen and sweet smelling powders and made to look as lifelike as possible. Then it was wrapped in linen bands, the quality of the linen used depending upon the purse of the family.

"Each separate limb of the deceased was dedicated to a particular divinity by the aid of holy oils, charms and sentences; a specially prepared cloth was wrapped round each muscle, every drug and bandage owed its origin to some divinity, and the confusion of sounds, of disguised figures, and of various perfumes, had a stupefying effect on those who visited this chamber. It need not be said that the whole embalming establishment and its neighborhood was enveloped in a cloud of powerful resinous fumes, of sweet attar, of lasting musk, and of pungent spices."

Prayers and magical charms were said, scarabs and amulets enclosed, and finally the body was placed in a coffin so constructed that it would stand upright, as though the person were standing erect. It was then taken home, and lamentations were made for some days. These finally gave way to festivals. Banquets were held in honor of the mummy, which was placed near the table and offered portions of food. Sometimes mummies were kept in the home for a long time, and were worshipped with the household gods. When at length the day for burial came, the family and friends accompanied the body across the Nile to the Necropolis. They took offerings with them,—food, furniture, toilet articles, and some literature—certainly some pages from the Book of the Dead. All the way across the river, the women wept. That the exhibition of grief might be sufficient, wailing women were hired to increase the lamentations.

Seeing the sun which they worshipped disappear each night in the west, the Egyptians grew to think that it went to a mysterious country, the land of Osiris. In course of time they located the land of the Blest in the west, and whereever possible, placed their tombs facing the west—the direction which the departed took for his long journey. All through the river ride the women cried: "To the West; to the West!"

Upon reaching the place of burial, the priest performed certain ceremonies. Then the mummy in its coffin, and the jars containing the vital organs, were sealed up in the chamber prepared to receive them.

There were always three essential parts to an Egyptian tomb: the chapel, or room used by the relatives to worship the deceased and bring him offerings; the sepulchral chamber which contained the mummy; and the serdab, or secret cell, where images of the deceased were sealed up for the ka to look upon, since the features of the earthly body were now changed by death. This secret chamber was connected by a small aperture with the chapel, in order that the smoke of burning incense and proffered prayers might be the more easily experienced by the Ka. On the west wall of the tomb was the stela, or a false door, upon which was engraved the name of the deceased, his parentage, titles, and a record of the offerings made to his ka. In early times offerings alone were made with no record of them, but as the people grew more enlightened, they realized that a time must come when even the best known would be forgotten and neglected. Therefore they conceived the notion of enumerating the articles of food contributed, believing that the ka would look upon the record and be satiated through the ages.

Compared to the earthly abode, which was temporary, the tomb was eternal; hence the care that was lavished upon the tomb by the Egyptians. While yet young, a man began to build his final resting place. If he died before it was completed, some relative supervised its completion, but in most cases tombs left thus unfinished show signs of hasty conclusion. The survivor was chiefly interested in his own tomb, and could give but passing attention to that of the departed.

In the Old Empire, tombs were constructed of brick masonry. The mummy was placed some distance below the brick work which was elevated a few feet above the ground. During the Middle Empire, grotto tombs came into favor. These were hewed out of the living rock. A large excavation was made and chambers were sometimes formed by masonry, sometimes hollowed from the rock itself. It was during this period that pictures of food offerings were made in addition to the food formerly offered alone. During the New Empire tombs were generally cut in rocks, and now it became customary to have the heart removed from the deceased and placed in a jar. The idea of reward and punishment was emphasized. " From the calm assurance of purely material happiness which the earliest Egyptian loved to dwell on, there developed a keener sense of the trials through which the soul must pass, together with a higher ideal of the future life, a strong conviction of the moral qualities and acts essential to the justification of the individual. Later this spiritual degenerated into a reliance upon ritual and formulas in a merely magical sense."[1]

The nature of the burial depended upon the means of the family. The middle class interment was less pretentious than that of the noble, and the poor appropriated some old, neglected tomb, or paid for space in a public tomb. Even in such cases, some offerings were made. The burial of royalty was splendid, as tombs recently discovered in the Valley of the Kings have attested. Furniture, receptacles, toilet articles—even a boat and a chariot were in some cases provided.

In the tombs of the wealthy were enclosed little images of servants, or "answerers." To the unimaginative Egyptian, the future world could only be a place, like his own Egypt, where he would sow and reap, under conditions most favorable. Water would be plentiful, and work would be so easy that it would be a joy to perform it. This satisfied the masses, who knew only how to reap and sow. But the wealthy had not been accustomed to cultivate the soil in this life and were not pleased with the prospect of doing so through countless ages. Lest such menial tasks be required of them in the realm of Osiris they had with them these images of servants— these answerers—who might respond when they were called upon: "Here am I, thy servant." Thus the noble would have his work performed by others, as it had always been.

Amulets and scarabs were also deposited with the mummy. The amulets were charms supposed to bring good luck, and the scarabs had a deeper significance. The word *scarab* means

[1] Blimmer: Essays on History, Religion and Art of Ancient Egypt.

beetle. A certain kind of beetle deposited its eggs in the sand. From the earth, in course of time, a fully developed beetle would come forth. The Egyptians, who knew nothing of insect life, believed the beetle, long since dead, had the power of restoring itself to life anew. Hence the scarab was an emblem of the resurrection and immortality. Just as the cross is a symbol dear to the hearts of Christians, so, to the followers of the Egyptian religion, the scarab was significant. It was made of various kinds of stone, variously colored, and was worn by the Egyptian during life, and buried with him at death. During periods when religious revivals were strong, large numbers of these emblems were produced; during ages when greater indifference to religious matters were shown, fewer seem to have been made. As little Greek vases have been found in all lands where Greek merchantmen went, so the Egyptian trade of antiquity can be traced by the little scarabs. Large collections of them have been made in recent years, and many are exhibited today in museums.

In the New Empire, when it became necessary to remove the heart of the deceased, a sacred scarab was substituted in its place. The idea prompting such action was that the heart was sinful, and if removed, might not be able to testify against its owner. The scarab, being a symbol of faith, might be of some assistance.

A copy of the Book of the Dead was supplied the deceased because it contained a list of the dangers his soul would have to meet in journeying to the abode of Osiris. The topography of the future world was included and all invocations to be uttered at different stages of the progress were given. Only with a perfect knowledge of all these things could the soul hope to reach the land of the blest. Advice was given him about meeting the forty-two judges of the western world, who judged him for forty-two sins. If his good deeds outweighed his shortcomings, he remained forever with Osiris; otherwise he was transformed into some unclean animal, and never knew the joys of eternal life.

It has been estimated that some 200,000,000 people died in Upper Egypt during its active history and found a resting place in the favorite strip of desert less than 450 miles in length. Of course only the most substantial of the tombs are preserved. The dryness of the country has helped to preserve ancient monuments.

It is small wonder that to the very poor, whose huts have always been in the Necropolis—the wealth concealed in tombs has always been a strong temptation. Records reach through the Middle and New Empires testifying that robbers pillaged tombs for jewelry and gold, and today the Arab traffics constantly in the spoils of the tombs—above which, in many cases, he lives.

THE FUNERAL PROCESSION: THE WEAPONS AND JEWELS.

CHAPTER XVI.

Excavations in Egypt.

We have spoken frequently of recent discoveries in Egypt, and of objects found within old tombs. The question naturally arises: Who makes these discoveries, and under what circumstances are the secrets of the tombs revealed?

Modern excavations in Egypt are of recent date. In 1798 the military expedition of Napoleon Bonaparte drew attention to Egyptian monuments. One of his soldiers, excavating for some fortifications in the delta, discovered a stone covered with an inscription, and this was preserved. Being found near the mouth of the Rosetta river, it was called the Rosetta stone. The stone had been inscribed during the reign of Ptolemy III., a Greek king. Because some of his subjects in Egypt were Greeks and some Egyptians, he had caused the decree to be inscribed (1) in Greek, (2) in hieroglyphics, (3) in demotic. The Greek sentences were easily read, and since it seemed probable that the other writing simply repeated the decree, scholars set to work to decipher it. By 1832 they had prepared an Egyptian grammar and vocabulary.

The earliest attempt at systematic investigation was begun in 1822, when the government of Tuscany sent a number of scholars into Egypt to study inscriptions. Champollian and Rosellini were among them. In 1840 Germany sent out an expedition under the leadership of Lepsius. This party began work at Memphis, among the pyramids. In course of time the Tuscan expedition supplied volumes of copied inscriptions and explanatory material.

August Marietta went to Egypt in 1850 and was active there until 1880. He made the first great discovery when he came upon the burial place of the Apis bulls in Memphis. Sixty-four tombs were found, together with amulets and funeral ornaments. In 1857 he was made director of a new museum, which was founded at Cairo. He received the monopoly of the right to excavate in the vicinity of Thebes, and while he allowed others to study what was unearthed under his direction, he would not permit them to do any excavating. Maspero succeeded him as curator of the Cairo Museum. Into this museum has been placed all the great finds of recent years and here one who would make detailed study of ancient Egypt must go.

As a result of his explorations in the valley of the Nile, and of his personal knowledge of all gifts made to the Cairo Museum, Maspero has prepared many books pertaining to the life of the ancient Egyptians. His conclusions are drawn entirely from the revelations of old monuments and remains, and are of first importance.

Means have been provided by the Egyptian Exploration Fund and by the Egyptian Research Account to make it possible for young students to undertake explorations in behalf of public museums. Nothing found by those thus engaged can be sold, whether publicly or privately, but must be presented to some museum where people generally can have an opportunity to see and examine such objects. Reports of all discoveries are published at the earliest possible moment. In marked contrast to such generous principles have been the undertakings carried on by many who have used recovered objects for their personal profit, or have withheld knowledge of them indefinitely.

W. M. Flinders Petrie, professor of Egyptology in University College, London, took charge of the expedition sent out by the Egypt Exploration Fund in 1884. Later he organized the Egyptian Research Account, in order to give young students an opportunity to do active work themselves. In late years Petrie has carried on his efforts alone. On the basis of his observations, discoveries and knowledge, he has prepared a history of Egypt, recently published. This is a chronological account of royal tombs unearthed by him, rather than a complete history of Egypt's development.

Gardner, Griffith and Naville have been sent out at different times by the Egypt Exploration Fund, and have each prepared reports of their finds.

The Tell el Amarna Letters should be mentioned with the great finds in Egypt. In 1887-8, Arabs, who were carrying off bricks for their houses, came upon a record chamber, containing many hundred letters inscribed on bricks. They were shown to experts who did not appreciate their value. They were put in sacks and carried around, from one place to another, with the hope of making something from their sale. When many of them had been ground to powder and others were hopelessly ruined, they were bought up by museums at London, Berlin, St. Petersburg and Cairo. They have since been translated and it appears that they belonged to the record chamber of the capital built by Amenhotep IV., and called by him the Horizon of the Solar Disk. As now translated, they are found to be letters written during the peaceful reign of Amenhotep III. and early in the reign of Amenhotep IV.; others recount the North Syrian war, and certain others, the Palestine war. They reveal the condition of the empire during the reign of the fanatical king who attempted to bring about a religious revolution at home, while hostile tribes assailed his empire on the east. The Tell el Amarna letters have done much to clear up a portion of Egyptian history, previously not understood. Their revelations have been supplemented by two wonderful discoveries made within the last two years: the discovered tomb of the parents of Queen Tiy—mother of Amenhotep IV., in 1905, and early in 1907, the tomb of Queen Tiy herself. These finds are so remarkable that we may well give them brief consideration.

In recent years, Theodore M. Davis has undertaken systematic excavations in the Valley of the Kings—the great Necropolis west of Thebes—for the benefit of the Cairo Museum. This work has been directed by Archaeologist Quibell, maintained by the present Egyptian government.

Quoting from one who was present at the exciting moment when the tomb of Queen Tiy's parents was opened:

"Squeezing their way between the wall and rock ceiling, M. Maspero and Mr. Davis were soon in the midst of such a medley of tomb furniture that, in the glare of their lighted candles, the first effect was one of bewilderment. Gradually, however, one object after another detached itself from the shimmering mass, shining through the cool air, dust-free and golden. Against the wall to the left stood a chair, and beyond it a gilded coffin-cover lay upside down. In it was a conventional mask that gleamed golden through dark veiling; and the mummy whose head this mask had covered lay farther off, its body partly incased in gilded openwork. Against the wall to the right leaned two 'Osiris beds,' flat surfaces on which seed had been sown, which in sprouting, had outlined the figure of the god. Not far off, along the wall opposite the door, stood a row of sentry-boxes, each containing a statuette. In front of these rose the outermost case for a mummy. To the left stood a bed. Nearer again lay a silvered mummy case; and on this, and on a mummy beyond it, the second in the tomb, a shaft of cold blue light struck down from the outer day.

"By day-light then, mingled with the light of flickering candle flames, the discoverers examined the second mummy. By candle light alone they searched the first. Both had been plundered by the thief of long ago. Throwing the mummy cases hither and yon, he had taken from both mummies everything of intrinsic value except a plate of gold closing the aperture through which the heart of one had been removed by the embalmers. Not a jewel, and only part of one necklace, remained of all those with which the dead must once have been bedecked. But if such trophies were lacking, others of surpassing splendor and significance still packed the tomb-chamber, from wall to wall. In the bottom of a mummy-case, from which the thief had removed the cover, he had left a cushion and a graceful alabaster vase. In another mummy-case he had neglected an alabaster jar and the cover of an embroidery-box which he must have carried across the chamber to a second bed, on which it now lay beside a superb gilded chair. Near by, where the floor suddenly fell one deep step to a lower level, he had thrown, among a multitude of sealed jars, half of the gilded openwork casing which had encircled one of the mummies. Near these jars again he had propped a coffin-cover against one corner of the tomb. Here, too, he had left a third bed and one of the most important finds in the tomb, a chariot, the curving front and wheel-rims of which shone through the darkness golden and scarlet.

"Except for its broken pole and the partly bare spokes of its gilded wheels, this chariot was in perfect condition; with the yoke already found in the corridor and a whip soon to be discovered, it lacked nothing to be complete.

"Maspero studied the hieroglyphics on their gleaming

mummy-cases. 'Tioua,' he read after a time; and after further study he went on, 'Ioua, hereditary prince, chief friend among the friends of the sovereign.' There were the names of the dead in the tomb; and these dead, as Maspero therefore knew, had been the parents of Tiy, a queen of the eighteenth dynasty, whose changing of the national religion had once caused such uproar and violence that the burial of her parents in the sacred Valley of the Kings would have had to be hasty and secret.

"The probable history of the tomb, accordingly, was clear. During a period of unrest Queen Tiy, who wished a royal burial for her father and mother, either chose an old tomb on which the work had been abandoned or stopped work on one which was being hewn out. In it she had placed the mummies, with their funeral offerings, till the tomb could be reopened and finished, or its contents transferred to a fitter resting place. Quiet times had perhaps never returned during her reign; and however that may be, the tomb had been reopened, not by Queen Tiy, but first by a robber, and now at last, by modern archaeologists."[1]

Even more gratifying than the discovery just recounted was the finding of Queen Tiy herself. Again we can get into the spirit of the discovery best by reading the description of an eye-witness:

"The excitement of entering a newly opened tomb is naturally considerable; but when the first inscriptions to be seen revealed the fact that the tomb of Queen Tiy, which had been so long sought for, had been found, a glamour was added to the moment which will not easily be forgotten by any of the party. Inside the tomb chamber the gold covered coffin and outer coffin, gleaming in the light of the electric lamps, formed a sight of surprising richness. The mummy of the queen protruded from beneath the lip of the beautiful coffin, which was made in human form. A vulture-headed diadem of gold could just be seen passing around her head, and one could see here and there the shining sheets of gold in which the body was wrapped. There must have been thousands of dollars worth of gold-foil and leaf in the chamber, and the post-Akhnaton officials seem to have carried away

[1] Century, Nov., '05.

many of the portable gold ornaments, probably amounting to many times that value. In a recess cut in the wall of the chamber stood four fine canopic vases of alabastrum, containing the queen's heart and intestines; and in one corner of the room there were several charming little pots and toilet utensils of blue glazed ware. One of these, in the form of a graceful girl carrying a pot upon her shoulder, is perhaps the most perfect specimen of miniature figure-molding known in Egypt.

"After the tomb had been opened for a few hours, the air, of course, became very much better, but its bad effects on the antiquities was at once discernible. Even before the first quick record had been finished, some of the scenes on the gold showed signs of dropping to pieces.

"It is to be hoped that most of the antiquities will be able to travel to Cairo, though their fragile condition makes it difficult to deal with them. Probably much of the rotten wood work, and even some of the fine reliefs on the gold-leaf, will have to be left in the tomb, which will be closed with Portland cement."[2]

Greatest care has to be exercised to protect finds from the Arabs. In spite of the vigilance of the government, pilfering of the old Necropolis is constantly carried on. Every fragment or curio which might bring profit is snatched up by those in the employ of speculators.

Difficulties Confronting the Explorer.

Petrie has given in detail many of the difficulties which have confronted him in his excavations among ancient Egyptian tombs. On one occasion, in preference to living in an Arabian village, he hunted out an old tomb, occupied the three chambers above, where the deceased had been fed and worshipped, and with his guide as a guard in an adjoining tomb, found the place secure and comfortable.

A little account of his experience in the summer of 1888, while excavating in the Fayoum, will give us some notion of the perplexities that often beset the archaeologist. Whenever possible, quotation is made from Petrie's own report. The district he selected—the Fayoum—calls to mind Amenem-

---
[2] Century, Sept., '07.

het III., who first irrigated the region and thus added materially to the arable land of his country. To this particular section Petrie was drawn, because, as he explains: "The exploration of the pyramids of this district was my main object, as their arrangement, their dates, and their builders were yet unknown."[3]

"So soon as we began to turn over the soil we found chips of sandstone colossi; the second day the gigantic nose of a colossus was found, as broad as a man's body; then pieces of carved thrones, and a fragment of inscription of Amenemhet III. It was evident that the two piles of stone had been the pedestals of colossal seated monolithic statues, carved in hard quartzite sandstone, and brilliantly polished. These statues faced northward, and around each was a courtyard wall with sloping outer face and red granite gateway in the north front. The total height of the colossi was about 60 feet from the ground. The description of Herodotus, therefore, is accounted for; and it shows that he actually saw the figures, though from a distance, as any person who visited them closely would not have described them in such a manner."[4]

Petrie took his corps of native workmen next to Hawara, for the pyramids there had not been opened in modern times. Finding no trace of an entrance, they tunneled for many weeks in the solid tomb. Finally a small opening was effected into the old chamber of the tomb, and there, by the flickering light of a candle, could be seen two empty sarcophagi. A modern canal has saturated this part of the land and the explorer was obliged to wade through mud to the tombs.

Quoting from his description of what was found: "The pyramid had been elaborately arranged so as to deceive and weary the spoilers, and it had apparently occupied a great amount of labor to force an entrance." After explaining a dozen ways they had tried and failed, he says: "At last the way had been forced by breaking away a hole in the edge of the glassy-hard sandstone roofing block, and thus reaching the chamber and its sarcophagi. By a little widening of the spoilers' hole I succeeded in getting through it into the chamber. The water was up to the middle of my body, and so

---

[3] Petrie: Ten Years' Digging in Egypt, 81.
[4] Ibid, 82.

the exploration was difficult; but the floor was covered with rubbish and chips, which might contain parts of the funeral vessels, and therefore needed searching. The first day I got the coveted prize, a piece of alabaster vessel with the name of Amenemhet III., proving finally to whom the pyramid belonged. Still there was a puzzle as to the second sarcophagus, which had been built up between the great central one and the chamber side. On clearing in the chamber which led to the sepulchre, however, a beautiful altar of offerings in alabaster was found, covered with figures of the offerings all named, over a hundred, and dedicated to the king's daughter, Neferuptah. The chamber itself is a marvellous work; nearly the whole height of it is carved out of a single block of hard quartzite sandstone, forming a huge tank in which the sarcophagus was placed. No trace of inscription exists on either the walls or the sarcophagi; and but for the funeral furniture, even the very name would not have been recovered."[5]

Next they located what had in all probability been the old Labyrinth. No trace of the building itself could be discovered, but the vast extent showed it to have been larger than any temple known in Egypt. Pliny, a Roman historian, has told us that for centuries this Labyrinth served as a quarry for this section of the country, and that a small town of quarrymen lived near by.

In the cemetery of Hawara, Petrie made some explorations. He succeeded in finding one tomb, which had been missed by the spoilers—this naturally was the coveted find. It belonged to the twenty-sixth dynasty, a period of the decline of Egyptian power. It was the tomb of a great noble, Horuta. Standing deep under water, it was more difficult to manage than usual.

"But the sarcophagus itself was most difficult to open. The lid block was nearly two feet thick, and almost under water. It was too heavy for us to move entire, so some weeks were spent in cutting it in two. One piece was then raised, but it proved to be the foot end; and though I spent a day struggling with the inner coffins, sitting in the sarcophagus up to my nose in water, I yet could not draw them out from under the rest of the stone lid. So after some days the men

---
[5] Petrie: Ten Years' Digging in Egypt, 86.

raised that, enough to get one's head in between the under side of it and the water; and then I spent another gruesome day, sitting astride of the inner coffin, unable to turn my head under the lid without tasting the bitter brine in which I sat." At last the coffin was recovered. " Anxiously opening it, we found a slight inner coffin, and then the body of Horuta himself, wrapped in a network of beads of lazuli, beryl, and silver, this last decomposed. Then came the last and longed-for scene, for which our months of toil had whetted our appetites—the unwrapping of Horuta. Bit by bit the layers of pitch and cloth were loosened, and row after row of magnificent amulets were disclosed, just as they were laid on in the distant past. The gold ring on the finger which bore his name and titles, the exquisitely inlaid gold birds, the chased gold figures, the lazuli statuettes delicately wrought, the polished lazuli and beryl and carnelian amulets finally engraved, all the wealth of talismanic armory, rewarded our eyes with a sight which has never been surpassed to archaeological gaze. No such complete and rich a series of amulets has been seen intact before; and as one by one they were removed all their positions were recorded, and they may now be seen lying in their original order in the Ghizeh Museum."[6]

We have noted repeatedly the various articles found within the tombs, such as funeral furniture, vases, food, and amulets. Some rather unusual disclosures were brought to light in this old cemetery in the Fayoum. Children's toys, and their personal belongings were found entombed with their mummies. One tomb of a much later date than yet mentioned—of Roman Egypt indeed—contained one of the books of the Iliad. More valuable than any of these were wreaths of flowers with which the dead had been adorned. These were perfectly dried and from them and accounts given us by Pliny, the ancient flora of Egypt has been worked out by the patience and painstaking of noted botanists.

[6]Petrie: Ten Years' Digging in Egypt, 93, ff.

DESCRIPTIONS OF EGYPT.

I.

The Nile had overflowed its bed. The luxuriant corn fields and blooming gardens on its shores were lost beneath a boundless waste of waters; and only the gigantic temples and palaces of its cities (protected from the force of the water by dikes), and the tops of the tall palm-trees and acacias could be seen above its surface. The branches of the sycamores and plane-trees drooped and floated on the waves, but the boughs of the tall silver poplars strained upward, as if anxious to avoid the watery world beneath. The full moon had risen; her soft light fell on the Libyan range of mountains vanishing on the western horizon, and in the north the shimmer of the Mediterranean could faintly be discerned. Blue and white lotus flowers floated on the clear water, bats of all kinds darted softly through the still air, heavy with the scent of acacia-blossom and jasmine; the wild pigeons and other birds were at roost in the tops of the trees, while the pelicans, storks and cranes squatted in groups on the shore under the shelter of the papyrus reeds, and Nile-beans. The pelicans and storks remained motionless, their long bills hidden beneath their wings, but the cranes were startled by the mere beat of an oar, stretching their necks, and peering anxiously into distance, if they heard but the song of the boatmen. The air was perfectly motionless, and the unbroken reflection of the moon, lying like a silver shield on the surface of the water, proved that, wildly as the Nile leaps over cataracts, and rushes past the gigantic temples of Upper Egypt, yet on approaching the sea by different arms, he can abandon his impetuous course, and flow along in sober tranquility.

On this moonlight night in the year 528 B. C. a bark was crossing the almost currentless canopic mouth of the Nile. On the raised deck at the stern of this boat an Egyptian was sitting to guide the long pole-rudder, and the half naked boatmen within were singing as they rowed.

As Phanes uttered these words they landed at the garden wall, washed by the Nile. The garden of Rhodopis was as full of sound, and scent and blossom as a night in fairy land. It was one labyrinth of acanthus shrubs, yellow mimosa, the snowy gueldres rose, jasmine and lilac, red roses and laburnums, overshadowed by tall palm-trees, acacias and balsam-trees. Large bats hovered softly on their delicate wings over the whole, and sounds of mirth and song echoed from the river.

This garden had been laid out by an Egyptian, and the builders of the Pyramids had already been celebrated for ages for their skill in horticulture. They well understood how to mark out neat flower-beds, plant groups of trees and shrubs in regular order, water the whole by aqueducts and fountains, arrange arbors and summer-houses, and even inclose the walks with artistically clipped hedges and breed gold-fish in stone basins.

At noon on the following day the same boat, which, the evening before, had carried the Athenian and the Spartan, stopped once more before Rhodopis' garden. The sun was shining so brightly, so warmly and genially in the dark blue Egyptian sky, the air was so pure and light, the beetles were humming so merrily, the boatmen singing so lustily and happily, the shores of the Nile bloomed in such gay, variegated beauty, and were so thickly peopled, the palm-trees, sycamores, bananas and acacias were so luxuriant in foliage and blossom, and over the whole landscape the rarest and most glorious gifts seemed to have been poured out with such divine munificence that a passerby must have pronounced it the very home of joy and gladness, a place from which sadness and sorrow had been forever banished.

—*An Egyptian Princess.*

Descriptions of Egypt. II.

The feast of Neith, called in Egyptian "the lamp-burning," was celebrated by a universal illumination, which began at the rising of the moon. The shores of the Nile looked like two long lines of fire. Every temple, house, and hut was ornamented with lamps, according to the means of its possessors.

The porches of the country houses and the little towers on the larger buildings were all lighted up by brilliant flames, burning in pans of pitch and sending up clouds of smoke, in which the flags and pennons waved gently backward and forward. The palm-trees and sycamores were silvered by the moonlight and threw strange fantastic reflections onto the red waters of the Nile—red from the fiery glow of the houses on their shores. But, strong and glowing as was the light of the illumination, its rays had not power to reach the middle of the giant river where the boat was making its course and the pleasure party felt as if they were sailing in dark night between two brilliant days. Now and then a brightly lighted boat would come swiftly across the river and seem as it neared the shore to be cutting its way through a glowing stream of molten iron.

Lotus-blossoms, white as snow, lay on the surface of the river, rising and falling with the waves and looking like eyes in the water. Not a sound could be heard from either shore. The echoes were carried away by the north wind and the measured stroke of the oars and the monotonous song of the rowers were the only sounds that broke the stillness of this strange night—a night robbed of its darkness.

The pyramids lay on the left bank of the Nile, in the silver moonshine, massive and awful, as if bruising the earth beneath them with their weight; the giant graves of mighty rulers. They seemed examples of man's creative power and at the same time warnings of the vanity and mutability of earthly greatness. For where was Chufu[1] now—the king who had cemented that mountain of stone with the sweat of his subjects? Where was the long-lived Chafra[2] who had despised the gods, and, defiant in the consciousness of his own strength, was said to have closed the gates of the temples in order to make himself and his name immortal by building a tomb of superhuman dimensions? Their empty sarcophagi are, perhaps, tokens that the judges of the dead found them unworthy of rest in the grave, unworthy of the resurrection, whereas, the builder of the third and most beautiful pyramid, Menkera,[3] who contented himself with a smaller monument, and reopened the gates of the temples, was allowed to rest in peace in his coffin of blue basalt.

There they lay in the quiet night, these mighty pyramids,

[1] Khufu. [2] Khafre. [3] Menkure.

shone on by the bright stars, guarded by the watchmen of the desert—the gigantic sphinx—and overlooking the barren rocks of the Libyan stony mountains. At their feet slept the mummies of their faithful subjects.

But their boat sped on before the north wind; they left the city of the dead behind them and passed the enormous dikes built to protect the city of Menes from the violence of the floods; the city of the Pharaohs came in sight, dazzlingly bright with the myriads of flames which had been kindled in honor of the goddess Neith, and when at last the gigantic temple of Ptah appeared, the most ancient building of the most ancient land, the spell broke, their tongues were loosed, and they burst out into loud exclamations of delight.

It was illuminated by thousands of lamps; a hundred fires burned on its pylons, its battlemented walls and roofs. Burning torches flared between the rows of sphinxes which connected the various gates with the main building, and the now empty house of the god Apis was so surrounded by colored fires that it gleamed like a white limestone rock in a tropical sunset. Pennons, flags and garlands waved above the brilliant picture; music and loud songs could be heard from below.
—*Egyptian Princess.*

Descriptions of Egypt. III.

By the walls of Thebes—the old city of a hundred gates—the Nile spreads to a broad river; the heights, which follow the stream on both sides, here take a more decided outline; solitary, almost cone-shaped peaks stand out sharply from the level background of the many-colored limestone hills, on which no palm-tree flourishes and in which no humble desert-plant can strike root. Rocky crevasses and gorges cut more or less deeply into the mountain range, and up to its ridge extends the desert, destructive of all life, with sand and stones, with rocky cliffs and reef-like, desert hills.

Behind the eastern range the desert spreads to the Red Sea; behind the western it stretches without limit, into infinity. In the belief of the Egyptians beyond it lay the region of the dead.

In the fourteenth century before Christ—for to so remote

a date we must direct the thoughts of the reader —impassable limits had been set by the hand of man, in many places in Thebes, to the inroads of the water; high dykes of stone and embankments protected the streets and squares, the temples and the palaces, from the overflow.

Canals that could be tightly closed up led from the dykes to the land within, and smaller branch-cuttings to the gardens of Thebes.

On the right, the eastern bank of the Nile, rose the buildings of the far-famed residence of the Pharaohs. Close by the river stood the immense and gaudy temples of the city of Amon; behind these and at a short distance from the Eastern hills— indeed at their very foot and partly even on the soil of the desert—were the palaces of the king and nobles, and the shady streets in which the high narrow houses of the citizens stood in close rows.

Life was gay and busy in the streets of the capital of the Pharaohs. The western shore of the Nile showed quite a different scene. Here too there was no lack of stately buildings or thronging men; but while on the further side of the river there was a compact mass of houses, and the citizens went cheerfully and openly about their day's work, on this side there were solitary splendid structures, round which little houses and huts seemed to cling as children cling to the protection of a mother. And these buildings lay in detached groups.

And even more dissimilar were the slow-moving, solemn groups in the road-ways on this side, and the cheerful, confused throng yonder. There, on the eastern shore, all were in eager pursuit of labor or recreation, stirred by pleasure or by grief, active in deed and speech: here, in the west, little was spoken, a spell seemed to check the footsteps of the wanderer, a pale hand to sadden the bright glance of every eye, and to banish the smile from every lip.

And yet many a gayly-dressed bark stopped at the shore, there was no lack of minstrel bands, grand processions passed on to the western heights; but the Nile boats bore the dead, the songs sung here were songs of lamentation, and the processions consisted of mourners following the sarcophagus. We are standing on the soil of the City of the Dead of Thebes.

Nevertheless even here nothing is wanting for return and

revival, for to the Egyptian his dead died not. He closed his eyes, he bore him to the Necropolis, to the house of the embalmer, or Kolchytes, and then to the grave; but he knew that the souls of the departed lived on; that the justified absorbed into Osiris floated over the Heavens in the vessel of the Sun; that they appeared on earth in the form they chose to take upon them, and that they might exert influence on the current of the lives of the survivors. So he took care to give a worthy interment to his dead, above all to have the body embalmed so as to endure long; and had fixed times to bring fresh offerings for the dead, of flesh and fowl, with drink-offerings and sweet-smelling essences, and vegetables and flowers.

Neither at the obsequies nor at the offerings might the ministers of the gods be absent, and the silent City of the Dead was regarded as a favored sanctuary in which to establish schools and dwellings for the learned.

So it came to pass that in the temples and on the site of the Necropolis, large communities of priests dwelt together, and close to the extensive embalming houses lived numerous Kolchytes, who handed down the secrets of their art from father to son.

Besides these there were other manufactories and shops. In the former, sarcophagi of stone and of wood, linen bands for enveloping mummies, and amulets for decorating them, were made; in the latter, merchants kept spices and essences, flowers, fruits, vegetables and pastry for sale. Calves, gazelles, goats, geese, and other fowl were fed on inclosed meadow-plats, and the mourners betook themselves thither to select what they needed from among the beasts pronounced by the priests to be clean for sacrifice, and to have them sealed with the sacred seal. Many bought only a part of a victim at the shambles—the poor could not even do this. They bought only colored cakes in the shape of beasts, which symbolically took the place of the calves and geese which their means were unable to procure. In the handsomest shops sat servants of the priests, who received forms written on rolls of papyrus which were filled up in the writing room of the temple with those sacred verses which the departed spirit must know and repeat to ward off the evil genius of the deep, to open the gate of the under-world, and to be held righteous before Osiris and the forty-two assessors of the subterranean court of justice.

What took place within the temples was concealed from view, for each was surrounded by a high inclosing wall with lofty, carefully closed portals, which were only opened when a chorus of priests came out to sing a pious hymn, in the morning to Horus the rising god, and in the evening to Tum the descending god. As soon as the evening hymn of the priests was heard, the Necropolis was deserted, for the mourners and those who were visiting the graves were required by this time to return to their boats, and to quit the City of the Dead. Crowds of men who had marched in the processions of the west bank hastened in disorder to the shore, driven on by the body of watchmen who took it in turns to do this duty and to protect the graves against robbers. The merchants closed their booths, then embalmers and workmen ended their day's work and retired to their houses, the priests returned to the temples, and the inns were filled with guests, who had come hither on long pilgrimages from a distance, and who preferred passing the night in the vicinity of the dead whom they had come to visit, to going across to the bustling noisy city on the further shore.

The voices of the singers and of the wailing women were hushed, even the song of the sailors on the numberless ferry-boats from the western shore of Thebes died away, its faint echo was now and then borne across on the evening air, and at last all was still.

Uarda.

KARNAK.

"I am Karnak, and a thousand million men have lived and died
  Since open have my gates been thrown for kings through them to ride:
My massive walls have echoed to the tread of Egypt's hosts,
But now they are a skulking place for goblins and for ghosts."

"I stand once more among those mighty columns, which radiate into avenues from whatever point one takes them. I see them swathed in coiled shadows and broad bands of light. I see them sculptured and painted with shapes of gods and kings, with blazonings of royal names, with sacrificial altars and forms of sacred beasts, and emblems of wisdom and truth.

The shafts of these columns are enormous. I stand at the foot of one—or of what seems to be the foot; for the original pavement lies buried seven feet below. It casts a shadow twelve feet in breadth—such a shadow as might be cast by a tower. The capital that juts out so high above my head looks as if it might have been placed there to support the heavens. It is carved in the semblance of a full-blown lotus, and glows with undying colors—colors that are still fresh, though laid on by hands that have been dust these three thousand years and more. It would take not six men, but a dozen, to measure round the curved lip of that stupendous lily.

"Such are the twelve central columns. The rest (one hundred and twenty-two in number) are gigantic, too, but smaller. Of the roof they once supported, only the beams remain. Those beams are stone carved and painted, bridging the space from pillar to pillar, and patterning the trodden soil with bands of shadow.

"Looking up and down the central avenue, we see at the one end a flame-like obelisk; at the other, a solitary palm against a back-ground of glowing mountain. To right, to left, showing transversely through long files of columns, we catch glimpses of colossal bas-reliefs lining the roofless walls in every direction. The king, as usual, figures in every group, and performs the customary acts of worship. The gods receive and approve him. Half in light, half in shadow, these slender, fantastic forms stand out sharp and clear and colorless; each figure some eighteen or twenty feet in height. They could scarcely have looked more weird when the great roof was in its place and perpetual twilight reigned. But it is difficult to imagine the roof on and the sky shut out. It all looks right as it is; and one feels, somehow, that such columns should have nothing between them and the infinite blue depths of heaven.

"How often has it been written, and how often must it be repeated, that the great hall at Karnak is the noblest architectural work ever designed and executed by human hands? One writer tells us that it covers four times the area occupied by the cathedral of Notre Dame in Paris. Another measures it against St. Peter's. All admit their inability to describe it; yet all attempt the description. To convey a concrete image of the place to one who has never seen it, is, however, as I have said, impossible. If it could be likened to this place or that, the task would not be so difficult; but there is, in truth, no building in the wide world to compare with it. The pyramids are more stupendous. The colosseum covers more ground. The parthenon is more beautiful. Yet in nobility of conception, in vastness of detail, in majesty of the highest order, the hall of pillars exceeds them every one. This doorway, these columns, are the wonder of the world. How was that lintel-stone raised? How were these capitals lifted? Entering among those mighty pillars, says a recent observer, 'you feel that you have shrunk to the dimensions and feebleness of a fly.' But I think you feel more than that. You are stupefied by the thought of the mighty men who made them. You say to yourself: 'There were indeed giants in those days.'

"It may be that the traveler who finds himself for the first time in the midst of a grove of *Wellingtonia gigantea* feels something of the same overwhelming sense of awe and wonder; but the great trees, though they have taken three thousand years to grow, lack the pathos and the mystery that comes of human labor. They do not strike their roots through six thousand years of history. They have not been watered with the blood and tears of millions. Their leaves know no sounds less musical than the singing of the birds, or the moaning of the night-wind as it sweeps over the highlands of Calaveras. But every breath that wanders down the painted aisles of Karnak seems to echo back the sighs of those who perished in the quarry, at the oar, and under the chariot-wheels of the conqueror."

Memphis.

"And this is all that remains of Memphis, eldest of cities—a few huge rubbish-heaps, a dozen or so of broken statues, and a name! One looks round and tries in vain to realize the lost splendors of the place. Where is the Memphis that King Mena[1] came from Thinis to found—the Memphis of Chufu[2] and Chafra,[3] and all the early kings who built their pyramid-tombs in the adjacent desert? Where is the Memphis of Herodotus and Strabo? Where are those stately ruins which, even in

[1] Menes. [2] Khufu. [3] Khafre.

the middle ages, extended over a space estimated at half a day's journey in every direction?' One can hardly believe that a great city ever flourished on this spot, or understand how it should have been effaced so utterly. Yet here it stood— here where the grass is green, and the palms are growing, and the Arabs build their hovels on the verge of the inundation. The great colossus marks the site of the main entrance to the Temple of Ptah. It lies where it fell, and no man has moved it. That tranquil sheet of palm-fringed back-water, beyond which we catch a distant glimpse of the pyramids of Gizeh, occupies the basin of a vast artificial lake excavated by Mena.

"No capital in the world dates so far back as this or kept its place in history so long. Founded four thousand years before our era, it beheld the rise and fall of thirty-one dynasties; it survived the rule of the Persians, the Greek and the Roman; it was, even in its decadence, second only to Alexandria in population and extent; and it continued to be inhabited up to the time of the Arab invasion. It then became the quarry from which old Cairo was built; and as the new city rose on the eastern bank the people of Memphis quickly abandoned their ancient capital to desolation and decay.

"Memphis is a place to read about, and think about, and remember; but it is a disappointing place to see. To miss it, however, would be to miss the first link in the whole chain of monumental history which unites the Egypt of antiquity with the world of today. Those melancholy mounds and that heron-haunted lake must be seen, if only that they may take their due place in the picture gallery of one's memory."

—*A Thousand Miles Up the Nile.*

A Hymn to the God Ra.

Incline thine ear towards me, thou rising Sun,
Thou who dost enlighten the two lands with beauty;
Thou sunshine of mankind, chasing darkness from Egypt!
Thy form is as that of thy father Ra rising in the heavens,
Thy rays penetrate to the farthest lands.
When thou art resting in thy palace,
Thou hearest the words of all countries;
For indeed thou hast millions of ears;
Thine eye is clearer than the stars of heaven;
Thou seest farther than the Sun.
If I speak afar off, thine ear hears;
If I do a hidden deed, thine eye sees it.
O Ra, richest of beings, chosen of Ra,
Thou king of beauty, giving breath to all."

AN OLD KINGDOM BOOK OF PROVERBS.

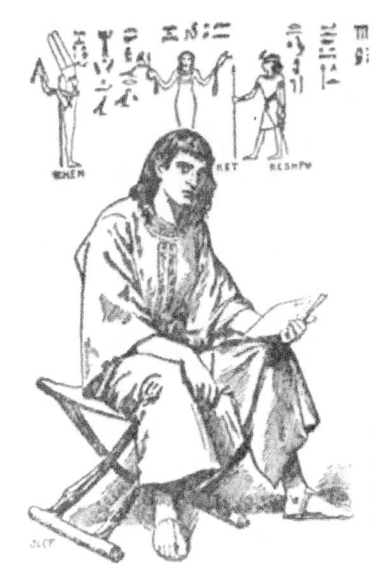

There is preserved in the Bibliothèque Nationale at Paris, a papyrus roll, which was discovered at Thebes by M. Prisse, and is now distinguished by his name. It was first described in 1857 by M. Chabas. The papyrus dates from the beginning of the Middle Kingdom (*Ca.* 2100 B. C.), and belongs to the rather extensive didactic literature of the Egyptians. According to the Egyptian custom, the words of the book were put into the mouth of a sage of the olden time, Ptah-hotep by name, who was said to have lived in the time of King Assa of the Fifth Dynasty (*Ca.* 2600 B. C.). There is no reason for doubting the correctness of the tradition. Of course it is not to be supposed that all of the proverbs really go back to Ptah-hotep. The author is stated to have been 110 years old, and his book opens with a remarkable description of old age. It proceeds in a style which recalls the Proverbs of Solomon, the Greek didactic poems, and even the homely "Poor Richard." It inculcates obedience, diligence, patience, and other virtues belonging to an official or servant. The Papyrus Prisse also contains the Proverbs of Kagemni, vizier of King Snefru (*Ca.* 2900 B. C.) of the Fourth Dynasty.

Precepts of Ptah-Hotep.

The words of the Lord Prefect Ptah-Hotep, who lived in the reign of Assa, King of Northern and Southern Egypt, who liveth forever.

Thus saith the Lord Ptah-Hotep: O Lord Osiris, whose feet are upon the crocodiles!

A man waxeth old, his strength decayeth, he getteth in years, his youth fadeth away:

Day by day the heart of an old man fainteth and is troubled:

His eyes see not, his ears hear not, his power is lessened and abated:

Behold, his mouth speaketh not as of yore, his mind is feeble, and remembereth not the deeds of yesterday:

Yea, his whole body is afflicted, good is to him as evil, his tongue savoreth no longer.

Alas, the old age of a man is full of misery, his nostrils drink not the breath of heaven, his lungs wax feeble, he delighteth neither to stand nor to be seated.

Who shall give unto my tongue authority to utter unto the young men the counsels from of old? or who vouchsafeth unto me to declare the counsels received from on high?

O Lord Osiris, let thy favor be poured out upon thy servant, and suffer that these evils be removed from those who are unenlightened.

Then answered the Lord Osiris and said: Instruct them in the counsels from of old; for verily, wisdom from of old maketh the weak strong; knowledge giveth freedom to him that heareth; wisdom cries aloud, and the ear is not satisfied with hearing.

Here beginneth the book of the wise sayings of the Lord Prefect Ptah-Hotep, the first-born, the son of the King, the well-beloved of the Lord:

That the ignorant and the foolish may be instructed in the understanding of wisdom.

Whoso giveth ear, to him shall these words be as riches;

To him who heedeth them not, to the same shall come emptiness forever.

Thus speaketh he, giving counsel unto his son.

Be not thou puffed up with thy learning; honor the wise, neither withhold thou honor from the simple.

The gates of art are closed unto none; whoso entereth thereat, though he seeketh perfection, yet shall he not find it.

But the words of wisdom are hid, even as the emerald is hid in the earth, and adamant in the rock, which the slave diggeth up.

Yield unto him whose strength is more than thine, who falleth upon thee in anger: be not thou inflamed, neither lay thy hands upon him; so shalt thou escape calamity.

He is froward, it shall not profit thee to contend against him; be contained, and when he rageth against thee, oppose him not; so in the end shalt thou prevail over him.

If one rail against thee, and flout thee, answer him not again, but be as one who cannot be moved; even so shalt thou overcome him. For the bystanders shall declare that he who, being provoked, holdeth his tongue, is greater than he who provoketh; and thou shalt be honored of those who have understanding.

If thou do evil, being thereto commanded by one having authority over thee, the gods shall not condemn thee.

Know the master, and the slave: be not froward: obey and reverence him to whom is given dominion over thee:

None may know adversity, when it cometh, nor prosperity, when it shall relieve him, for the will of fate is hid from all:

But he that abuseth his servant shall be confounded, and God who gave him authority shall suddenly take it away; and great shall be his overthrow.

Be diligent, and do more than thy master commandeth thee; for the slothful servant shall be discomfited, and he that is idle shall be chidden.

See thou neglect not thy household; if thou find opportunity to increase thy wealth improve it; business begetteth business, but poverty is the lot of the slothful.

The wise traineth his child to walk devoutly and to serve the Lord; he maketh him obey his law, and do that which is bidden; so shall the love of the father be justified.

The son of a man is flesh of his flesh and bone of his bone; let not thy heart be cold towards him. But if he be froward, and transgress thy law, and, being tempted of evil, turn himself from thy instruction, then do thou smite the mouth that smote thee.

Delay not to bring the erring to obedience, and to chastise the rebellious; so shall he not stray from the path of righteousness, nor stumble among pitfalls.

Hide not thy path, let not thy way be hidden; though thou stand in the council of thy master, declare the truth that is in thee.

Be not as those who go backward, who eat the words of their own mouth, lest peradventure they offend:

Be not like unto them; feigners, answering, He that perceiveth the error of others, the same is wise: when the wise man uplifteth his voice against error, deny him not, but keep silence; for surely none but the wise have understanding.

If thou be wise guard thy house: honor thy wife, and love her exceedingly: feed her belly and clothe her back, for this is the duty of a husband.

Give her abundance of ointment, fail not each day to caress her, let the desire of her heart be fulfilled: for verily he that is kind to his wife and honoreth her, the same honoreth himself.

Withhold thy hand from violence, and thy heart from cruelty; softly entreat her and win her to thy way; consider her desires, and deny not the wish of her heart.

Thus shalt thou keep her heart from wandering; but if thou harden thyself against her, she will turn from thee. Speak to her, yield her thy love, she will have respect unto thee; open thy arms, she will come unto thee.

Blessed is the son who gives ear to the instruction of his father, for he shall escape error.

Train thou thy son to obedience; his wisdom shall be pleasing unto the great.

Let his mouth have respect to thy sayings; by obedience shall his wisdom be established. Day by day shall his walk be perfect; but error shall be the destruction of fools. The ignorant and the froward shall be overthrown, but knowledge shall uplift the wise.

He that lacketh prudence and inclineth not his ear to instruction, the same worketh no good. He thinketh to discover knowledge in ignorance, and gain in that which profiteth nothing; he runneth to mischief, and wandereth in error, choosing those things which are rejected of the prudent; so subsisteth he on that which perisheth, and filleth his belly with the words of evil. Yea, he is brought to shame, seeking to be nourished with whatsoever the wise hold in abomination, shunning profitable things, led astray by much foolishness.

THE VOYAGE OF THE SOUL.

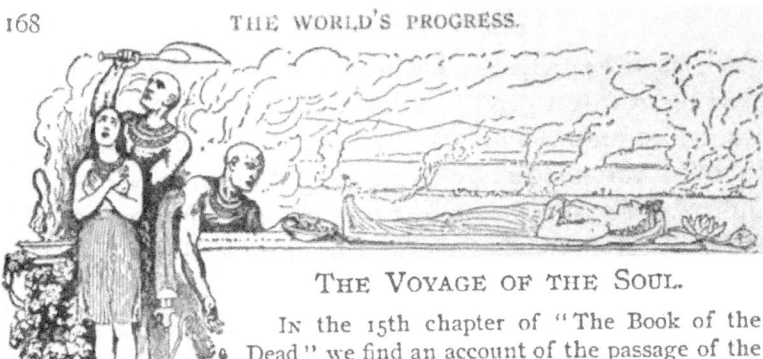

In the 15th chapter of "The Book of the Dead" we find an account of the passage of the soul in a boat across the firmament, to the abode of the blessed.

This fable reappears in the religious writings of other nations, as, for instance, in the Greek story of Charon, ferrying departed spirits across the Styx, and in the traditions of the ancient Mexicans. The soul is called by the Egyptians Osiris, in connection with the proper name of the individual (N), to indicate that the latter already partakes of the divine nature. Ra is the sun-god, approaching the west. The following translation is by P. Le Page Renouf:

Here is the Osiris N.

Come forth into Heaven, sail across the firmament and enter into brotherhood with the stars, let salutation be made to thee in the bark, let invocation be made to thee in the morning bark. Contemplate Ra within his Ark, and do thou propitiate his orb daily. See the fish in its birth from the emerald stream, and see the tortoise and its rotations. Let the offender (the dragon) fall prostrate, when he meditates destruction for me, by blows on his backbone.

Ra springs forth with a fair wind; the evening bark speeds on and reaches the Haven. The crew of Ra are in exultation when they look upon him; the Mistress of Life, her heart is delighted at the overthrow of the adversary of her Lord.

See thou Horus at the look-out at the bow, and at his sides Thoth and Maat. All the gods are in exultation when they behold Ra coming in peace to give new life to the hearts of the Chu, and here is the Osiris N along with them.

[*Litany.*]

Adored be Ra, as he setteth in the land of Life.
Hail to thee, who hast come as Tmu, and hast been the creator of
    the cycle of the gods.

Give thou delicious breezes of the north wind to the Osiris N.

Hail to thee, who hast come as the Soul of souls, revered in Amenta,

Hail to thee, who art above the gods, and who lightenest up Tuat with thy glories,

Hail to thee, who comest in splendor, and goest around in thine orb,

Hail to thee, who art mightier than the gods, who art crowned in Heaven and King in Tuat,

Hail to thee, who openest the Tuat and disposest of all its doors,

Hail to thee, supreme among the gods, and weigher of words in the nether world,

Hail to thee, who art in thy Nest, and stirrest the Tuat with thy glory,

Hail to thee, the great, the mighty, whose enemies are laid prostrate at their blocks,

Hail to thee, who slaughterest the Sebau and annihilatest Apepi (the dragon).

[After each invocation, the italicized line is repeated.]

Horus openeth: the Great, the Mighty, who divideth the earths, the Great One who resteth in the Mountain of the West, and brighteneth up the Tuat with his glories and the Souls in their hidden abode, by shining into their sepulchres.

By hurling harm against the foe thou hast utterly destroyed all the adversaries of the Osiris N.

THE SOUL'S DECLARATION OF INNOCENCE.

This declaration was to be made by the soul in the Judgment Hall of Osiris in the presence of the council of forty-two gods. The heart being weighed against the symbol of truth and found correct was then restored to the deceased who entered upon the life of the blessed.

"O ye Lords of Truth! I have brought you truth.
I have not privily done evil against mankind.
I have not afflicted the miserable.
I have not told falsehoods.
I have had no acquaintance with sin.
I have not made the laboring man do more than his daily task.
I have not been idle.
I have not been intoxicated.

I have not been immoral.
I have not calumniated a slave to his master.
I have not caused hunger.
I have not made to weep.
I have not murdered.
I have not defrauded.
"I have not eaten the sacred bread in the temples.
I have not cheated in the weight of the balance.
I have not withheld milk from the mouths of sucklings.
I have not slandered any one.
I have not netted sacred birds.
I have not caught the fish which typify them.
I have not stopped running water.
I have not robbed the gods of their offered haunches.
I have not stopped a god from his manifestation.
I have made to the gods the offerings that were their due.
I have given food to the hungry, drink to the thirsty, and clothes to the naked.
I am pure! I am pure!"

WEIGHING THE HEART IN THE JUDGMENT HALL OF OSIRIS.

THE ADVENTURES OF THE EXILE SANEHAT.[1]

(2000 B.C.)

THE fact that three copies of this tale have been found indicates that it was popular. Sanehat was a high official, and probably a member of the royal family; but on the death of King Amenemhet, the founder of the twelfth dynasty, Sanehat, fearing for his life, fled to Syria and lived there many years. In his old age he desired to return, that he might die in his native land. The narrative was probably prepared for inscription on the wall of his tomb. The translation is from W. M. Flinders Petrie's "Egyptian Tales."

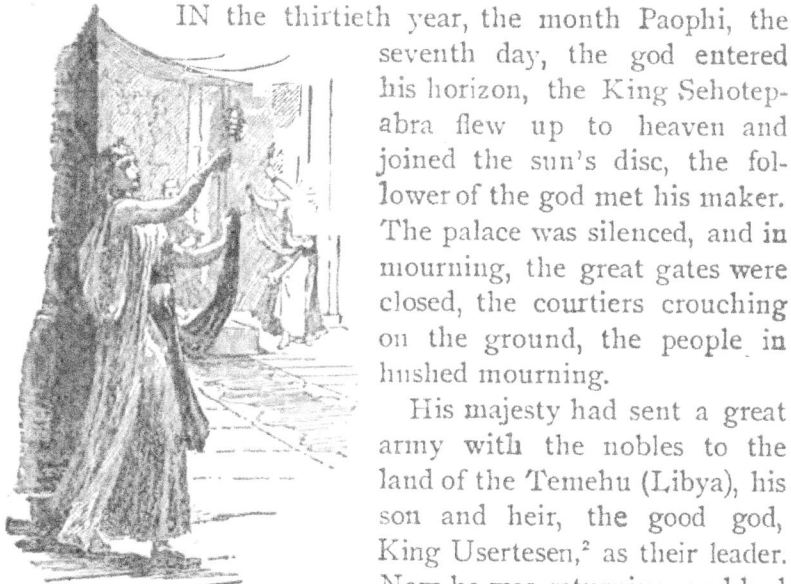

IN the thirtieth year, the month Paophi, the seventh day, the god entered his horizon, the King Sehotepabra flew up to heaven and joined the sun's disc, the follower of the god met his maker. The palace was silenced, and in mourning, the great gates were closed, the courtiers crouching on the ground, the people in hushed mourning.

His majesty had sent a great army with the nobles to the land of the Temehu (Libya), his son and heir, the good god, King Usertesen,[2] as their leader. Now he was returning, and had brought away living captives and all kinds of cattle without end. The councillors of the palace had sent to the West to let the king know the matter that had come to pass in the inner hall. The messenger was to meet him on the road, and reach him at the time of evening: the matter was urgent. "A hawk had soared with his followers." Thus said he, not to let the army know of it. Even if the royal sons who commanded in that army sent a message, he was not to speak to a single one of them.

But I was standing near, and heard his voice while he was speaking. I fled far away, my heart beating, my arms fail-

---

[1] More correctly rendered as Sinuhe.
[2] Sesostris.

ing, trembling had fallen on all my limbs. I turned about in running to seek a place to hide me, and I threw myself between two bushes, to wait while they should pass by. Then I turned me toward the south, not wishing to come into this palace—for I knew not if war was declared—nor even thinking a wish to live after this sovereign. I turned my back to the sycamore, I reached Shi-Seneferu, and rested on the open field. In the morning I went on and overtook a man, who passed by the edge of the road. He asked of me mercy, for he feared me. By the evening I drew near to Kher-ahau (Cairo) and I crossed the river on a raft without a rudder. Carried by the west wind, I passed over to the east to the quarries of Aku and the land of the goddess Herit, mistress of the red mountain. Then I fled on foot, northward, and reached the walls of the prince, built to repel the Sati. I crouched in a bush for fear of being seen by the guards, changed each day, who watch on the top of the fortress. I took my way by night, and at the lighting of the day I reached Peten, and turned me toward the valley of Kemur. Then thirst hasted me on; I dried up, and my throat narrowed, and I said, "This is the taste of death."

When I lifted up my heart and gathered strength, I heard a voice and the lowing of cattle. I saw men of the Sati, and one of them—a friend unto Egypt—knew me. He gave me water and boiled milk, and I went with him to his camp; they did me good, and one tribe passed me on to another. I passed on to Sun, and reached the land of Adim (Edom).

When I had dwelt there half a year Amu-an-shi—who is the prince of the Upper Tenu—sent for me and said: "Dwell thou with me that thou mayest hear the speech of Egypt." He said thus for that he knew of my excellence, and had heard tell of my worth, for men of Egypt who were there with him bore witness of me. Behold he said to me, "For what cause hast thou come hither? Has a matter come to pass in the palace? Has the king of the two lands, Sehetepabra, gone to heaven? What has happened about this is not known." But I answered with concealment, and said, "When I came from the land of the Temehu, and my desires were there changed in me, if I fled away it was not by reason

Copyright by Underwood & Underwood, N. Y.
HAREM WINDOW AND COURT.

of remorse that I took the way of a fugitive; I have not failed in my duty, my mouth has not said any bitter words, I have not heard any evil counsel, my name has not come into the mouth of a magistrate. I know not by what I have been led into this land." And Amu-an-shi said, "This is by the will of the god (King of Egypt), for what is a land like, if it know not that excellent god, of whom the dread is upon the lands of strangers, as they dread Sekhet in a year of pestilence?" I spake to him, and replied, "Forgive me, his son now enters the palace, and has received the heritage of his father. He is a god who has none like him, and there is none before him. He is a master of wisdom, prudent in his designs, excellent in his decrees, with good-will to him who goes or who comes; he subdued the land of strangers while his father yet lived in his palace, and he rendered account of that which his father destined him to perform. A king, he has ruled from his birth; he, from his birth, has increased births, a sole being, a divine essence, by whom this land rejoices to be governed. He enlarges the borders of the South; but he covets not the lands of the North; he does not smite the Sati, nor crush the Nemau-shau. If he descends here, let him know thy name, by the homage which thou wilt pay to his majesty. For he refuses not to bless the land which obeys him."

And he replied to me, "Egypt is indeed happy and well settled; behold thou art far from it, but whilst thou art with me I will do good unto thee." And he placed me before his children, he married his eldest daughter to me, and gave me the choice of all his land, even among the best of that which he had on the border of the next land. It is a goodly land; Iaa is its name. There are figs and grapes; there is wine commoner than water; abundant is the honey, many are its olives; and all fruits are upon its trees; there is barley and wheat, and cattle of kinds without end. This was truly a great thing that he granted me, when the prince came to invest me, and establish me as prince of a tribe in the best of his land. I had my continual portion of bread and of wine each day, of cooked meat, of roasted fowl, as well as the wild game which I took, or which was brought to me, besides what my dogs captured. They made me much butter, and prepared milk of all kinds. I passed many years, the children that I had became great, each ruling his tribe. When a messenger went or came to the palace, he turned aside from the way to come to me; for I helped every man. I gave water to the thirsty, I set on his way him who went astray, and I rescued the robbed. The Sati who went far, to strike and turn back the princes of other lands, I ordained their goings; for the Prince of the Tenu for many years appointed me to be general of his soldiers. In every land which I attacked I played the champion, I took the cattle, I led away the vassals, I carried off the slaves, I slew the people, by my sword, my bow, my marches and my good devices. I was excellent to the heart of my prince; he loved me when he knew my power, and set me over his children when he saw the strength of my arms.

A champion of the Tenu came to defy me in my tent: a bold man without equal, for he had vanquished the whole country. He said, "Let Sanehat fight with me;" for he desired to overthrow me, he thought to take my cattle for his tribe. The prince counseled with me. I said, "I know him not. I certainly am not of his degree, I hold me far from his place. Have I ever opened his door, or leaped over his fence? It is some envious jealousy from seeing me; does he think that I am like some steer among the cows, whom the bull overthrows? If this is a wretch who thinks to enrich himself at my cost, not a Bedawi fit for fight, then let us put the matter to judgment. Verily a true bull loves battle, but a vain-glorious bull turns his back for fear of contest; if he has a heart for combat, let him speak what he pleases. Will God forget what he has ordained, and how shall that be known?" I lay down; and when I had rested I strung my bow, I made ready my arrows, I loosened my dagger, I furbished my arms.

At dawn the land of the Tenu came together; it had gathered its tribes and called all the neighboring people; it spake of nothing but the fight. Each heart burnt for me, men and women crying out; for each heart was troubled for me, and they said, "Is there another strong one who would fight with him? Behold the adversary has a buckler, a battleaxe, and an armful of javelins." Then I drew him to the attack; I turned aside his arrows, and they struck the ground in vain. One drew near to the other, and he fell on me, and then I shot him. My arrow fastened in his neck, he cried out, and fell on his face: I drove his lance into him, and raised my shout of victory on his back. Whilst all the men of the land rejoiced, I, and his vassals whom he had oppressed, gave thanks unto Mentu (the god of war). This prince, Amu-an-shi, embraced me. Then I carried off his goods and took his cattle, that which he had wished to do to me, I did even so unto him; I seized that which was in his tent, I spoiled his dwelling. As time went on I increased the richness of my treasures and the number of my cattle. . . .

[But at last the exile desired to return to his native land, and sent a petition to the King of Egypt, asking permission.]

Then the majesty of King Kheper-ka-ra, the blessed, spake upon this my desire that I had made to him. His majesty sent unto me with presents from the king, that he might enlarge the heart of his servant, like unto the province of any strange land; and the royal sons who are in the palace addressed themselves unto me.

Copy of the decree which was brought to lead me back into Egypt.

"The Horus, life of births, lord of the two crowns, King of Upper and Lower Egypt, Kheper-ka-ra, son of the Sun, Amen-em-hat, ever living unto eternity. Order for the follower Sanehat. Behold this order of the king is sent to thee to instruct thee of his will.

"Now, although thou hast gone through strange lands from Adim to Tenu, and passed from one country to another at the wish of thy heart—behold, what hast thou done, or what has been done against thee, that is amiss? Moreover, thou reviledst not; but if thy word was denied, thou didst not speak again in the assembly of the nobles, even if thou wast desired. Now, therefore, that thou hast thought on this matter which has come to thy mind, let thy heart not change again; for this thy Heaven (queen), who is in the palace is fixed, she is flourishing, she is enjoying the best in the kingdom of the land, and her children are in the chambers of the palace.

"Leave all the riches that thou hast, and that are with thee, altogether. When thou shalt come into Egypt behold the palace, and when thou shalt enter the palace, bow thy face to the ground before the Great House; thou shalt be chief among the companions. And day by day behold thou growest old; thy vigor is lost, and thou thinkest on the day of burial. Thou shalt see thyself come to the blessed state, they shall give thee the bandages from the hand of Tait, the night of applying the oil of embalming. They shall follow thy funeral, and visit the tomb on the day of burial, which shall be in a gilded case, the head painted with blue, a canopy of cypress wood above thee, and oxen shall draw thee, the singers going before thee, and they shall dance the funeral dance. The weepers crouching at the door of thy tomb shall cry aloud the prayers for offerings: they shall slay victims for thee at the door of thy pit; and thy pyramid shall be carved in white stone, in the company of the royal children. Thus thou shalt not die in a strange land, nor be buried by the Amu; thou shalt not be laid in a sheep-skin when thou art buried; all people shall beat the earth, and lament on thy body when thou goest to the tomb."

When this order came to me, I was in the midst of my tribe. When it was read unto me, I threw me on the dust, I threw dust in my hair; I went around my tent rejoicing and saying, "How may it be that such a thing is done to the servant, who with a rebellious heart has fled to strange lands? Now with an excellent deliverance, and mercy delivering me from death, thou shalt cause me to end my days in the palace."

I made a feast in Iaa, to pass over my goods to my children. My eldest son was leading my tribe, all my goods passed to him, and I gave him my corn and all my cattle, my fruit, and all my pleasant trees. When I had taken my road to the south, and arrived at the roads of Horus, the officer who was over the garrison sent a messenger to the palace to give notice. His majesty sent the good overseer of the peasants of the king's domains, and boats laden with presents from the king for the Sati who had come to conduct me to the roads of Horus. I spoke to each one by his name, and I gave the presents to each as was intended. I received and I returned the salutation and I continued thus until I reached the city of Thetu (Thebes).

When the land was brightened, and the new day began, four men came with a summons for me; and the four men went to lead me to the palace. I saluted with both my hands on the ground; the royal children stood at the courtyard to conduct me: the courtiers who were to lead me to the hall brought me on the way to the royal chamber.

I found his majesty on the great throne in the hall of pale gold. Then I threw myself on the ground; this god, in whose presence I was, knew me not. He questioned me graciously, but I was as one seized with blindness, my spirit fainted, my limbs failed, my heart was no longer in my bosom, and I knew the difference between life and death. His majesty said to one of the companions, "Lift him up, let him speak to me."

The royal children were brought in, and his majesty said to the queen, "Behold, Sanehat has come as an Amu, whom the Sati have produced."

She cried aloud, and the royal children spake with one voice, saying before his majesty, "Verily it is not so, O king, my lord." Said his majesty, "It is verily he." Then they brought their collars, and their wands, and their sistra * in their hands, and displayed them before his majesty; and they sang—

" May thy hands prosper, O king;
  May the ornaments of the Lady of Heaven continue.
  May the goddess Nub give life to thy nostril;
  May the mistress of the stars favor thee, when thou sailest south
      and north.
  All wisdom is in the mouth of thy majesty;
  Thy uræus † is on thy forehead, thou drivest away the miserable.
  Thou art pacified, O Ra, lord of the lands;
  They call on thee as on the mistress of all.
  Strong is thy horn. Thou lettest fly thine arrow.
  Grant the breath to him who is without it;

---

* The sistrum was a musical rattle, usually consisting of a thin oval metal band, crossed with metal rods and having a handle. See cut, p. 39.

† The serpent, with raised, projecting head, which was an emblem of sovereignty.

Grant good things to this traveller, Sanehat the Pedti, born in
    the land of Egypt,
Who fled away from fear of thee,
And fled this land from thy terrors.
Does not the face grow pale, of him who beholds thy countenance;
Does not the eye fear, which looks upon thee?"

Said his majesty, "Let him not fear, let him be freed from terror. He shall be a Royal Friend amongst the nobles; he shall be put within the circle of the courtiers. Go ye to the chamber of praise to seek wealth for him."

When I went out from the palace, the royal children offered their hands to me; we walked afterwards to the Great Gates.

Years were removed from my limbs: I was shaved, and polled my locks of hair; the foulness was cast to the desert with the garments of the Nemau-shau. I clothed me in fine linen, and anointed myself with the fine oil of Egypt; I laid me on a bed. I gave up the sand to those who lie on it; the oil of wood to him who would anoint himself therewith. There was given to me the mansion of a lord of serfs, which had belonged to a royal friend. There many excellent things were in its buildings; all its wood was renewed. There were brought to me portions from the palace, thrice and four times each day; besides the gifts of the royal children, always, without ceasing. There was built for me a pyramid of stone amongst the pyramids. The overseer of the architects measured its ground; the chief treasurer wrote it; the sacred masons cut the well; the chief of the laborers on the tombs brought the bricks; all things used to make strong a building were there used. There were given to me peasants; there was made for me a garden, and fields were in it before my mansion, as is done for the chief royal friend. My statue was inlaid with gold, its girdle of pale gold; his majesty caused it to be made. Such honor is not done to a man of low degree.

May I be in the favor of the king until the day shall come of my death.

THE SONG OF THE HARPER.

(Sixteenth century B.C.)

The Song of the Harper was found in the tomb of the priest Neferhotep, near Thebes. It was designed to be sung on the anniversary of his death. He is shown sitting with his wife, son and daughter, while the harper chants. Other copies of this song have come down to us. *Ra* or *Re* is the general appellation of the Sun-god; *Tum* or *Tmu* denotes the Sun setting; *Shu* is the light of the Sun in its life-giving function.

Neferhotep, great and blessed, sleepeth; we protect his sleep.
Since the day when Ra began his race, and Tum hastened to its ending, fathers have gone down to death, and children have arisen in their place.
Even as Ra has his birth in the morning, fathers beget sons;
Even as Tum begetteth night, mothers conceive and bring forth;
The breath of the morning is in a man's nostrils;
Man that is born of a woman vanisheth when his race is run.

Holy Father, vouchsafe that the day return with blessing;
Smell thou the fragrant oils that we pour on thy altars, receive the flowers that we bring for an offering.
Lo, thy sister dwelleth in thy heart as in a temple;
Give these lotus flowers into her arms, place them in her bosom;
Lo, she sitteth at thy right hand; let the harp and the sound of singing be pleasing unto thee, and drive sorrow away.
Rejoice even unto the day when we, pilgrims, enter Amenti, welcomed by him who went before us.

Vouchsafe, O Lord, that the day come quickly;
Pure of heart and deed was he whom we loved:

The life of earth passeth away, even so passed he away;
Behold, he was, and he is not, and no man knoweth his place.
So hath it been, since Ra went forth, O Man, and so shall it be forever.
The eyes of a man are opened, and are quickly closed again.
His soul drinketh of the sacred waters, he drinketh with them that are gone of the waters of the River of Life.

Give unto the poor, who cry to thee when the harvest faileth; so shall thy name be magnified forever.
And to the feast of thy sacrifice multitudes shall come, worshipping;
And the priest, clothed with a panther's skin, shall pour out wine unto thee;
And shall offer cakes, and sing songs before thy altars,
In that day when thy servants stand before Ra, the Sun-god.
Shu shall bring forth the harvest in its season,
And glory shall be thine, but destruction shall overtake the wicked.

Return quickly, O Neferhotep, let the day of thy honor return:
Lo, the works which thou didst upon earth, thou didst leave them in the day of thy going;
Rich wast thou, but of thy riches only these ashes are left.
In the day of thy going thou tarriedst not, nothing didst thou save in that day:
Yea, though a man have much grain, yet the day of his poverty shall come;
Death regardeth not his riches; Death heedeth not the pride of a man.

Friends, the day of your going shall come; let your hearts have understanding.
Whither ye go, thence shall ye not return forever.
The upright man shall prosper, but the transgressor shall perish.
Be ye just, for the just man shall be blessed.
But neither the brave man, nor he that feareth, nor he that hath friends, nor the forsaken one,
None shall escape the grave, no man small prevail against Death.
Vouchsafe unto us, therefore, of thine abundance, and be thou blessed forever of Isis.

PRESENT-DAY EGYPT

Alexandria.

Where East and West Meet.

ALEXANDRIA is the great commercial center of the southern Mediterranean. Approached from the sea, the coast is so level that the city is not visible until the harbor is almost reached. Modern docks and warehouses are crowded along the shore.

In spite of its modern appearance, Alexandria is an old city, founded by Alexander the Great, in 332 B. C. He evinced his usual insight and good judgment in the site chosen, it being sufficiently far west to escape the deposits brought down by the Nile and carried to sea by its various outlets. The only important city of all those founded by the great conqueror, Alexandria became a center of culture and education. Scholars and men of genius were encouraged to come here by the Ptolomies, who were determined to make the place a second Athens. A museum was founded and a library established, some 900,000 rolls of manuscript being accumulated. This we may feel sure embraced the wealth of ancient learning.

When the city was besieged by the Romans in the time of Cæsar, this priceless collection of books was destroyed. The loss to the future was irreparable. However, an earnest effort was put forth to replace as many as possible of the writings, and for years scribes copied precious rolls sent them from other educational centers and from private collections. Indeed, it was plainly hinted by those best informed that the originals were never returned to rightful owners, but that copies were invariably returned and the original kept to grace the public library. When Omar overcame Egypt in the seventh century, he proclaimed the Koran sufficient for all, saying that it included whatever wisdom men needed. Whereupon he commanded the destruction of this second library.

It is recorded that the contents were distributed among four thousand public baths of Alexandria and that fires were kept burning for six months before the books were consumed. Lovers of antiquity can never cease to regret these two wanton wastes of ancient literature.

Pompey's Pillar* may be seen towering high above the city as one draws near. While its significance is not absolutely proved, nevertheless it is thought to have been erected in honor of Diocletian in the third century. It is made of red granite and was originally crowned by a statue. Aside from it and the catacombs, there is little to suggest the venerable age of the place. The catacombs were used here, as in Rome, by early Christians for interment.

In many respects Alexandria is like certain European cities. Its streets are well paved, it has broad avenues in its newer sections, and the local activities center around a great public square, named after Mohammet Ali, who loved the place and did much to beautify it. Except for the ruinous policy of Saïd and Ismail, who involved their country in heavy debt, Alexandria would be a very wealthy metropolis, for its yearly shipment of cotton alone is nearly one million bales. Nevertheless, while as conspicuous a commercial center as Liverpool, its commerce is slight compared to what it was before shipping interests were diverted around the Cape of Good Hope.

In no other locality can one see such a meeting of the nations. All languages are heard in a general babel around the harbor and in the streets. Numbering about three hundred and forty thousand people, its population includes Asiatics and Europeans of every description, who offer a striking contradiction to Kipling's couplet:

> "For East is East, and West is West,
> And never the twain shall meet."

Cairo.

The ride from Alexandria to Cairo leads across the level plains of the delta. Fields of grain, occasional palms, scatter-

---

* The shaft is erroneously associated with Pompey.

ing villages of mud huts, and the ever-evident canals make up the landscape. As one draws near the city a sight of the Pyramids is gained; then the suburbs of Cairo appear.

Unlike Alexandria, Cairo is a comparatively modern city. The seaport was twelve hundred years old before a stone of Cairo had been set in place. Now having a population of about six hundred thousand, it, too, shows great diversity of people. While the Arabs make up the bulk of the inhabitants, representatives of all countries and climes are seen. The domed mosques stand on every hand, monuments to the teachings of Mohammed.

Much as Venice attracts artists by its lavish display of color, Cairo also offers visions for one who is skillful with the brush. Its sapphire skies, gorgeous sunsets with their marvellous after-glow, the gleaming sands of the desert and Pyramids turned to gold in the setting sun, are intoxicating. It is the land of Arabian Nights, and slight imagination is required to make the visitor fancy himself back in story land. Strange and unfamiliar sights greet him everywhere; even the odor of the oriental city, incapable of description, is present when darkness has eliminated many of the scenes, and slumber has lessened many of the sounds.

Although few spend much time in Alexandria, all visitors to Egypt devote as many days or weeks as may be possible to Cairo. From there one may visit the great Pyramids, going by train if limited in point of time; going by donkey or camel if fond of following historic customs. Here, too, one starts upon the trip up the Nile, without which any visit to Egypt would be incomplete. The bazaars afford much entertainment for the sojourner in Cairo. Even those who for some reason have made this city their abode for a protracted time never tire of the street scenes or the bazaars. Unlike our shops, each bazaar displays in a series of booths one commodity; rugs and carpets have a bazaar given up to them alone; jewels and ornaments are displayed at another, and so on. It would seem as if each article was priced according to the purse of the customer. It is impossible in oriental lands to shop expeditiously, as in western countries. The oriental makes bargains with his customers; he names a price considerably larger than he expects to receive; the would-be customer names another considerably less than he expects to pay; and sometimes for hours the bickering is continued, each satisfied in the end and probably far better pleased than if the matter had been speedily adjusted.

Many festivals are observed in Egypt. The year is lunar: if New Year's Day be ascertained, it is very easy to account for the months, each being twenty-eight days in length. Within a period of thirty-three years a complete circuit is made and another begun. The fact that a given holiday was celebrated last year in one month proves immediately that this year it will fall at another time. Mohammedan feasts and fasts are strictly observed. The month of Ramadan is the holy month, corresponding in some measure to our Lent. None of the faithful will allow a morsel of food or a drop of water to pass their lips during that month from sunrise to sunset. But the moment the golden orb has fallen below the horizon the feasting begins, often to last throughout the night. When this month of daily fasting falls in the hot summer-time, the mortality is very great, not only because of immoderate indulgence through the night, but because of the suffering for lack of water through the day.

The yearly departure of the caravan for Mecca is a remarkable sight. Every true Mohammedan hopes to some day make a pilgrimage to Mecca — the sacred city of his prophet. Each year those who are able set out upon their journey. A carpet which has been woven for this purpose is sent to the sacred shrine, to take the place of the one placed there the previous year. The procession of pilgrims winds through the streets of Cairo, witnessed by the entire population, who throng the streets to catch sight of the carpet and, if possible, to touch it. Reaching Mecca, the carpet which has absorbed holiness during the past year is torn up, the pieces being distributed among the pilgrims, who treasure them as their dearest possessions.

Upon his return home, each pilgrim is looked upon with envy and honor by his Mohammedan brethren. He and all who behold him know that his entrance into Paradise is secure; henceforward he is distinguished for his piety, and those less fortunate can but dream of the day when they, too, may be able to follow his worthy example.

The Egyptian Museum.

Only in comparatively recent years have antiquities been adequately prized or cared for. Early in the nineteenth century Lord Elgin, then on diplomatic service to Turkey, was so dismayed by the spectacle of Parthenon fragments lying about unprotected on the Acropolis at Athens, that he succeeded in obtaining permission from the Sublime Porte to remove them to England. Subsequently the British Museum purchased them from him for much less than had been the expense incurred in removing and exporting them from Greece. Similarly, valuable recoveries in Egypt were left for private individuals to take away as they saw fit; sometimes they were finally collected by national museums, but quite as often they became the possessions of the favored few, or in some cases were even wholly lost.

In 1863 Mariette obtained the exclusive right to excavate in Egypt. He also awakened the government to the need of placing all recoveries under its exclusive control. Since the time of Napoleon scarcely a vessel had left Alexandria without carrying some priceless treasure to be added to the collections of the Louvre or the British Museum. In 1878 Mariette founded the Egyptian Museum at Balak, and for a long time it was known as the Balak Museum.

Although small and without the slightest protection against fire, it nevertheless provided a place for antiques; some were merely stored in sheds, for lack of room, and others remained unclassified because there was no opportunity to display them. In 1889 the need for another building was keenly felt. Egypt could not build at this time, but the Palace of Gizeh was placed at the disposal of the collection. While somewhat larger than Balak, it was neither commodious nor safe.

On the first day of April, 1897, the corner stone of a national museum was laid in Cairo by the Khedive. This substantial and fireproof building, constructed at a cost of almost $900,000, was completed November 15, 1902, and is now the repository of the largest and most valuable collection of Egyptian antiquities in the world.

This museum has been fortunate in its curators—all men of scholarly attainments and well versed in Egyptian history.

Mariette was succeeded by M. Maspero, whose voluminous work upon Egyptian history is well known to many. Later he resigned this position to resume his literary work in Europe, only to return by a fortunate circumstance in 1899, in time to supervise the transfer of the many priceless treasures to their present abode.

Leaving the busy streets of Cairo, one turns from Mohammedan to ancient Egypt. On every hand the past looms up; pharaohs and beings of a period far remote populate this little world, and so far as life can express itself in material things, these are available for examination and study. The plan followed in the arrangement is the chronological one used also in the earlier buildings. The heavier objects have been given place on the ground floor; the lighter and smaller articles on the floor above. The first six rooms on the ground floor are devoted to the remains of the Old Empire—particularly of the fourth, fifth and sixth dynasties. The diorite statue of Khafra, so often shown in prints, is here; also the squatting statue of a scribe, second only in beauty to the one in the Louvre. The next series of rooms are given over to the remains of the Middle Empire. The statue of Amenemhet III, of the twelfth dynasty, is worthy of special mention. Moreover, statues and sphinxes of the Hyksos period are also found here.

The New Empire left evidences of regal splendor, eclipsing all earlier periods; gilded chairs, chariots, dishes of gold and silver, as well as statues of the kings themselves attract attention. Other rooms record Egypt's decay—when Ethiopians ruled the land; the period of Egyptian Renaissance, productive of wonderful sculpture; the coming of Alexander and Greek supremacy; the period of Roman rule; and finally Byzantine Egypt.

The second floor is the treasure house for the more varied remains. One may see the mummies of the priests of Ammon, funerary furniture, dolls and other toys, alabaster vases, domestic furniture, funerary barks, terra-cottas of the Græco-Roman period, statues of the gods, amulets and "answerers" and, most imposing of all perhaps, the royal mummies.

In one of the rooms is an example of the finest surviving Egyptian painting: a picture of geese feeding. This, like other paintings of ancient Egypt, was found in an old tomb.

The *Galerie des Bijoux* is also on this upper floor. Some of its wonderful treasures rival the workmanship of Tiffany; others are even more perfect. The stones most frequently used were lapis lazuli, carnelian, jasper and garnets. The favorite ornaments were rings, collars, chains, amulets and bracelets.

One might spend months in this museum and fail to exhaust its marvels. Few can do this, and for those whose visit to Cairo must be brief, it is better to see only a little and see it well than to attempt to hurriedly pass through all the rooms. The British Museum, the Louvre and the Metropolitan Museum in New York all have departments of Egyptian antiquities.

Since the work of excavation and discovery still goes on, it may reasonably be expected that further light will be thrown upon the past by the labor of the next few years. For this reason only recent publications regarding the Nile dwellers have any great value.

The Suez Canal.

The Suez Canal has been the cause of Egypt's late international importance. It exemplifies several striking paradoxes. Opposed bitterly by England at first, it is now largely under her control; made possible by the heavy investments of the viceroy of Egypt, this country has no shipping today to profit by the canal nor does it receive any benefit whatever because of it. On the contrary, it has been the real cause of Egypt's loss of independence. Before the building of the canal began Egypt had no debt; while the viceroy acknowledged the suzerainty of the Sultan of Turkey, in a large measure he was free to conduct all internal affairs, and hoped in time to gain full sovereignty. The enormous amounts supplied by Viceroy Saïd for the canal with the idle hope of dazzling the eyes of Europe were the first of a long series of extravagances which so burdened his country with debt that progress finally ceased and activities became paralyzed. To protect their subjects, who had loaned money at a rate of interest prohibited in their own lands, European countries stepped in and assumed control of Egyptian finances. Today it is impossible to foresee how Egypt can regain the independence she has lost.

In ancient times canals provided Egyptians access to the Red Sea. When the expedition was made to Punt during the early years of the New Empire, it is probable that ships built at Thebes were dispatched directly to the sea by means of some constructed water way. Again, we know that a canal was built two or three hundred years before the Christian Era and that Cleopatra tried to save the remnant of her fleet after the battle of Actium by means of it; but owing to its impaired condition and the low water at that season, her attempt failed.

When Egypt became a Roman province a water way connecting the Red and Mediterranean seas was projected but not constructed. Napoleon was quick to see its opportunities during his Egyptian campaign and set his engineers to work upon the plan, which was abandoned upon his withdrawal from Africa. The idea prevailed that the two seas were of different levels. In 1847 England, France and Austria sent out a commission to ascertain the facts, and their surveys proved that the levels were the same. However, nothing was done and the matter was forgotten save by a French engineer by the name of De Lesseps, who continued to brood over the undertaking. In 1856, having unusual opportunities to cultivate the acquaintance of Viceroy Saïd, De Lesseps obtained from him a concession for the construction of a canal to join the Red Sea and the Mediterranean, it being distinctly stated that this should cost Egypt nothing, that fifteen per cent of the profits should fall to her share, and that in ninety-nine years, upon payment of the actual improvements made by the canal company along the banks, the canal should revert to Egypt. To prevent the importation of vast hordes of laborers, Saïd agreed to supply peasant labor at a nominal price, De Lesseps and his associates to provide them with adequate food and care; likewise to bring fresh water to the scene of action for their use. The concession was made conditional to the approval of the Sultan of Turkey, suzerain of Egypt, whose consent was to be obtained by De Lesseps without mediation of the viceroy.

When it came to procuring capital sufficient to promote the enterprise, De Lesseps found it far more difficult than he had imagined. England had completed a railroad from Alexandria to Suez in 1858 and vigorously opposed the canal project; private funds might have been forthcoming from Englishmen but for the fact that the government disapproved so heartily; French capital was needed largely at home. The canal company issued 400,000 shares, which for some time went begging. De Lesseps finally persuaded Saïd to take 177,662 shares, which marked the beginning of Egypt's enslavement and at the same time the beginning of De Lesseps' success. Stock was readily sold now, and in 1859 the digging began.

In 1863 Saïd died and Ismail became viceroy of Egypt. He fell into the mistake of his predecessor and became a willing victim for the canal company. The work upon the canal was but one-fourth completed; twenty-five thousand peasants had been impressed every three months, but their insufficient food and cruel treatment had resulted in the death of thousands. Protests were made by civilized countries everywhere—particularly did the English government take a stand for humane conditions, "her philanthropy and political interests being roused to simultaneous action."

It is amusing to review articles written during the years when the canal was first discussed as a possibility, then as an actual undertaking. The following lines have been taken from a magazine published in 1860:

"We have once more to advert to the monster folly of the nineteenth century. It is now understood that our government perceives the wisdom of leaving a project so insane to the fate and ridicule which inevitably await it. It was their opposition alone that gave it any importance, and by exciting the national prejudices of France, enabled the projectors to raise funds which they never could have got without it. . . .

"The project is to cut a ship canal three hundred feet wide and thirty feet deep over ninety miles of flat sand. As the level of the Mediterranean and the Red Sea are the same, the canal will be near thirty feet below the level of both, and hence it will be a stagnant and in all likelihood a pestilential ditch.

"The Suez Canal will be begun but never completed nor half completed. Its wreck, as useless as the Pyramids, but far less interesting, will like to be exhibited to posterity probably under the name of the 'French Folly.' "*

England's appeal to the Sublime Porte to have the work upon the canal stopped brought to light the fact that the Sultan's sanction to the undertaking had never been procured. The work done so far had followed very primitive methods, peasants digging the sand up by handsful, putting it in palm-leaf baskets and carrying these up the steep bank to empty. France made great effort to obtain the Sultan's approval, for the situation was critical. His reply was that he confirmed the concession granted by Viceroy Saïd, but that the work henceforth should not be done by impressed peasants. The company's treasury was again empty; it chose to hold the viceroy responsible for the predicament caused by the withdrawal of the peasants and brought him a bill for damages. The claims made could not have been substantiated in any court, for there was no contract, and the concession distinctly stated that the canal was to cost Egypt nothing. However, the viceroy was peculiarly situated; he was dreaming of a day when he might shake off the suzerainty of Turkey and be recognized by the powers as a monarch of independent might. Moreover, he valued the friendship of France—which was to cost him dear. He had been educated in Paris and hoped to make Cairo the Paris of Egypt. Refusing to pay the damages asked, De Lesseps prevailed upon him to submit the matter for arbitration and—strange as it may seem—the emperor of France was agreed upon, his judgment to be final. Napoleon III ruled that the clause wherein the viceroy had agreed to provide peasant labor amounted to a contract; that by the decree of the Sultan this labor was now unavailable; hence the company had suffered severe loss. The fact that the water was already filtering in from the sea, necessitating the use of dredges, was not brought to light. Not only sustaining the company's claim, he added other injuries which they had overlooked. The result was that the viceroy paid a large amount, which added to Egypt's rapidly increasing debt, and at the same time enabled the canal company to continue operations.

* Living Age, December, 1860.

In 1869 the canal was finished, and its completion was celebrated by sumptuous festivities. The Empress of France, Emperor of Austria, Crown Prince of Prussia, Prince of Wales, and many other important members of royalty were present. Forty-eight ships were required to convey the guests thither; the celebration lasted one month — the entire cost defrayed by the viceroy, or the Egyptian government. It amounted to about $21,000,000. It was for this occasion that Verdi wrote his opera Aïda, the great Egyptologist Mariette Bey studying ancient costumes and settings to give added interest and reality, while the Egyptian Museum supplied jewels for the gifted musicians brought from various parts of Europe to present the opera.

A few years later it was found that the debt of Egypt amounted to over $450,000,000. Securities for this vast amount were held by English, French and German subjects. Even the stipulated fifteen per cent of the canal profits had been used as security; the Nile valley suffered from insufficient water supply, and the inflated price of cotton, obtaining during the Civil War in the United States, fell. In the face of impending ruin, something had to be done. At the clamorous demands of Europe, the Sultan deposed Ismail, whose reckless policy, together with that of Saïd, had brought this overwhelming trouble upon his country. The British government bought the stock held by the viceroy—177,662 shares—for $20,000,000, thus obtaining a controlling voice in the company. France and England established what was known as the "dual control" in Egypt, which continued until the revolt of 1882, at which time France refused to go to the extreme of bombarding Alexandria and withdrew—thus ending her control in Egyptian affairs. Since 1882 English "occupation" has continued and bids fair to continue for an indefinite time. It is even now evident that if the canal reverts to the Egyptian government upon the expiration of ninety-nine years, this may be a very different government from that which gave the original concession.

From the standpoint of commercial history, few events have been more signal than the completion of the Suez Canal. Heretofore vessels have saved little except time by making use of it, for the tolls exacted have been equal to the expense of about three thousand miles ocean travel. One dollar and ninety cents per vessel tonnage and two dollars per passenger, crews excepted, have been required, thus making the cost of large vessels passing through amount sometimes to $10,000; $400 has been charged for a small yacht. However, it is now contemplated to make the tolls for both Panama and Suez canals uniform—one dollar and twenty cents per vessel tonnage and no charge for passengers being the proposed change. The distance has been greatly reduced by means of the canal; from England to Bombay lessened from 10,860 to 4,620 miles; from New York to Bombay from 11,520 to 7,920 miles.

The Suez Canal is one hundred miles in length, four hundred twenty feet wide surface measure, and one hundred eight feet on the bottom; it was originally twenty-seven feet nine inches deep but has been since dredged to a depth of thirty-one feet, lakes making it deeper in some places. It takes about fifteen hours and forty minutes to pass through, electricity making night passage possible.

The majority of ships passing through fly under the English flag; next in number are those sailing under the French flag; fewer still belonging to Germany. Except for passenger vessels and men of war, few United States crafts have been seen in these waters. However, in view of the opening of Panama, the shipping of this country may be expected to rapidly increase.

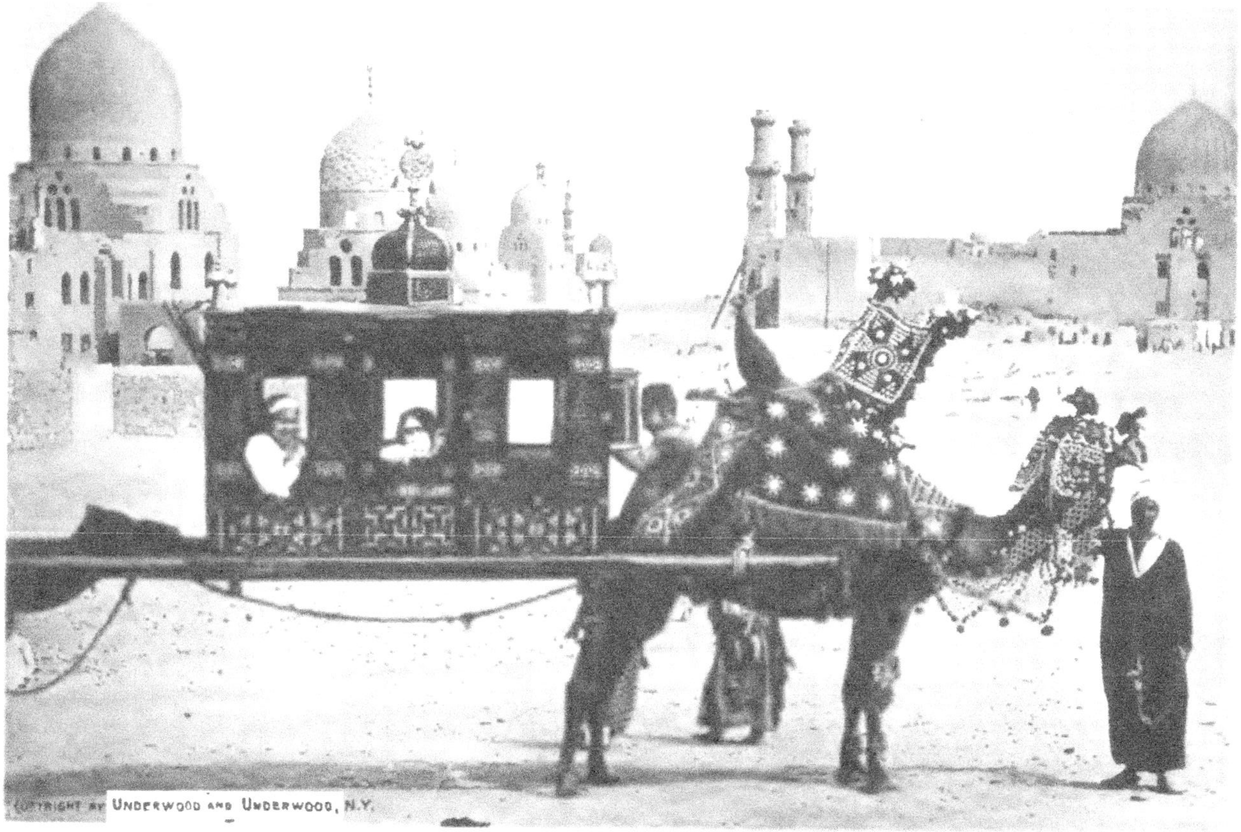
COPYRIGHT BY UNDERWOOD AND UNDERWOOD, N.Y.

BABYLONIA AND HER NEIGHBORS

PREFATORY CHAPTER

THE interpretation of the present is to be sought in the light of the past. *Ex oriente lux* (light out of the east) is an old and familiar saying. In the last century there flashed from this quarter a light that astonished the world, and like the wise men of old, it came from the valley of the Tigris and Euphrates. The consequent increase in our knowledge has revolutionized much of the thought of the past, and so quietly has this been done that none but those who have been more particularly interested in the new discoveries are aware of the importance and extent of the changes made. Our views of ancient history, literature, life, religion have been greatly altered and enlarged.

Europe and America have been for almost two millennia under the potent spell and inspiration of a little people who lived at the eastern end of the Mediterranean. Prophets and teachers arose among them who lifted the world off its hinges, set Greece, the home of intellect, to thinking anew, and uttered their messages through the successors of the Caesars. A wonderful people, indeed! How are they to be explained? Most certainly we must seek for their explanation in the light of their antecedents and racial affinities. It was, and is, no more possible to understand them and correctly interpret their literary remains, the Bible, apart from a knowledge of the great family of which they formed numerically only an insignificant part than it would be to understand the spirit and thought of the people of the United States if the early relations to Great Britain were unknown or ignored. The Old Testament, in the book of Genesis, records that the ancestors of the Hebrews emigrated from Ur of the Chaldees, an ancient city, even in the days of Abraham, of southern Babylonia and a principal seat of the worship of the moon-god, Sin. But of the great family of the Semites—the Arabians, Babylonians, Assyrians, Canaanites, Aramaeans, Syrians, etc., little was known a century ago. Practically all scholarly interest in this group until the middle of the nineteenth century was confined to the literature and civilization of the Arabs since the Mohammedan era.

No better evidence of the universal ignorance of this past, extending down to modern times, can be found than in Sir Isaac Newton's "Chronology of Ancient Kingdoms Amended," published in 1728. This foremost scholar of his day writes, page 268: "However we must allow that Nimrod founded a kingdom at Babylon, and perhaps extended it into Assyria; but this kingdom was but of small extent, if compared with the empires that rose up afterwards; being only within the fertile plains of Chaldea, Chalonitis, and Assyria, watered by the Tigris and Euphrates; and if it had been greater, yet it was but of short continuance, it being the custom in those early ages for every father to divide his territories amongst his sons. So Noah was king of all the world, and Cham was king of all Afric, and Japhet of all Europe and Asia Minor." Nimrod, Noah, Ham and Japhet were all as truly historical persons to the great scientist Newton and his age as were David, Isaiah and the apostle Paul.

More than a century and a half have passed since this famous son of a Lincolnshire farmer wrote his Chronology, but the limitations under which he wrote were destined to remain for succeeding historians until quite recently. Even trained historians have found it difficult within the last two or three decades to adjust themselves to the new discoveries. Not long ago serious writers contended that the world was created 4004 B.C., in six days of twenty-four hours each, and anathemas were in store for those that questioned it. Writing in 1855, Professor Lewis in his "Six Days of Creation," declares that the Biblical story of the Creation was given "by inspiration to the earliest times, and to the earliest men, and in the earliest language that was spoken on the globe."—Hebrew! Less than twenty-five years ago one of the present writers' colleagues in a theological seminary, was teaching his students that the use of the plural name for God in Hebrew, and the thrice repeated "Holy, holy, holy," furnished collateral evidence in support of the doctrine of The Trinity. He was quite unaware that the polytheistic Assyrians used the same thrice repeated *ashru, ashru, ashru,* in praise of their gods.

This however is only another proof of the common origin of the Semitic peoples, a reminder of the days when the tribes were not dispersed, and Abraham had not yet gone forth from the gates of Ur. Scholars of today have found that the substance of the first twelve chapters of Genesis is also recorded in the literature of other Semitic tribes, the Babylonian narrative being strikingly similar to that of the Hebrews. The other stories lack the lofty spiritual quality of the Old Testament narrative, as the Hebrew writers were untouched by the polytheism of their neighbors. The Semitic race has always been preeminently religious, and though the Assyrians and Babylonians failed to spiritualize their beliefs, as did the Hebrews, their cosmologies show the traces of their common origin. There we find Adam and Eve, under the names of Adapa or Eabani and Ukhat, created out of clay, and other similarities, too numerous to mention here. The point is that we have in these records valuable material on the period before the Hebrews were called to be a separate nation, and we can better estimate their remarkable qualities.

Owing to the political relations into which the people of Israel and Judah were brought to the empires of the Tigris and Euphrates valley, the compilers of the historical books of The O. T., and the prophets have given us incidental, valuable, but not always unprejudiced notices of their kinsmen to the East. The II. Book of Kings touches upon some noteworthy events from the time of Tiglathpileser II. including the fall of Israel and Judah. Characteristic of these notices is the complete omission of Sargon's name except in Isaiah 20:1, where until the discovery of the inscriptions it was thought to be an official title, although he was the one who completed the conquest of the northern kingdom, the "House of Omri," as he calls it, and deported its inhabitants. It is difficult indeed for an Assyriologist to imagine an Assyrian *rabshak* speaking to the messengers of Hezekiah as that officer is reported to have done in II. Kings 18:25f.: "Am I now come up without the Lord against this place to destroy it? The Lord said unto me, Go up against this land and destroy it." This Yahwe (Lord) Isaiah declares the Assyrian blasphemed, an act, which, to say the least, was more in accord with his usual temper. Yahwe was no more in the estimation of Sennacherib than the gods of the petty principalities of Hamath and Arpad. The truth seems to be that the writer in the book of Kings makes the *rabshak* speak as he is alleged to have spoken just as the Babylonian priests declared that Cyrus had been called to the conquest of Babylon by the Babylonian god Marduk.

The books, especially of Isaiah, Jeremiah, Nahum and Ezekiel, contain some interesting material upon the cultus of Babylonia. It is, however, the darker features that the prophets delight to draw, and the picture they present to us does not in all points resemble the one we find in the palaces of the kings. The animus displayed toward the enemy is far removed from the precept which enjoins that he shall be loved. The fourteenth chapter of Isaiah is a standing witness to the correctness of this observation. It is a magnificent paean of prophetic feeling, but it is necessary to observe that the fate of Nabonidus, the last king of Babylon, was not so wretched as here described. When Cyrus conquered the city he made Nabonidus governor. It may, however, be that this perfervid and vengeful utterance of irrepressible joy related originally to Sargon II., king of Assyria, conqueror of Samaria, who, as his successor Sennacherib tells us "was not buried in his house," and that after the fall of Babylon the latter name was interpolated. At all events this king, unlike "the kings of the nations," did not "sleep in his own house" (vss. 18-19), and the introductory verses are obviously late. Optimistic and pessimistic patriots who writhed under the domination of a foreign power, religious zealots conscious of their possession of a purer and practically religious faith, it is little wonder they portrayed only the harsher features of their spoilers and conquerors.

The apocalyptic book of Daniel, so long interpreted as a sober recital of historic events, is distinctly and admittedly at variance on some points with the monumental records of Nebuchadnezzar, Nabonidus, and Cyrus. It would, however, be an unjustifiable inference were any one to conclude from the foregoing that the records of the Old Testament had all, or in great measure, been relegated to the hazy region of myth and fiction by the revelations of the contemporary records of the monuments. The historical presentation of events from the age of

Saul onwards has on the whole received welcome corroboration. The inscriptions on stone and clay have confirmed the story of the parchment rolls, completing, amending, elucidating it and always enabling us to interpret it more accurately.

Sufficient has been said in the foregoing to suggest the far-reaching importance of Babylonian and Assyrian archaeology and literature for the understanding of the Old Testament. We are able now not only to bring new material in contemporary documents to aid us in its study, we are able also to interpret the life and thought of its people in the light of the larger history, political, institutional, social, moral, legal and religious, of the great family to which Israel belonged. The life of the various members of the ancient semitic stock has been illuminated by the discoveries which began with Botta and Layard. The conditions existing in Canaan prior to the conquest, for example, became clear only with the discovery of the Tell-Amarna tablets in 1887. They were found in the palace of Amenophis on the bank of the Nile about 180 miles south of Cairo and they cast an unexpected light upon the period of the Exodus. Israel, her history, her conquests, her captivities and her religion no longer stand as things apart in which the supernatural has been imminent and active in a manner nowhere else discoverable in the history of the race. A "Thus saith Jehovah" differs from a similar utterance from the gods of Israel's neighbors, but it is rather in the character of the prophet than in the understanding of the people.

While the Old Testament gave us some information about Babylonia and Assyria prior to the discoveries of their own monuments, a brief account of which is given in the following pages, it must be admitted that it has gained by these discoveries incomparably more than it gave. But we have learned not only about Israel and the Bible, we have learned also much about the earlier Amoritic inhabitants of Palestine who had entered there and spread into Egypt and Babylonia as early as the second half of the third millennium B.C. Much has been won from these records about Egypt and Ethiopia, about the peoples of Arabia, the Hittites, the Aramaeans, Armenians, Elamites, Medes and Persians as well as the early inhabitants of Babylonia, the Sumerians, the original inventors of the cuneiform writing, which was a later development of pictographic symbols. We have learned with astonishment of the advances made in Babylonia in early times in the arts and architecture. Deprived by the nature of his country, in which wood and stone were not to be found, we read of Gudea (Circa 3000 B.C.) bringing diorite from Magan, West Arabia, for his sculptures, some of which are now to be seen in the Louvre collection. The skill of the lapidarist in connection with the cunningly engraved cylinder seals is today the admiration of the best workers in the art of engraving, and the wounded lioness from the palace of Ashurbanipal in the seventh century B.C. is the best portrayal of animal life that has come to us from ancient times. As Professor Sayce has recently shown, the lamp in use in Greece in the historical age, and not before, and later borrowed by the Romans, and after the Greek conquest, by the Egyptians, was Babylonian in origin and a common utensil in Mesopotamia prior to the fourteenth century B.C. The composite symbols of Babylonia were adopted by the people of Western Asia. The eagle of the southern city-kingdom of Lagash (Telloh) was transported to the Hittites. The eagle symbol, wherever found, double-headed or single, is a bird from the land of Paradise. The winged horse is found upon Hittite seals, and from Asia passed over the Hellespont and became the Greek Pegasos. The native fetish deities of Asia Minor were replaced by gods in human form, and the idea of a trinity, or triad of deities, followed in the wake of Babylonian culture. In architecture the Babylonians invented the arch. This achievement had always been attributed to the Etruscans on the basis of the statements of the classical writers. But it was used by the Babylonians, as we now know, three thousand years before there is any evidence of its use on classical soil. Columnar construction dates back to the same period. Both the arch and the column were found in the buildings unearthed a few years ago at Nippur by the expeditions from the University of Pennsylvania. Owing to the dearth of wood and stone these pioneers in the arts of civilization were forced to have recourse to clay, the only material available. They therefore invented the pillar made of brick. Babylonia was the land *par excellence* of brick buildings. Their land abounded in asphaltum and this they used instead of mortar, as the Hebrew writer tells us they did when they built the tower of Babel, "the temple with the lofty tower," in Babylon. "Their technical skill rested on scientific principles no less unattainable in modern architecture than the Grecian idea of beauty in the plastic art. The buildings which they constructed with brick must have been built according to rules and laws unknown to modern architecture, which views many of these ancient works with the same astonishment as is evoked by the pyramids of Egypt." Babylonia can at least claim to have made early advances in astronomical observations. The movements of the heavenly bodies were carefully watched from the earliest times and records made of them. Even in the late Roman period the Chaldeans were still looked upon as the founders of astronomy. It is true that Egypt had also at a very early age successfully cultivated this science and had introduced a practical calendar which began the year on the day when Sirius was first observed on the eastern horizon at sunrise 4200 years before the Christian era. Some Egyptologists hold that this calendar was the precursor of the Julian, which in turn was modified by Pope Gregory in 1582, thus giving us the Gregorian calendar which was adopted in England by the Calendar Amendment Act of 1751. But it is more probable that we are indebted to the Babylonians for our calendrical system, Greece and Rome borrowing from them. The naming of the days of the week after the sun and moon gods and the five planets known to them seems beyond dispute. It was they who divided the circle into 360 degrees in connection with their sexagesimal system of numerals, the day into 24 hours, and the hour into 60 minutes. The faces of our watches bear daily and hourly witness to our obligations to this old people of the land of Shinar. There are 24 hours in the day, but our time-pieces divide them into two periods of 12 hours each, just as the Babylonian day was reckoned as 12 *double* hours. By what routes and means these transfers of scientific achievements were made from the mother-land of science to the peoples of Europe we are not yet able to decide. Further discoveries, however, will doubtless reveal still more clearly the historic connections of modern culture with the people of the Tigris and Euphrates valley who themselves speak of their cities as "ancient" before the deluge.

All of this increase of knowledge hinted at in the preceding paragraphs, and all too briefly sketched in this work, is the acquisition of our own times. The Greeks, who in haughty disdain regarded all others as "barbarians," knew little of this ancient of days—nothing whatever of the great ruler Sargon I. or Hammurabi, imperialist and great law-giver fifteen hundred years before the enactment of the laws of Draco and Solon at Athens.

Among the Greek writers Herodotus is the only one that can be considered as a direct source. He may have visited Babylon about the middle of the fifth century B.C. Much of what he has written, however, is clearly a matter of hearsay or romancing. The judgment passed on him by his contemporaries and successors was certainly not without foundation. His critics accused him, as the Arabian historians did Ibn Ishaq, the biographer of Mohammed, of direct falsification, and even a superficial study of his writings is sufficient to prove that the accusation was not without apparent warrant. One seeks in vain, for example, in the Babylonian literature for evidence of the custom, which he describes as one of the most beautiful and wisest of the Babylonians, of putting the marriageable girls once a year upon the market to be sold to the highest bidders! Naively he adds that this was an earlier custom that was no longer practised in his time. Of the history of Babylon he knew little— of its latest rulers and even of the great Nebuchadnezzar he had not an inkling as Tiele, the Dutch historian, has said. Ctesias, the Carian physician who lived for seventeen years at the Persian court of Artaxerxes Mnemon in the fourth century, did not know that Babylon had an independent existence. Those who followed were for the most part merely excerptors from those who preceded them. In view of the paucity and unreliability of the sources an impenetrable veil was drawn between us and the ancient orient. At last it has been lifted, and in the language of the old poets of Babylon, "brother again sees brother."

CLAY JARS OF CHALDEA.

BABYLONIA AND ASSYRIA

CHAPTER I.

Early Civilization of Asia.

IN STUDYING the history of Babylonia and Assyria, our attention is drawn to one of the earliest inhabited portions of the globe—so far as is now known: to the valley of the Euphrates. Biblical tradition favored the view that this was the Cradle of the Human Race. Here the Yahvistic writer placed the fabled Garden of Eden, the best explanation he could devise for the origin of mankind. The valley was a regular thoroughfare for early tribes journeying to and from Arabia, and reaching out to the east, west, or north for new homes, often remaining for long succeeding generations in the fertile region itself. It was a land where men of various tongues and dialects met, only to again diverge. The effort of the Hebrew to explain how so many languages had come into being resulted in the story of the Tower of Babel. Before the beginnings of the Hebrew race as distinct from the general Semitic family, an old civilization had developed here in Chaldea. In connection with his worship, the Chaldean built high ziqqurats—temple-towers of from three to seven platforms, rising one above the other, each platform smaller than the one below. The story handed down from one generation of the Hebrews to another was that the Chaldeans had once tried to build a tower to reach the very heavens. Alarmed at their presumption, God confounded their speech so they could no longer understand one another. Thus was man punished and thus the various speeches originated.

In following the history of the mixed race known as the Babylonians, and of those who pressed north of the home-country to found the state of Assyria, we shall become acquainted with the only great nation of antiquity whose civilization may have been older than that of the Egyptians. We have no reliable record of the Chinese until late in the third millennium, and their civilization, if more ancient still, was isolated at least, and affected no other people. When Thutmose I. penetrated to the valley of the Euphrates, some years after the expulsion of the Hyksos, he came upon a nation, of whose culture, script, and language, as the recently discovered Tell-el-Amarna tablets indicate, were already familiar to his own people.

The recorded life of Egypt reaches back more than 6,000 years; civilization in Mesopotamia may have been more ancient. Many monuments have been unearthed in the sites of ancient cities which throw light upon great antiquity. In Egypt visible monuments have borne witness through long succeeding centuries of early strength; in Babylonia and Assyria the very site of cities was forgotten, and men no longer remembered where these two influential powers of antiquity had developed. Though in the last century only anything like a complete history of Egypt has been possible, yet evidences of a nation long since extinct, were preserved in temples and tombs, and hieroglyphics covering walls and columns indicated that whoever should discover their meaning would learn of their mighty builders. Far different was the case of Babylonia and Assyria. They too had once been proud and wealthy nations, taking foremost rank; their cities filled the valleys of the Euphrates and Tigris, and their fertile fields yielded even more abundantly than the rich Nile valley. Their palaces rose to the glory of their kings, and their commerce penetrated to every corner of the ancient world. Then changes came upon the life of antiquity. New peoples pushed to the front; the tide of commerce shifted into other channels. These nations were conquered by their yet stronger neighbors, and their temples and palaces, built not of enduring stone but of perishable brick, fell into heaps of nameless mounds. When the waters of the mighty rivers were no longer guided through canals to irrigate the land, the soil ceased to be productive. Desert sands spread over the desolate region and reclaimed wide areas which became the tenting ground for nomadic tribes. The very words of the late writer in the Book of Isaiah concerning these nations rang true through the ages:

"And Babylon, the glory of kingdoms, the beauty of the Chaldees' excellency, shall be as when God overthrew Sodom and Gomorrah. It shall never be inhabited, neither shall it be dwelt in from generation to generation: neither shall the Arabian pitch tent there; neither shall the shepherds make their fold there. But wild beasts of the desert shall lie there; and their houses shall be full of doleful creatures; and owls shall dwell there, and satyrs shall dance there. And the wild beasts of the islands shall cry in their desolate houses, and dragons in their pleasant palaces; and her time is near to come, and her days shall not be prolonged.

"Then shall the Assyrian fall with the sword, not of a mighty man; and the sword, not of a mean man, shall devour him; but he shall flee from the sword, and his young men shall be discomfited. And he shall pass over to his stronghold for fear, and his princes shall be afraid of the ensign."[1]

Nineveh, the capital of Assyria, disappeared suddenly. In Alexander's day its site was unknown. Babylon, however, was not destroyed by Cyrus, but continued its importance until the rise of its rival Seleucia, and was still inhabited in the Middle Ages. But the two nations were forgotten in the west for hundreds of years. Then with the dawn of peace and order in Europe during the later Middle Ages, came the desire to know about the past. Monks who made pilgrimages to the Holy Land, during the twelfth and thirteenth centuries, sometimes pressed farther east, and made mention of strange mounds seen in the valleys of these ancient rivers. Travelers told of curious inscriptions found among the ruins there. In rare cases, they even went to the length of copying one or two, with greater

---

[1] Isaiah 13, 19-22; 31, 8-9. NOTE.—This is the A. V. version. It should read:
The Assyrian shall fall by a sword, not a man's,
And a sword, not a human one, shall devour him.
[And he shall flee from the face of the sword,
And his brave ones shall become tributary,
And his rock he will run by in terror,
And his princes in fright shall abandon their flag.]
The destruction is to be *supernatural*, according to Isaiah. The lines in brackets are probably a later addition.—(CRAIG.)

or less accuracy. It was left finally for the eighteenth century to locate the old sites of Babylonian cities, and for the nineteenth century to discover the hidden meaning of the wedge-shaped letters inscribed upon their ruins.

To the patient efforts of the men who persisted in their difficult and often disheartening task of unearthing ruins, and to the scholars who toiled year after year to read the forgotten language these ruins brought to light, we owe most that is now known regarding the early inhabitants of the Euphrates valley. These nations, so long destroyed, their cities, so long abandoned, we shall try to bring before us as they have been reconstructed by historians in more pretentious volumes. Naturally, any account of the Babylonians and Assyrians will involve some consideration of their neighbors, whose civilizations developed by their side, and whose fortunes frequently mingled with theirs.

The Recovery of Forgotten Cities.

Were we to proceed at once to the development of the Babylonian and Assyrian states without first pausing to note what far-reaching efforts have been made to read their early civilization from their remains, entombed within the earth, we would deprive ourselves of one of the most interesting pages in modern historical research.

Since the middle of the twelfth century we find references made to the ruins of Babylon and Nineveh, by monks and travellers who greatly confused the ancient cities, repeatedly mistaking Baghdad for Babylon. In 1613 there was published by an English nobleman an account of his distant travels. "Sir Anthony Sherley; His Relation of His Travels into Persia." This is what he wrote of these ancient capitals: "I will speak . . . of Babylon; not to the intent to tell stories, either of the huge ruins of the first Towne or the splendour of the second, but because nothing doth impose anything in man's nature more than example—to shew the truth of God's word, whose vengeances, threatened by His Prophets, are truely succeeded in all those parts. .

"All the ground on which Babylon was spred is left now desolate; nothing standing in that Peninsula between the Euphrates and the Tigris, but only part, and that a small part, of the greate Tower, which God hath suffered to stand (if man may speake so confidently of His greate impenetrable counsels) for an eternal testimony of His work in the confusion of Man's pride, and that Arke of Nebuchadnezzar for as perpetual a memory of his greate idolatry and condigne punishment. . . .

"Nineve, that which God himself called That greate Citie, hath not one stone standing which may give memory of the being of a towne. One English mile from it is a place called Mosul, a small thing, rather to be a witness of the other's mightinesse and God's judgment than of any fashion of magnificence in itselfe." [2]

These words struck the note which was to lead to extensive labors for discovery. Europe was at the time passing through a period of deep religious fervor, which was felt in many classes of society and walks of life, and people who cared not at all for the history of ancient nations were roused by the possibility offered to verify statements found in the Old Testament and prove its inspiration by showing the fulfillment of its prophecies. Although nothing of importance was accomplished at this time, the religious motive survived.

The first systematic investigation was made by Claudius James Rich, appointed in 1811 as resident of the East India Company at Baghdad. He made a thorough examination of all the large mounds in that particular locality and prepared a survey of the most important ones. This proved very useful to those who came later to the field. He had besides made a small collection of finds at Hillah and Mosul—a box only three feet square—which were sent with his charts to the British Museum. These later furnished the inspiration to further exploration.

In 1842 the French government sent Paul Emil Botta to Mosul as consular agent, and his name was destined to be connected with all discoveries made in Assyria during the early part of the nineteenth century. Stimulated by Julius Mohl, who had examined Rich's meagre but suggestive finds, he was the first to actually dig into the mounds of ruins. After coming upon nothing noteworthy during three months' excavation in Kujundjik, a peasant told him that strange objects had been

[2] Sherley: His Relation of His Travels Into Persia.

found at Khorsabad, about four hours to the northeast, and thither Botta sent his workmen.

The poor Arabian laborers of this region are ignorant Mohammedans, and they suspected that Botta was digging for gold, while they conceived the unique idea that the fragments bearing inscriptions, now and then brought to light, were charms which in some way guided him on to hidden treasure. The Turkish Pasha put all possible obstacles in his way, but the very first shaft Botta sank came upon the walls of an old palace—a find especially valuable at a time when only the most enthusiastic scholars had faith in the undertaking, and people generally regarded the project as misguided. No less than 209 rooms were laid bare by Botta and his successor, Victor Place.

Austen Henry Layard, an English boy of Huguenot descent, had devoured all available books of travel and adventure. He came to the work of Assyrian exploration as an enthusiastic young man about the time of Botta's widely noised discovery. On November 9, 1845, Mr. Layard began to excavate at Nimrud, some distance south of Nineveh, and before the first day's work was done he had the promise, and, in part, the satisfaction of realizing his "visions of palaces under ground." He had discovered the North-West palace of Nimrud, built by Ashurnatsirpal, 884-861 B.C., upon the foundations of one laid by Shalmeneser, 1300 B.C. After a little more than a year and a half he returned to England having discovered no less than three palaces. The funds necessary for his work were obtained from Sir Stratford Canning, the English ambassador at Constantinople.

In 1849 excavations were begun again with the assistance of Hormuzd Rassam at the expense of the British Museum. "The excavations carried on under these auspices, and with the powers Layard then possessed, were successful beyond his wildest dream. As the trenches followed round the walls of room after room they uncovered great slabs of alabaster, with which the chamber walls were wainscoted, and these were found to be richly carved in relief with scenes of hunting, of war, and of solemn ceremony. The very life of palace, camp and field in Assyrian days came back again before the astonished eyes of the explorer, while these received an addition to their verisimilitude by the discovery in some of the ruins of pieces of iron which had once formed parts of the same kind of armor as that portrayed on the reliefs, together with iron and bronze helmets, while in others were found vases and ornamentally carved pieces of ivory. Here were the pictures and there were the objects which they represented. As the trenches were dug deeper or longer, monuments carved or inscribed were found daily."[3]

Whatever objects could be transported were sent to the British Museum in London, and went far to arouse interest and thus secure funds to enable Layard to continue his operations. During this expedition the palace of Sennacherib, the walls of which had been partly laid bare during the first period, was still further explored, and in addition to the valuable bas-reliefs an ancient library, consisting of thousands of clay tablets, was found in two of the rooms, and this was greatly increased by Rassam's discovery of the North-West palace in 1854.

In 1850 William K. Loftus began his labors in this field, but none of his discoveries proved so valuable as his descriptions of various mounds, used as guides to this day. Concerning the appearance of the mounds he wrote: "I know of nothing more exciting or impressive than the first sight of one of these great Chaldean piles looming in solitary grandeur from the surrounding plains and marshes. A thousand thoughts and surmises concerning its past eventful history and origin—its gradual rise and rapid fall—naturally present themselves to the mind of the spectator. The hazy atmosphere of early morning is peculiarly favorable to considerations and impressions of this character, and the gray mist intervening between the gazer and the object of his reflections imparts to it a dreamy existence. This fairylike effect is heightened by mirage, which strangely and fantastically magnifies its form, elevating it from the ground, and causing it to dance and quiver in the rarefied air. No wonder, therefore, that the beholder is lost in pleasing doubt as to the actual reality of the apparition before him."[4]

Of all the Assyrian discoveries which were crowded into the last century, unquestionably the most important was made

[3] Rogers: Hist. of Babylonia and Assyria, 154.
[4] Loftus: Travels and Researches in Chaldea and Susiana.

by Rassam in 1852 and 1853 when he laid bare the magnificent palace of Assurbanipal, in which was found the royal library. Here the king had caused to be collected tablets embodying the literature of both Babylonia and Assyria, and numberless royal inscriptions of both states, from the earliest time. Owing to the circumstance of their having been inscribed upon tablets of clay, many had been destroyed as the building in which they were kept fell in ruins. Many were found in an almost perfect state of preservation and thousands of others have since been joined by the patient labors of scholars. At this point Assyrian excavations largely ceased, for it was felt that unless some understanding of these tablets could be gained, it was scarcely worth while to amass more of them at such great outlays. Archæologists realized that the inscriptions must be deciphered before funds would be forthcoming for fresh undertakings.

We have seen how difficult a task Egyptologists had in discovering the meaning of the hieroglyphics, and how the Rosetta stone, giving one decree in three different languages, at last led to an understanding of the whole. The Babylonians and Assyrians used a series of wedge-shaped letters or symbols, which has given the name *cuneiform* to their written language. These wedge-shaped signs were impressed on the clay by a stylus, and several of them are united to form a *syllabic* character. There are about 400 of these complex syllabic signs in the syllabary, instead of 26 letters as in English. Where the writing on the tablets is very close, as it frequently is, it is often very difficult to read the signs correctly. In the earlier Babylonian period, moreover, the form differs from that of the later Babylonian and Assyrian period. To make the reading still more puzzling they are polyphonic, *i. e.*, have several syllabic values, and are also used ideagraphically, *i. e.*, may be used for entire words. If we should read b either b, p, m, d, etc., and also for break, run, beside with only the context to guide us we would have a parallel case. There was no Rosetta stone to help this time, and the tablets long remained sealed books. We have only to look at a page of the characters to wonder that their meaning at last dawned upon the tireless workers.

Prominent among linguists engaged upon Assyrian inscriptions were Sir Henry Rawlinson, Fox Talbot, Jules Oppert, and a talented Irish scholar by the name of Hincks. At last translations of certain inscriptions were offered by these men, but critics looked at the apparently meaningless signs and questioned the versions rendered. At least, they insisted, there was no way to prove that a meaning had not been worked into them, rather than out of them.

Finally it was suggested that a single inscription, hitherto unread, be sent to the four scholars just mentioned, and that they be asked to return their renderings sealed, to a committee appointed to examine them. To the amazement of the world, the translations made were almost identical, differences occurring in those portions which the translators themselves had marked as uncertain. This was, indeed, a triumph for students of the Assyrian language, and compelled a general agreement that the cuneiform tongue had at last been mastered. Rapid advances were made after this test, which was made in 1857. The translation of numerous tablets was at once eagerly begun.

George Smith, a young man engaged to copy inscriptions required by Rawlinson for some material he was about to publish, was not content to copy meaningless signs, but set to work to understand them. So rapidly did he advance in mastering the language that he became most helpful in classifying the tablets stored in the British Museum. In connection with his work there one incident deserves notice.

The clay tablets had been removed as carefully as possible from the ruins of the library at Nineveh, and had been brought to the London Museum with as little mishap as could be expected. Some were perfect, some partly missing, some in fragments. One day George Smith came upon a deluge story which so strongly resembled the version given in the Old Testament that he was struck by the similarity. Now recent years have disclosed that the flood legend has been common among all Semitic peoples, but the fact was not established in the middle part of the last century. Finding many portions of the story lacking, Smith felt that he would like to go in search of them. The whole affair was widely published, and Edwin Arnold, then editor of the Daily Telegraph of London, became interested in it. Through his influence the Telegraph offered five thousand guineas to pay the expenses of an expedition to Nineveh, under the direction of George Smith, to recover, if possible, the missing portions of the story. In 1872, accordingly, Smith started out upon his search for the "Deluge Fragments," under contract to telegraph his experiences and discoveries to the London paper. When he actually came upon a fragment of the deluge epic, it was regarded in England as a great and unexpected triumph. Two other fragments were found, and then the Telegraph, probably thinking it had been sufficiently advertised, decided that its venture had succeeded, and Smith was recalled. Returning in 1873, he died in Assyria three years later of a fever contracted in the marshy, fever-breeding country.

In recent years, excavations have been carried on in the valley of the Euphrates under auspices of the University of Pennsylvania. Most of this work has been done at Nippur, and accounts of the discoveries have been published. An agreement was made with the Turkish government to the effect that all remains uncovered be turned over to the Imperial Museum at Constantinople. So generous did the leaders of this college band prove in aiding the Turks to classify objects found, accepting no remuneration for their services, that the Sultan was pleased to present a large number of them to the Museum of the University of Pennsylvania, where they are today exhibited.

TRANSPORT OF TIMBER FOR SARGON'S PALACE.
(The God Ea, represented in the lower left-hand corner as half man, half fish, escorts the fleet.)

CHAPTER II.

SOURCES OF BABYLONIAN AND ASSYRIAN HISTORY.

In considering the four important sources of Babylonian and Assyrian history, we may note first, Old Testament writings.

Unquestionably the Bible has gained more through Assyrian excavations than it has itself contributed to the history of that country. As has been said before, the Old Testament consists of Hebrew writings which portray various phases of Hebrew life, and mention is made of other nations only when the Chosen People by force of circumstances were thrown in direct contact with them. Since their kingdom was overcome by Babylonians, we could scarcely expect Hebrew writers to hold unprejudiced opinions regarding their own conquerors; nevertheless whatever facts concerning them crept into their writings have been verified by modern discovery.

Much is often revealed in a few words, as is characteristic of Biblical expression. For example, see how much is condensed in the following sentence: "And the king of Egypt came not again any more out of his land: for the king of Babylon had taken from the river of Egypt unto the river Euphrates all that pertained to the king of Egypt."

Not alone have the facts recorded in the Old Testament proved useful to those engaged in reconstructing the history of the Tigris-Euphrates nations, but the desire of religious adherents to confirm the truth and accuracy of ancient Hebrew writings has served as an incentive both to those who did the work and to those who by contributions made the task possible.

The writings of the early Greeks concerning Babylonia and Assyria supply another source. Berosus was a Babylonian priest connected with a temple sacred to Bel. He lived during the fourth century before Christ, when Babylonia and Assyria had become Greek provinces. For the Antiochus he wrote a lengthy history of his country, which would have been of greatest value to us had it been preserved.

Unfortunately it was destroyed, and only excerpts, made by Polyhistor and Apollodoras of the first century B.C., are now in existence.

Herodotus devoted more than twenty chapters of his first volume to Babylonia, but owing to certain faults we have found characteristic of his writings, he has led some scholars to even declare that he never saw the country at all. While they cannot be wholly depended upon, his writings have some value. Other Greek writers have thrown so little light on Babylonian life that we shall not consider them here at all.

Thirdly, we may mention Egyptian records as a source for Mesopotamian history. The Egyptian hieroglyphics and the cuneiform symbols of the Assyrian tongue were translated about the same time, so that little actual help was gained through Egyptian sources. Nevertheless, campaigns waged by Egyptian kings within the very borders of Asiatic countries, with detailed accounts as set forth upon the walls of Egyptian temples, cannot fail to aid in the reconstruction of Assyrian growth and development.

Lastly and most important of all are the monuments and remains unearthed in Mesopotamia itself. More than one hundred thousand clay record tablets have been recovered; temples and palaces have been excavated, and within these were found alabaster slabs carved with many scenes characteristic of Assyrian life; armour, utensils and numerous other articles have each thrown some light upon the ancient civilization. The value of this first hand, or original material, is priceless indeed, since without it no detailed knowledge of these old kingdoms could ever have been hoped for. Explorations among the ruins are still carried on, and it is possible that the present century may add much to what has already been gained concerning the ancient dwellers in the once fertile valleys of the Euphrates and Tigris.

PHYSICAL GEOGRAPHY OF BABYLONIA AND ASSYRIA.

If you will look closely at a map of the eastern hemisphere, you will see that a great tract of desert extends across northern Africa, and reaching beyond the Mediterranean Sea, the Isthmus of Suez and the Red Sea, traverses the entire width of Asia to the Pacific Ocean. This desert waste is so broken by plateaus and mountain ranges that its vast extent is scarcely realized. Rivers occasionally cross it, producing fertile valleys which, generally speaking, support the life of the whole area.

We are now concerned with the location and topography of the ancient Babylonian and Assyrian kingdoms, and of those districts lying adjacent. North of the Persian Gulf some considerable distance, we find the Armenian mountains. These ranges are loftier than most in Western Asia, piercing high above the eternal snow-line. During winter their sides and gorges are massed with snow, which melts rapidly with the warmth of spring and heat of summer. The drainage of the mountains has resulted in many streams, which unite to form the Euphrates on the western slopes, and on the eastern slopes, form the Tigris. Ages ago these two rivers emptied into the Persian Gulf at points some distance from each other. But such heavy deposits of rich mountain loam have been brought down by the streams, that they have extended the land far into the gulf, pushing the water back for some hundred miles. Joining one another in the area thus formed, the waters of the two streams reach the gulf today as one mighty river with many mouths. We may judge how great changes this land-building process has wrought by the fact that the town of Ur, now nearly two hundred miles from the gulf, was a sea-port at the time of which we are now studying. The annual increase of the land is about 115 feet.

Herodotus' statement that "Egypt is the gift of the Nile," might have been made with equal truth of the Euphrates and Babylonia. Here again an annual overflow refreshes a valley, while in antiquity a network of canals provided water, fertility, and humidity for districts sloping off gently on either side.

Today this territory is held by the Turks, and with their ruinous policy of trying to extract all possible revenue from their lands while doing nothing to improve them, the old canals are abandoned, none others take their place, and the rivers wander today at will, leaving part of the area parched and unproductive, and converting the rest into fever-breeding swamps and marshes.

The Euphrates is the longer of the two rivers. Taking

its rise west of a lofty mountain, it receives several tributaries near its source, but none join it during the last eight hundred miles of its course. The snows melt gradually; in March the stream begins to overflow its channel; high water mark is reached by the first of June, and July finds the waters receding. This river is very winding in its course, at one place being but one hundred miles from the Mediterranean Sea and near Babylon running along within twenty-five miles of the Tigris, only to immediately branch off again to the south. Its entire length is about eighteen hundred miles, and most of the water is spent before it reaches the Gulf.

The Tigris is somewhat different from its sister stream. Its name signifies "the swift," or the "arrowy," and indicates its rapid current, whereas the Euphrates flows more gently. Not so broad as the Euphrates, the Tigris is much deeper. On the east of the high mountains wherein this river has its rise, spring comes quickly; the water rises rapidly, and the period of its overflow is short. Beginning to rise in March, the first of May sees the high water mark, and by the last of June the stream is fast finding its usual volume.

The territory between the Tigris and Euphrates the Greeks called Mesopotamia, meaning "between two rivers," but they applied the name to the northern portion of the district—the home of the Assyrians. As generally used to-day, the term Mesopotamia signifies the whole region.

The southern portion, bordering on the Persian Gulf, has a deep alluvial soil, built up by the yearly deposit of the rivers. Like the valley of the Nile, it has been the repository of fine silt. This portion from its capital city Babylon was called Babylonia. As we might expect, this was the country first settled because it was the more accessible. Its wide, monotonous plains, enriched with the fertile mountain loam, afforded the most productive farm lands in the world. Herodotus told of their prodigious yield of grain: "This territory is of all that we know the best by far for producing grain; as to trees, it does not attempt to bear them, either fig, or vine or olive, but for producing grain it is so good that it returns as much as two-hundred-fold for the average, and, when it bears its best, it produces three-hundred-fold. The blades of the wheat and barley there grew to be four fingers broad; and from millet and sesame seed, how large a tree grows, I know myself, but shall not record, being well aware that even what has already been said relating to the crops produced has been enough to cause disbelief in those who have not visited Babylonia." Theophrastus wrote: "In Babylon the wheat fields are regularly mown twice, and then fed off with beasts to keep down the luxuriance of the leaf; otherwise the plant does not run to ear. When this is done the return in lands that are badly cultivated is fiftyfold, while in those that are well farmed it is a hundredfold."

The land of Babylonia has been happily compared with the southern half of our state of Louisiana, which it resembles in marshy districts. Again it might be likened to the Egyptian Delta, being of course, larger,—something like Denmark in point of area. Possessing no rocks or mountains, the country seemed at first to be devoid of building material. It has been supposed that its primitive people first sheltered themselves in huts built of reeds which grew abundantly along the river banks. After awhile it was discovered that clay mud furnished a fair material when shaped into bricks and dried in the sun. A more enduring brick was later made by baking the brick in ovens. This oven-baked brick as well as the sun-dried brick constituted the great building material of Babylonia for all subsequent time.

The district north of the alluvial line, enclosed by rivers and mountains, in time became the kingdom of Assyria. This region differed greatly from the southern land. It was made up of low ranges on the north, rolled gently to the south, and supplied excellent pasturage. Stone and material suitable to building purposes were available, but the people, accustomed to the clay bricks of their old home in Babylonia, never made use of the more substantial building stuff. Indeed the Assyrians were not at all of an inventive mind, as another illustration will plainly show. In Babylonia, because the ground was low and level, the people were obliged to construct artificial heights for building sites, thus to escape marshy exhalations and troublesome insects. They erected huge piles of sun-dried brick and crowned these with their palaces and temples.

Now the Assyrians were in the beginning colonists who had gone out of the mother state to find less populated regions farther north. There were hills and elevations in abundance in Assyria, but holding to the custom they had so long followed, they continued to construct great foundations of bricks for their buildings. It is curious indeed to find them, throughout their history, expending time, labor and resources to produce what nature had already provided.

Assyria was somewhat larger than Babylonia, and has been compared to the state of Illinois in size. While the northern mountains and the Gulf afforded definite boundaries, the limits to the east and west were never certain and both Babylonians and Assyrians pushed out in each direction as they became more powerful, contracting again if their strength weakened. On the west a desert separated them from the Mediterranean, and while various tribes held the country east of the Tigris in early times, the Medes later conquered the region east of Assyria, and Persia reached away to the southeast.

There are two seasons in these valleys—the rainy period, lasting from November to March, and the dry season, filling out the remainder of the year. Babylonia was never subject to the cold storms of Assyria, and the kings of the latter country, after they conquered Babylonia, frequently maintained winter palaces in the old capital, Babylon. Summer is intensely hot near the Gulf. In recent years this has been a serious obstacle to confront those carrying on excavations here.

In ancient times an extensive system of canals and ditches made it possible to keep the land under constant cultivation, thus preventing in a large measure the sand storms that now spread over the country, causing much suffering and even death. Under Turkish rule at present, the whole region is left desolate.

In spite of Herodotus to the contrary, certain kinds of trees grew in Babylonia. The fig, apple, almond and walnut were native. The date palm ministered to the wants of the people in manifold ways. An old Persian poem sung of its 360 uses, while the Greeks claimed that it supplied the Babylonians with bread, wine, vinegar, honey, rope, fuel, wood for furniture, and food for cattle. A wide variety of grains and vegetables were produced.

STORY OF BABYLONIA AND ASSYRIA. 217

Wild animals were plentiful. The Mesopotamian lion was thought milder than its jungle cousin. Buffaloes were domesticated. Leopards, hyænas, wild boars, gazelles, foxes and hares were found, while birds and fishes abounded.

Altogether this was a spot where life was favorable for man, and it was natural that wandering tribes that came thither should soon abandon their roving habits for the surer livelihood promised by a fixed home.

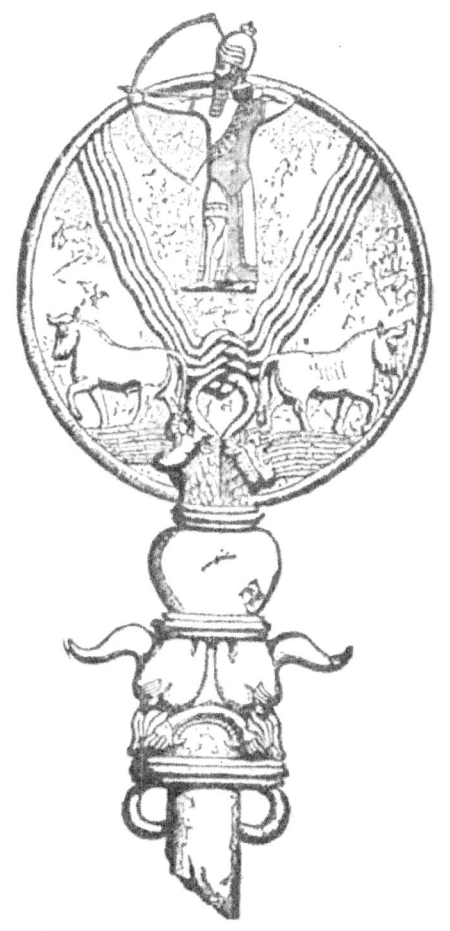

SARGON'S STANDARD (WITH FIGURE OF ASSHUR).

CHAPTER III.

Prehistoric Chaldea.

We have already noted that prehistoric periods are those preceding written records. Uncertainty enters into all attempts to reconstruct such a period for any people, and especially has this been true of Babylonia. However, when the library of Nineveh was unearthed, tablets were discovered which shed some light on those remote ages.

The land we call Babylonia was once called Chaldea. So we shall call it during its prehistoric age—as we call the British Island Britain in the beginning of its history, and later, England. By the term Chaldea we are to understand that portion of the valleys which extended around the Persian Gulf. It was inhabited at the earliest period known. Probably its first settlers were a branch of the Turanian or Yellow Race, to which the Chinese, Japanese, Monguls and present-day Turks belong. That the Chaldeans came from some other locality into this land is not doubted, but whence they came is not known.

The southern part of Chaldea was called Shumir—the Hebrews writing it *Shinar;* the land immediately north they called Accad. The dwellers in both districts came from the same stock and spoke practically the same language. The name *Accad* means mountains, or highlands, and it has been surmised that it may have attached to the inhabitants from some earlier home.

These early people may have migrated to Chaldea five or six thousand years before the Christian era. Of their coming and first settlements, nothing is known. When we first learn of them, they had reached quite a degree of civilization, having canals for irrigating the lands unreached by the river; they had also devised the cuneiform system of writing—an advance on the picture system, earlier in use.

The history of their strange symbols was probably this: in ages bygone they had invented a system of picture writing, as all primitive people seem to have done. As they advanced, too much time was required to copy the elaborate pictures in their entirety, and so the principal outlines were used to represent the pictures themselves. When these people migrated to Chaldea, and were reduced to clay tablets on which to write, it was easier to make straight lines than curved ones. In this way the written language continued to undergo changes until it was eventually made up of wedge-shaped symbols, one of the clear results of the use of the clay tablets.

Our principal knowledge concerning the Chaldeans pertains to their religion, which is believed to have been one of the earliest religions of the world.

The religious instinct seems to have been inborn with man. Some form and degree of worship has been found among all primitive people and is cruder or more elevated according to the stage of development. Primitive man felt himself able to cope with many of the conditions around him, but he soon found that the very agencies which helped might also injure him. The sun, whose light and warmth gave life to his growing crops, might also wither them with its intense heat. The rain which renewed and refreshed the fields, might come in torrents and lay them low. Gradually all these agencies were regarded as *Beings,* which must be importuned. The religion of the Chaldeans taught man how to guard himself against the harmful forces in the world, and every animate and inanimate thing was endowed with a spirit.

A series of tablets treating of this ancient religion was recovered by Rassam, and they fall into three divisions: those treating of "Evil Spirits," others concerning diseases, and last, those devoted to prayers and hymns of praise.

The Accadian conceived of the earth as resembling a huge, inverted bowl. The thickness represented the earth's crust; the hollow beneath was thought of as a bottomless pit, destined to be the final dwelling place of man, and was the abode of demons. Above the earth were two heavens; the higher, supported by a lofty mountain; the lower containing seven kind and friendly planets, which wandered at will through its wide domains. Opposed to these were seven fiery phantoms. Over all dwelt the great Spirit Ana.

"Between the lower heaven and the surface of the earth is the atmospheric region, the realm of Mermer, the Wind, where he drives the clouds, rouses the storms, and whence he pours down the rain, which is stored in the great reservoir of Ana, in the heavenly Ocean. As to the earthly Ocean, it is fancied as a broad river, flowing all around the edge of the imaginary inverted bowl; in its waters dwells Ea, the great Spirit of the Earth and Waters, either in the form of a fish, whence he is frequently called "Ea the fish," or "the exalted fish,' or on a magnificent ship, with which he travels around the earth, guarding and protecting it.

"The minor spirits of the earth are not much spoken of except in a body, a sort of host or legion. All the more terrible are the seven spirits of the abyss, the Maskim, of whom it is said that, although their seat is in the depths of the earth, yet their voice resounds on the heights also; they reside at will in the immensity of space, 'not enjoying a good name either in heaven or on earth.' Their greatest delight is to subvert the orderly course of nature, to cause earthquakes, inundations, ravaging tempests."[1]

The Maskim were ever feared and hated as is shown by the following, translated from one of the tablets:

"They are seven! they are seven!—Seven are they in the depths of Ocean,—seven they are, disturbers of the face of Heaven.—They arise from the depths of Ocean, from hidden lurking-places.—They spread like snares.—Male they are not, female they are not. Wives they have not, children are not born to them.—Order they know not, nor beneficence;—prayers and supplications they hear not. Horses grown in the bowels of the mountains—foes of EA—they are throne-bearers of the gods—they sit in the roads and make them unsafe.—The fiends! The fiends! They are seven, they are seven, seven are they!

"Spirit of Heaven, be they conjured! Spirit of Earth, be they conjured!"

[1] Ragozin: Chaldea.

A Charm.

Seven are they, they are seven;
  In the caverns of ocean they dwell,
They are clothed in the lightnings of heaven,
  Of their growth the deep waters can tell;
Seven are they, they are seven.

Broad is their way and their course is wide,
  Where the seeds of destruction they sow,
O'er the tops of the hills where they stride,
  To lay waste the smooth highways below, —
Broad is their way and their course is wide.

Man they are not, nor womankind,
  For in fury they sweep from the main,
And have wedded no wife but the wind,
  And no child have begotten but pain,—
Man they are not, nor womankind.

Fear is not in them, nor awe;
  Supplication they heed not, nor prayer,
For they know no compassion nor law,
  And are deaf to the cries of despair, —
Fear is not in them, nor awe.

Cursed they are, they are cursed,
  They are foes to wise EA'S name;
By the whirlwind are all things dispersed
  On the paths of the flash of their flame,—
Cursed are they, they are cursed.

Spirit of Heaven, oh help! Help, oh Spirit of Earth!
  They are seven, thrice said they are seven;
For the gods they are Bearers of Thrones,
  But for men they are Breeders of Dearth
And the authors of sorrows and moans.
  They are seven, thrice said they are seven.
Spirit of Heaven, oh help! Help, oh Spirit of Earth!

—Rendered into verse by Dyer.

Besides these seven hated ones, there were numberless demons who could work all manner of evil for man. They were invisible and brought sickness, sorrow, insanity, and grief. No house was secure against them, and no bolt strong enough to keep them out.

To contend against so much evil, it was necessary to employ conjurers and those skilled in magic, who by incantations and mixtures of herbs might discover the demons and put them to flight. Like the Egyptians, the Chaldeans believed that when one was ill, a demon had taken possession of his body, which must be driven out before recovery would be possible. As a result of this belief, the science of medicine never developed in Babylonia. Even in its advanced period, magicians treated the sick.

Charms and talismans were in great demand to ward off demons. They were worn by the living and adorned the dead. Many articles of furniture were made to serve two purposes—as household conveniences or ornaments, and talismans. Thus the winged bulls which have been found guarding the portals of royal palaces were placed there to keep out demons who would manage in some way to creep in unless prevented by eternal vigilance.

It was believed that certain of these demons were so forbidding in aspect that should they but catch sight of their own faces, they would be frightened away. Therefore a most dreadful demon was fashioned, as terrible and fierce as human ingenuity could conceive. This impersonated the south-west wind—the wind which brought burning heat and drought in its wake. An image thus made was placed in southwest windows, with the hope that the approaching demon might look upon himself and flee in terror.

As time went on, the Chaldeans progressed in their religious beliefs, and the third series of tablets record prayers and hymns of adoration.

Nothing was more natural than that they should worship the sun, as a manifestation of divinity which provided heat, light and life itself, for the children of the earth. Some of these hymns are beautiful in their conception.

"O Sun, I have called unto thee in the bright heavens. In the shadow of the cedar art thou; Thy feet are on the summits—The countries have wished for thee, they have longed for thy coming, O Lord! Thy radiant light illumines all countries. Thou makest lies to vanish, thou destroyest the noxious influence of portents, omens, spells, dreams and evil apparitions; thou turnest wicked plots to a happy issue.

"O Sun! thou hast stepped forth from the background of heaven, thou hast pushed back the bolts of the brilliant heaven,—yea, the gate of heaven. O Sun! above the land thou hast raised thy head! O Sun! thou hast covered the immeasurable space of heaven and countries!"

The sun disappeared at evening tide, and during the night contended with the spirits of darkness. Some other protection was needed for man while darkness reigned. So fire was brought into existence, and was also regarded as worthy of worship:

"Thou who drivest away the evil Maskim, who furtherest the well-being of life, who strikest the breast of the wicked with terror,—Fire, the destroyer of foes, dread weapon which drivest away Pestilence."

Certain wandering Turanian tribes today cling to a religion much like the one so briefly described. Like their remote ancestors, they have conjurers instead of priests.

When they had reached this stage of development, the Chaldeans were overpowered by a vast barbaric horde.

THE STORY OF GENESIS RELATIVE TO THE FIRST SETTLEMENT IN SHUMIR.

"And the whole earth was of one language, and of one speech. And it came to pass, as they journeyed from the east, that they found a plain in the land of *Shinar;* and they dwelt there. And they said one to another, Go to, let us make brick, and burn them thoroughly. And they had brick for stone, and slime had they for mortar. And they said, Go to, let us build us a city and a tower, whose top may reach unto heaven; and let us make us a name, lest we be scattered abroad upon the face of the whole earth. And the Lord came down to see the city and the tower which the children of men builded. And the Lord said, Behold, the people is one, and they have all one language; and this they begin to do; and now nothing will be restrained from them, which they have imagined to do. Go to, let us go down and there confound their language, that they may not understand one another's speech. So the Lord scattered them abroad from thence upon the face of all the earth; and they left off to build the city. Therefore is the name of it called Babel;[1] because the Lord did there confound the language of all the earth; and from thence did the Lord scatter them abroad upon the face of all the earth.

"And Nimrod was a mighty hunter before the Lord; wherefore it is said, Even as Nimrod the mighty hunter before the Lord. And the beginning of his kingdom was Babel, and Erech, and Accad, and Calneh, in the land of Shinar. Out of that land went forth Asshur, and builded Nineveh, and the city Rehoboth, and Calah. And Resen between Nineveh and Calah; the same is a great city.

"And Terah took Abram his son, and Lot the son of Haran, his son's son, and Sarai his daughter-in-law, his son Abram's wife; and they went forth with them from Ur of the Chaldees, to go into the land of Canaan; and they came unto Haran, and dwelt there."—*Genesis* 10 *and* 11.

The first great Semitic invasion took place probably about the beginning of the fourth millennium B.C., and it seems impossible to assign to it a more definite date. The later Babylonians, like the Chinese, gave great antiquity to their nation, reckoning back into hundreds of thousands of years. Their beginnings belonged to so remote a time that adding years inconceivably was but another way of saying that certain events happened very long ago, so long, indeed, that no record or monument remained to give evidence of events which had survived only in stories handed down, from father to son, for thousands of generations.

Like the Hebrews and Arabs, these people belonged to the Semitic race, and from whence they came has long been a matter of conjecture. Scholars are now agreed that Arabia had been their home and that there they had lived as shepherds and herdsmen. They poured in overwhelming forces into the

---

[1] This is a late popular etymology. Babel means "the gate of God," and has no connection with the Hebrew verb *balal* "to confound."

land of Chaldea, killing some of the inhabitants, driving others out of the country, and assimilating the rest.

The Chaldeans had reached a much higher degree of culture than their conquerors, who rapidly took on the civilization of their adopted country. As in England the Saxon and Norman for some generations after the conquest pursued each his native life and customs, little influenced by the other, so in Chaldea at first the Semitic herdsman followed his pastoral life outside the brick-walled cities of the Chaldeans.

Some have thought that an invasion of Cushites, or Ethiopians, had preceded the invasion of the Semites in Chaldea, and have claimed that the language, customs and culture in the land when conquered by the Semites was the result of a blending of Turanian and Ethiopian. The theory has been vigorously opposed by other authorities who contend that the invading Semites found only pure Turanian stock. However that may be, the civilization and culture of Chaldea, whether simply Turanian, or Turanian-Cushite, was soon taken on by the newcomers. Adopting the Chaldean language, they used it for all their inscriptions, writings and literature. Even after the speech of the people had become quite a different tongue, as a result of its assimilation with the Semitic, still in all written records the early Chaldean language—or Sumerian, as it is generally called—was alone used. Assyriologists have often noted that "while the language was Sumerian, the spirit of the writings was Semitic."

Because the land of Chaldea was so accessible, and offered advantages so superior to surrounding countries—plentiful water and a fertile soil,—it became a veritable bee-hive of humanity. When the Semites first came thither, they were a fierce, warlike people; but soon, under new conditions, they became peace-loving, as the Turanians before them had been. Shortly they were unable to hold the valley against new tribes that unceasingly swarmed into the country.

Prior to 2000 B.C. Ashur had been settled probably in part at least, by emigrants from the south who may have united with other Semites from North Mesopotamia and in time they founded the state of Assyria. Somewhat later, the ancestors of the Hebrews, according to one of the O. T. traditions, departed from the land of Chaldea for Harran in Mesopotamia, and later entered Canaan, on the east coast of the Mediterranean Sea. Each of these little bands founded states which developed such peculiar characteristics, that after the lapse of a few ages, it would scarcely have occurred to an observer that the ancestry, early environment, and traditions of all had been the same.

It was not strange, then, that the Hebrews of later time, trying to account for the diversity of languages and nations, made this swarming valley the site of the scattering of the tribes and the confusion of tongues.

Those who remained in Chaldea became a peaceful farming people, caring not at all for war. The Assyrians, while of the same stock, developed very differently. There were several reasons for this. First, their country was less accessible than Chaldea, whose shore was washed by the Persian Gulf, and so it suffered less from invasions, and was allowed to keep a more purely Semitic civilization. Again, having gone out from Chaldea before they became devoted to peaceful pursuits, the Assyrians retained and fostered their original warlike dispositions. The more temperate climate of Assyria was more invigorating and produced men of greater endurance than did the kingdom to the south.

Both Chaldea and Assyria alike, developed small states, each led by a city in which had been built a temple sacred to some local deity. Each community was presided over by one who combined the duties of king and priest.

Such was the condition of affairs when the first written records, more or less complete, bring some degree of certainty and less conjecture into the development of these nations. And here we arrive at the beginning of Mesopotamian history, properly so-called.

A JAR-SHAPED COFFIN OF CLAY.

CHAPTER IV.

CITY-STATES BEFORE THE RISE OF BABYLON.

We have seen that the Chaldeans were in time assimilated with the invading Semites, producing eventually a new nation. It is not to be supposed that this was at once accomplished, or that the dawn of authentic history found such a process completed. Rather, the Chaldeans held tenaciously to the south, the Semites kept farther to the north, and for many centuries the two races fought for dominance in the valley.

As early as 4500 B.C., a record inscribes one as "king of Kengi," but his kingdom probably included but a few cities added to his own.

Several cities had been founded at a remote time and these now grew rapidly in importance. Each was built around a temple dedicated to some particular divinity. Eridu worshipped the god EA, father of waters; Ur was sacred to Sin, the moon-god, and later kings, of the dynasty of Ur, added the name Sin to their own, as for example, Ine-Sin, Pur-Sin. Larsam was sacred to the sun-god Shamash; Uruk to the goddess Ishtar; Nippur to En-lil, father of the gods, and so on. Each city believed that its god—Bel or Lord—was the greatest of all gods, and often its inhabitants were inspired to go out to conquer other cities and territories in order to extend the prestige of the local deity. Probably at the same time the people were stimulated to fight because certain cities had grown up in the very heart of the fertile valley, while others had been obliged to locate in poorer sections. Naturally these last looked with envious eyes upon the richer soil of their neighbors, and desired to win it for themselves. Each city watched for the first sign of weakness in her sister cities, and when it appeared, tried at once to incorporate them into her own domains.

The political history of the Euphrates valley before the

dominance of Babylon is the history of these cities as they grew into little states. Some grew strong; others weakened and became tributary to the more vigorous few.

En-shag-kush-ana, "Lord of Kengiu," was the name of the first king to appear in the Babylonian records. Erech was probably his capital, and Nippur the religious center of his little kingdom. We have already connected Nippur with the excavations made by the University of Pennsylvania. The ruins there unearthed have enabled scholars to understand in the main sacred cities of Babylonia. En-shag-kush-ana was priest as well as king. Although his race was not mentioned, he was probably a Chaldean, like the people over whom he ruled.

A little to the north, a Semitic kingdom with the city Kish as its head, was growing rapidly in power, and threatened to absorb even Erech itself. On this account, Chaldeans attacked it and gained the victory, whereupon their god, En-lil of Nippur was celebrated in festival and his temple received numerous trophies of the triumph, since he had enabled those of the south to overcome the cruder Semitic city.

Their defeat only led the Semitic kingdom of Kish to strengthen its forces, and about 4000 B. C., under leadership of Lugalzaggisi, the vigor of the new race overcame the nearly expended force of the Chaldeans. This conquering Semitic king set forth his position thus: "Lugalzaggisi, king of Erech, king of the world, priest of Ana, hero of Nidaba, son of Ukush, he who is looked upon favorably by the faithful eye of En-lil.

"When En-lil, Lord of the lands, invested Lugalzaggisi with the kingdom of the world, and granted him success before the world, when he filled the land with his power, and subdued the country from the rise of the sun to the setting sun—at that time he straightened his path from the lower sea of the Tigris and Euphrates to the upper sea, and granted him the dominion of everything from the rising sun to the setting of the sun, and caused the countries to dwell in peace."[1]

For some generations the Semites now held the valley and the Chaldeans are lost sight of in surviving records.

[1] Hilprecht: Old Babylonian Inscriptions.

Then a southern kingdom, Shirpurla, with Sungir its chief city, became strong enough to throw off Semitic rule. This victory of the Chaldeans was widely celebrated in the annals of the waning race. Not only did they now gain the upper hand of all the cities in the valley, but they pushed into Elam, a kingdom to the east and dominated both it and its tributary lands.

While comparisons in history may sometimes be misleading, they often aid the student to better understand certain conditions. There is some similarity between these two races in this valley contending for supremacy—the stronger being sometimes held in check, the weaker gradually losing ground—in certain aspects, it calls to mind the period in English history when Saxons, Jutes and Angles struggled for leadership. The Saxons had developed the higher civilization; the Danes were the more vigorous and aggressive. Sometimes the Saxons would be able to set up their king, again the Danes would enthrone one of their number. Now the waning light of Saxon power would seem to be well-nigh spent, when suddenly it would burst out again with a flame that would illumine all England, only again to be eclipsed by the fresh strength of the other nation. Not to push the comparison further, either country offers a fair example of the usual course events take whenever two races, somewhat equal in strength, seek to gain the upper hand in a given territory.

A northern city, hitherto unmentioned, was to give the palm once more to the Semitic. Agade, the home-city of Shargani-shar-ali, or Sargon I.

Many legends cluster around this king, an early Semitic hero. Since our knowledge of him comes mainly through legendary sources, it is difficult to separate the grain from the chaff. A tradition which in the course of history has been related many times of men in many lands, was told first of this Semitic king.

"Sargon, the powerful king, King of Agade, am I.

"My mother was of low degree, my father I did not know.

"The brother of my father dwelt in the mountain.

"My city was Azupirani, situated on the banks of the Euphrates.

"(My) humble mother conceived me; in secret she brought me forth.

"She placed me in a bask-boat of rushes; with pitch she closed my door.

"She gave me over to the river, which did not (rise) over me.

"The river bore me along; to Akki, the irrigator, it carried me.

"Akki, the irrigator, brought me to land.

"Akki, the irrigator, reared me as his own son.

"Akki, the irrigator, appointed me his gardener.

"While I was gardener, Ishtar looked on me with love.

"Four years I ruled the kingdom."[2]

Sargon I. and his son, Naram Sin, had great capacity for organization. They were prolific builders, and bricks have been found bearing their names and titles. The material for their temples they brought some distance—the famous cedars of Lebanon forming the beams. Sargon was called "Lord of Nippur, Shirpurla, Kish, Babylon and Uruk. Naram Sin extended his sway to the Mediterranean on the west, east into Elam, and south into Arabia and the isles of the Persian Gulf. He took for the first time the title: " King of the Four World-Regions. His vast kingdom thus built up disappeared, however, as quickly as it came into being, and after some changes, Ur became the capital center. Three thousand eight hundred B. C. has been accepted as the date of Sargon's reign and this is the first definite date in Babylonian history.

The kings of the Ur dynasty erected several temples, and because Ur was easy of access, they imported many of their building materials. Dolerite was brought from Arabia, cedar from Syria, gold and precious stones from the east. This town was sacred to Sin, the moon-god, and several hymns praising this deity have been found.

Isin, Erech, and other cities strove now for leadership, and internal dissensions offered opportunity for the Elamites on the east, now advancing on a wave of prosperity, to invade the land. It is known that they advanced as far as Erech, and carried off a statue of the goddess Nana. They set up their own king, whose line continued on the throne for some time. One of these invading kings called himself: " exalter of

---

[2] Trans. quoted by Goodspeed: Hist. of the Bab. and Assy., p. 62.

Ur, king of Larsa, king of Sumer and Accad." Under Elamite administration, temples were built and the religious and commercial centers continued to grow.

Of this whole period Maspero has said: "We have here the dust of history rather than history itself; here an isolated individual makes his appearance in the record of his name, to vanish when we attempt to lay hold of him; there the stem of a dynasty which breaks abruptly off, pompous preambles, devout formulas, dedications of objects of buildings, here or there the account of some battle, or the indication of some foreign country with which relations of friendship or commerce were maintained—these are the scanty materials of which to construct a narrative."

To summarize the period as a whole, we may note that thus far no united kingdom had been evolved. To weld that together was the work of the next period. This was, on the other hand, an age of city-states, each one contesting for leadership. While the struggle began with the mere hope of annexing cities in the valley, it expanded to include outlying lands as well. The assimilation of the two races was, generally speaking, effected, and henceforth the Chaldeans disappear as a distinct element of the country, having been absorbed politically by the Semites.

A Part of a Hymn to the Moon-God.[3]

(Composed in the city of Ur before the age of Abraham.)

Father, long-suffering and full of forgiveness,
Whose hands uphold the life of all mankind!
First born, omnipotent, whose heart is immensity,
There is none who may fathom it!

In heaven, who is supreme?
Thou alone, Thou art supreme.
On earth, who is supreme?
Thou alone, Thou art supreme.

As for Thee, Thy will is made known in heaven,
And the angels bow their faces.
As for Thee, Thy will is made known upon earth,
And the spirits kiss the ground.

[3] Translated by Sayce.

CHAPTER V.

Dominance of Babylon, 2100-1100 B.C.

In early times Babylon had not been a city of sufficient size to demand royal attention. No king had thought it of enough importance to include with his enumerated possessions, although in all probability, it was founded as early as 4000 B.C.—perhaps earlier still. Sumu-abi was its first king, but of him and his immediate successors, we know little. The sixth king was destined to bring greatness to his city and to the whole country—for it was he who united the many states of Babylonia into one strong kingdom and drove the usurping Elamites from the throne.

"Hammurabi, sixth king of Babylon, ruled in the twenty-first century B.C. His reign and the reigns of his family were regarded by the Babylonians as their "Golden Age." Down to the last days of Babylon, Babylonian kings emulated his example, modelling even their inscriptions after his.

How Hammurabi freed the land from Elamite rule is not known, but his name was soon established as an able soldier. He assumed the titles: King of Sumer and Accad, King of the Four-Quarters of the World, King of Babylon. Having annexed all the little city-states to his original kingdom of Babylon, the capital city gave its name to the whole country. To make this union lasting, Hammurabi himself appointed officers of administration for each political division of the kingdom, and so made the entire system dependent upon the government at the capital. The pre-eminence now given the capital turned the tide of commerce and traffic from other places and made Babylon the great center, not only for matters of government, but for industrial and social life as well.

Hammurabi was not only a distinguished warrior, but a statesman. When he had made secure his recently united kingdom, he turned to internal improvements. A post-envoy system for royal messages was established. This tended to make the roads and highways between different parts of the country safe. He established royal granaries in the valley of the Euphrates—as we have found them maintained in the valley of the Nile—to store grain for use in time of famine.

As each succeeding city was exalted to leadership in Babylonia, we have found that the patron deity of that community rose to highest place in the pantheon. Originally, Marduk was accorded a minor position in the category of gods. By enabling Babylon to gain supremacy over all other cities, he had now proven himself greatest of all gods; so while Nippur and other religious centers, long established, retained their deities and their cults, there came forward a large priesthood devoted to the worship of Marduk. These priests, centered as they were around Babylon, probably had much to do with that city's rapid progress in becoming the center of culture, art and literary effort. Long years after, when the kings of warlike Assyria had added Babylonia to their numerous possessions, they turned to the archives of this city for its literary productions and one of the most productive periods was the reign of Hammurabi.

Perhaps the most stupendous undertaking of this king was the construction of a vast canal which reclaimed a large tract of land, long unproductive. An inscription left by him has been found, and sets forth his effort in this fashion:

"Hammurabi, the powerful king, king of Babylonia, when Anu and Bel gave unto me to rule the land of Sumer and Accad, and with their scepter filled my hands, I dug the canal Hammurabi, the Blessing-of-Men, which bringeth the water of the overflow into the land of Sumer and Accad. Its banks upon both sides I made arable land; much seed I scattered upon it. Lasting water I provided for the land of Sumer and Accad. The land of Sumer and Accad, its separated peoples I united, with blessings and abundance I endowed them, in peaceful dwellings I made them to live."[1]

He was a tireless builder, spending much care in repairing old temples and constructing new ones. Indeed King Hammurabi stands forth, after four thousand years have passed, as a ruler of exceptional executive ability. Prosperity long attended his people because of the personal supervision he gave to all branches of the administration.

[1] Quoted in Rogers: Hist. of Baby. and Assy., 391.

Among the lasting benefits assured his subjects was means of getting legal redress. A court of appeals was instituted at Babylon to which any citizen might come to state his wrongs. He codified the laws of the land in 282 laws and inscribed them on monoliths, one of which was found ten years ago in Susa, whither it had been carried by the Elamites about 1100 B.C. In the prologue to the Code he states, "When Marduk sent me to rule the people . I established law and justice in the land and promoted the welfare of the people."

Long after his death his son and successors reaped the benefits of Hammurabi's splendid rule, and the memory of his strength and capacity held the country in check as long as his house endured. Probably for some time before the close of this prosperous era, which came to an end cir. 1700 B.C., mountaineers threatened the eastern borders, and the death of the last king of the dynasty was the occasion for an invasion of the Kassites, a people who emerged from Elam-Media. They seem to have been one of the many bands of mountaineers who gained a livelihood from the products of the mountainous regions and by frequent plundering raids directed against those living on either side of their strongholds. They well knew that Babylon's long devotion to the arts of peace had weakened her military strength, and regarded the time as favorable for winning the fertile valleys for themselves. At all events, they placed their king upon the throne. The inhabitants of southern Babylonia were never possessed of strong patrotism. So long as the land was allowed to rest in peace and the taxes were not increased, there seems to have been no especial interest on the part of the people generally as to who wore the crown. The material development of the country did not suffer long on this occasion, and for nearly 600 years the Kassite dynasty ruled in Babylon. They rapidly took on the culture of their newly acquired state, built temples and directed their attention to the prosperity of the land. As time went on, they wellnigh ceased to be regarded as usurpers. One of their kings set forth his titles thus: "I am Agumkakrime, the son of Tashshigurumash; the illustrious descendant of god Shuqamuna; called by Anu and Bel, Ea and Marduk, Sin and Shamash; the powerful hero of Ishtar, the warrior among the gods.

"I am a king of wisdom and prudence; a king who grants

hearing and pardon; the son of Tashshigurumash; the descendant of Abiru . the crafty warrior; the first son of the great Agum; an illustrious, royal scion who holds the reins of the nation (and is) a mighty shepherd.

"I am king of the country of Kashshu and of the Akkadians; king of the wide country of Babylon, who settles the numerous people in Ashnunak; the King of Padan and Alman; the king of Gutium, a foolish nation; (a king) who makes obedient to him the four regions, and a favorite of the great gods."

This enumeration of tributary lands shows these kings to have been good warriors.

For a hundred years before the end of the Kassite dynasty, the kingdom of Assyria, founded before 3000 B.C. in all probability, was growing in strength and importance. When the Babylonians were unable to hold out against invading kings, naturally the Assyrians felt in no way bound to render the tribute they had paid Babylonia to usurping foreigners, and took advantage of the occasion to assert their sovereignty.

As has been previously noted, the Assyrians were of pure Semitic stock, and, as their own artists represent them, apparently had not intermarried with the Chaldeans, as the Semites farther south had done. They were warlike in disposition, and knew neither the luxuries of the southern state nor its enervating climate. They had even become powerful enough to make treaties with the rulers of Babylon regarding disputed lands, and this fact in itself was significant. For some considerable period after the invasion of the Kassites, Assyria was concerned with her own affairs, but the time was coming when she would make her power felt in the mother country.

Generally speaking, the Kassite rule was an age of peace. Among the Tell el Amarna letters, unearthed upon the ancient site of the "Horizon of the Sun's Disk," correspondence has been found between some of these Asiatic rulers and the kings of Egypt. The letters open with the preliminaries customary in oriental correspondence: "To Kadashman-Bel, king of Kardunyash, my brother; thus saith Amenophis, the great king, the king of Egypt, thy brother: with me it is well. May it be well with thee, with thy house, with thy wives, with thy children, with thy nobles, with thy horses and with thy chariots, and with thy land may it be well; with me may it be well, with my house with my wives, with my children, with my nobles, with my horses, with my chariots, with my troops, and with my land, may it be very well." Regarding this particular letter and others of the same period, Rogers says: "No historical material of great moment is offered in these letters. They reveal a period of relative peace and prosperity, and deal, in considerable measure, with the little courtesies and amenities of life. It is, for example, curious to find the Babylonian king reproving the king of Egypt for not having sent an ambassador to inquire for him when he was ill. When kings had time for such courtesies, and could only excuse themselves for failing to observe them on the ground of their ignorance of the illness, and the great distance to be covered on the journey, there must have been freedom from war and from all distress at home and abroad."[1]

It was not destined to long continue peaceful, however. By 1285 B.C. the Assyrian king felt himself powerful enough to invade Babylonia. Penetrating even to the capital itself, he carried away the statue of the god Marduk—a great indignity. He allowed the Babylonia king to become his vassal. This state of affairs continued for seven years, whereupon the Babylonians succeeded in driving the Assyrians north again, taking from them some of the territory they had seized. When next the Assyrians threatened, the Semites instituted a revolution, forced the Kassites from the throne, and established the dynasty of Isin.

Now began the struggle for supremacy in the valley, waged by two great nations. The strength of Babylonia was waning, but their king, Nebuchadnezzar I., held the kingdom together with a strong hand. He only delayed the inevitable. The future belonged to the more vigorous kingdom to the north, and to her power Babylonia soon fell subservient.

To follow the main thread of activity in the Euphrates valley, we must now turn to Assyria, while the life so characteristic of Babylon continued until it could be said: "No capital in the world has ever been the center of so much power, wealth, and culture for so vast a period of time."

[1] Rogers: Hist. of Baby. and Assy., Vol. I., p. 418.

WINGED LION.

CHAPTER VI.

Beginnings of the Assyrian Empire.

The beginnings of the Assyrian state are lost in obscurity. Nineveh was possibly founded before 3000 B. C., but like Babylon, its origin is not known. Asshur was long the important city of the country, overshadowing the later capital.

About 1490 B. C. Thutmose III. pushed into Asia and roused the western portion of that continent with his conquests. Assyria, like many other weak states, hastened to send gifts to the conquering pharaoh. These signified submission, and Thothmes gave no further evidences of his military power. The next mention of Assyria occurs when the state had become sufficiently important to enter into a treaty with the Kassite king of Babylonia, regarding disputed territories. As we have already noted, Assyria, long subservient to the older kingdom, felt in no way bound to submit to the foreign rule of Kassite princes, and had already established her own independence, which was acknowledged by the Babylonian king when he negotiated a treaty with her. Later, the daughter of an Assyrian king was married to the king of Babylonia. Their son came to the throne at an early age, and the Babylonians, seeing an intrigue to allow Assyrian influences to dominate their land, made way with the boy-king, substituting another in his place. Thereupon the Assyrian ruler, grandfather of the murdered prince, invaded Babylonia, killed the monarch popularly crowned, and placed his own candidate upon the throne. The result of this Assyrian interference was not immediately important, but it was the first of a long series of difficulties between the two countries, which ended ultimately in the recognition of the Assyrian king as ruler of Babylonia as well.

About 1290 B. C., troubles having again arisen, the northern king came once more to the city of Babylon, this time carrying away the statue of the god Marduk, as we have already seen. He left Assyrian officials in the land as his representatives. Seven years later, these were driven out by a popular uprising of the Babylonians, who seized certain outlying districts which had recently been appropriated by the Assyrians. When the Kassite princes were finally dethroned, Nebuchadnezzar I., of the dynasty of Isin, was strong enough to hold the Babylonian state intact against the power which constantly threatened at the north.

To this point we had come in the preceding chapter, and this recast of the situation is made that we may have its essential features clearly in mind.

Coming now to the reign of Tiglath-Pileser I., 1120 B.C., we meet one of the great warriors of antiquity, and with his administration, a new era opened for Assyria. The first five years of his reign were occupied with campaigns to the north, east, and west, in which directions tribes had been menacing the borders of his kingdom. In these campaigns we see the beginnings of those cruel, relentless punishments, amounting often to mere savagery,—which fill the pages of Assyrian history. These were meted out to all who failed to submit to Assyrian arms. An inscription commemorating the victories of the warrior says: "With their corpses I strewed the mountain passes and the heights. I took away their property, a countless booty. Six thousand warriors, the remnant of their army, who had fled before my arms, embraced my feet. I carried them away and counted them among the inhabitants of my own land." And again: "In those days, Asshur, the Lord, sent me, who knows no victor in war, no rival in battle, whose rule is righteous over the four quarters of the world, towards distant kingdoms on the shores of the Upper Sea, which knew not submission, and I went forth. Across impracticable heights and through precipitous defiles the inside of which no king had beheld before, I passed. Through sixteen mountain ridges I marched in my chariot where the ground was good; where it was inaccessible, I cleared away with axes, and bridges for the passage of my troops I constructed excellently well. I crossed the Euphrates. Twenty-three kings of the land of Nairi, assembled their chariots and troops in the midst of their countries and came forth to do battle against me. By the impetuous onslaught of my mighty arms I conquered them. I destroyed their numerous armies like Raman's thundershower; with the corpses of their warriors I strewed the mountain heights and the enclosures of their cities as with straw. Their 120 chariots I destroyed in the battle; sixty kings of the lands of Nairi, with those who had come to their assistance, I pursued to the Upper Sea. Their great cities I took, their spoils, their possessions I carried off, their towns I burned with fire, I destroyed, laid them waste, made heaps of them and land for the plough. Numerous herds of steeds, colts, calves, and implements without number I carried home. The kings of the lands of the Nairi my hand captured alive, all of them. To these same kings I granted favor. Captive and bound, I released them before Shamash, my lord, and made them swear allegiance forever. Their children, the offspring of their royalty, I took as hostages. I imposed on them a tribute of 1,200 steeds and 2,000 bulls and dismissed them to their respective countries. The vast lands of Nairi I took in all their extent, and all their kings I brought low to my feet."

When five years, filled with similar campaigns, had passed, a large number of tribes paid tribute to Assyria. Before this period, Calab had served as capital. Tiglath-Pileser now rebuilt Asshur. Rare trees were brought from conquered lands, to beautify the town. Temples were restored, to the honor of the gods. Of the restoration of the temple of Ana and Adad, the king caused to be inscribed: " I built it from foundation to roof larger and grander than before, and erected also two great towers, fitting ornaments of their great divinities. The splendid temple, a brilliant and magnificent dwelling, the habitation of their joys, the house for their delight, shining as bright as the stars on heaven's firmament and richly decorated with ornaments through the skill of my artists, I planned, devised, and thought out, built and completed. I made its interior brilliant like the dome of the heavens; decorated its walls like the splendor of the rising stars, and make it grand with resplendent brilliancy. I reared its temple towers to heaven, and completed its roof with burned brick; located therein the upper terrace containing the chamber of their great divinities; and led into the interior Anu and Adad, the great gods, and made them to dwell in their lofty house, thus gladdening the heart of their great divinities."[1]

The memory of this stern warrior lived long after his death, holding tribes in subjection and enabling his successors to rule

[1] Quoted in Goodspeed, p. 171.

in comparative peace. The greatness of the future kingdom has been attributed in no small measure to the foundations laid by Tiglath-Pileser I.

A period of reaction followed. Tribute, which had been paid only for fear of a strong, well disciplined army, was no longer forthcoming. Babylonia and Assyria have left so few records for these years that they are almost sure to have been years of inaction. On the alluvial bottoms of Babylonia, a new dynasty arose, known as the dynasty of the Sea Lands. Both the rulers and the subjects they governed were comparatively newcomers, who easily gained the upper hand in the decadent state, especially as no interference came from Assyria.

While the inertia of Babylonia allowed the latest comer to rule, so the inaction of Assyria allowed countries on the west— Syria and Palestine—to gain strength. On the north, the Armenians, a nation of traders, extended their territories and their commercial affairs.

In 950 B. C. Tiglath-Pileser II. became king. From this time forward records become more numerous, and we are able to trace the stages of development with greater accuracy. Assyria once more wakened to her possibilities, while Babylonia continued in her helpless, prostrate condition. Nothing of note is chronicled until Asshur-natsirpal III. became king in 885 B. C. He promptly marched against the earlier conquered tribes on the north who no longer paid their tribute. He slaughtered a goodly number at the start, and this report spread like wildfire among the tribes, who hastened to send gifts. For some years he continued to bring countries under tribute, quelling revolts with such severity as only an Assyrian could have directed. One inscription is sufficient to let us understand his customary procedure:

"I drew near to the city of Tela. The city was very strong; three walls surrounded it. The inhabitants trusted to their strong walls and numerous soldiers; they did not come down or embrace my feet. With battle and slaughter I assaulted and took the city. Three thousand warriors I slew in battle. Their booty and possessions, cattle, sheep, I carried away; many captives I burned with fire. Many of their soldiers I took alive; of some I cut off hands and limbs; of others the noses, ears, and arms; of many soldiers I put out the eyes. I reared a column of the living and a column of heads. I hung up on high their heads on trees in the vicinity of their city. Their boys and girls I burned up in the flame. I devastated the city, dug it up, in the fire burned it; I annihilated it."[2]

Babylonia and nations on the east united against the relentless conqueror, but in vain. They were defeated and some of their cities laid waste.

Having carried on campaigns in this fashion for some time, Asshur-natsirpal found himself at the head of a large army, well disciplined, invincible, inured to slaughter and devastation—a menace to the state if kept idle, and if disbanded, removing at a stroke the fear which prompted the payment of tribute.

Something should perhaps be said of tribute, which we find kings demanding of all subjected people. The habit of compelling the payment of tribute was tolerated only in an age when might made right. None of the earliest nations gave anything in exchange for tribute exacted. No effort was made to defend tributary tribes from the attacks of other tribes. Tribute was merely the price paid by a people for the privilege of being in other respects left alone. A king who dreamed of a wide reaching empire, tried to bring as many nations as possible under his tribute. The payment of this tribute was the formal acknowledgment of the emperor's over-lordship. Until the age of Persian dominance, no monarch was able to do much more than compel the annual payment in joining alien territories to his own. Assyria attempted on a smaller scale what Persia effected, but little more than the *conception* of a great empire was contributed by Assyria; it was given reality by Persian conquerors.

Asshur-natsirpal realized the only course open to him was that of conquest, and to that he now turned. Setting out for the west, his march was a continual triumph. His reputation was so well established, and the strength of his army so well understood that tribes on either side sent gifts as soon as he drew near.

Reaching the Euphrates, he was unable to make any ade-

[2] Quoted in Goodspeed, p. 197.

quate provision for the transportation of his troops. The Assyrians were an inland people and knew nothing of maritime affairs. Each soldier was expected to get himself across the stream, partly swimming, partly buoyed up by inflated skins of animals.

Drawing near the Mediterranean Sea, he found that commerce occupied the people in that region to the exclusion of war. Indeed, they would pay heavily to avoid war, which seriously interfered with their trade. The king of the Hittites —once a nation of importance but at this time retaining little of its former strength—stated his position very frankly. His policy was direct and simple. He was willing to pay down the sum of twenty talents of silver, one hundred talents of copper, two hundred and fifty talents of iron, along with chains and beads of gold and much other treasure, if he were simply let alone. National pride counted for nothing. The primary desire was to get the Assyrians out of the country as soon as possible; and well might they pay a heavy tribute to gain such a boon as that."[3]

It was apparent that there would be no particular opportunity for military skill against people of such convictions as these. The Assyrian army moved on and at length drew near the green slopes of the Lebanon, in sight of the Mediterranean waters, dotted over by Phoenician ships, busily plying their trade. While no city was besieged, no blood shed, the effect was marked upon the entire region. All acknowledged Asshurnatsirpal as conqueror. In some cases, Assyrian officials were stationed to keep the home government in touch with these distant parts; in other places, Assyrian colonists were induced to settle, far from their native homes. Cities were walled by the labor of Assyrian soldiers, and were temporarily protected by Assyrian fortifications. While such demonstrations had a lasting effect on the western states, the Assyrian king, on his part, was deeply impressed by one thing, and this omened ill for their future; the people of this region cared more to protect their commerce than their country. They valued the protection of their wares above the honor and independence of their respective states. We shall see that this one fact as understood by the Assyrian king developed a definite western policy.

[3] Rogers: Hist. of Baby. and Assy., Vol. II, 64.

Unable to supply military action for his troops, the king set them to cutting down trees—cedar, cypress, and juniper. These were taken to Assyria. The army returned home without approaching Damascus, where opposition was certain to be strong. Too much glory had been won to have it overshadowed by any chance issue.

While the western conquest had been in progress, officers at home had been carrying out the king's plans by rebuilding Calah, and constructing a large canal. The king now returned to personally supervise the construction of a royal palace.

"A palace for my royal dwelling-place, for the glorious seat of my royalty, I founded forever and splendidly planned it. I surrounded it with a cornice of copper. Sculptures of the creatures of land and sea carved in alabaster, I made and placed them at the doors. Lofty doorposts of   wood I made, and sheathed them with copper and set them up in the gates. Thrones of costly woods, dishes of ivory containing silver, gold, lead, copper, and iron, the spoil of my hand, taken from conquered lands I deposited therein."

In 860 B. C. Asshur-natsirpal died, leaving the future to regard him as the most ferocious king in all Assyrian history; yet he had accomplished more for his country than any of his predecessors, and left it more united and in a more prosperous condition. His son, Shalmaneser II., like the father, found himself obliged to keep an army active, collecting tributes and making fresh conquests. He repeated the westward march, and met an alliance formed against him at Damascus. To that city's forces were joined those of Israel and of Phoenicia. While their armies were defeated, no tribute was exacted, and this fact in itself shows that the victory was not complete.

This first coalition formed against Assyria, made up of Mediterranean peoples, is important. Such a union might have effectually stayed the great military power of the age had not jealousies among the states themselves hindered permanent union. By 846 B. C. the alliance had been broken, and Jehu of Israel sent gifts to the Assyrian ruler. This furnished him his first hold on the independence of the Hebrews.

The next hundred years saw a union of Babylonia and Assyria, and an attempt, on the part of one king at least, to blot out all differences between the two peoples by showing among other things that their religions were the same. To give weight to the claim, he constructed temples in Nineveh, after the model of those of Babylon.

In the following chapter we shall note the height of Assyrian dominance and the proudest years of her history.

FLOCKS AND CAPTIVE WOMEN CARRIED AWAY.

CHAPTER VII.

Assyria—A Powerful Empire.

A dynasty of weak kings followed and seemed to be leading Assyria on to ruin, but in 746 B. C. the people rose up in rebellion, driving them out and crowning a ruler selected by themselves. It is supposed that the one they chose had already proven his worth and capacity either at the head of a large division of the army, or possibly in the management of some Assyrian province. In any event, he was firmly established at once and spent no time trying to inspire his subjects with awe. His own name has not been recorded but he took the crown name of Tiglath-Pileser III., seeking to emulate him who had borne it first. He is the Pul of the Old Testament.

Babylonia demanded first attention. The Armenians had established themselves in the southern part of the kingdom and threatened to crush out the old life and culture by their rapidly increasing numbers.

Tiglath-Pileser III. was hailed by the native Babylonians as a deliverer. Forcing the usurpers back, he divided the former kingdom into four provinces, placing Assyrian governors over each. He also brought many captives into these provinces to make their homes, hoping in this way to weaken the national spirit which tried every little while to gain back old-time freedom for the state.

The Medes on the east required some curbing, but their independence was not destroyed. These matters attended to, Tiglath-Pileser III. was free to give attention to the west.

The city of Arpad stood in the way of Assyrian progress and since it refused tribute, it was besieged. The plucky town held out for two long years, but when finally taken, was laid waste with great slaughter. All neighboring tribes hastened to send tribute, and were incorporated into the Assyrian empire.

Heretofore we have seen people brought under tribute and some faint efforts made to hold them. Now we have reached the imperial period of Assyrian development when the government, established at home, sought to increase its actual possessions abroad, and to bind them to the original kingdom with strong ties.

An alliance had been made among the sea-coast states, with Judah at the head. This had been formed, of course, to stay the western tide of Assyrian power. Notwithstanding, the king of Samaria yielded the moment the Assyrian army drew near, paying the tribute with no display of force. Judah alone seems to have remained unyielding and undisturbed. Thirty thousand captives were brought into these districts to find new homes, while many of the natives were deported to make room for them.

Several methods were employed by Assyria to make conquests lasting. If a tribe or city acknowledged the Assyrian king as conqueror, no recourse was made to arms; an annual tribute was usually imposed and an Assyrian governor placed in the territory to hold revolts in check and to generally represent the empire, of which the province was now a part. The native king was frequently allowed to rule over the people, even though his main duty in some instances seems to have been to raise the required tribute. If, on the other hand, a tribe or city resisted, a war or siege followed. One battle might reduce a tribe to submission; in the case of a city, all supplies were shut off, and eventually the inhabitants would be starved into surrender, whereupon, the city was often made "land for the plough" by the exasperated king, and the people subjected to all sorts of cruel punishments.

When a kingdom was conquered, it was thought desirable to destroy its old patriotism by removing all chances for its development. With that end in view, some of its citizens would be sent out of the country to seek homes in other lands, while those from distant regions would be brought in to take their places. Naturally the newcomers knew nothing of the traditions of their newly found country and cared not at all to fight for them. In this way, nations ceased to retain their venerated customs, but as the kings often record: "I made them all to speak one language"—and that Assyrian. One far-reaching effect of this policy was that when a revolt did break out in some district, it no longer spread like wildfire in all directions, but the governor of the province was himself able to put down any uprising, and the colonists recently imported, caring nothing for the older inhabitants, could be depended upon to help him.

Tiglath-Pileser III. turned now to Gaza, whose king fled to Egypt there to get aid in behalf of his state. Deserted, the city soon surrendered and the Assyrian king, having sent the old gods home to Assyria, installed Assyrian gods in the temples. Thence he marched to Palestine.

He who had held out against Assyria before was dead and a weak king now ruled in Judah. Had the kings of Samaria and Damascus formed an alliance with Judah, the power of Assyria might yet have been broken; instead they united their forces to invade Judah and appropriate the territory of the weak king for themselves. Isaiah, the great statesman of the Hebrews, counselled the ruler in vain. To protect himself against his aggressive neighbors he appealed to Assyria for help. This drew Tiglath-Pileser III. to Samaria and Damascus, while Judah, sending gifts, was not at this time molested. The Samarians themselves rose up against their king. Having killed him, they asked the Assyrian ruler to allow Hoshea to rule over them as an Assyrian vassal. This sifted the opposition down to Damascus, which city prepared for a siege. Some five hundred outlying towns were laid waste and their inhabitants sent into other districts. Not all the army being constantly required to guard the besieged town, part of the troops marched into Arabia, demanding tribute and receiving it. In 732 B. C. Damascus fell and became an Assyrian province.

By this time, Babylonia was in a state of turmoil. Under Assyrian government the people had at first been free to develop their arts of peace, and literature had flourished. Then the Chaldeans to the south, established originally in the region around the gulf, known once as Chaldea—tried again to rule the land. In 726 B.C. Tiglath-Pileser III. marched into Babylonia, where, taking the hands of the god Marduk, he was crowned king of Babylonia. According to the ancient custom, he who wore this crown must return each year and celebrate this same ceremony. Two years later Tiglath-Pileser having again performed the rites, died before the year elapsed.

During the short reign which followed interest again reverted to the west. Hoshea refused to pay tribute in 725 B.C., looking to Egypt for help. He was taken captive and Samaria made ready for a siege. Strange to say, the town held out for three years and the king of Assyria died before it was taken. Sargon II. at once succeeded. (722-705 B. C.) He again was not of royal blood and he too chose a popular crown name.

Samaria soon fell, and quite possibly neither the besieging army or the stricken town knew of any change in rulers. Twenty-seven thousand two hundred and ninety of the inhabitants of Samaria—the flower of the land,—were deported to the Median mountains, while colonists were brought in from Babylonia and other provinces to take their places. This loss it was impossible to retrieve. Assyrian governors were set over the land, now merely an Assyrian province.

In 721 B. C. attention focused once more in Babylonia, where the Chaldeans had again usurped the crown. In the battle Sargon waged, the result was so indecisive that neither side gained much. The usurpers were simply checked.

Suddenly an alliance was formed in the west, made up of stricken Samaria, Damascus and Gaza. Sargon marched rapidly west before their armies were ready, and defeated them separately and carried "the ten tribes into captivity." Now again more strangers were brought in, and more citizens sent out. It is little wonder, after all these mixtures of peoples, that in later years the Jews regarded the Samarians as not of their kin, but an inferior race, so that in the time of Christ one could say: "How is it that thou, being a Jew, askest drink of me, which am a woman of Samaria? For the Jews have no dealings with the Samaritans!"

It was during this campaign that the Hittite king was taken prisoner and his kindgom, once so powerful, was merged into the Assyrian Empire.

Not long after, Hezekiah, king of Judah, attempted to stir up an opposition to the Assyrian tribute payment. Isaiah, the far-seeing statesman, again counselled against it,—vainly to be sure, yet constantly, for this was an unfavorable moment. As might have been foreseen, the coalition was short-lived.

Sargon's work in time of peace was extensive. He built a palace, like his predecessors, but outdoing them, he constructed a royal city for its location. This was a custom new in Assyria, but we have seen that it was usual in Egypt, during the Middle and New Empires. Choosing a spot not far from Nineveh, at the base of a mountain, he had a rectangular area laid out, its corners pointing to the four cardinal points. First temples were built to the gods, whose favor he sought in every possible way, even going to the length of paying for the site of the city, and compensating those who asked no money. After the temples, the palace itself arose—built of ivory, palm-wood, cedar, cypress, having gates of wood overlaid with bronze. The eight gates of the city were named for the eight leading divinities, the walls for Asshur, and the ramparts for Niveb. An invocation was inscribed to the gods: "May Asshur bless this city, and this palace! May he invest these constructions with an eternal brightness! May he grant that they shall be inhabited until the remotest days! May the sculptured bull, the guarding spirit, stand forever before his face! May he keep watch here night and day, and may his feet never move from this threshold!" The palace is said to have contained "twenty-four bulls in relief and two miles of sculptured slabs." Since the work was only begun in 712 B. C., and he came to reside within in 707 B. C., he was apparently able to command a large army of workmen. This was the palace whose ruins Botta unearthed in 1846, and each part remaining appeared to be as perfect as workmanship could make it.

The new city was peopled in a unique way. "People from the four quarters of the world, of foreign speech, of manifold tongues, who had dwelt in mountains and valleys,
whom I, in the name of Asshur my lord, by the might of my arms had carried into captivity, I commanded to speak one language and settled them therein. Sons of Asshur of wise insight in all things, I placed over them, to watch over them; learned men and scribes to teach them the fear of God and the King."

It is supposed that Sargon II. was murdered in 705 B. C. and his son Sennacherib succeeded to the throne. He had observed his father's difficulties in keeping order in Babylonia, and had concluded before ever he came to the throne that to indulge the pride of Babylon by longer conforming to her venerated custom of crowning her king each year—thus requiring his annual appearance,—was mere folly. He believed that Babylonia, whatever her history, was now an Assyrian province, and hence the king of Assyria was her king. So he himself did not go at all to Babylon, but was merely crowned in Nineveh as King of Assyria. Now the Babylonians, far from submitting to this train of logic, in course of a brief time, crowned their own king. Thereupon the Chaldeans, ever watchful for an opportunity to re-establish their power, set up a ruler in the same country, farther south. In 702 B. C., because of this confusion, Sennacherib marched to Babylon, laid waste many Chaldean cities, deported 200,000 people and crowned as king a young nobleman, Babylonian by birth but educated at the Assyrian court. Having so vigorously asserted his strength, he was soon needed in the west.

The situation there was critical. Hezekiah, king of Judah, had successfully conducted a war against the Philistines, and was therefore regarded by his subjects as a great and mighty warrior. There was a strong faction in the kingdom who opposed the annual payment of tribute to Assyria and who believed that against them also Hezekiah might assert himself and free them from this hated tribute service. Isaiah, understanding the vast difference in the resources of the two countries, counselled against a war, but it remained for future generations to discern the clear, far sighted reasoning of this statesman, and the king, even had he chosen to heed good counsel, was shortly plunged into a war which was the popular demand of his people. Jerusalem prepared for a siege, and water was brought into the city from some distance by an aqueduct. Egypt promised aid, for the Ethiopian king who ruled that country and the native princes who were struggling to regain the throne, all felt that an opportunity opened in this way to win glory in Asia which should serve as a lever to them at home. Judah had yet to learn how fallen was this ancient state and how incapable of giving material assistance.

The rebellion spread, for freedom was dear to nations in those days when submission meant at least heavy tributes, and often deportation and a dismantled country. In the city of Ekron the people, stirred by a hope of independence, seized the Assyrian governor and led him captive to Hezekiah. As usual, the Assyrian king made forced marches and appeared before he was expected and before the armies were massed, so he had the less difficult task of defeating each nation separately. Tyre, one of the rebel cities, was first attacked. It was not possible to materially injure her, since her defenses on the sea were strong; Sidon surrendered and an Assyrian ruler was set over the city; now many of the allies were consumed with fear and dropped out of the coalition, sending tribute with all haste. In Ekron those who had led the rebellion were killed or deported. As had long been the case, the Assyrian king was meeting with brief resistance. Judah held out, however. Hezekiah watched for re-enforcements from Egypt, but before they drew near, Sennacherib opened battle, winning with heavy losses. Hezekiah withdrew his forces into Jerusalem to undergo a siege, while the Assyrian army turned to meet Egyptian allies and captured the leaders. Forty-six cities around Jerusalem were taken, and when it seemed futile to longer hold out, Hezekiah sent an embassy to Sennacherib to ask for terms of peace. A sum of money approaching $1,000,000 in our money, was demanded, and although it was raised with difficulty in Judah, it was paid over to the conqueror. However, Hezekiah did not come out to meet Sennacherib and acknowledge him as overlord, and the Assyrian king, feeling that his victory was yet indecisive, dispatched his most trusted generals to demand the surrender of Jerusalem. Meanwhile he marched with the great mass of Assyrian forces to intercept more Egyptian armies now approaching. Encamping at Pelusium, a place noted for its plagues before that day and since, the army was stricken in the night. In a few days only a remnant of the great force remained and a homeward march was begun at once.

The Hebrews, according to their custom, interpreted this issue to signify direct intervention of Providence in their behalf. Instead of being led captives of Assyrian provinces and having their land devastated, they gained fame and glory by the expedition. The Egyptians also claimed a victory— all because of the pestilence.

The two accounts of the campaign, the Hebrew version of the story as chronicled in the Old Testament, and the Assyrian version, as translated from their tablets, are both so interesting that we quote them at length. Such differences as they show are easily explained in view of the standpoints of each writer.

Returning home, Babylonia was found to be in a state of insubordination, having once more asserted her independence. Sennacherib now placed his own son on the throne, but still difficulties multiplied. At last the Babylonians united with the Chaldeans, their long-sworn enemies, against Assyria. At this juncture, in 689 B. C., Sennacherib determined to strike at the root of the trouble. He marched into the land and set fire to the city of Babylon, after plundering its temples and palaces. Over the desolate site of the city he then turned a canal, converting the region into a swamp.

It is almost staggering even at this remote time to think of the pride and glory of Babylonian life, the splendor of its palaces, the wonder of its temples, being thus wantonly destroyed. Long periods of peace in the kingdom had given opportunity for art and literature to develop, and there can be no question that countless records of priceless worth were destroyed by the deed of this fierce Assyrian. The culture of Babylonia had indeed succumbed to the barbarism of Assyria. The inhabitants—scholars, artists, artisans, were taken captives, and deported to various points of the empire.

The following reign saw all that was possible done to atone for this reckless act, but far beyond what we can now calculate, the loss was irreparable.

Hebrew Account of the War with Assyria.

"Now in the fourteenth year of King Hezekiah did Sennacherib, king of Assyria, come up against all the fenced cities of Judah, and took them. And Hezekiah, king of Judah, sent to the king of Assyria to Lachish, saying, 'I have offended; return from me: that which thou puttest on me will I bear.' And the king of Assyria appointed unto Hezekiah, king of Judah, three hundred talents of silver and thirty talents of gold.

"And Hezekiah gave him all the silver that was found in the house of the Lord, and in the treasures of the king's house. At that time did Hezekiah cut off the gold from the doors of the temple of the Lord, and from the pillars which

Hezekiah, king of Judah, had overlaid, and gave it to the king of Assyria.

"And the king of Assyria sent Tartan and Rabsaris and Rab-shakeh from Lachish to King Hezekiah with a great host against Jerusalem. And they went up and came to Jerusalem. And when they were come up they came and stood by the conduit of the upper pool, which is in the highway of the fuller's field. And when they had called to the king, there came out to them Eliakim, the son of Hilkiah, which was over the household, and Shebna the scribe, and Joan the son of Asaph, the recorder.

"And Rab-shakeh said unto them: Speak ye now to Hezekiah, Thus saith the great king, the king of Assyria: What confidence is this wherein thou trusteth? Thou sayest (but they are vain words) I have counsel and strength for the war. Now on whom dost thou trust, that thou rebellest against me?

"Now, behold, thou trusteth upon the staff of this bruised reed, even upon Egypt, on which if a man lean, it will go into his hand, and pierce it: so is Pharaoh, king of Egypt, unto all that trust on him.

"But if ye say unto me, We trust in the Lord our God: is not that he, whose high places and whose altars Hezekiah hath taken away and hath said to Judah and Jerusalem, Ye shall worship before this altar in Jerusalem?

"Now, therefore, I pray thee, give pledges to my lord the king of Assyria, and I will deliver thee two thousand horses, if thou be able on thy part to set riders upon them. How then wilt thou turn away the face of one captain of the least of my master's servants, and put thy trust on Egypt for chariots and for horsemen? Am I now come up without the Lord against this place to destroy it? The Lord said to me, Go up against this land, and destroy it.

"Then said Eliakim, the son of Hilkiah, and Shebna, and Joan, unto Rab-shakeh, Speak, I pray thee, to thy servants in the Syrian language; for we understand it: and talk not with us in the Jews' language in the ears of the people that are on the wall. But Rab-shakeh said unto them, Hath my master sent me to thy master, and to thee, to speak these words? hath he not sent me to the men which sit on the wall? Then Rab-shakeh stood and cried with a loud voice in the Jews' language, and spake, saying, Hear the word of the great king, the king of Assyria: Thus saith the king, Let not Hezekiah deceive you: for he shall not be able to deliver you out of his hand. Neither let Hezekiah make you trust in the Lord, saying, The Lord will surely deliver us, and this city shall not be delivered into the hand of the king of Assyria: Harken not to Hezekiah: for thus saith the king of Assyria, Make an agreement with me by a present, and come out to me, and then eat ye every man of his own vine and every one of his own fig-tree, and drink ye every one the waters of his cistern: Until I come and take you away to a land like your own land, a land of corn and wine, a land of bread and vineyards, a land of oil, olive and of honey, that ye may live, and not die: and harken not unto Hezekiah, when he persuadeth you, saying, The Lord will deliver us. Hath any of the gods of the nations delivered at all his land out of the hand of the king of Assyria? Where are the gods of Hamath, and of Arpad? where are the gods of Sepharvaim, Hena, and Ivah? have they delivered Samaria out of mine hand? Who are they among all the gods of the countries, that have delivered their country out of mine hand, that the Lord should deliver Jerusalem out of mine hand? But the people held their peace, and answered him not a word: for the king's commandment was, saying, Answer him not.

"And Hezekiah prayed before the Lord, and said, O Lord our God, I beseech thee save thou us out of his hand, that all the kingdoms of the earth may know that thou art the Lord God, even thou only. Therefore thus saith the Lord concerning the king of Assyria, He shall not come into this city, nor shoot an arrow there, nor come before it with shield, nor cast a bank against it. By the way that he came, by the same shall he return, and shall not come into this city, saith the Lord. For I will defend this city, to save it, for mine own sake, and for my servant David's sake.

"And it came to pass that night that the angel of the Lord went out, and smote in the camp of the Assyrians an hundred fourscore and five thousand: and when they arose early in the morning, behold they were all dead corpses.

"So Sennacherib, king of Assyria, departed, and went and returned and dwelt at Nineveh."—*II. Kings*, 18 *and* 19.

Concerning the Revolt of Judah: From an Assyrian Tablet.

"But as for Hezekiah of Judah, who had not submitted to my yoke, forty-six of his strong walled cities and the smaller cities round about them, without number, by the battering of rams, and the attack of war-engines, by making breaches by cutting through, and the use of axes, I besieged and captured. Two hundred thousand, one hundred and fifty people, small and great, male and female, horses, mules, asses, camels, cattle and sheep, without number, I brought forth from their midst and reckoned as spoil. (Hezekiah) himself I shut up like a caged bird in Jerusalem, his royal city. I threw up fortifications against him, and whoever came out of the gates of his city I punished. His cities, which I had plundered, I cut off from his land and gave to Mitinti, King of Ashdod, and made his territory smaller. To the former taxes, paid yearly, tribute, a present for my lordship, I added and imposed on him. Hezekiah himself was overwhelmed by the fear of the brilliancy of my lordship, and the Arabians and faithful soldiers whom he had brought in to strengthen Jerusalem, his royal city, deserted him. Thirty talents of gold, eight hundred talents of silver, precious stones, couches of ivory, thrones of elephant skin and ivory, *ushu* and *urkarinu* woods, of every kind, a heavy treasure, and his daughters, his palace women, male and female singers, to Nineveh, my lordship's city, I caused to be brought after me, and he sent his ambassador to give tribute and to pay homage."

CHAPTER VIII.

Last Years of Assyrian Greatness.

"And it came to pass, as Sennacherib was worshipping in the house of Nishroch his god, that Adrammelech and Sharezer his sons smote him with the sword: and they escaped into the land of Armenia. And Esarhaddon his son reigned in his stead." Thus did the Hebrew chronicle the death of Sennacherib, and since Assyrian tablets recounting the dire plot have long since been destroyed, we are thrown wholly upon the fact as stated without explanation or detail.

Esarhaddon, who succeeded to the throne in 680 B. C., had already acted as regent in Babylonia, and had there acquired deep veneration and love for the Babylonian past, as well as for its life and culture. He wished to win the favor of its people, scattered though they were, and so in addition to being crowned king of Assyria, he had himself proclaimed viceroy of Babylonia, for this office would not require his annual presence in celebration of the yearly rites. Thus had his grandfather done, and Sennacherib only had ruthlessly thrust aside the national prejudice. His father had laid Babylon waste, changing its very site into a swamp and scattering its proud people to the four winds. Esarhaddon immediately planned to rebuild the city and so far as possible, bring those departed back to their old homes.

In an age given over to cruelty, devastations, selfish plots and intrigues, it is surprising to find that this king allowed no reflections to be cast upon his father's memory by condemning his Babylonian policy. He had it set forth on tablets that the gods had been displeased with the wrong doing of Babylon, and that a king, merely their instrument, had in this way visited divine wrath upon the heads of the people; while now, he, Esarhaddon, again acting as agent for the gods, ready once more to give their favor in hope of future obedience, would now rebuild the ancient capital.

Slowly the city rose, more splendid and magnificent than before. First the old temples were replaced, and around these the city came into being. Chaldeans had taken possession of the land after the nation was disrupted. The new king now forced them back, restoring property wherever possible to its rightful owners.

Such being the situation at home, abroad the state of affairs was critical. Tyre had not submitted, nor Judah. Sidon no longer paid tribute. Vast sums of money were needed to carry on the gigantic building project, and these commercial sea-port towns offered a rich reward to the conqueror.

Having heard that Esarhaddon was determined to make a westward march, the sea-coast cities prepared to offer resistance. Sidon was besieged and held out for nearly three years. When at last it fell into the hands of the exasperated Assyrians, it was utterly destroyed. Both king and soldiers were infuriated by the long delay and plundered until weary. The walls of the town were broken down and cast into the sea; the luxurious homes of the merchantmen were stripped of their wealth and razed to the ground. The entire city was blotted out of existence. Then the king set about erecting a new town on its site, naming it for himself, and peopling it with those taken captive in the nearby mountains while the siege was carried on. Over all he placed an Assyrian governor, and then set out for Nineveh.

Reaching his capital, he made a triumphal entry, laden with spoils, captives and cattle. Some of the noblest citizens of Sidon swelled his train. Gold, silver, precious stones, rare woods, dress-stuffs,—these had fallen to his share after three years of waiting.

The siege of Tyre had been begun about the same time that Sidon was attacked, but Tyre was more favorably situated. She could not be cut off from the sea and so could not be starved into submission. Baal was king and he proposed to hold out against the besiegers. The Assyrians walled up the land side of the city and it was wholly cut off from its land commerce, so in the long run, it would have to yield. After a time, the siege was raised, but over-land commerce was no longer possible.

Esarhaddon knew well that the frequent disturbances in Syria which so annoyed him and had so troubled previous reigns, were largely instigated by unceasing efforts of Egypt to stir the cities to rebellion, hoping in some unquiet times that she might gain a foothold in western Asia and share in the plunder of Syria, as pharaohs in early times had done. To understand her position it is necessary to go back and see how Egypt had fared after losing first place among the nations.

The Ethiopians, having taken on Egyptian culture and customs centuries before, had gained political control as the country weakened. Native princes gained power in the nomes and tried incessantly to regain possession of the throne. As usual there was so much personal jealousy among them that concerted action was impossible. Egypt's name had stood for power and great resources so many centuries, that even though the state was weak—even tottering within, abroad it was still judged by its former strength. Assyrian rulers had doubtless known better its truer condition, for Sennacherib's generals told those of Judah that looking thence for aid was like leaning on a bruised reed.

Esarhaddon determined to strike at the root of Syrian dissension, and in 673 B. C. led an army for the first time in Assyrian history against Egypt. An army met his own outside the borders and the result was indecisive. The Assyrians did not enter the land at all. Three years later they defeated an Egyptian army sent to meet them, crossed the border now unhindered, and marched rapidly to Memphis. The city, wholly unprepared for such unexpected attack, fell at once into their hands. It was plundered generally and laid waste. Unquestionably much of great historic value was wantonly destroyed by soldiers who were allowed to pillage at will. Statues of gods were removed to Nineveh, together with great booty—and this was the work of a man who deplored the loss of Babylon, and had undertaken to rebuild a capital not yet known when Memphis stood the wonder of the world!

The Assyrians never outgrew their ferocity, their savage thirst for ravage and murder, and their culture in Assyria's most enlightened days was but a veneer encasing old tendencies, characteristics and desires.

Over the twenty-one nomes, native princes were allowed to rule, as vassals of an Assyrian governor, set over the whole land. The king further undertook to change the names of ancient towns, giving them Assyrian names, but this never became a change at all—simply a useless attempt.

The youngest world-power had now conquered the oldest. Surely these were years wherein chart-makers would have had a sorry time trying to indicate a nation's possessions.

On its homeward march the Assyrian army made a raid into Arabia, but desert marches told quickly on the soldiers, and no lasting results came of it.

At this point Assyrian possessions—even the original kingdom itself—were threatened alarmingly by a migration starting from the southern portion of present Russia. Thither had come the Medes in an early day, and now thousands upon thousands came pouring eastward in search of new and less crowded homes. It was hopeless to stay such an onset of troops—it would wear out many an army. Places vacated today would be filled shortly by those pressing in the rear. Besides, these people had no plan of conquest or occupation of the land. They simply spread out like so many hungry cattle, seeking food where it might be found. All that could be done was to turn aside the main stream of progress. These new comers settled down in Syria, reaching east to the land of the Medes and far beyond it. In spite of watchful care, many fertile lands were lost to Assyria.

In 668 a second Egyptian campaign was planned by the king, but before starting out, he had his son, Asshur-banipal, recognized as regent of Babylonia. This was to cause much trouble in the future, because it once more divided the now united country, and made an opportunity for old jealousies to creep in again. On the march, Esarhaddon died, leaving the future to regard him as noblest among Assyrian kings— the most just and fair-minded of his race.

Asshur-banipal who succeeded to the throne in 668 B. C., was naturally fond of learning and was a prodigious book-collector. By using that term for Assyrian days we mean of course a collector of clay tablets whereon were inscribed literary productions.

The Egyptian campaign had already opened, for it was plain that the conquests of two years before were practically lost. Sea-coast towns in Egypt submitted at once. Little opposition was encountered in the Land of the Pyramids, and Assyrian government was soon re-instated. The suspicion of the generals was awakened by the simplicity of their task and withdrawing their army, they loitered not far away. No sooner had they left than the Assyrian government, tolerated in the presence of the army, was thrown off and old forms instituted. Now it was the Egyptian's turn to be surprised when the army, supposed to be far on its homeward march, reappeared in the land. The revolt was quickly put down, and the leaders killed with as great cruelty as ever blackened Assyrian pages.

In 660 B. C. Egypt declared her independence and this was the first great loss of the Assyrian empire, soon to be followed by many more.

Probably before this Tyre had been forced to yield, and the king had sent his son and daughter to the Assyrian court as an indication of submission.

A raid was made into Media, some of its cities being taken and their inhabitants deported. For such experiences the Medes grew to hate the Assyrians with increasing fervor. Asshur-banipal was finding some difficulty in holding together the empire of his fathers, and when revolts occurred, they were put down with greatest severity.

Babylonia had maintained peace for fifteen years, but the people clung to the traditions of their early history, and harked back to a time when Babylon was the greatest city of the world. Now, except for freedom from tribute, they ranked as any other Assyrian province. Encouraged by the feelings of those under him, the prince-regent conceived the notion of stirring up all the provinces to revolt at the same time, hoping that Babylonian independence might be gained in time of confusion. He was urged on to this course, which was misguided and ill timed, with little chance for success. Its only hope lay in keeping secret the plot so far as the Assyrian king was concerned. There were, however, many who would gladly try to benefit themselves by unearthing any plan for revolt. There might also be governors of provinces sufficiently far-sighted to have nothing to do with any treasonable plot, and these could not be expected to guard such a secret.

At last the Chaldeans on the south, Palestine, some provinces of Syria and some Arabian tribes, promised help. The Babylonians were destined to learn how different was that from actually giving it. To allay any suspicions Asshurbanipal might have, an embassy of Babylonian nobles visited his court to give him assurance of his brother's loyalty. When the news came that the Babylonians had seized Ur and Uruk, the Assyrian king was much astonished. He spent some little time in complaint of his faithless brother; an inscription ran:

"At that time Shamash-shum-ukin, the faithless brother, to whom I had done good, and whom I had established as king of Babylon, and for whom I had made every possible kind of royal decoration, and had given him, and had gathered together soldiers, horses, and chariots, and had intrusted them to him, and had given him cities, fields, and woods, and the men dwelling in them, even more than my father had commanded—even he forgot that favor I had shown him, and he planned evil. Outwardly with his lips he spoke friendly things, while inwardly his heart plotted rebellion."

Asshur-banipal waited for a favorable omen before starting out to quell the rebellion, and it came at last in this way: "In those days a seer slept in the beginning of the night and dreamed a dream, thus: 'On the face of the Moon it is written: Whoever deviseth evil against Asshur-banipal, king of Asshur, makes enmity, a violent death I appoint for them. With the edge of the sword, the burning of fire, famine, and the judgment of the Pest-god, I will destroy their lives.' This I heard and trusted to the will of Sin, my lord. I gathered my army; against Shamash-Shum-ukin I directed the march."

Help came to the revolting Babylonians from few of the promised allies. Arabia, Chaldea, and the land of the Elamites sent troops, but in the battle waged they suffered fearful defeat. Babylon underwent a severe siege and at last the king committed suicide. Then the gates of the city were thrown open and great was the slaughter. Asshur-banipal had himself proclaimed king, and pushed on to punish the allies for their part in the rebellion. Much of the land of the Elamites was laid waste, and left smoking by this man who patronized learning. The weakening of these people left Assyria open to attacks later from the Medes.

The later years of Asshur-banipal's reign were filled with peaceful interests. He rebuilt the great palace of his father, and in one of its upper chambers was amassed the great number of tablets, referred to as the library of Nineveh. In 626 B. C. the king died.

Our knowledge of the reigns immediately following is scanty. Babylonia asserted her independence and the Assyrian king had a difficult task to hold the empire together. Determined to recover the kingdom to the south, he marched against its capital while its king was distant with his army. Cut off from Babylon, the king appealed to the Medes for aid. They cared not at all to help the Babylonian, but they hated with undying hatred the very name of Assyria. Their numbers had often been increased by refugees, driven from their homes by Assyrian armies, and they themselves had experienced defeat at the hands of Assyrian troops. The possibility of crippling the great power of Asia stimulated them to aid the Babylonians. They soon repulsed the Assyrian army near Babylon and drove it north. Still they pursued the fleeing army and forced the king and his army to retire into Nineveh. At last the fate the Assyrians had so often meted out to others was measured out to them. Great wealth was stored in Nineveh, and this the besieging army wished for themselves. The walls were strong and were long defended, but an assault finally carried all before it. Nineveh, built by the wealth of spoils, beautified by plunder from the known world, became the spoils of the Medes, who stripped the temples and palaces and then set fire to the city.

Nineveh fell in 606 B. C. The Assyrians were scattered to the four winds and grass grew over the once smoking ruins. Two hundred years later, when Xenophon led his army over this spot on his return to Greece, none knew that they passed over the site of the once great world-city.

The civilization developed by the Babylonians had been passed on to the Assyrians. It was now left a heritage for the Chaldeans, to whom descended the legacies of both countries, and in turn they dominated the valley of the Euphrates. As for Assyrian greatness, so far-reaching and wide, the Hebrew told the story in poetic language centuries ago, and today none could set it forth more vividly.

"Behold, the Assyrian was a cedar in Lebanon with fair branches, and with a shadowing shroud, and of an high stature; and his top was among the thick boughs. The waters made him great, the deep set him up on high, with her rivers running round about his plants and sent out her little rivers unto all the trees of the field. Therefore his height was exalted above all the trees of the field, and his boughs were multiplied, and his branches became long because of the multitude of waters, when he shot forth.

"All the fowls of heaven made their nests in his boughs, and under his branches did all the beasts of the field bring forth their young, and under his shadow dwelt all great nations. Thus was he fair in his greatness, in the length of his branches; for his root was by the great waters. The cedars in the garden of God could not hide him: the fir trees were not like his boughs, and the chestnut trees were not like his branches; nor any tree in the garden of God was like unto him in his beauty. . All the trees of Eden, that were in the garden of God, envied him.

"Strangers, the terrible of the nations, have cut him off, and have left him: upon the mountains and in all the valleys his branches are fallen, and his boughs are broken by all the rivers of the land; and all the people of the earth are gone down from his shadow, and have left him. Upon his ruin shall all the fowls of the heaven remain, and all the beasts of the field shall be upon his branches. To the end that none of all the trees by the waters exalt themselves for their height, neither shoot up their top among the thick boughs, neither their trees shall stand up in their height, all that drink water: for they are delivered unto death, to the nether parts of the earth, in the midst of the children of men, with them that go down to the pit."—*Ezekiel* 31.

CHAPTER IX.

The Chaldean Empire in Babylonia.

We have found frequent mention of the Chaldeans, and it is now necessary to understand just what was their position at the fall of Nineveh.

The Chaldeans of this period were descendants of the Semitic invaders, who settled in the Sea-lands, including parts of eastern Arabia as well as lands in Babylonia washed by the Persian Gulf. Originally a pastoral people, they had taken to trade and though long in Babylonia, they had not mingled greatly with others. They looked with envious eyes upon the fertile valley of the Euphrates and coveted the wealth of its cities. On this account they would willingly follow any leader who might enable them to gain these lands and riches for themselves. Because such a victory would unquestionably give kingship over the people, many of their princes made efforts to gain political control, causing no end of trouble to the Babylonian or Assyrian officials in charge of maintaining the peace. This makes clear the motive prompting the numerous attempts to usurp the government, already noted.

The old Babylonians had received so many infusions of blood from the Elamites, Kassites, and colonists settled in their territory by different Assyrian rulers, that the pure Babylonian stock no longer existed to any extent, although Babylonian ideas, culture and characteristics had been absorbed by those who came to dwell in the land. The empire which now grew up in the valley was essentially Chaldean. It has been called the New Empire of Babylonia.

Upon the death of Asshur-banipal, he who had previously been king-regent asserted himself as king of Babylonia, and so Nabopolassar has sometimes been called the founder of the New Chaldean Empire, although in truth he was merely one who declared Babylonian independence at a time when none were strong enough to dispute the claim. The empire, established in this way, followed Babylonian precedence in all matters. The kings concerned themselves with war only when compelled to do so, their works being works of peace—the building of temples, the construction of canals.

One foreign war of some importance occurred during the first reign—the reign of Nabopolassar. Necho II., pharaoh of Egypt, desired to regain those Asiatic possessions which Thothmes III. and later warrior kings had won for the Nile kingdom. To this end he led an army north, demanding the submission of the sea-coast towns. Gaza was quickly won, and this city was key to the east. Tyre and Sidon would pay tribute to any nation rather than have their commerce again destroyed by war. Judah alone resisted. Too long had this little country held out against a various enemy to yield tribute upon demand. Josiah was now Judah's king. He led an army against the Egyptian forces but was repulsed and he himself killed. In confusion the Hebrew army fled to Jerusalem where a younger brother of Josiah was proclaimed king. The Egyptian pharaoh now collected a heavy fine from the people of Judah and he named a king for them in place of the one just popularly crowned.

The old Assyrian empire, so long the fear of all nations, was now under control of three distinct peoples: the Chaldeans held the Euphrates valley, the Medes held the north, and Egypt had appropriated western Syria. Now the pharaoh determined to further extend his empire. He would reach the very banks of the Euphrates. This plan threatened the Chaldean state, and Nabopolassar being too old to undertake active service in the field, sent his son Nebuchadnezzar to meet the Egyptian force. This was soon put to flight. The Babylonian prince pursued and had not word come of the death of the king, his father, the Babylonian army would have been able to march victorious into Egypt. It was, however, more important to hold the kingdom at home than to pursue fleeing troops abroad, so the prince went home to be crowned Nebuchadnezzar II., king of Babylonian, and to enjoy one of the longest reigns in Babylonian history. The city of Babylon became his pride, and the erection of temples and palaces attracted him more than conquests.

Notwithstanding, the kingdom of Judah compelled attention by refusing after three years' peace to longer pay tribute.

The war-party in this little state seems often to have been strong and always to have been eager for independence, while its adherents were generally so blinded by their own enthusiasm that they were unable to estimate correctly their probable chance for success. Isaiah had long been dead. Jeremiah held his place of influence and he labored diligently to show his people the folly of their intent. He succeeded only in drawing censure upon himself and in 597 B. C., Nebuchadnezzar sent an army to besiege Jerusalem. The Judean king Jehoiakim, suddenly died, and a youth about eighteen years of age ascended the throne. He thought best to surrender, whereupon he, his mother and court, were taken as captives to Babylon, together with 7,000 soldiers and 1,000 artisans. The remainder of the inhabitants were left to pay tribute and remain subservient to Babylonian rule.

In Egypt, Hophra had come to the throne. Like his predecessor, he longed for Syrian possessions, and now tried to stir up the sea-coast states to rebellion. No folly could have been plainer—for Judah it meant destruction itself to set its strength against the forces of Babylonia. Jeremiah thundered his bitterest reproaches. He sought vainly to bring his countrymen to their senses and save them from utter ruin. But the spirit of rebellion was abroad, and many times it has spread similarly through a land, drawing to its cause voices seldom heard, and kindling a desire which cannot be put down by cool argument and reason. So Jeremiah continued to grow in disfavor, and was finally held a prisoner by those he tried to aid.

It has been pointed out with much force that the stricken nation of Judah had become the prey of neighboring tribes and that an insufferable situation impelled it to war, but Babylonia could alone protect it, and Babylonian protection was not to be won by rebellion against its rule. Egypt was to again prove the "bruised reed" which would fail utterly when leaned upon.

From the Babylonian standpoint the situation was this: here was a little state which for hundreds of years had been the center of western dissensions. Its revolts had already cost Babylonia and Assyria dear in fighting men and tiresome sieges, and now it must be forever quelled if attention was to be given to home affairs. Crippling its strength would not avail, for that had been already tried. Trusting to the vows of its kings was manifestly useless, since the king who led the revolt had sworn by his mighty God to be faithful to Babylon. That solemn pledge he had now broken. Nothing short of laying waste the land and scattering the people would apparently put an end to the trouble.

Moab, Ammon, Tyre and Sidon were now in league with Judah and Egyptian aid was promised. The war party in Jerusalem went about shouting that Jehovah was with them—no matter, seemingly, what folly they undertook.

In 587 B. C. the Babylonian army besieged Jerusalem, intending to starve the city into submission. The siege was raised when Egyptian reinforcements drew near, long enough to defeat them and send them home in confusion. Then it went on again. In 586 B. C. the Babylonians broke through the walls of Jerusalem and the city was destroyed. The king who had broken faith was taken to Babylon and blinded, while his sons were slain. Such punishments as these had not been common with the old Babylonians, and they show that the Chaldeans were not of the ancient temperament,—merciful and kind. The best citizens of Jerusalem were taken captives, while the poorer ones were left to cultivate the soil. The great prophet Jeremiah was thought to be friendly to the government of Babylon, and was given permission to go where he would. He remained with the stricken band of Hebrews, who soon after journeyed into Egypt.

Tyre, as an ally, was besieged but here the problem of cutting the city off from outside communication again arose. The siege lasted for thirteen years and in the end the city paid tribute. In 567 B. C. Nebuchadnezzar's army invaded Egypt, but it was merely a raid to terrorize the Egyptians and put an end to Egyptian interference.

The king was now free to give his energy to internal affairs, and his attention was chiefly centered in building and beautifying Babylon. Notable among his undertakings were the walls of the city—counted among the seven wonders of the world. They were so well constructed that had they been defended, the city could never have been taken save by treachery inside the capital itself. In 562 B. C. Nebuchadnezzar died—the last great king of an ancient nation.

Of the following reign little is known, the king being assassinated in the second year of his rule. Two other uneventful reigns followed, and then Nabonidus ascended the throne. This man was a student—not a king. He did one good service for future ages; being devoted to rebuilding the temples of the gods, he had his workmen excavate deep down into the old foundations of the temple of the sun-god in Sippar, which he says had not been seen for 3200 years, for the record-tablet, always placed in the corner. Then he caused a new tablet to be inserted, repeating the history of the temple and enumerating his repairs. Modern excavators have been greatly aided by these tablets of Nabonidus. While he was thus absorbed, his country was fast plunging on to ruin. His was an age when the mere existence of a nation depended upon its aggressive policy. While the entire resources of the country were being expended upon shrines sacred to the gods, there was neither time nor money for the maintenance of an army. Matters were allowed to take their own course for awhile, and later the king's son, Belshar-usur, or Belshazzar, was left to manage government concerns. For this reason, the Hebrews recorded him as the last Babylonian king, while in truth his father bore the kingly title.

Even when danger threatened the state to such an extent that the scholar-king himself, poking around among his ancient record-tablets, was finally forced to take notice of it, he gave no thought to his kingdom or his subjects, but was simply alarmed for the safety of his statue-deities. These he had hurried into the capital from all parts of the land. So occupied was he lest perchance a god or two might some way escape him, that he had no time to prepare the city for attack, and in the end Babylon, the pride of its age, came into the hands of the conqueror without a blow!

The fact was that there were many within the kingdom who would gladly welcome outside interference. The Hebrews had settled down in their quarter and had become the leading people of commerce and loaners of money. One commercial firm alone—Egibi & Sons—filled a place for that age not unlike the modern Rothschilds. These people, who may have been of Jewish descent, hated the king who had destroyed their city of Jerusalem and his descendants, and would willingly help any one who might rob Babylonion kings of their empire. It has been surmised that for aid rendered they were allowed to go back to their own country and rebuild Jerusalem on its early site.

Not only were the Hebrews an element to be reckoned with; the priests of the Babylonian gods had been repeatedly offended by Nabonidus, and they too joined the opposition, beyond doubt.

So great a city as Babylon had never before existed. No city since has had so long a history, and yet, without a blow struck in its defense, it passed into the possession of a people just taking on the ways of civilized life. It was little wonder that it fell shortly into ruins, soon to be grass-covered and like Nineveh, forgotten!

Since 606 B. C. the Medes, conquerors of Assyria, had been extending their territory. They were now a people of strength, united under King Astyages.

In the land earlier called Elam, now Persia, a great conqueror appeared—Cyrus the Great. He defeated the Medes under Astyages, and so rapidly did his empire come into being, that all civilized nations were roused to the danger of a world-conqueror. In 546 B. C. Egypt, Babylonia, Lydia and Sparta arrayed their forces against Cyrus, to check his power, but his camels put their cavalry to flight, and he won the decisive battle. Having annexed Asia Minor, he turned to Babylon. As we have seen, the city of Babylon might have held out indefinitely against attack, but when Belshazzar led an army against a detachment of Persian troops, none were left to defend the capital. The old tale of Herodotus that Cyrus turned the Euphrates out of its course and entered the city through its channel, is mere fiction. Such exertion was unnecessary, for the city gates swung open wide to the conqueror.

And thus we come to the end of the political history of the Tigris-Euphrates states—a mere skeleton of framework, which we can now fill out with some account of their social, industrial and religious life.

ASSYRIAN PALACE AT NINEVEH.

CHAPTER X.

The Babylonian and Assyrian Compared.

To understand the Babylonian, we must take into consideration both the nature of his country and the origin of his race. Apart from these two important factors, the marked differences between himself and his Assyrian brother would not be clear.

We have found that Babylonia was an alluvial plain, sloping gently to the Persian Gulf, and made fertile by the annual overflow and deposits of two rivers. As in Egypt, so here remarkable yields of grain rewarded the sower if he but supplied necessary moisture by maintaining a system of well-regulated canals. Regarding the origin of the Babylonians, we found that they sprang from a union of Semitics with the earlier Turanian settlers of the country, receiving later infusion of blood from the Kassites and Elamites. This intermingling of races and peoples resulted in a nation whose characteristics differed widely from the purer Semitic stock that peopled Assyria.

"The Babylonian was a stout, thick-set man, somewhat short, with straight nose, wide nostrils, and square face. The Assyrian, on the other hand, was tall and muscular, his nose was slightly hooked, his lips were full, his eyes dark and piercing. His head and face showed an abundance of black curly hair.

"The Babylonian was essentially an irrigator and cultivator of the ground. The cuneiform texts are full of references to the gardens of Babylonia, and the canals by which they were watered. It was a land which brought forth abundantly all that was entrusted to its bosom. But the fear of floods and the reclamation of the marsh lands demanded constant care and labor, the result being that the country population of Babylonia was, like the country population of Egypt, an industrious peasantry, wholly devoted to agricultural work, and disinclined to war and military operations. In the towns, where the Semitic element was stronger, a considerable amount of trade and commerce was carried on, and the cities on the sea-coast built ships and sent their merchantmen to distant lands.

"The character of the Assyrian was altogether different from that of the Babylonian. He was a warrior, a trader, and an administrator. The peaceful pursuits of the agricultural population of Babylonia suited him but little. His two passions were fighting and trading. But his wars, at all events in the later days of the Assyrian Empire, were conducted with a commercial object. It was to destroy the trade of the Phœnician cities and to divert it into Assyrian hands, that the Assyrian kings marched their armies to the west; it was to secure the chief highways of commerce that campaigns were made into the heart of Arabia and Assyrian satraps were appointed in the cities of Syria. The Assyrian was indeed irresistible as a soldier, but the motive that inspired him was as much the interest of the trader as the desire for conquest."[1]

Side by side with the Babylonian's farming concerns, grew his love for study and his development of the peaceful arts. An elementary education was general in Babylonia. As industry and commerce brought wealth and created thus a leisure class, education and learning flourished in Babylonian cities. Schools grew into prominence, and in the realm of astronomy and certain of the sciences, some advance was made by which the Greeks later profited. Quite the reverse was true in Assyria. A feverish desire for commercial gain and for military conquest prevented progress in the arts of peace. Learning was confined to a few—professional scribes supplied secretaries for the state and even wrote private letters for private citizens. When the luxuries of the ancient world could be won as tribute, the Assyrian scorned to produce them for himself. With blood unmixed with any peace-loving people, he retained the characteristics of his earlier Arabian home. He left the cultivation of the country to slaves and dwelt in cities, when war and trade left him intermittent periods at home.

Both Babylonian and Assyrian were religious, but here

[1] Sayce: Social Life Among the Assyrians and Babylonians, 13.

again we find differences due to environment. The Babylonian, inheriting the conjuring and magic of the earlier Chaldean, possessed a religion which held him in constant dread of demons. The greatest aid and solace his religion afforded was to assist him in driving away foes which assailed him at every turn. The Assyrian on the contrary, showed the same proud bearing in his religious concerns as in other aspects of life. Asshur was his mighty God, strong in battle and unequaled in courage. Firm in his conviction that Asshur would give him victory, he went forth, like his Hebrew brother, to overcome all others and destroy other gods which offended the true God.

In origin and traditions alike, the Assyrian and the Hebrew in early times present many similarities, and the religion of the one is comparable at many points with that of the other.

Houses.

It is supposed that in earliest times the dwellers in the Euphrates valley built their huts of reeds which grew in profusion along the river and the canals. These in time were replaced by huts of sun-dried brick. We have already learned that the low level plains of Babylonia afforded little or no stone for building purposes. Oven-dried brick was the most substantial building material known and this was so costly, on account of the scarcity of fuel, that only the temples, kings' palaces, and homes of the wealthy were made of it. The great majority of houses then, were constructed of clay mud, shaped in bricks and dried in the sun.

The more pretentious dwellings of nobles and kings were placed on artificially constructed heights—huge piles of brickwork, in order to raise them above the gnats and the malaria-breeding fogs of the marshes. The huts of the poor were located wherever opportunity offered. While these contained but one or two rooms with small apertures in the clay walls for windows, and had no floor save the ground, the houses of the wealthy were frequently several stories high, the upper floors being reached by outside stairways. The use of the arch was known in Babylonia from 4000 B.C., a perfect keystone example having been found at Nippur by the University of Pennsylvania expedition. Windows were furnished with tapestries to exclude the storms and intense heat of noonday. Flat roofs supplied a place for the women to perform many household duties, or, if these were performed by slaves elsewhere, they sat here to embroider their tapestries and to chat with their friends. Here too, on hot nights, mattresses were thrown down for the hours of sleep.

Wherever possible a garden surrounded the house. The pride of the Babylonian, as of the Egyptian, was his carefully tended garden, whether it was a tiny plot of land or a vast overhanging terrace like that of Babylon's queen.

Streets were narrow and exceedingly dirty, for into them all refuse and rubbish from the houses accumulated. We learn that sometimes the entire street would be filled up to the very doors of the dwellings, and then, instead of clearing them out, an upper story was added to the houses, new doors provided, and the occupants started anew on a fresh elevation.

In homes of the wealthy the furniture was simple, and in the huts of the poor it was scanty indeed. Chairs, stools, and tables were in use; a mat often constituted the bed, although pictures of most uncomfortable looking bedsteads have been preserved, these being possessed only by the wealthy.

The Assyrians who went from Babylonia into their northern land, took with them the habits and customs there acquired. While stone was plentiful, they used it only for foundations, or for the less important portion of their buildings, continuing to make mud brick for the rest, as they had done before. While hills and elevations were now available on every hand, they still erected huge piles of brick or stone and crowned these by their buildings. The Assyrian blood, unmixed with other tribes or peoples, produced no ingenuity, no inventive genius. The Assyrian remained an imitator—never a creator. For this reason, we find close similarity between the houses of the two countries.

Certain features which became inseparable with later architecture had their beginnings in Babylonia. In early times the roof which covered the mud hut was supported by dried palm stems; gradually a more substantial support was substituted, and in this way the column had its origin and was adopted and improved upon by the Greeks. Again, interior house decoration may be traced back to these Babylonian houses built of brick. In houses of the well-to-do, the unsightly bricks were covered by a coating of stucco and upon this were painted various scenes and ornamentations. In Assyria, slabs of soft lime-stone were used instead of the stucco, and figures of horses and men, hunting scenes and battles, were carved in bas-relief upon them. Indeed much of our knowledge concerning the life of the people has been gained from a study of the reliefs discovered in buried palaces.

Regarding the daily lives of those who dwelt within these mud brick houses, we have less detailed information than concerning the ancient Egyptian. Fewer scenes of ordinary life were painted in the Tigris-Euphrates valleys, and whatever was entrusted to the clay stood far greater chance of being destroyed than that committed to Egyptian stone.

Family Life.

In considering the family life, the position accorded to woman and the marriage laws and regulations are of first importance.

In early times in Babylonia, a man received a dowry with his wife. Polygamy was not infrequent but a strong check was placed upon it by requiring the husband, in case of divorce, to return the wife's dowry to her and allow her to return home or maintain her own establishment. The income from the dowry was enjoyed by both husband and wife, but it remained the portion of the wife and could be willed according to her pleasure. In case of a woman's second marriage, her first dowry belonged to her, subject to the claim of her children for one-half of its value.

In both Babylonia and Assyria married women enjoyed many liberties. They might carry on business enterprises, borrow or loan, manage their own property and dispose of it at their will. They could seek justice in the courts, and if they belonged to the middle classes, could come and go at pleasure. The women of noble families were more carefully guarded, and seldom appeared unattended in public.

Girls who were not provided with dowries might be purchased and so become superior slaves of their husbands. Children might be sold by their parents and brothers might sell their sisters, but in these countries, slaves were not despised as inferiors and inhumanly treated. They were often adopted into families, and since those of noble birth were not infrequently taken captives in war, the slave might be superior to the owner. However, this last was not so common in Mesopotamia as it was later in Rome. The fact which alone assured slaves of good treatment was that there was generally no race difference to engender feeling betwen slave and master. Indeed one case is cited in those days of quickly reversed fortunes, where the slave in a few years became the master and his former owner became his property!

Marriage was both a civil and a religious ceremony, and the contract was signed in the presence of a priest. In a code of Babylonian laws compiled about 2250 B. C., a law provided that "If a man has taken a wife and has not executed a marriage-contract, that woman is not a wife." Another provided for one who is helpless: "If a man has married a wife and a disease has seized her, if he is determined to marry a second wife, he shall marry her. He shall not divorce the wife whom the disease has seized. In the home they made together she shall dwell and he shall maintain her as long as she lives."[2]

Both sons and daughters could inherit property, and according to Babylonian law, whosoever possessed property, could will it, or dispose of it, with certain well established restrictions. In case there were no children to inherit an estate, it was a common practice to adopt them. Thus families were prevented from dying out.

Children were cared for, sent to school, taught trades or professions, and probably a certain amount of family life was enjoyed while they were growing up. The rights of each member of the family were definitely recognized by law. Home life as we today understand the phrase, was unknown in antiquity.

We can contrast the condition in Babylonia, where the individual, instead of the family, was recognized by the law to that in Rome of a later time, when the family was the unit of the state, and the pater familias managed all family affairs without state interference or restriction.

[2] Johns: Babylonian and Assyrian Laws, Contracts and Letters, 56, 58.

CHAPTER XI.

Morality of the Ancient Babylonians.

For some years past, the French explorer De Morgan has been making extensive excavations at Susa, the capital of ancient Persia, and before the rise of Persia, the capital of Elam as early as 3000 B. C. In the winter of 1901-1902, having removed layers of earth containing ruins of Persian palaces, he reached deposits contemporary with some of the old Elamite kings. Here was discovered a stone monument inscribed with the code of Hammurabi. As we have seen, this king ruled Babylonia about 2000 B. C. He it was who united all the little city-states into one kingdom with its capital at Babylon. Proving himself a statesman as well as a warrior, he devoted himself to the welfare of his subjects. He repaired old canals and constructed new ones, restored the temples and above all, gave the country a uniform system of laws. These laws were not made by Hammurabi—generally speaking at least. They had been long established by custom and he merely codified such customs and earlier decisions into a system so that justice might be administered alike throughout the realm. The laws were then inscribed upon stone slabs and erected at certain places where the people could read them, and those who felt themselves injured might know what redress lay open to them.

The particular stele unearthed by De Morgan had been set up originally in the town of Sippara. Later Elamite kings became powerful enough to invade Babylonia and lay the country under tribute. During this period, one Elamite king had removed the stone monument from Sippara and taken it home with his spoils. It had graced his triumphal procession upon his return and was set up at his capital. 49 columns of inscription were engraved upon it, but the Elamite king caused 5 to be removed and the stone to be re-polished, in order that his name might be therein inserted. For some reason this was forgotten or omitted.

Of the 282 laws once carved upon the stele, all are still legible. Their discovery is most important for the history of ancient Babylonia, as it has enabled scholars to reconstruct the standards of morality and justice current when the country came into its first strength and power. We may be sure that these laws were in vogue much earlier than the time of Hammurabi and they lived on with little change for many years after. They without doubt furnished the basis for the legal code throughout the history of Babylonia, and without some knowledge of them we would never have been able to understand the civilization of the country as it is known today. It is comparable to the "Mosaic Code," which is made up of different strata from different periods, cir. 1000 B.C. to 500 B.C. The similarity between the two codes harks back to an early period when the two peoples had not yet left their Arabian home, and indicates general Semitic customs. Hammurabi's code " is concerned little, if at all, with religious matters; the chief content is almost entirely civil and criminal, dealing with such subjects as marriage, the family, property rights, agricultural and commercial activities."

It is on the basis of these laws now translated that the morality of the ancient Babylonians has been worked out. We find that the people were on the borderland of retaliation, and punishments often took the form of fines. There was still the old tribal " group responsibility "—that is, the children often had to suffer for the sins of the father. Distinction was now made between intentional and unintentional injury. Trial by ordeal was sometimes allowed, especially when magic was thought to have been used. Death was a frequent punishment. Banishment might be inflicted. On the whole, the practices in Babylonia, before and after 2000 B. C., were not so severe as those common in England a century ago, when petty larceny was met by extreme punishment.

The Babylonians carried the idea of contract and written agreement farther than any other ancient people. Understandings which are today made verbally between men were inscribed on clay tablets, duly impressed by the seals of the parties concerned, and carefully preserved. We find the law required receipts and written contracts as early as 2000 B. C. For example, "If a merchant has given to an agent corn, wool, oil, or any sort of goods to traffic with, the agent shall write down the money value, and shall return that to the merchant. The agent shall then take a sealed receipt for the money that he has given to the merchant. If the agent forgets and has not taken a sealed receipt for the money he gave to the merchant, money that has not been acknowledged by receipt shall not be put down in the accounts."[1] Regarding money given bankers: "If a man has given another gold, silver, or any goods whatever on deposit, all that he gives shall be shown to witnesses, and take a bond and so give on deposit. If he has given on deposit without witnesses and bonds, and has been defrauded where he made his deposit, he has no claim to prosecute."[2]

"An eye for an eye, and a tooth for a tooth" was demanded by the Code of Hammurabi.

"If a man has knocked out the eye of a patrician, his eye shall be knocked out.

"If he has broken the limb of a patrician, his limb shall be broken.

"If he has knocked out the eye of a plebeian or has broken the limb of a plebeian, he shall pay one mana of silver.

"If a patrician has knocked out the tooth of a man that is his equal, his tooth shall be knocked out. If he has knocked out the tooth of a plebeian, he shall pay one-third of a mana of silver.

"If a man has struck another in a quarrel, and caused him permanent injury, that man shall swear, 'I struck him without malice,' and shall pay the doctor."[3]

Theft at a fire was made a capital offense. "If a fire has broken out in a man's house and one who has come to put it out has coveted the property of the householder and appropriated any of it, that man shall be cast into the self-same fire."[4]

Fees of the surgeon were graded by law, and severe penalties were inflicted for unskillful operations. Probably these were not strictly enforced but were intended to prevent malpractice.

Marriage laws and regulations governing inheritance were necessarily definite in a country where a man might have more than one wife. Since perpetuation of a family through

---

[1] Johns: Babylonian and Assyrian Laws, Letters and Contracts; Hammarabi's Code, 104, 105. [2] Ibid., 122, 123. [3] Ibid., 196, 197, 198, 201, 206. [4] Ibid., 25.

adoption was frequent, laws protected both foster children and foster parents.

"If a man has brought up a child, whom he has taken to be his son, but has not reckoned him with his sons, that foster child shall return to his father's house

"If a craftsman has taken a child to bring up and has taught him his handiwork, he shall not be reclaimed. If he has not taught him his handicraft, that foster child shall return to his father's house."

Injury which today would necessitate the payment of damages, in ancient Babylonia might even be punished with death. "If a builder has built a house for a man, and has not made his work sound, and the house he built has fallen, and caused the death of its owner, that builder shall be put to death. If it is the owner's son that is killed, the builder's son shall be put to death.

"If he has caused the loss of goods, he shall render back whatever he has destroyed. Moreover, because he did not make sound the house he built, and it fell, at his own cost he shall rebuild the house that fell."

Workmen were required to do faithful work or make good consequent losses. "If a boatman has built a boat for a man, and has not made his work sound, and in that same year that boat is sent on a voyage and suffers damage, the boatman shall rebuild that boat, and, at his own expense, shall make it strong, or shall give a strong boat to the owner.

In a land where the cultivation of the soil was the great industry, naturally many regulations refer to the lease of ground and the rent to be paid by the farmer to the owner of the estate. Because the very production of the soil depended upon the maintenance of canals, neglect in the care of the dikes was severely punished.

"If a man has hired a field to cultivate and has caused no corn to grow on the field, he shall be held responsible for not doing the work on the field and shall pay an average rent.

"If a man has given his garden to a gardener to farm, the gardener, as long as he holds the garden, shall give the owner of the garden two-thirds of the produce of the garden and shall take one-third himself.

"If a man has neglected to strengthen his dike and has

not kept his dike strong, and a breach has broken out in his dike, and the waters have flooded the meadow, the man in whose dike the breach has broken out shall restore the corn he has caused to be lost. If he be not able to restore the corn, he and his goods shall be sold, and the owners of the meadow whose corn the water has carried away shall share the money.

"If a man has opened his runnel for watering and has left it open, and the water has flooded his neighbor's field, he shall pay him an average crop."

That justice might be administered uniformly throughout the realm, courts were established in different cities, and Hammarabi insured the well-being of his subjects by further creating a court of appeals, held in Babylon. To this superior court anyone, thinking himself unfairly treated in the lower courts, might have a hearing. Perjury was severely punished.

"If a man has borne false witness in a trial, or has not established the statement that he has made, if that case be a capital trial, that man shall be put to death.

"If he has borne false witness in a civil law case, he shall pay the damages in that suit." Judges were always restricted by law and were held to strict account in administering justice. Any suspicion of bribery expelled the judge from his seat.

"If a judge has given a verdict, rendered a decision, granted a written judgment, and afterwards has altered his judgment, that judge shall be prosecuted for altering the judgment he gave and shall pay twelvefold the penalty laid down in that judgment. Further, he shall be publicly expelled from his judgment-seat and shall not return nor take his seat with the judges at a trial."

Other public servants were required to deal justly with the people. Governors of provinces who oppressed the inhabitants or in any way were unjust to those dependent upon them, laid themselves liable to a death sentence if charges against them could be proven.

In the light of these laws we would conclude that the Babylonians had reached a high stage of morality when authentic history of their kingdom begins. Honesty, truth, fair-dealing,—these were demanded by the laws of the realm, and penalties attached to crimes violating them. One who was injured must bring his cause before a judge and allow disinterested persons to render a decision. Instead of retaliation upon the assailant, money was sometimes received as compensation for injury. In more flagrant cases, the law imposed the penalty of death. A man could not slander his neighbor without risk of punishment.

"If the claimant of lost property has not brought the witnesses that know his lost property, he has been guilty of slander, he has stirred up strife, he shall be put to death.

"If a man has not his witnesses at hand, the judge shall set him a fixed time not exceeding six months, and if within six months he has not produced his witnesses, the man has lied; he shall bear the penalty of the suit."

Protection was assured the weak and helpless by this code. It was customary to receive hostages as security for debt—the debtor's son and slave. Such a hostage was entitled to fair treatment and a law made it an offense to misuse him. "If a hostage has died of blows or want in the house of the creditor, the owner of the hostage shall prosecute his creditor, and if the deceased were free-born, the creditor's son shall be put to death; if a slave, the creditor shall pay one-third of a mana of silver, furthermore, he shall lose whatever it was that he lent."

Regarding intemperance among the Babylonians, they used beer freely, but appear to have gone to no such excesses as were common among the Egyptians. The price of beer was fixed by law and an overcharge was punishable by drowning.

The morality of the people seems to have been very slightly influenced by their religion. While all Semitics have been strongly religious people, the Babylonians had reached a certain degree of secularism in their religion. Their temples were financial centers for the country and were of more direct interest to the people because from them they might negotiate small loans to tide them over emergencies perhaps than because the deity of the locality had there his center of worship.

A lengthy prologue setting forth the titles of Hammurabi and the gods that gave him power, preceded his code of laws. These were followed by an epilogue similar in nature. The king calls down curses upon any future ruler who should cause his wholesome regulations to be altered. "In the future, in days to come, at any time, let the king who is in the land, guard the words of righteousness which I have written on my stele. Let him not alter the judgment of the land which I judged nor the decisions I decided. Let him not destroy my bas-relief. If that man has wisdom and is capable of directing his land, let him attend to the words which I have written upon my stele, let him apprehend the path, the rule, the law of the land which I judged, and the decision I decided for the land, and so let him guide forward the black-headed race; let him judge their judgment and decide their decision, let him cut off from his land the proud and violent, let him rejoice in the flesh of his people."[5]

Blessings were given him who should respect this code of laws and terrible curses heaped upon any who might disregard it. Much of Babylonia's prosperity appears to have resulted from the enforcement of these impartial judgments.

[5] Johns: Babylonian and Assyrian Laws, Letters and Contracts; Hammarabi's Code, 104, 105.

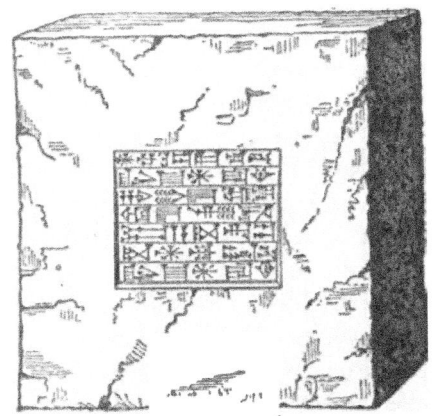

BABYLONIAN BRICK. THE KING'S NAME AND TITLES WERE INSCRIBED ON EACH BRICK.

CHAPTER XII.

Literature and Learning.

The Babylonians produced quite an extensive literature. Their writings treated of religion, mathematics, astronomy, astrology and geography, while some attempt was made to explain animal and plant life. History in Babylonia was limited almost wholly to royal inscriptions and lists of kings. In Assyria, on the other hand, the greater portion of the literature related to history, and the kings set forth the happenings of their reigns with directness and considerable detail. Diplomatic affairs, correspondence with Babylonia and foreign provinces, official letters, tribute lists and royal decrees, make up a large part of the surviving tablets.

We have already spoken of the library of Asshurbanipal, or the Ninevan library, and have seen what a world of light was thrown upon Assyrian civilization when its surviving tablets were at last deciphered. Babylonia maintained libraries, however, before Nineveh was founded.

These clustered, for reasons which we shall soon see, around the temples. At Erech were early collected writings which were concerned with the religion of the ancient Chaldeans, together with the myths and legends of the country. So many tablets were preserved in this temple that Erech was called the "city of books." A library, rich in mathematical lore, grew up at Larsa, another at Nippur, and still another at Cathah. Smaller libraries were attached to all the great temples.

When we speak of "libraries" in Mesopotamia, collections of clay tablets are meant. Rooms were frequently provided within the temples for the storing of these clay books. The size of the tablet varied greatly. The largest were flat and about 9 by 6½ inches; smaller ones were slightly convex, while tiny ones, not more than one inch long, containing but a line or two, have been found. Sometimes the lettering is so fine that it could have been done only with the aid of a lens, and it cannot be read without one.

In these valleys, the cheapest, most available writing material was the soft clay, ever in evidence. When bricks had been partially dried in the sun, a substance was formed which readily received impressions, and these became firm as the tablet hardened. Both sides and sometimes the edges as well, were written upon, and little pegs of wood provided legs for the brick to rest upon when reversed, that the soft impressions might not be injured. To make the whole proof against fire and water, it was finally baked in an oven. When so treated, a material was made which proved more enduring against action of the elements than either parchment or papyrus.

It is quite certain that papyrus and possibly parchment as well were used for writing purposes, especially in the later period, but no fragment of either has survived.

Certain disadvantages attached to the cheap tablets. They were heavy and unwieldy to hold or carry, but more especially, they allowed no embellishments or lengthy descriptions. Owing to the laborious method of transcribing records, everything was of necessity abbreviated and simplified. Thus we see how one thing acts upon another—the country afforded only clay tablets for writing material; these, limited because of size and weight, curtailed speech and so influenced the style of expression.

Occasionally one tablet constituted a book, but more often several tablets were needed to contain the entire writing. Thus the Deluge Story is the eleventh tablet, or chapter, of a series numbering twelve in all. Seventy tablets composed a single work on astronomy, while the three books comprising the earliest religious texts covered 200 tablets. Each tablet was carefully numbered and known by the first line of the book; as, for example, one work treated on the creation and began: "Formerly that which is above was not yet called the heaven;" so the first tablet of the series was entitled: "Formerly that which is above, No. 1;" the second, "Formerly that which is above, No. 2," and so on through the entire series.

The ancient Chaldeans believed that literature and the art of writing were gifts from the gods, and in the myth which to them explained how knowledge came into the world, it was numbered among the things taught them by the Man-

MUSICIANS AND ATTENDANTS IN THE GARDEN OF ASSHURBANIPAL.

Fish, Oannes. This is the myth as Berosus told it: "There was originally at Babylonia a multitude of men of foreign race who had colonized Chaldea, and they lived without order, like animals. But in the first year (of the new order of things) there appeared from out the Persian Gulf where it borders upon Babylonia, an animal endowed with reason, who was called Oannes. The whole body of the animal was that of a fish, but under the fish's head he had another head, and also feet below, growing out of his fish's tail, similar to those of a man; also human speech, and his image is preserved to this day. This being used to spend the whole day amidst men, without taking any food, and he gave them an insight into letters, and sciences, and every kind of art; he taught them how to found cities, to construct temples, to introduce laws and to measure land; he showed them how to sow seeds and gather in crops; in short, he instructed them in everything that softens manners and makes up civilization, so that from that time no one has invented anything new. Then, when the sun went down, this monstrous Oannes used to plunge back into the sea and spend the night in the midst of the boundless waves, for he was amphibious."

It was believed that learning and letters were under the special protection of the gods, and for this reason it was fitting to preserve books in the temples. The libraries thus established were cared for by scribes and were open to the public. Many were engaged constantly in copying, repairing and taking care of the tablets. An order of celibate priests, not unlike the monks of the Middle Ages, devoted itself to the task of book-making, regarding the work as a pious undertaking.

Among the most ancient books recovered is one containing bits of folk-lore, popular songs and maxims. One of the maxims runs:

"Like an oven that is old
 Against thy foes be hard and strong."

A fragment of a ploughman's song says:

"My knees are marching—my feet are not resting;
With no wealth of thy own—grain thou makest for me."

The Creation legends were among the most ancient writings.

"A plant had not been brought forth, a tree had not been created.
A brick had not been made, a beam had not been formed.
A house had not been built, a city had not been constructed.
A city had not been made, earthly things had not been made glorious.
Nipur had not been built, (its temple) E-kura had not been constructed.
Erech had not been built, (its temple) E-Ana had not been constructed.
The deep had not been made, Eridu had not been constructed.
As for the glorious temple (of Eridu), the house of the gods, its seat had not been made.
The whole of the lands, the sea also, (had not been formed).
When within the sea the current was
In that day Eridu was made. E-Sagila was constructed,
E-Sagila which the god Lugal-du-azagga founded within the deep;
Babylon (also) was built, E-Sagila was completed.
The gods and the spirits of the earth were made altogether.
The glorious city, the seat of the joy of their hearts, supremely they proclaimed.
Merodack (Marduk) bound together the slime before the water.
Dust he made and he poured it out with the flood.
The gods were made to dwell in a seat of joy of heart.
He created mankind.
The god Aruru, the seed of mankind, they made with him.
He made the beasts of the field and the living creatures of the desert.
He made the Tigris and Euphrates, and set (them) in (their) places
Well proclaimed he their name.
The ussu-plant, the dittu-plant of the marshland, the reed and the forest he made.
He made the verdure of the plain;
The lands, the marshes, and the greensward also;
Oxen, the young of the horse, the stallion, the mare, the sheep, the locust;
Meadows and forests also.
The he-goat and the gazelle brought forth to him.'"

[1] George Smith: Babylonia, 46.

Babylonian myths often took the form of epics. The epic of Gilgamesh was popular. Twelve tablets composed it, each corresponding to a zodiacal sign. The Deluge Story made up the eleventh chapter. Another epic, the Descent of Ishtar into Arallu, or Hades, was well known. Ishtar, herself a goddess, mourned a departed god, her consort, so greatly that she braved the terrors of the underworld to find him and to carry him water from the fountain of life, that he might rejoin her. This was the earliest form of a myth which later appeared in many lands.

Astronomy had its birth in astrology—the so-called science which sought to discover the influences of the planets upon the destinies of mankind. This science was firmly believed in and strongly supported for centuries after the Christian era, and has its followers even today.

Mathematics had a similar beginning. Geometrical figures were used for augury. In arithmetic, 60 was a favorite number for computation, and the division of a circle into seconds, minutes and degrees, dates from this time.

Geography consisted merely of lists of seas, mountains, rivers, waters, nations, and cities then known. Grammars and dictionaries were plentiful because they were needed even at that time for an understanding of a language, already " dead," but still the language of literature.

In the realm of history, royal inscriptions may be included. With the rise of Assyria these came to be more complete. Fewer set phrases, copied by each king from most ancient times, were used and more information was included concerning the subject at hand. For example, an inscription of Tiglathpileser I. (about 1100 B. C.) filled eight sides of a clay cylinder, and contained 809 lines. It consisted of (1) an invocation to the gods who had given him power; (2) set forth his titles and summed up the deeds of his reign; (3) 500 lines recounted the campaigns of his first year; (4) 200 lines described his royal hunts and his temples built and restored; (5) finally a blessing was pronounced upon those who shall honor his deeds and a curse is given those who ignore them.

Both nations loved justice and delighted in formality. All kinds of agreements were put into writing and were duly witnessed. To the original code of laws in Babylonia, court decisions were added and together comprised the later law of the land. All important cases were abstracted and the decision of the judges given at length on tablets which have been preserved in many cases with the signature of the judge. The judges were appointed by the king. Priests were eligible, but others often served. There was probably a court in the vicinity of every important temple, which has given a general impression that the priests took entire charge of court proceedings.

Education was much more widely diffused in Babylonia than in Assyria. In the former country both girls and boys seem to have received some elementary training in the art of reading and writing. Schools for the training of scribes were maintained in connection with each of the great temples. Tutors were doubtless employed in families of the nobility, but little is known of the training of the young. The art of writing was a difficult one to master and required the memorizing of a large number of symbols. There must have been much truth in the sentence found often in the children's copy-books: "He who would become a scribe must rise with the dawn." In the school of Sippara a tablet has been found which is supposed to have been either a medal or a diploma given by the school. An inscription upon it reads: "Whosoever has distinguished himself at the place of tablet writing shall shine as the light." The calling of the scribe was an honorable one and his social position was good.

One indication that people of the better classes in Babylonia could write is to be found in the number of personal letters which have been found. These are not written, as in Assyria, in one uniform handwriting, but show many variations and degrees of perfection.

In Assyria writing was a profession, and only tradespeople whose business compelled them to understand rudimentary writing, public officials and the upper classes understood the art. Public scribes wrote many private letters, much in the same way as a lawyer of today might draw up some document, and to the letter so written, the sender affixed his seal.

Learning was limited in the northern kingdom to the favored few. Some of the kings were book collectors. This was notably true of Assurbanipal who sent his men everywhere to gather up tablets of worth and antiquity.

Letters which have been translated help to bring these early days before us. This one was probably sent by a lover to the object of his adoration:

"To Bibea say, thus saith Gimil-Marduk: May Shamash and Marduk for my sake preserve thy health forever. I have sent for thy health. Tell me how thou art. I went to Babylon and did not see thee. I was greatly disappointed. Send me the reason of thy leaving, and let me be cheered. In Marchevan do thou come. For my sake keep well always."[2]

The next is written by the captain of a river barge to King Sennacherib, concerning the transporting of colossal bulls.

"To the king my lord, thy servant Asshur-mukin has ordered me to transport in boats the colossal bulls and cherubim of stone. The boats are not strong enough and are not ready. But if a present be kindly made to us, we will see that they are got ready, and ascend the river."

If the writer of the third failed to have his request granted, it could scarcely be for lack of persistence in making it known. It is a letter written by a tenant to his landlord, and belongs to the age of Abraham:

"To my lord say, thus saith Ibgatum thy servant: As, my lord, thou hast heard, the enemy has carried off my oxen. Never before have I sent to thee, my lord. Now I have caused a letter to be brought to thee, my lord, Do thou, my lord, send me one young cow. I will weigh out and send five shekels of silver to thee, my lord. My lord, what thou sayest, under the command of Marduk, thy protector, what pleases thee, no one can hinder thee, my lord. My lord, do thou make her worth the five shekels of silver that I have weighed out and sent to thee. Do thou, my lord, treat seriously this request, do not trifle with my wish. Let my lord not wonder at this request, which I send my lord. I am thy servant. I will do thy will, my lord. As to the young cow, which thou, my lord, dost send, let her be on credit, and either to Basu, or wherever is convenient to my lord, do thou send. With Iliikisham, my brother, let the young cow come. And I, in order that my lord should quickly consent and send the young

---

[2] Johns: Baby. and Assy. Laws, Letters and Contracts, 336.

cow, will forthwith weigh out and send fifteen shekels of silver to thee, my lord."[3]

Sayce has suggested that the five shekels of silver was the amount he paid annually for the lease of his farm, and that he sent it at this time to further influence the landlord to grant his request. Another interpretation has been put upon it that he sent the five shekels as a payment down, but did not propose to pay the full price until he saw the particular cow sent him.

Letters were enclosed generally in an envelope of clay. Powdered clay was sprinkled over the letter to prevent its clinging to the cover. Because the envelope of clay had to be broken before the letter was read, safety and privacy was proven by the unbroken cover. Again the tablet upon which the letter was inscribed was sometimes covered with a linen wrapper and the ends held by a seal—a lump of clay pressed down with the impression of the seal upon it. Few of these clay or linen envelopes have been found, for they were regarded as valueless and were cast aside. A very fair postal system was maintained in Mesopotamia.

"Babylonian and Assyrian letters were treated much as ours are when they are put into a post-bag to which the seals of the post-office are attached. There were excellent roads all over Western Asia, with post-stations at intervals where relays of horses could be procured. Along these all letters to or from the king and the government were carried by royal messengers. It is probable that the letters of private individuals were also carried by the same hands. The civilized and oriental world was bound together by a network of postal routes over which literary intercourse was perpetually passing. They extended from the Euphrates to the Nile and from the plateau of Asia Minor to the confines of Arabia. These routes followed the old lines of war and trade along which armies had marched and merchantmen had traveled for unnumbered generations. The Tell-el-Amarna tablets show that letter-writing was not confined to Assyria and Babylonia on the one hand, or to Egypt on the other. Wherever the ancient culture of Babylonia had spread, there had gone with it not only the cuneiform characters and the use of clay as a writing material, but the art of letter-writing as well."[4]

[3] Johns: Baby. and Assy. Laws, Letters and Contracts, 334.
[4] Sayce: Life and Customs in Baby. and Assy., 228.

Fifteen hundred and seventy-five letters alone were found in the library of Asshurbanipal, unearthed by Layard. This great Assyrian king sent scribes throughout Babylonia to visit ancient temples and copy tablets on which were preserved ancient writings. Some thirty thousand were collected before his death and they treated of all subjects known at that time. It was remarkable that when this splendid palace fell into ruins, many of these tablets remained uninjured, and, having laid undisturbed for twenty-five hundred years, were finally brought to light some fifty years ago to give the world of today their old-time messages.

Deluge Story—Column III.

"The surface of the land like fire they wasted;
they destroyed all life from the face of the land;
to battle against men they brought the waters.
Brother saw not his brother; men knew not one another.

In heaven the gods feared the flood and
hastened to ascend to the heaven of Anu.
The gods, like dogs in the kennel, crouched down in a heap.
Six days and nights
the wind, the flood, and the storm go on overwhelming.
The seventh day, when it approached, the flood subsided, the
storm which had fought against men like an armed host
was quieted. The sea began to dry, and the wind and the flood
 ended.
I beheld the sea and uttered a cry,
for the whole of mankind was turned to clay;
like trunks the corpses floated.
I opened the window, and light smote upon my face;
I stopped and sat down; I wept;
over my face flowed my tears.
I beheld a shore beyond the sea;
a district rose twelve times distant.
On the mountain of Nizir the ship grounded;
the mountain of Nizir stopped the ship, and it was not able to
 pass over it.

The first day, the second day, the mountain of Nizir stopped the ship.
The third day, the fourth day, the mountain of Nizir stopped the ship.
The fifth day, the sixth day, the mountain of Nizir stopped the ship.
The seventh day when it approached
I sent forth a dove, and it left. The dove went in and returned
and found no resting place, and it came back.
Then I sent forth a swallow, and it left. The swallow went and returned,
and found no resting place, and it came back.
I sent forth a raven, and it left.
The raven went, and saw the going down of the waters, and it approached, it waded, it croaked; it did not return.
I sent the animals to the four winds; I sacrificed a sacrifice
I built an altar on the peak of the mountain.
I sent vessels . . . by sevens;
underneath them I spread reeds, cedar-wood, and herbs.
The gods smelt the savour; the gods smelt the good savour; the gods gathered like flies over the sacrifices.
Thereupon the great goddess at her approach
lifted up the mighty bow which Anu had created according to his wishes.
These gods, by my necklace, never will I forget."

ISHTAR. FROM AN ASSYRIAN CYLINDER.

CHAPTER XIII.

Clothing.

The Babylonians and Assyrians were very fond of dress. There were three essentials to Mesopotamian dress, and accessories depended upon the taste and purse of the wearer. A head-dress, a tunic and a robe were the main features of one's apparel, although all were not of necessity worn by the lower classes. The head-dress was frequently of felt and was some times quilted; the tunic was generally made of linen when worn in Babylonia and of wool in Assyria; the robe was long, falling to the ankles; it was often of wool and was finished with a deep fringe. The tunic and some times the robe as well were belted at the waist by a wide and elaborate girdle. Women's garments were similar to those worn by men, but their robes fell in more ample folds. Naturally fashions changed and a garment worn in the days of the Semitic invasion would have appeared odd and out of date in the age of Asshurbanipal.

Early portraits of kings show them clad in thick quilted skirts falling to the ankles, while quilted turbans covered their heads. Later robes took the place of the skirt. Parasols were carried in Babylonia as protection against the heat, but in Assyria they gradually became the privilege of the royal family. In portraits of later Assyrian kings, the parasol is frequently shown. This custom may have been borrowed from Persia.

Ordinarily no head-dress was worn by the lower classes in Babylonia unless, perhaps, to denote some special calling. Certain musicians appear with caps. The devotees of fashion probably donned head-dresses at pleasure.

Jewelry was popular with both men and women, even the poor being adorned with necklaces, bracelets, anklets. Shoes and sandals were seldom worn in the southern kingdom. In Assyria, naturally a colder climate brought about some variations of dress. High boots and leather breeches were worn by the soldiers of later periods; shoes were needed to protect the feet from frosty ground, and cloaks were required in addition to the usual robe.

Embroidered and imported robes, smart hats and other details of wearing apparel were characteristic of later periods when wealth and leisure gave opportunity for such indulgences. Certain it is that the simple tunic sufficed in early days, and rank was indicated by its greater or abbreviated length.

The ancient Chaldeans or Sumerians always shaved their heads and faces. Influenced by this custom, the Babylonians did not wear long beards. The Assyrians, more purely Semitic, wore long ones and had hair dressers largely in the place of barbers, who curled both their beards and hair.

A word should be said of the costumes of the priests. They may always be distinguished on the monuments by their long, flounced robes, reaching nearly to the ground. Because the goat was an animal of special sanctity, a goat-skin was invariably thrown over the shoulder—quite as the Egyptian priest wore the skin of a leopard.

In connection with the jewelry worn by men, we may consider the little cylinders which served as seals. In Babylonia, because of the scarcity of stone, even tiny pebbles were valued, and it came to be the custom to have these cut in cylindrical shapes by expert stone-cutters. An opening was made throughout their length to allow a cord or chain to pass through. This attached the cylinder to the owner's wrist. Upon the round surface of the cylinder were engraved various designs and figures, and a few words explaining the identity of the wearer, name of his father and other noteworthy facts regarding him. His name was affixed, and with this he stamped his letters and all documents. To be without a cylinder was almost as inconvenient as to be without a name. The very poor, who could not afford such a seal, were obliged to make a nail-mark in the soft clay, while some one wrote the name of the person to whom that particular mark belonged. The possessor of a cylinder had only to pass it over the clay and his signature was made. Many of these little cylinders have been recovered, and some lack the name of an owner, showing that they had been made by a gem-cutter, but had not yet found a buyer.

Food.

Food was easily obtained in Mesopotamia, and consisted mainly of grains and dried fish. Cereals were made into little cakes and seasoned with dates or some other fruit. Fish and fowl were plentiful; many kinds of fruits and vegetables were grown, and wine and beer were universally used. Lacking the tomb-pictures of Egypt, we know less about the food and its preparation in the Euphrates valley.

Sports and Pastimes.

For our knowledge of ancient Babylonian and Assyrian life, we are dependent largely upon scenes depicted on palace walls, especially the walls of royal dwellings. These scenes commemorate the doings of the king particularly, and where laborers, slaves and the common people are shown at all, they are seen at work, building palaces and temples, marching to battle, swelling the triumphal processions, or they are cultivating the fields, storing away the grain—all to the glory of the realm and consequently to the king. Naturally then, we know little about the pastimes of the masses. They no doubt thronged the streets on festivals, for then they were free from work. Even labor on royal palaces—always pushed with all possible speed—was then suspended. Every day in the year had its own significance, but five days each month were of particular importance, being sacred to the gods, and were duly observed. Worship and merry-making were in a measure mingled. Other days for popular observance were those in which the king and the army returned from successful wars. A triumphal procession passed slowly through the streets on its way to the temple, where thanksgiving was rendered the gods who had made victory possible. Such occasions were always holidays, and the people in gay attire, gathered to witness the home-coming of their sovereign, and to gaze in wonder at the booty and the captives.

Two recreations pictured on the palace walls were enjoyed only by the nobles and the wealthy classes—the hunt and the banquet. In modern times, when those in high position have occasionally laid down important matters for a brief while to seek recreation in hunting, fishing and out of door life, they have taken opportunity to throw off much of the conventionality surrounding their every-day life and have found some diversion in "roughing it,"—in sharing the varying fortune likely to befall those who leave the certain comforts of home for the uncertain conditions to be met away from the centers of civilization. Such was not at all the case with the kings of Assyria when they left their capitals to hunt the lion in its distant jungles and marshes. In the palace of Sennacherib and Asshurbanipal, hunts have been depicted throughout their progress. We may see the king marching out of the city in his state chariot, his charioteer at his side, while behind him an attendant holds high an embroidered parasol over his kingly head to protect him from the rays of the sun. Nobles accompany him on horses and they, together with the guards and retinue of servants, make up a small army. Goats and cattle are driven along, that his majesty and his nobles may have fresh milk and meat throughout their absence; a sumptuous tent shelters the king when the procession stops for the night, while each noble tries to pitch his tent near the more splendid one of his king. Maspero has graphically described the hunt. Some wild oxen have been discovered, and the king gives chase:

"In less time than we can speak, three of the bulls are rolling on the ground, pierced with several arrows; the four others but slightly wounded, turn round and gallop towards the river. Asshurbanipal follows the largest of them, which he is almost sure is wounded in the shoulder; then gradually he overtakes it, skillfully drives his chariot beside it without checking speed, and laying aside his bow, grasps one of the poignards he wears in his belt. With one hand he seizes one of the animal's horns, with the other he plunges his weapon into his neck; the short, wide blade divides the spine, between the neck and shoulder, the bull falls like a stone. A flight of arrows arrests the fugitives before they can reach the water; the whole herd is killed, except the old bull that escaped at first.

"The return to the camp is a triumphal march. As soon as the sentinels signal the arrival of the party, soldiers, slaves, women, all who are not bound by etiquette or military duty, hurry to meet it, and form two lines, watching the procession. The sight of the seven bulls, each carried by five or six men, almost causes them to forget the respect due to royalty. They exclaim upon the size of the animals, the strength of their horns, the savage aspect given by their manes; they praise their master's skill, and loudly thank the gods who have favored him with such rare and terrible game. Asshurbanipal has left his chariot in front of his tent, and now prepares to return thanks for his success to the lord Asshur and the lady Ishtar. Two priests with their harps are waiting to commence the hymns of praise. The bearers place the oxen side by side in a single line. The king, accompanied by his fly-flap and sunshade-bearers, stands on the right, the bow in his left hand. He takes the cup full of sacramental wine, which the vizier presents to him, touches it with his lips, then partly empties it over the victims whilst the musicians play. The same evening a messenger will start for Nineveh to have the new exploit graven upon stone. The picture will portray the departure, the chase, the death, the solemn entry, and an inscription placed above the last scene will tell posterity the name of the victor. 'I, Asshurbanipal, king of multitudes, king of Assyria, whose power is secured by Asshur and Beltis, I have killed seven oxen; I have strung the mighty bow of Ishtar, queen of battles, against them, I have made an offering over them and poured wine upon them.'

"On the following day the dogs rouse three lions from their jungle. These are killed after having made a desperate resistance. 'The three bodies are carried back to the camp, then presented to Ishtar with the same ceremonies that had celebrated the triumph over the wild bulls, and the sculptors were ordered to represent the hand-to-hand struggle of the sovereign and his savage foe. 'I, Asshurbanipal, king of peoples, king of Assyria, alone on foot, in my majesty, I seized a lion of the desert by the ear; and by the mercy of Asshur and Ishtar, queen of battles, I pierced its loins with my lance, with mine own hands.'"[1]

A banquet sometimes celebrated the return from a fine and successful hunt, but it faded into insignificance when compared with the one held after the return from a war of pillage and conquest. The entire population of the capital became temporary guests of the king.

---
[1] Maspero: Ancient Egypt and Assyria, 260.

"After the procession, the day is passed in a perfect frenzy of joy by the whole nation. It is customary for all the inhabitants of the city, slaves and freemen, to eat and drink at the king's expense during the festival; this is a method of giving them a share of the booty. For seven days the palace gates are open to all comers. Many colored stuffs suspended over the walls by means of ropes have transformed the courts into immense banqueting halls. The crowd is coming and going from morning till night; the people install themselves upon state-seats and ask for whatever they like; the slaves have orders to give them anything they wish for, and to bring each person whatever he desires as many times as he asks for it. Women and children are admitted to these festivals as well as men. The soldiers kept in barracks by their duty are not forgotten; the king sends them the food and wine they cannot fetch for themselves in so great profusion that they have nothing to regret. The loaves disappear by thousands, by thousands also the oxen, sheep, goats, and birds of all kinds are sacrificed to satisfy the public appetite. But what they eat is nothing to what they drink. The Assyrian is sober in ordinary life, but he does not know how to stop if he once allows himself any excess. Wines of Assyria and Chaldea, wines from Elam, wines from Syria and Phoenicia, wines from Egypt, the skins are emptied as soon as opened, without visibly quenching the universal thirst. After one or two days no brain is strong enough to resist it, and Nineveh presents the extraordinary spectacle of a whole city in different degrees of intoxication; when the festival is over, several days are required before it resumes its usual aspect.

Whilst the people are becoming tipsy outside, Asshurbanipal feasts the leading chiefs and the ministers of state within the palace. Unlike the common people, the nobles eat but little, so that few dishes of meat are set before them, but cakes and fruits of different kinds, grapes, dates, apples, pears, and figs are brought in continual relays, by long lines of slaves. On the other hand, they drink a great deal—with more refinement, perhaps, than the common people, but with equal avidity.

The only persons who do not drink, or who drink little, through the necessity of retaining their sobriety, are the guards, the servants and the musicians. No festival is complete without the presence of singers, and the king's musicians conscientiously perform their finest melodies. Perhaps some one listened to them at the beginning of the feast, but now that the great silver bowls have been filled and emptied several times, their music is literally wasted. They may sing out of tune, or remain silent, just as they please, no one will listen or care.

The court poet has placed the recital of the hero's life and exploits, from the hour of his birth until the day of his triumph, in his own mouth. He concluded by saying:

"'I am a strong warrior, beloved of Asshur and Ishtar, the child of royalty. The gods have been gracious to me. The wheat has grown to five cubits, and its ears of corn are always one cubit long; during my reign, abundance has overflowed; during all the years of my reign, the divine blessing has been poured out upon me like a heavy dew. The gods have raised me higher than any king ever ascended before me. Whilst Asshur and Ishtar support me, who can prevail against me? My power is everlastingly founded by their hands, the duration of my race is established; they shall reign for many days, and for everlasting years.'"[2]

---

[2] Maspero: Ancient Egypt and Assyria, 368, ff.

ASSYRIAN KING IN ROYAL ROBES.

CHAPTER XIV.

Architecture and Decoration.

Architecture is evolved from religion as well as from nature. Generally speaking, we find temples of worship to be the first buildings erected by every people.

Because the Babylonians were limited by lack of other material to sun or kiln-dried brick, and the Assyrians, devoid of originality, limited themselves to the same baked clay, we would scarcely expect to find pleasing or artistic buildings in either state. Even in the dwellings of rich and poor, the great difference was one of size. It was impossible to make a clay wall very ornate, but the wealthy could have more walls and broader expanse of bricks. Size, or hugeness, then, signified superiority. It naturally followed that the temple, the noblest structure attempted by the Mesopotamians, was especially large, being called by a word which meant "mountain house."

Large tracts of land were dedicated to the temples. Having been consecrated by libations of wine, oil and honey, the temple proper, consisting of halls or rooms surrounding an inner court, was first erected. Near this arose the ziggurat or tower, and many smaller buildings, not unlike private dwellings. These served as residences for the priests, for the temple school, store-houses for the sacred oil and other articles pertaining to worship, and many other purposes. The entire area was enclosed by a wall, and was ordinarily remote from the noises of the city. Within this large enclosure other walls surrounded buildings of special sanctity and importance. Within the temple proper was an inner room where the statue of the god was kept. This corresponded to the "holy of holies" in a Jewish synagogue, and was entered only by the priest or king.

The ziggurat or mountain house—for this alone was massive and high—built as symbolic of the mountain form which the whole earth was supposed to assume, was a tower, sometimes three, sometimes five or even seven stories high. The remains of one of these ziggurats was discovered by Dr. Peters and his explorers at Nippur, and is supposed to have been built as early as 2700 B. C.

The ziggurat at Borsippa had a base of earthwork 272 feet on each side, and was 26 feet high. Above this foundation arose two stories, 26 feet in height, each 42 feet less on a side than the story below. Four stories, each 15 feet high, followed, decreasing 42 feet on a side like the lower ones, and the last, or seventh, story, was just 29 feet square. Stairways wound around the outside of the tower, and it was thought pleasing to the gods that worshippers should ascend to the top. Each story was sacred to some particular god whose statue it contained while the shrine of the most important deity was placed on top. Sometimes each story was painted a different color.

The mass of worshippers, however, assembled at the temple rather than the tower, and offerings were made at the base of the ziggurat instead of at the top.

It was the ambition of the kings that the inner walls of their buildings, whether temples or palaces, should "shine like the sunlight," and to this end gold, silver and precious stones lent their gleams and glows to mural decorations.

Next in importance to the temples were royal palaces, and in Assyria, where religion was given less prominence, the temple was a mere adjunct of the palace. Here again, a large inner court was surrounded by halls and rooms. The palace court was paved and decorated and upon the inner walls of the palace the skill of the artist was expended. The floors were made of tiles, and these followed ingenious patterns. Sometimes the floors were formed of bricks or tablets covered with inscriptions deeply cut; then molten metal—brass or bronze—was poured over the whole, and filling the depressions, caused the entire floor to look like a curious and intricate design.

It was comparatively easy to lay floors and raise walls of bricks, but it was quite another thing to make roofs of them. The longest rafters were obtained from the cedars of Lebanon and these ranged from 30 to 40 feet in length. This practically determined the width of the halls and rooms, which seem to have been even four times their width in length.

The monotony of the inner walls was relieved by alabaster reaching around the halls from twelve to fifteen feet above the floors, and held in place by strong iron clamps. On this soft, yielding substance were portrayed scenes in the life and exploits of the king—his campaigns, hunts, works of peace, and acts of worship. These were executed in bas-relief after the slabs were fitted into place. Above them extended a frieze perhaps three feet in width, made of tiles painted in delicate colors and laid in such a way as to form a picture or design. We miss the gaudy colors so popular in Egypt. It has been well said that the Assyrian artist sought to please by the elegance of his forms and the harmony of his hues—not to startle by a display of bright and strongly contrasted colors. The palace of Sennacherib, second only to the temple of Karnak in grandeur—covered an area of eight acres, and contained some eighty apartments. The palace of Sargon at Khorsabad had no less than 209 rooms. Of the scenes depicted on the slabs of alabaster in the state apartments Rawlinson writes at length: "The most striking characteristic of Sennacherib's ornamentation is its strong and marked realism. Mountains, rocks, trees, roads, rivers, lakes were regularly portrayed, an attempt being made to represent the locality, whatever it might be, as truthfully as the artist's skill and the character of his material rendered possible. The species of trees is distinguished, gardens, fields, ponds, reeds, are carefully represented; wild animals are introduced, as stags, boars and antelopes; birds fly from tree to tree, or stand over their nests, feeding the young who stretch up to them; fish disport themselves in the water; fishermen ply their craft; boatmen and agricultural laborers pursue their avocations; the scene is, as it were, photographed, with all its features.

"In the same spirit of realism, Sennacherib chooses for artistic representation scenes of a commonplace and everyday character. The trains of attendants who daily enter his palace with game and locust for his dinner, and cakes and fruit for his dessert, appear on the walls of the passages exactly as they walked through his courts bearing the delicacies in which he delighted. Elsewhere he puts before us the entire process of carving and transporting a colossal bull, from the first removal of the huge stone in its rough state from the quarry to its final elevation on a palace mound, as part of the great gateway of a royal residence. We see the trackers dragging the rough block, supported on a low flat-bottomed boat, along the course of a river, disposed in gangs, each gang having a costume of its own which probably marked its nation, under taskmasters armed with staves, who urged on the labor with blows. The whole scene must be represented, and so the trackers are there, to the number of three hundred, each delineated with as much care as if he were not the exact image of ninety-nine others. We then observe the block transferred to land, and carved into the rough semblance of a bull, in which form it is placed on a rude sledge and conveyed along level land by gangs of laborers, arranged nearly as before, to the foot of the mound at whose top it has to be placed. The construction of the mound is elaborately represented. Brickmakers are seen moulding the bricks at its base, while workmen with baskets at their backs, full of earth, brick, stone, or rubbish toil up the ascent—for the mound is already half raised—and empty their burdens out upon the summit. The bull, still lying on its sledge, is then drawn up an inclined plane to the top by four gangs of laborers, in the presence of the monarch and his attendants. After this the carving is completed, and the colossus, having been raised into an upright position, is conveyed along the surface of the platform to the exact site which it is to occupy."

Guarding the portals of the palaces stood the winged bulls and lions, in pairs. They were thought to ward off demons and to inspire awe in those who beheld them. They were formed with five legs, in order that the spectator, whether he viewed them from the front or side, might still see the usual four. Speaking of these great stone creatures, Layard wrote: " I used to contemplate for hours these mysterious emblems, and muse over their intent and history. What more noble forms could have ushered the people into the temple of their gods? What more sublime images could have been borrowed from nature by men who sought, unaided by the light of revealed religion, to embody their conception of the wisdom, power and ubiquity of a Supreme Being? They could find no better type of intellect and knowledge than the head of a man; of strength, than the body of a lion; of rapidity of motion than the wings of a bird. These winged human-headed lions were not idle creations, the offspring of mere fancy; their meaning was written upon them. They had awed and instructed races which flourished three thousand years ago. Through the portals which they guarded, kings, priests, and warriors had borne sacrifices to their altars long before the wisdom of the East had penetrated to Greece, and furnished its mythology with symbols long recognized by the Assyrian votaries.

"They may have been buried, and their existence may have been unknown before the foundation of the Eternal City. For twenty-five centuries they had been hidden from the eye of man, and they now stood forth once more in their ancient majesty. But how changed was the scene around them! The luxury and civilization of a mighty nation had given place to the wretchedness and ignorance of a few half-barbarous tribes. The wealth of temples and the riches of the great cities had been succeeded by ruins and shapeless heaps of earth. Above the spacious hall in which they stood the plow had passed and the corn now waved. Egypt has monuments no less ancient and no less wonderful, but they have stood forth for ages to testify her early power and renown, while these before me had but now appeared to bear witness, in the words of the prophet, that once 'the Assyrian was a cedar in Lebanon with fair branches. . . . Now is Nineveh desolate and dry like a wilderness, and flocks lie down in the midst of her.'"

Babylon was probably the most beautiful city of antiquity. Nebuchadnezzar II. surrounded the capital with walls of such solidity that it is supposed the city could never have been taken by assault. His father began the fortifications, and it was left for the greatest Babylonian king to complete them and make them even more secure. Between the outer and inner walls, wide distances were left. Here trees and gardens were planted. This space was provided for nearby villagers in times of siege, and it was also intended that here fields of grain might be grown to sustain the population under such trying conditions.

Herodotus described these walls: "And here I may not omit to tell the use to which the mould dug out of the great moat was turned, nor the manner wherein the wall was wrought. As fast as they dug the moat, the soil which they got from the cutting was made into bricks, and when a sufficient number were completed, they baked the bricks in kilns. Then they set to building and began with bricking the borders of the moat, after which they proceeded to construct the wall itself, using throughout for their cement hot bitumen, and interposed a layer of wattled reeds at every thirtieth course of the bricks." According to this writer the outer wall was 14 miles in circumference, 93 feet thick, and 370 feet in height, but it is supposed that he included the city of Borsippa, across the river, within the length of wall, and no doubt he computed the height to include the lofty towers built at intervals along the wall, to give sentinels a wide outlook over the country. These walls the Greeks included among the wonders of the world, and probably ancient warfare could not have destroyed them.

The Hanging Gardens of this great city were also enumerated among the world's wonders. These are said to have been built by Nebuchadnezzar for his Median queen, who wearied of the dull, flat country of Babylonia, and pined for her mountain home. The lowest terrace arose some 500 feet square, and three other terraces, supported by arches and pillars, were constructed above it, each smaller than the one beneath. These four platforms or terraces were covered with soil drawn up in carts, and the earth was deep enough to grow large trees, as well as all kinds of plants and vines. A pump house was located on top, water being drawn from the river and forced all through the structure, while the pipes were carefully concealed. Broad stairways led up to the uppermost terraces where a residence was built for the favorite queen. Hanging gardens had been built in Nineveh by former kings, but none so splendid as these nor on so gigantic a scale. Seen from afar, overtowering the high walls of the city, their height accentuated by the vast expanse of level land, the effect was that of a low mountain, clothed in verdure and scenting the breeze with the blended fragrance of its beautiful flowers.

The population of Babylon was probably above 500,000 and the city contained more wealthy families than any other in Asia. The houses of these added to the beauty of the place, while two royal palaces, one on either side of the Euphrates, exceeded all former splendor in the southland. Streets were laid out at right angles, and the more important ones terminated in high gates leading out of the city walls. These gates were made of cedar and covered with bronze plates. Well might

Nebuchadnezzar exclaim: "Is not this great Babylon, which I have built for the royal dwelling-place, by the might of my power, and for the glory of my majesty?" And again: "For the astonishment of men I built this house; awe of the power of my majesty encompasses its walls. The temples of the great gods I made brilliant as the sun, shining as the day. In Babylon alone I raised the seat of my dominion, in no other city!"

DECORATION IN ENAMELED TILES ON ONE OF THE GATES OF THE HAREM IN SARGON'S PALACE.

CHAPTER XV.

Religion.

We have learned something of the primitive religious ideas of the Chaldeans, or Sumerians, who originally occupied Babylonia. However, when the Babylonian religion is mentioned, reference is made to the later faith of the valley, and this resulted from a blending of the Sumerian beliefs and the religious system brought in by the Semitic invaders.

The original inhabitants of the country, in their attempt to explain the forces of nature, had conceived that spirits belonged to animate as well as inanimate objects, and that these spirits had power to bless or injure. The rain could refresh the crops or it might wash them out of the earth; the sun could cause the grain to germinate or in a day could dry it up with withering heat. The evil which each spirit was likely to do so far exceeded the good that gradually these spirits were thought of as demons. It was a demon which took possession of a man and made him ill. Famines were brought by the south-west wind. In short, demons threatened on every hand, and only a diligent use of charms and frequent incantations could protect humanity and enable each to live out his days amidst such imminent dangers.

Now it is evident that there is no trace of our conception of a god in all this, but the early Sumerians had also their gods which were likewise personifications of nature, and these were later adopted by the Babylonian Semites, who also took over the earlier beliefs about the various spirits. In the course of perhaps several hundred years from the blending of the two beliefs, with such changes as growing intelligence brought, the religion of the Babylonians was evolved.

The Semites who pushed north and founded the state of Assyria, took with them the religion of the southern kingdom.

In explaining further the religion of the southland, we must remember its early political situation. Instead of one united kingdom, it was made up of a number of little states under leadership of cities. The leading cities had grown up around the temple of some protecting deity whose favor was believed to extend over the immediate vicinity. Thus, for example, Sin, the Moon-god, was not only the patron deity of Ur, but of the whole state of which Ur was the capital city. To exalt its god, a state would reach out to incorporate another. The people thus conquered did not cease to worship their former deity but now gave homage to the god of their conquerors as well. When several little states were united, the greatest of their gods was the god of their strongest city, since he had clearly demonstrated his power by giving victory over the rest. In truth, it should be explained that such was the official god, for without doubt the masses knew little of political absorption and worshipped the god of their infancy rather than new gods honored by the state.

In course of various unions, En-lil or Bel became the most important god in Babylonia and remained so until Babylon gained supremacy over all other states. Then Marduk, her ancient god, was given first place.

A brief consideration of the leading Babylonian gods will help us to gain some insight into these early ideas and conceptions. As early as 3500 B. C., En-lil or Bel was worshipped in Nippur. The very name testifies to its Sumerian origin. Lil signifies *demon,* and En-lil was the *chief of spirits.* In one of the earliest inscriptions in Sumerian he is mentioned with *Anna* and *Enki,* the gods of heaven and the abyss. These three made up the original triad and as such they continued throughout the later period as Bel Anu and Ea. Nippur became a strong political center and this made Bel principal god of the land until his powers were transferred to Marduk. Bel's consort, like the consorts of all Babylonian gods, was but a weak reflection of the god himself.

Eridu was a seaport. Ea, god of "that which is below," was its local deity. He was first considered as god of the earth but the water was of greater commercial importance and gradually he grew to be regarded as god of the deep. From merely a local god, protecting Eridu, he extended his sway over all waters. In both Larsa and Sippar the sun-god Shamash, known among the Sumerians as *Utu,* was honored. No other deity enjoyed such continued popularity as the "god of day." From the earliest to the latest period he was hailed as the "god that gives light and life to all things, upon whose favor the prosperity of the fields and well-being of man depend." As light is opposed to darkness, so again light reveals wrong doing; for this reason this god of light became associated with justice. Sin, the Moon-god, was given prominence over Shamash, so far as official order of deities was concerned. Some renown attached to him because he was the father of Ishtar. Indeed from being the father of many gods and goddesses, he was remembered as father of this brilliant goddess, greater than all others. Sin was worshipped more extensively in early times.

Ishtar, supreme goddess, mother of the gods, was first conceived as a mild, sympathetic mother-spirit, a goddess of love and care. In Assyria, however, she was regarded as goddess of war and battle, and was associated with Asshur in that connection. Nabu, the wise, all-knowing god, sacred in Borsippa, was also popular in literature and learning. In addition to being patron of intelligence and wisdom, he was also patron of agriculture. When his favor was given, storehouses were heaped high with grain; when his favor was withdrawn, famine afflicted the land. From the twelfth century B.C. onwards his name appears in royal names such as Nabo-polasar, Nebuchadnezzar, Nabo-nidus, and in the ninth century B.C. the worship of this god only was preached: "Put thy trust in Nebo; trust not in another God." The long proper names so contantly found in both Babylonia and Assyria were always compounded from several words and had some particular meaning—as, Sennacherib, or more correctly Sin-akhi-irib, meaning "Sin has multiplied brethren;" Buzur-Asshur—"a stronghold is Asshur;" Sargon or Sargina—Sar meaning king and gin, to establish, "I am the established king."

Anu was the god of the heavens; Ramman the god of storm, and both held important places in the myths and stories of the people. In later times Ea was a deity of wide dominion. Father of Marduk, he was god of humanity. He gave wisdom, and as god of water, fountains were sacred to him. Oannes or Fish-Man was simply a name given him by Greek travellers. In time he was regarded as god of civilization, and nothing could have been more natural, for over the waters he protected came civilization to Chaldea, and progress was facilitated by navigation. Great works of art were ascribed to him; likewise he was god of the smith and of the sculptor.

The great bulls were works of his hand. He was probably made father of Marduk in later years, when Babylon's god had been given first place in the nation, and the only way to reconcile all that was believed of Ea was to show that as father, his wisdom had descended to his son, Marduk.

In addition to these leading deities, there was a host of minor ones but their enumeration would be useless for our purposes. One tablet in the British museum contained originally the names of nearly 1,800 gods. They were early local gods, and as their states were added to the kingdom, they were included in the temple lists to pacify their worshippers.

The religious faith and worship for any one district was not complicated. Each little community had its patron deity and paid scant attention to the numerous gods of temple lists.

In Assyria the political situation had been far different. No large number of petty states, each with its religious system, had united to form the kingdom; consequently we miss the numerous gods found in Babylonia. Asshur was the one great god of the northern people. Alone he stood, god of all. When Assyria entered upon her military career, Asshur was regarded as god of war, and because of repeated victory, grew very popular in this conception. His standard was carried into battle to encourage the soldiers; knowing that his mighty power was with them, they could not fail. The standard of Asshur, one of the earliest ensigns of the battle field, has its own interest for us. On top of a long pole, guarded on either side by huge wings, perhaps the wings of the eagle, a circle enclosed the figure of an archer, shooting an arrow. Seen afar by faltering troops, the standards of the national god gave new strength and inspired fresh hope of victory.

The similarity between the religion of the Assyrians and the Hebrews has frequently been noted. Both nations were Semitic and hence their inheritances were the same. Their origin and early home was identical. The Hebrews, in course of their wanderings and experiences, grew to worship one God to the exclusion of all others. The Assyrians retained their warlike disposition, and worshipped one God as greater than all others, but they allowed other deities to be honored as well. Both nations with great regularity ascribed all their victories to the divinity they worshipped—nay, more by far, they attributed all their slaughters to the same deity. The Hebrews, during the period when as tribes they struggled for existence, treated their enemies with great cruelty. This was done, they insisted, to appease their God, or generally in furtherance of his direct command. Their brethren, the Assyrians, proceeded in exactly the same manner, and all their ruthless deeds were done to gratify Asshur and avenge the insults done him by revolts against his strength. One divinity commanded the outrages as much as the other, and they were but expressions of an early and barbarous development.

Among the masses, the sacrifice was unquestionably that feature of worship best understood. It seems to have been an instinct born in man to make offerings to appease the wrath of a god, and to seek by the same means to win his favor. The priests acted as mediators between the people and the divinity. To a priest, the farmer, laborer, and slave as well as the noble and prince, brought each his offering, and such portions as were considered sacred were offered upon the altar.

As the Egyptian provided food for the ka of the deceased, so also the Babylonian provided it for the zi of his dead. It is possible that the belief in the shadowy ka came originally from the valley of the Euphrates.

Gods were supposed to visit their shrines at intervals and so food was placed for them. The masses of the people were so ignorant that it is entirely probable they regarded the image of the god as the god himself, and that they thought these images of clay and stone actually devoured the food they brought.[1] The more enlightened had no such crude notions, but realized that the god-spirit was something apart from anything they saw and worshipped. If we substitute the name of the Hebrew deity in place of the Babylonian god, worshippers of Judah might have used some of the hymns of prayer and praise used in Babylonia:

"The heart of my lord is wroth; may it be appeased!
O lord, my sins are many, my transgressions are great!
The sin that I sinned I knew not,
The transgression I committed I knew not,
The lord in the wrath of his heart has regarded me,
God in the fierceness of his heart has revealed himself to me.

[1] See the apocryphal story of Bel and the Dragon.

I sought for help and none took my hand;
I wept, and none stood at my side;
I cried aloud, and there was none that heard me.
I am in trouble and hiding; I dare not look up.
To my god, the merciful one, I turn myself, I utter my prayer;
The sins I have sinned turn into a blessing;
The transgressions I have committed let the wind carry away!
Strip off my manifold wickedness as a garment!
O my god, seven times seven are my transgressions: forgive my sins!"

Another, written first to Sin of Ur, and later incorporated into the hymns of the nation:

"Father, long-suffering and full of forgiveness,
Whose hand upholdeth the life of all mankind!
First-born, omnipotent, whose heart is immensity, and there is none who may fathom it!
In heaven who is supreme? Thou alone, thou art supreme!
On earth, who is supreme? Thou alone, thou art supreme!
As for thee, thy will is made known in heaven, and the angels bow their faces.
As for thee, thy will is made known upon earth, and the spirits below kiss the ground."

Elsewhere we find Ashur appealed to as "lord of the gods, *who has created himself.*"

Services were many. Each day required its own offerings and ceremonies. The changes of the moon were watched and accompanied by peculiar services. Taboos were placed on certain days and on these no work was permitted.

The priesthood was large. Besides the chief priests, there were elders, anointers,—who anointed the images of the gods and the vessels of the temple with sacred oil; priests who presided over the oracles and whose function it was to ascertain auspicious times for war and other prodigious undertakings, and seers, who interpreted dreams.

Revenues of the temples came from offerings and more regularly, from the tithe, a tax paid by both king and subjects. In this way, the temples controlled property. Their lands were usually rented out.

When Babylonia reached her age of greatest prosperity, the religion of the land had been greatly secularized, and the temples were important for their business significances quite as much as for their religious features. " The temple exerted an overwhelming financial influence in smaller towns. Only in certain large cities was it rivalled by a few great firms. Its financial status was that of the chief, if not the only, great capitalist. Its political influence was also great. This was largely enlisted on the side of peace at home and stability in business." Its great possessions resulted from the daily and monthly payments, from lands dedicated to the temple by devout ones, and from careful investment of revenues.

"The temple was also a commercial institution of high efficiency. Their accumulations of all sorts of raw products were enormous. The temple let out or advanced all kinds of raw material, usually on easy terms. To the poor, as a charity, advances were made in times of a scarcity or personal want, to their tenants as part of the metayer system of tenure, to slaves who lived outside its precincts, and to contractors who took the material on purely commercial terms. The return was expected in kind, to the full amount of advance, or with stipulated interest.

"The temples did a certain amount of banking business. By this we mean that they held money on deposit against the call of the depositor. Whether they charged for safe-keeping or remunerated themselves by investing the bulk of their capital, reserving a balance to meet calls, does not appear.

"In certain circumstances the king's officials might borrow of the temples. Some kings laid hands on the treasure of the temple for their own use. Doubtless this was done under bond to repay. The cases in which we read of such practices are always represented as a wrong.

"The temple could act in all the capacities of a private individual or a firm of traders."[1]

The religion of Mesopotamia did not require the believer to preserve his dead, as in Egypt. Cremation was almost always resorted to, and for this reason we lack the tomb-finds, so elucidating in Egypt. The body was made ready for burial, with some food and other necessities, then it was partially burned, at least, and the remains entombed. The conditions of the country in Babylonia made cremation almost a necessity.

---
[1] Johns: Baby. and Assy. Laws, Contracts and Letters, 211.

While some degree of purity was occasionally reached in Mesopotamian conceptions of religion, and far-sighted and high-minded persons lived in both countries, there was much that was degrading in connection with the worship. All Babylonian classes were grossly superstitious and believed always in the demons. The incantations used to drive these away were not only countenanced by the priesthood, but were taught as a part of the established worship. Demons were of various kinds and possessed different degrees of power. They lurked in obscure places, ready to inflict themselves upon unhappy mortals. All diseases, all misfortunes were their doings. A sufferer exclaims:

> "They have used all kinds of charms
> to entwine me as a rope,
> to catch me as in a cage,
> to tie me as with cords,
> to overpower me as in a net,
> to twist me as with a sling,
> to tear me as a fabric,
> to throw me down as a wall."

To this the conjurer replies:

> "But I by command of Marduk, the lord of charms,
> by Marduk, the master of bewitchment,
> Both the male and female witch
> as with ropes I will entwine,
> as in a cage I will catch,
> as with cords I will tie,
> as in a net I will overpower,
> as in a sling I will twist,
> as a fabric I will tear,
> as a wall throw them down."

At this juncture, images of witches were burned by fire, having been tortured first by these specified actions.

The ritual set forth water as a purification for some bewitchment.

SOCIAL LIFE IN MESOPOTAMIA.

> "Glittering water, pure water,
> Holy water, resplendent water,
> The water twice seven times may he bring,
> May he make pure, may he make resplendent.
> May the evil spirit depart,
> May he betake himself outside,
> Spirit of heaven, be thou invoked!
> Spirit of earth, be thou invoked!

Another remedy was this:

> "White wool, which has been spun into thread,
> To attach it to his couch in front and at the top,
> Black wool which has been spun into thread
> To bind at his left side."[2]

In addition to long lists of formulæ for driving away the demons of sickness, and famine and misfortune, a countless number of omens had to be taken into account if one wished success to accompany his undertakings. Some of these concerned the movement of heavenly bodies.

> "The moon and sun are balanced.
> The subjects will be faithful
> The king of the land will reign for a long time."

Another brought a sense of danger in its day:

> "On the fifteenth day the sun and moon are seen together,
> A powerful enemy raises his weapons against the land,
> The enemy will smash the great gate of the city;
> The star of Anu appears bright—
> The enemy will devastate."

Or this:

> "The moon is seen out of season,
> Crops will be small.
> On the twelfth day the moon is seen together with the sun—
> A strong enemy will devastate the land."

[2]Jastrow: Babylonian Religion.

A numerous list of omens pertained to the doings of animals. Stray dogs might bring disaster if they entered houses in unusual ways, and yet it was necessary that they frequent the streets. By-ways that they left were not thought lucky. The following omens have been translated from old tablets:

"If a yellow dog enters a palace, it is a sign of distress.
　If a speckled dog enters a palace, the palace will give peace to the enemy.
　If a dog enters a palace and crouches on the couch, no one will enjoy that palace in peace.
　If a dog enters a temple, the gods will not enlarge the land.
　If a raven enters a man's house, that man will secure whatever he desires."

All kinds of dreams were carefully tabulated, and were noted from time to time in connection with events in the dreamers' lives:

"If in a dream a fish appear on a man's head, that man will be powerful."
"If a mountain appear on a man's head, that man will be without a rival."[a]

While all these omens were not directly connected with worship, they were consistent with the religious teaching of the time, and so are perhaps rightly considered here.

The Babylonians were more religious than the Assyrians and their government was far more bound up in religious ceremonies. One fact alone bears out this statement: In Babylonia the king must each year celebrate anew the ceremony of taking his temporal power from the god Marduk by taking the hands of the god's image. This service took place on New Year's day, and no matter what might be the situation in other parts of the empire, to Babylon the king must come and observe the ancient custom would he remain possessor of the kingly crown.

[a] Jastrow: Babylonian Religion.

ILU NABU- KU- DU- RI- UTSUR

ILU NA- BI- UM- KU- DU- UR- RI- U- TSU- UR

The name Nebuchadnezzar in two forms of writing—as found on brick and in inscriptions.

CHAPTER XVI.
THE LABORING CLASSES.

Both slave and free labor existed in Babylonia, but, as has been previously said, there was no special prejudice felt towards the slave. He was often of the same nationality as the owner, was trusted, and often adopted into the family. Parents sold their children into slavery, and in hard times men would even sell themselves to obtain food and shelter. On the other hand, slaves might become free men and might rise to positions of high importance in the state. Having been a slave left no stigma to one who later became free. The slave might accumulate money and so purchase his freedom; freedom might be secured to him because of adoption into a family. While still in servitude he might appear as a witness or party in a suit, and his testimony was valued as much as though he were free. Nevertheless, while enjoying privileges unusual to one in slavery, he was still but a chattel given as security for a debt, offered as part of a dowry, or again, his services might be hired out for a given period, his earnings to go to his owner.

Various measures were taken to protect the slave, as the Code of Hammurabi shows. Fines were imposed for any abuses suffered during a period when he was hired out. This served as a check upon those who otherwise might have caused him to overwork.

Slaves made up quite a portion of the laborers, both in Babylonia and Assyria, although in the latter country less friendly relations seem to have existed between slave and owner, for the great mass of Assyrian slaves had been taken captives in war, and were foreigners, unaccustomed to the ways of the land, and less devoted, probably, to the interests of those who owned them.

Few slaves were bought and sold with the land, and these generally belonged to temple lands. Private farms were worked by slaves privately owned.

Free labor was available, but as a consequence of slavery, wages were low. The grazers were generally free men; they received large herds of cattle and flocks of sheep from several owners, and these they pastured for months together on the west slope of the Euphrates. Because the herds required constant protection from nomadic tribes of the desert, the grazers had to be men of responsibility.

The oldest occupation of the Euphrates valley was agriculture. The soil yielded heavily and early won tribes away from their roving state. Taxes were always paid in kind, and grain was stored for times of scarcity in royal granaries.

For the Babylonian, the year opened in the fall—in Tisri (September), the month of harvest. When his crops were harvested, the farmer paid his tax; if the land was farmed out, the owner paid the tax and the tenant paid his rent. New contracts for land were made at this time of the year.

The ordinary arrangement between landlord and tenant seems to have been that he who rented should pay one-third of the year's produce for the use of the farm, and that he should keep all buildings and ditches in repair. This last stipulation was strongly enjoined, and a fine was inflicted did he fail in this particular.

During the portion of the year when the usual round of sowing and reaping ceased, the canals and ditches needed attention. The entire prosperity of the soil depended upon the maintenance of the irrigation system.

"Ploughing, harrowing, sowing, reaping, and threshing constituted the chief events of the agricultural year. The winters were not cold, and the Babylonian peasant was consequently not obliged to spend a part of the year indoors shivering over a fire. In fact fuel was scarce in the country; few trees were grown in it except the palm, and the fruit of the palm was too valuable to allow it to be cut down. When the ordinary occupations of the farmer had come to an end, he was expected to look after his farm buildings and fences, to build walls and clean out the ditches.

"The ditches, indeed, were more important in Babylonia than in most other parts of the world. Irrigation was as necessary as in Egypt, though for a different reason. The Chaldean plain had originally been a marsh, and it required constant supervision to prevent it from being once more inundated by the waters and made uninhabitable. The embankments which hindered the overflow of the Euphrates and Tigris and kept them within carefully regulated channels, the canals which carried off the surplus water and distributed it over the country, needed continual attention. Each year, after the rains of the winter, the banks had to be strengthened or re-made and the beds of the canals cleared out. The irrigator, moreover, was perpetually at work; the rainy season did not last long, and during the rest of the year the land was dependent on the water supplied by the rivers and canals. Irrigation, therefore, formed a large and important part of the farmers' work, and the bucket of the irrigator must have been constantly swinging."[1]

Large numbers of sheep were raised in these valleys, and the manufacture of wool into dress-stuffs, carpets, and tapestries, made Babylonia famous among the nations of her time. Her rugs and carpets were the pride of her people and large sums were paid for them. Scenes sculptured in bas-relief were seen in tapestries which lined the walls of wealthy homes. Vegetable dyes were used, and gayly colored flowers, bright hues and tints, made attractive decorations for interiors against dull back-grounds of brick. A large proportion of the industrial population was engaged in weaving, dyeing, and preparing these commodities for shops and other places of sale.

Because of the constantly growing demand for wool, many were induced to raise sheep and to trade in the raw wool. Records show that Belshazzar, son of the king and heir to the Babylonian throne, was a wool-merchant on a large scale, his commercial interests being, of course, managed by others.

The price of wool varied greatly, being sometimes high, sometimes low. It cost little in addition to the wages of the shepherd to pasture flocks west of the river during the greater part of the year, for pasturage there was free to all. For some months, to be sure, sheep had to be sheltered and fed inside enclosures, within or near the city. This was the costly part of sheep-raising.

When the flocks were driven into town, toll per head was exacted at the city gate. Lists of the various tolls collected

[1] Sayce: Baby. and Assy., 88.

and turned into the general treasury show them altogether to have been considerable; not only were they collected of all who passed through the gates but a bridge toll was paid by whoever passed over the bridge connecting Babylon and Borsippa, across the river; all ships and sailing crafts, moreover, paid a toll to pass under the bridge.

Enumerations of the trades of Babylonia have been found; these mention the trades of carpenter, smith, metal-worker, weaver, leather-worker, dyer, potter, brick-maker and vintner. The carpenter not only raised the beams and scaffolding of houses, but as well made whatever articles of furniture the times afforded. The brick-maker made tablets for inscriptions as well as bricks for building purposes. The brickyards were always on low land, near the river, where reeds, so useful in brick-making, were abundant. Building bricks were made in different sizes—some nearly a foot square by $2\frac{1}{2}$ inches thick; others about 15 by 15 and three inches in thickness. Chopped reeds were frequently mixed in the bricks themselves, and since the demand for them was constant, they were cultivated and grown in large areas. In a secluded corner of the brickyard, the fine tablets for literary purposes were produced; and here too, dishes and vases of pottery were molded and baked. Thus we see that great activity and divers interests attached to these yards given over to the manufacture of clay articles.

The leather worker found material in abundance, owing to the extensive cattle raising. Harnesses, saddles, and shoes, beautifully decorated, were chief among leather commodities.

The smith excelled in fashioning articles from gold, silver, copper and bronze. Ordinarily the metal was melted and run into molds of clay or stone. The customer usually furnished the ore and paid for the work upon it. Metal workers were held accountable for the excellence of their work, as is shown by guaranties found, whereby they promised to pay heavy fines if during a given term of years, their work should be found imperfect.

The people of Babylonia never succeeded in mastering the bas-relief work, so effectively used in Assyrian palaces. Enamelled tiles took the place of these, and they were either painted in some design and glazed, or simply tinted. "Quite as old as the trade of the carver in ivory was that of the porcelain-maker. The walls of the palaces and temples of Babylonia and Assyria were adorned with glazed and enamelled tiles on which figures and other designs were drawn in brilliant colors; they were then covered with a metallic glaze and fired. Babylonia, in fact, seems to have been the original home of the enamelled tile and therefore with the manufacture of porcelain. It was a land of clay and not of stone, and while it thus became necessary to ornament the plain mud wall of the house, the clay brick itself, when painted and protected by a glaze, was made into the very best and most enduring of ornaments. The enamelled bricks of Chaldea and Assyria are among the most beautiful relics of Babylonian civilization that have survived to us, and those which are now in the Museum of the Louvre are unsurpassed by the most elaborate productions of modern skill."

The trade of the vintner was lucrative. Wines were made from dates and grapes; beer was doubtless made from grain. It seems to have been the custom to supply laborers with beer with their daily rations.

Organizations among workmen corresponded to the guilds of later years. Those who would learn a trade, whether freemen or slaves, had to serve as apprentices a certain time and learn the work thoroughly.

Wages were always so low that they amounted to little. It has been estimated that the average wages of a workman was about 12s., or $3.00 a year; unskilled laborers were contented if merely supplied with food. In the reign of Cambyses a butcher is recorded to have been paid 75 cents for a month's work—freemen had always to compete with slave labor, and if only the employer furnished food and clothing, he could command any amount of labor.

Babylonia early exchanged her grain and dates for the products of other lands. For example, teak-wood and cotton were brought from Arabia, cedar from Lebanon, marble from the east, gold from the peninsula of Sinai. Sometimes the raw materials were made up in Babylonia and returned to the lands from whence they came together with grain, rugs and cloth of wool. Because of her geographical position, Babylonia was able to command an important commercial position, importing and exporting constantly.

"The mass of the people in Babylonia were employed in the two pursuits of commerce and agriculture. The commerce was both foreign and domestic. Great numbers of the Babylonians were engaged in the manufacture of those fabrics, particularly carpets and muslins, which Babylonia produced not only for her own use but also for the consumption of foreign lands. The ordinary trades and handicrafts practised in the East no doubt flourished in the country. A brisk import and export trade was constantly kept up, and promoted a healthful activity throughout the entire body politic. Babylonia is called 'a land of traffic' by Ezekiel, and Babylon 'a city of merchants.' The monuments show that from the very earliest times the people of the low country on the borders of the Persian Gulf were addicted to maritime pursuits and navigated the gulf freely, if they did not even venture on the open ocean.

"The products of the various countries of Western Asia flowed into Babylonia down the courses of the rivers. From Armenia came wine, gems, emery, and perhaps stone; from Phœnicia, tin, copper, musical instruments; from Media, silk, gold and ivory."[2]

The Professions: The Banker.

In ancient times, the money-lender was the banker, and lending money was foremost in Babylonian professions. Even members of the royal families were themselves heavy loaners and drew high rates of interest, although, to be sure, their business transactions were carried on by agents.

The rate of interest varied greatly, being generally higher in Assyria. In Babylonia it might be 20%, or again 16%, and was rarely as low as 10%. Cases are on record in Assyria where 25% and 33⅓% were exacted. As is still customary in the East, interest was computed monthly, and unless the borrower was well known and trusted, it was paid monthly. Security for the full amount was always required.

A great firm of Babylon held a position in that country corresponding to that held by the Rothschilds in England, loaning to the state as well as to private individuals. Personal deeds and documents belonging to citizens were stored in

---
[2] Rawlinson: Babylonia.

the well-protected chambers of this firm as they are today kept in safety boxes in bank vaults. Banking firms continued for generations, and immense numbers of wills, deeds of sale, business contracts, leases, tax certificates, loans and marriage agreements accumulated within their chambers.

SCRIBES.

While each one pleaded his own case ordinarily, in the courts of Babylonia, pleas were frequently thrown into form beforehand by a scribe. These scribes performed duties discharged in later times by attorneys at law, as well as those which would of necessity fall to their share. In Babylonia they acted as librarians, authors and publishers, multiplying copies of books and selling them. In Assyria, where the art of reading and writing was not so generally known, they acted as private clerks and secretaries to a wide extent.

MEDICINE.

We have noted early in our study that medicine had but a small part in Babylonian life. Charms, magic and incantations in a large measure took its place. However, with acquaintance with Egypt, came an impulse to learn of a science which occupied a more important position in the valley of the Nile. While physicians came into prominence in later years, they were never wholly depended upon. The doctor was called to act in unison with the magician and conjurer unless, as was often the case, he himself united the two arts of healing. Herodotus and other travellers have testified to cases similar to the following: " Pressing forward and peeping over the heads of the people, we see a man stretched upon a mattress, and apparently just about to die. A few weeping friends kneel at his side, and we learn that he has been brought from his home, and laid down in the public market place, in the vain hope that some one may propose a remedy which will save his life. This custom, so strange to us, is common in Babylon, they say. When all else has failed, when doctors and sorcerers have done their best, the sick person is transported to the open square, and advice is asked from the crowd which is sure to gather.

" Today, as ever, each has a different remedy to propose,

though all are agreed as to the cause of illness. A demon possesses the man, of that there is no question. 'Come away, little one!' cries an old woman, drawing back her grandson. 'Go not too near, lest the evil spirit leave the man, and seize upon thee. Often have I seen it. Bel be praised that I have his image!' And she draws forth a little clay image of Bel, and hangs it carefully on the neck of her grandson. 'Hast thou tried the wool of a young sheep?' asks a woman of the sick man's wife. 'Let a sorcerer tie seven knots in it, on seven moonlight nights. Tie the strands around thy husband's neck, around his limbs, around his head. So shall his soul not leave his body.'

"'Try the recipe of Asshurbanipal the Assyrian,' cries another. 'It is well known and never fails. Six different kinds of wood, a bit of snake skin, some wine, and a piece of ox flesh. Make a paste, and cause the sick man to swallow it.'[1]

"A man hurries up with a handful of clay, and molds a little figure which he displays as the image of the sick man. We cannot see the resemblance, but the crowd presses forward and watches his motions with eager curiosity. He calls for a cup of wine, pours part of it over the image, and after drinking the rest, mutters an incantation. All in vain, while he is yet speaking, the family of the sick man raises a chorus of wails, in which the crowd joins. The man is dead; no charm can avail him more."[2]

The Soldier.

We cannot speak of the vocation of the soldier as we speak of the regular professions of men, but any account of Assyria which failed to give some idea of the army, the very support and strength of that great empire, would be incomplete.

At first, as in Babylonia, the soldiers when needed were recruited from peasants in the field. When the war was over, they would return to their usual tasks. However, Assyria with her many conquests felt the need of trained soldiers, proficient in military tactics. To the standing army which grew into a strong body, warriors taken captive in other lands

---

[1] This reminds one of the snails, etc., that were crushed and brewed in small beer for rickets in New England. See Alice Morse Earle, "Customs and Fashions in Old New England."
[2] Arnold: Stories of Ancient Peoples, 123.

were added. In course of a few generations a formidable army was thus brought into being, and the calling of a soldier became a regular profession. Men were required to give evidences of skill before they could take commands of regiments and even before they could command a company of ten. Maspero has made an extended study of military affairs in Assyria and we can do no better than follow the results he has reached in his investigation:

"The Assyrian army is the best organized war machine that the world has yet seen.[1] It is superiority of weapons, not any superiority in courage and discipline, that has secured to the Ninevite kings since Sargon the priority over the Pharaohs of the Delta, of Thebes and Meroe. Whilst the Egyptians, as a rule, still fight without any protection, except the shield, the Assyrians are, so to speak, clothed in iron from head to foot. Their heavy infantry is composed of spearmen and archers, wearing a conical cap ornamented with two side pieces which protect the ears, a leather shirt covered with overlapping metal scales which protects the chest and the upper part of the arms, close fitting breeches, and boots laced in front. The spearmen carry spears six feet long, with an iron or bronze head, a short sword passed through their belt, and an immense metal shield, sometimes round and convex, sometimes rounded at the top and square at the bottom. The archers have no shields; they replace the spear by a bow and quiver, which hang over their back. Their light infantry also includes some spearmen, but they wear a helmet with a curved crest, and are provided with a small round wicker-work shield. The archers have no breastplate, and are associated either with slingers or with soldiers armed with clubs and double-edged axes.

"The spearmen and archers of the line are usually of Assyrian origin or levied in the territories that have been subject to Assyria for a long time; the other troops are often recruited amongst tributary nations, and they wear their national costumes. They are arranged in companies, and manœuvre with a regularity which foreigners themselves admire. . . . They march with extraordinary rapidity, leaving no stragglers or lame men behind them as they go,

[1] The narrative is set back in the days of Assyrian Empire.

and their generals are not afraid to impose fatigues upon them to which the soldiers of other lands would quickly succumb. They either ford the rivers or swim across them upon inflated skins. In wooded countries, each company sends forward a certain number of pioneers, who fell the trees and clear a path.

"The cavalry are divided into two corps, the chariot soldiers and the regular cavalry. The Assyrian war-chariot is much heavier and more massive than the Egyptian. Like the Egyptian chariots, the Assyrians always charge in a regular line, and there are few troops in the world that can resist their first shock. When a battalion of the enemy sees them coming, rapid and light, their darts pointed, their bows strung, they usually disband immediately after the first volley of arrows, and run away. The line is then broken, and the chariots disperse over the plain, crushing the fugitives beneath their wheels, and trampling them under their horses' feet.

"Formerly the chariots were very numerous in the Assyrian armies. They are less used at the present day, but tradition gives them the post of honour and the king or the chief general always reserves for himself the privilege of leading them into the fight. It is the distinguished branch of the service, the one in which the princes and great nobles prefer to serve, and its weight often decides the fate of the battle.

"Yet now the cavalry commences to rival it, if not in numbers, at least in importance. The horse was at first ridden bareback; now it is covered with one cloth, or with a complete caparison similar to that of the chariot horses. All the cavalry wear helmets and cuirasses like the infantry of the line, but they have no shields; they replace the floating petticoat by cotton drawers. One-half of them carries the sword and lance, the other half is armed with a bow and sword.

The lance is eight or nine feet long, the bow is shorter than the bow used by the infantry, and the arrows are scarcely three feet long. Formerly each mounted archer was accompanied by a servant, mounted like himself, who led his horse during the battle so as to leave both his hands free. The art of riding has made such progress during the last few years that the servant has become useless, and has disappeared from the armies. Now lancers and bowmen are all trained to guide their steed by the pressure of the knees, and they may be seen galloping with flying reins, shooting their arrows as they go, or else halting suddenly, they quietly discharge the arrow, then turn and gallop off again.

"The proportion of the different services is always about the same. There are, on an average, one hundred foot soldiers to every ten cavalry and every single chariot; the infantry is really the queen of the Assyrian battles."[5]

[1] Maspero: Ancient Egypt and Assyria, 320.

THRESHOLD—SLAB IN ASSHURBANIPAL'S PALACE.

CHAPTER XVII.

The Medes.

The Medes belonged to the Indo-European branch of the Aryan race. It is supposed that they came into Europe from the far east, and thence migrated to Asia, some time previous to 1000 B. C. They settled a mountainous tract to the east of Assyria, occupying a district rather larger than Babylonia and Assyria together. Because of its rugged mountains, narrow passes, and inclement winter weather, their country was easily defended against invaders. In the days of Assyrian dominance, the people of Media maintained uniform independence, notwithstanding the fact that military kings were annexing territories far and near with almost irresistible force. And so today, those who live in this district, remain comparatively free from the government which seeks to rule them.

For the history of this ancient nation we are thrown almost wholly upon the writings of Herodotus, Xenophon and other Greek travellers, for as yet no antiquarian has attempted to recover Median past from mounds of buried ruins. Indeed the country has never been left desolate like Babylonia, but its cities fell to the share of others, and later generations, finding material for new buildings in the structures of their predecessors, have left no mounds to allure the historian and archæologist. Since rich finds in other lands have in recent years thrown unexpected light upon the past, it has been surmised that beneath the present cities, in this land of ancient Media, might be recovered monuments of her early life. So far, however, other fields have proven more inviting to the explorer and the excavator.

In spite of the faults of credulence and exaggeration so characteristic of Herodotus, we must nevertheless turn to his writings and to those of Xenophon for Median history.

We have noted that during the eighth century, Assyria made a raid into Media. The independence of the people was not disturbed however. This verifies the statement of Herodotus that the Medians made good soldiers, hardy and well able to defend their land. They were trained to a life of physical activity, inured to the hardships of a rigorous climate. Charging on horseback at full speed, they made a formidable defense.

In their early conflicts they seem to have displayed excessive cruelty in war, showing no mercy to helpless women or innocent children. As for plunder, they cared little for it, and Isaiah refers to them as "the Medes who care not for silver, and as for gold, have no delight in it."[1]

By frequent plundering raids into their territory, the Assyrians incurred the lasting hatred of the Medes, who, urged on by a spirit of revenge, united in 606 B. C. under a Median prince to aid the king of Babylonia against the Assyrian monarch. Having defeated the army, the Medes pursued, and shut the Assyrian force within the walls of Nineveh. Thereupon they made an assault upon the defenses of the city and carried the day. The capital of Assyria and all the wealthy cities of the realm were overrun, plundered and burned, while the surviving inhabitants were so widely scattered that we hear no more about them.

Before this the Medes had cared little for luxury and ease, although they always delighted in a certain barbaric splendor. With the vast treasure of Nineveh their king now built a palace of extensive proportions. Its halls and pillars were of woods, its courts wide and the whole structure magnificent. No wood was left visible, all being concealed by a coating of silver tiles. Herodotus wrote thus of the palace walls:

"The walls enclose the palace, rising in circles, one within the other. The plan of the place is that each of the walls should out-top the one beyond it by the battlements. The nature of the ground, which is a gentle slope, favors this arrangement in some degree, but it was mainly effected by art. The number of the circles is seven, the royal palace and the treasuries standing within the last. Of the outer wall, the battlements are white; of the next, black; of the third, scarlet; of the fourth, blue; of the fifth, orange; all these are covered with paint. The last two have their battlements coated respectively with silver and gold."

We may gain some idea of the wealth represented by this

[1] Isa. 13, 17. The chapter is late, and, as Duhm says, the fact that the redactor ascribed it to Isaiah is instructive as regards the want of critical ability of the *diaskenasts*. Craig.

building when we learn that the king of Persia carried away the greater portion of the gold and silver decorations for his palace; Alexander the Great removed the silver tiling from the roof, and some seventy years later another conqueror found about $5,000,000 worth of gold and silver plating overlooked by his predecessors. While no former palace may have exceeded this in actual outlay of wealth, others may have been more artistic, for the Medes reached no special architectural skill.

After the Assyrian conquest, the Median nation soon became weak and degenerate. The people affected a life of luxury and idleness. The king lived amidst pomp and ostentatious seclusion; his courtiers and nobles gave themselves up to immoderate indulgences and amusements. While under Cyaxares and his father, Media had become a power in Asia, upon the death of this king, his son Astyages succeeded to the throne. He had grown up during the later years of ease and had no greater ambition than to rule the kingdom left him, no more animating impulses than to pass his days amid the ceremony and studied formality of the Median court. Astyages seems to have planned neither political activity nor personal diversion. He never joined in the hunts which were popular with his courtiers. Rather, he spent his leisure with such entertainment as his palace afforded and for his administration, depended wholly upon the reports of his officials. Such was Media when a Persian king, realizing the real situation, led an army against the country. In connection with our study of Persia we shall come again to the story of this conquest.

Polygamy was always allowed by the code of Median laws and morals, while women seem to have been treated with a certain chivalrous attention and deference. The civilization of the land was similar to that of Persia, which nation, it is supposed, sprang originally from the same stock. No greater difference existed betwen the two peoples than might be found between two modern Teutonic nations.

Education and learning was not valued in either country. Boys were taught to ride, to hunt, to shoot, and to become proficient in out of door sports rather than the arts of reading and writing.

The religion was akin to that of Persia, and the faith of the Persians was singularly pure. They like the Hebrews, worshipped one God. No degrading ceremonies and teachings attached to their forms of worship, as was the case in Egypt and Babylonia. The most ancient writings of the Zenda-Vesta appear to embody the faith of the Medes, and these will be considered in connection with the religion of Persia.

In conclusion, it may be said that the Medes were neither an inventive nor an ingenious people, nor did they develop a great civilization, culture, or literature. Indeed we are forced to the conclusion of Rawlinson: they scarcely contributed an idea or invention to the great store of knowledge transmitted by the past to the modern world.

RUINS OF PERSEPOLIS.

CHAPTER XVIII.

Persia Before the Age of Cyrus.

The origin and early history of both Medes and Persians were similar. When first the Persians are mentioned in Assyrian annals, they had migrated to the region east of Assyria, inhabiting an indefinite district which later became part of the Median state. At this time—about the ninth century before the Christian era—they were not united under one king, but each clan followed the leadership of a chosen chieftain. As a result of an Assyrian attack, more than twenty of these chiefs brought tribute and acknowledged the supremacy of the great king.

Nothing of importance is again heard of them until shortly before the fall of the Assyrian capital. They were then united into a kingdom, serving one ruler, and living in what has been called "Persia Proper," to distinguish the original state from the wide empire which was brought at length under Persian rule. While free to manage their internal affairs, they paid tribute to Media, now a vigorous and aggressive nation. It is plain then, that previous to the fall of Nineveh, the Persian state had taken no part in Asiatic affairs, and furthermore, was not yet free and independent. However, in less than one hundred years her people had gained control over the entire western portion of Asia, extending their rule from the Indus to the valley of the Nile, while only the little Greek nation held out against them on the west.

Before entering upon a study of this rapid imperial expansion, it would be well for us to get some general impressions of the comparatively small territory in which the various Persian tribes became welded into a united people, and of the conditions in the original kingdom wherein the principles which were to temporarily dominate the ancient world were developed.

Persia Proper consisted of an area of about 450 miles in length, and averaging 250 miles in width. It might have been roughly bounded on the south and west by the gulf which came to bear its name, while a desert reached off to the east and north, save where Persian territory touched upon the Median kingdom. A narrow strip of arid land lay between the gulf and a mountain range, making up perhaps one eighth of the entire area. The climate here is hot and dry, the soil marshy, producing little growth of any sort. The district east of this range was irregularly divided into highlands and valleys, lofty rocks and winding chasms. Wherever water was available, vegetation was luxuriant, making the wild scenery fantastic and attractive. Generally water was scarce, and most of the year the land lay parched and brown.

"The region east of the range is of varied character. In places richly fertile, picturesque, and romantic almost beyond imagination, with lovely wooded dells, green mountain-sides, and broad plains suited for the production of almost any crops, it has yet on the whole a predominant character of sterility and barrenness, especially towards its more northern and eastern portions. The supply of water is everywhere scanty. Scarcely any of the streams are strong enough to reach the sea. After short courses they are either absorbed by the sand or end in small salt lakes, from which the superfluous water is evaporated. Much of the country is absolutely without streams, and would be uninhabitable were it not for the subterranean channels of spring-water.

"The most remarkable feature of the country consists in the extraordinary gorges which pierce the great mountain-chain, and render possible the establishment of routes across that tremendous barrier. Scarped rocks rise almost perpendicularly on either side of the mountain streams, which descend rapidly with frequent cascades and falls. Along the slight irregularities of these rocks the roads are carried in zigzags, often crossing the streams from side to side by bridges of a single arch, which are thrown over profound chasms where the waters chafe and roar many hundred feet below. The roads have for the most part been artificially cut in the sides of the precipices, which rise from the streams sometimes to the height of 2,000 feet. Thus the country towards the edge of the plateau is peculiarly safe from attack, being defended on the north and east by vast deserts, and on the south by a mountain barrier of unusual strength and difficulty.

"It is in these regions, which combine facility of defence with pleasantness of climate, that the principal cities of the district have at all times been placed."[1]

It appears that nearly one-half of the kingdom was practically unsuited for habitation, being dry and producing little to sustain life. In these early times only two or three cities existed, small villages making up the remaining social centers, while peasants farmed limited portions of the outlying country where the water supply sufficed to maintain crops.

Various fruits abounded in the mountainous regions. Peaches were native to the soil. Grapes grew in profusion, and corn and vegetables were plentiful. Along the coast fish might be found in large quantities and constituted a staple article of food throughout the land. The natural conditions were not sufficiently favorable to allow heavy yields of grain or to make agriculture foremost among the nation's activities.

The Persians were active, vivacious people, lacking wholly the repose and dignified calm so characteristic of the English, for example. They concealed neither joy nor sorrow, and were immoderate in their expressions of both.

Learning and education were given little attention. It has become a trite and well-known saying that "Persian boys were taught to ride, to shoot, and to speak the truth." The religion of the people placed truth first among the virtues. Their steadfast fidelity to a promise excited wonderment among the nations. Physical, rather than mental, development was sought, and while in the nation's later life the people gave themselves up to indolence, passing the hours with personal adornment and feasting, these pastimes did not characterize their early years.

Like the Medes, Persian nobles had several wives, and polygamy was the rule rather than the exception. Women were kept in well-nigh complete seclusion, and no mention is made of them, nor are they seen in pictures adorning the palaces.

The attitude assumed toward the sovereign influenced the very character of the people. "The Persian king held the same rank and position in the eyes of his subjects which the great monarch of Western Asia, whoever he might be, had

[1] Rawlinson: Persia.

always occupied from time immemorial. He was the lord and master, absolute disposer of their lives, liberties, and property; the sole fountain of law and right, incapable himself of doing wrong, irresponsible, irresistible—a sort of God on earth; one whose favor was happiness, at whose frown men trembled, before whom all bowed themselves down with the lowest and humblest obeisance.

"The feeling of the Persian towards his king is one of which moderns can with difficulty form a conception. In Persia the monarch was so much the State, that patriotism itself was, as it were, swallowed up in loyalty; and an unquestioning submission, not only to the deliberate will, but to the merest caprice of the sovereign, was, by habit and education, so ingrained into the nature of the people that a contrary spirit scarcely ever manifested itself. In war the safety of the sovereign was the first thought, and the principal care of all. If the king suffered, all was lost; if the king escaped, the greatest calamities seemed light and could be endured with patience. The same cheerful submission characterized times of peace. It was here that their loyalty became a defect rather than a virtue. The voice of remonstrance, of rebuke, of warning, was unheard at Court. Tyranny was allowed to indulge unchecked in the wildest caprices and extravagances. The father, whose innocent son was shot before his eyes by the king in pure wantonness, instead of raising an indignant protest against the crime, felicitated him upon the excellence of his archery. Thus a tone of servility was engendered which, sapping self-respect, tended fatally to lower and corrupt the entire character of the people."[2]

Such were the tendencies of the embryo state which under the leadership of a great ruler was soon to burst into sudden and brilliant flower, absorbing in a single campaign nations which had never before been united.

Cyrus the Great and the Persian Empire.

In ages when monarchs were absolute in the foremost countries of the world, the personal ability of the king was a matter of far greater concern than we today realize. In modern times, political and social changes have had their be-

[2] Rawlinson: Persia.

ginnings in the conditions and desires of the people. In the remote years we are now studying, the people were less considered, and their wishes seldom heard. The personal character of the king determined the policy of the ancient state. We have already seen how the welfare—the very fate of Egypt, Babylonia and Assyria depended upon their rulers. Even more pronounced was this in Persia, where subjects, including nobles and princes, acted in unthinking submission to a degree unknown in other lands.

In taking up the career of Cyrus the Great we are largely dependent upon the writings of Herodotus and Xenophon. Of Herodotus we have learned something, and concerning Xenophon we may note that besides being a writer and a traveller, he was also an experienced and able general. Herodotus lived some fifty years after the death of Cyrus, and Xenophon was thirty years younger than Herodotus. Both Greeks wrote at length of the great Persian King.

When Astyages ascended the throne of Media, Persia was a mere tribute-paying kingdom, insignificant not only in political strength, but in social life, wealth, and culture. It is supposed that Cyrus was sent to the Median court as a hostage from a tribute land. His father ruled in Persia, and we are told that he was greatly impressed as a boy by the difference between the two countries. The subjects over whom his father ruled were many of them soldiers whose days were spent with training and physical exercise. They ate and drank moderately, and while they lacked the culture and refinement of the northern kingdom, they were just coming into the strength and vigour which the Medians lost upon their conquest of Assyria and subsequent abundance of wealth.

Tradition pictures the youth clinging to the simple habits of his early life, and caring little for the pomp and ceremony around him. He delighted in riding and liked the hunt best of all amusements, while he shortly became the companion of Astyages during the king's leisure hours, bringing refreshing life and boyish candor into a degenerate court.

Some years later Cyrus returned home and, shortly after, a faction of the Medes who had become devoted to the Persian prince and felt dissatisfied with the tyranny of their king, informed Cyrus that if he would bring an army against the

Medes, they would cause the Median forces to desert to him. Another account says that Cyrus himself planned the conquest while at the Median court, and having feasted his attendants and led them to drink heavily, escaped to Persia, where he soon persuaded his father to march against the Medes. In either case, it would seem that the prince had learned the true condition of degenerated Media, and determined to free his own land from the hated tribute service—establishing its independence.

In the battle which was waged against the two people, Astyages was taken captive, and when the majority of the soldiers went over to the Persian side, the remaining soldiers fled. Cyrus allowed Astyages to retain his own personal attendants, and permitted him to live in a style befitting his recent position. Under guard of Persian soldiers, he was free to go about at will.

It is probable that Cyrus had at first no greater ambition than to free Persia from tribute imposed by Media, but the desire for conquest once awakened never ceases while lands remain unwon. In conquering Media, all territories of Assyria fell to Cyrus' portion. The Medes had held lands to the river Halys on the northwest. Beyond this boundary stream the empire of Lydia had been growing under the rule of Crœsus.

Crœsus has become proverbial for his wealth. As he extended the boundaries of Lydia, he grew wealthier still, until his resources exceeded all estimate. Having lost a favorite son, he lived in seclusion until a sense of approaching danger roused him to defend his kingdom. The river Halys was a narrow stream—too small by far to prove a lasting barrier against an aggressive nation. To spare his land the ravages of war, Crœsus determined to invade the land of his rival. He thought best to consult the oracle at Delphi before entering upon such a serious campaign. Having sent costly presents to Delphi, Crœsus inquired whether or not it would be safe for him to proceed against Persia. The reply was that if Crœsus crossed the Halys and carried war into Persia, a mighty kingdom would be overthrown, and that he would do well to form an alliance with the strongest Greek state.

Regarding the answer as favorable, he sent word to Sparta

that, since he was advised by the Delphian oracle to seek the strongest Greek state as an ally, he solicited their assistance. These Spartans were unlike any soldiers we have yet met; they fought for glory, not for plunder. They were glad, of course, to be considered the strongest Grecian state, and sent the assistance asked. With such re-enforcements, Crœsus crossed the Halys and met Cyrus who had known of the Lydian movement and was ready for an attack. The battle was fought near Pterie; both sides lost heavily, and Crœsus thought Cyrus was too crippled to longer advance, so he himself returned to Sardis, his capital, to make plans for a new campaign the following year. Cyrus waited until the Lydian troops were largely disbanded, and then suddenly appeared before Sardis. Consternation swept over the Lydians, but they trusted to their cavalry which was numerous and well disciplined. Cyrus had also taken the Lydian cavalry into account, and had ordered his camels which carried the equipment of war, to face the horse, and if possible, to put them to flight. In the battle fought such was the result—the horses turned in confusion upon the charge of the camels, and the Lydian army withdrew into Sardis to undergo a siege. They expected to win in the long run, for they had sufficient stores of all kinds, and they hoped that outside aid would come sooner or later. Cyrus understood the danger of delay, and determined to carry the city by assault. By scaling a nearly perpendicular embankment, entrance to Sardis was gained, and Crœsus fell into the hands of the great Persian conqueror. He was given considerate treatment. Few cruelties disfigure the pages of Persian history, and never were severe punishments meted out wholesale to captives in war. Those who betrayed confidence were harshly dealt with, and rebels seldom escaped, but the Persians were generally fair-minded. Cyrus was uniformly mild and generous, lacking the inordinate pride of most Oriental monarchs, treating his subjects with kindness. Crœsus became one of his trusted companions, and accompanied him upon his later campaigns. The story of the funeral pyre is probably an invention of the Greeks, or, if it had any foundation whatever, it may be that Crœsus requested such an honorable end in preference to swearing allegiance to an unknown conqueror.

When measures had been taken for the government of Lydia, attention turned to Babylonia. There, as we have seen, the crown was worn by a king who was more interested in the temples of the gods than in the immediate welfare of his nation. His son Belshazzar made some defense outside the capital, but a faction within the city, out of sympathy with the existing government, allowed the Persians to take possession. Cyrus now allowed the Jews to return to Jerusalem and there to rebuild their temple and to make their homes in the land of their fathers. For this reason the Hebrews had only words of praise for Cyrus. To the number of 49,697, with their property and possessions, they set upon their long march—a peaceful band which encountered no opposition throughout its course. The event stands unparalleled in history.

Had Cyrus lived, he would doubtless have added Egypt to his empire. This was left for his son to accomplish. The great king fell fighting for territories in the north.

In conclusion, it may be said that Cyrus is the first great conqueror we have so far met who was kind and humane. His policy towards the conquered stands out in marked relief to the butcheries and punishments which characterized Assyria. Notwithstanding, all charges of selfish motives which have belonged to those who have sought to become world-conquerors, attach to Cyrus. Urged on by personal vanity and hope of becoming supreme, he considered only the final issue and allowed his ambition to triumph over his nobler nature. Some years later Alexander emulated his example, and one hundred years ago Napoleon undertook the same gigantic task—greater in his day—of building up a world-empire. The motives prompting all three were the same, and in each case the empires, so quickly brought into being, vanished as quickly as they arose.

CHAPTER XIX.

War with Greece.

Upon the death of Cyrus, in 529 B. C., his son Cambyses succeeded to the throne, while a younger brother Smerdis, was left to supervise certain provinces, according to his father's wishes. The conquest of Egypt had been planned by Cyrus and would undoubtedly have been undertaken by him had he lived. Cambyses at once began preparations to this end and these occupied some considerable period.

This young prince who had just come into absolute power, apparently inherited all his father's failings and few of his virtues. He had never learned to control himself and that omened ill for those who became his subjects. His jealousy, suspicion, cruelty, and arrogant pride contrasted strikingly with the generous, kindly temperament of Cyrus. Before setting out for Egypt, he had his brother secretly murdered. No rumor of this crime reached his subjects, however.

Egypt at this time was not able to defend herself against an army that had become experienced and confident under the command of Cyrus; consequently, the country fell rapidly into the hands of the new Persian king. Far from showing the leniency of his father toward the vanquished, he marked his victories with needless cruelty.

The two great powers of Africa besides Egypt were the states of Ethiopia in the south, and Carthage in the northwest. Of the former we learned something in The Story of Egypt; of the latter we shall learn later on. Suffice it to say here that the Carthaginians were colonists of the Phœnicians, and, like them, were traders whose commerce penetrated to all lands washed by the Mediterranean Sea.

When Egypt lay at his feet, Cambyses resolved to make himself supreme in the whole continent of Africa—only the northern portion of the continent was then known. Accordingly, he directed troops to advance against these two powers which he thought alone worthy of his notice. Now Carthage could only be taken by sea, and the king was limited to

Phœnician vessels, manned by Phœnician sailors. These men promptly refused to make war on their own colony, whose interests were so closely interwoven with those of their country. Their stand must have been united and firm, for Cambyses found himself obliged to abandon his project. The expedition to the south was disheartening. The Persian soldiers were unused to the hot sands and intense sun of Nubia and great loss and discouragement overtook the army. Those who withstood the heat were too exhausted by the march to accomplish anything. The king remained in Egypt. He was constantly haunted by his crime against his brother. He realized his unpopularity with his subjects, and feared that disaster would at any time overtake him. His fears were shortly reflected in his soldiers, who having learned that they were no longer led by one who could bring victory in the face of opposing obstacles, lost heart and fought indifferently.

Herodotus wrote at length concerning the conduct of Cambyses in Egypt and his stories were long credited. Tales were told of Cambyses' profaning Egyptian temples, desecrating the tombs of the dead, stabbing the apis-bull with his own sword, outraging the priests and inflicting such injury upon the nobles as only the madness which they attribute to him, could explain. In recent years these statements have been modified by investigation. An Egyptologist of first rank claims that the tale regarding the apis-bull was not well founded. Unquestionably Cambyses was brutal in his treatment of a mild and gentle people, and he may have easily incurred the wrath of the priesthood by his contempt for their religion, certain features of which he regarded as mere folly. It is also probable that his deeds have been greatly exaggerated by those who had cause to hate him for his interference with a land to which he had no just claim. Instead of being insane, he no doubt displayed his ungovernable temper and in moments of rage, gave orders which he would gladly have recalled in another mood.

While Cambyses loitered in Egypt, a report spread through the empire that Smerdis had been crowned, and that Cambyses need no longer be regarded as king. One of the Magians, a priesthood of Persia which represented a more material form of worship than the teachings of Zoroaster allowed, had attempted to usurp the throne in Cambyses' absence. The real king, feeling depressed with his partial victory, doubting the fidelity of his army, confessed the murder of his brother to his ministers. Having thus disclosed the presumption of the pretender, Cambyses committed suicide.

Darius, a prince of the house of Cyrus, was chosen to succeed. This was a choice likely to prove acceptable to the people, for he was the only legitimate heir to the throne. Herodotus explained with all gravity that the counsellors of state, of whose number Darius was one, agreed to determine the succession after this fashion: they would each go on horseback at sunrise to the city gate, and he whose horse neighed first should be proclaimed king!

The Magian was Killed.

When the people finally learned the truth and realized how great a deception had been practised, they turned against his priesthood and instigated a general massacre. The worship they had established was cast aside and the purer faith of ancient Persia was restored. The pretender had compelled the Jews to cease labor on the new temple they were building in Jerusalem. Darius gave them permission to continue. So similar were the religions of the Hebrews and Persians, that there could be no friction between the two nations on that ground in an age when nearly all religions were polytheistic.

Darius was long occupied with internal disturbances. Revolts were put down with severity. When the government of the empire was firmly established, it was superior to any before known in Asia. The whole empire was divided into satrapies, or provinces—each under a resident governor; these governors made frequent reports to the capital and the opportunity for revolts was slight.

Internal concerns thus settled, Darius turned to conquest. He conducted a campaign in the east, pushing Persia's possessions to the banks of the Indus.

It was natural that the king should have cast longing eyes westward, toward the beautiful isles and states of Greece. Long before the age of Cyrus, Greek colonists had settled in Asia Minor. They had fallen to the share of Persia when Lydia was conquered, and Darius had organized their local government so completely that the freedom-loving Greeks were oppressed by it and in 500 B. C. revolted. These Greek cities appealed to Athens for aid in their struggle for liberty. A few soldiers were sent, and with such aid they displaced the Persian government and destroyed Sardis. Darius sent an army to put down the revolt, and the city which had led the struggle was destroyed. The king of Persia now determined to punish Athens for having given help to the revolting Greek cities of Asia Minor. Accordingly, he fitted out an expedition to conquer Greece. The naval forces were wrecked in a storm and the land forces were routed by hostile tribes en route. A second expedition was prepared, more numerous and better equipped than the first. Before dispatching it, however, Darius sent heralds to the various Greek states to inquire if they would submit peacefully. They replied with great scorn. In 490 B. C. the Persian king sent 300,000 soldiers to conquer Greece. The battle of Marathon was fought, and owing to the skill of Miltiades, the Greeks won. Four years later Darius died and Xerxes ruled in his stead. To him was left the duty of wiping out the inglorious defeat of the Persian arms. Not until 480 B. C. were the armies ready for what was expected to be a great conquest.

It has been said that never in the history of the world has such a motley array of soldiers been gathered together under one commander. All nations subservient to Persia were represented, and while Herodotus may have overstated their number, we may accept his statement that it was the largest force ever thus far marshalled together. At the defense of Thermopylæ the Persians learned the character of their opponents. A little band of three hundred Spartans under command of Leonidas held the entire Persian army at bay in a narrow pass for two days. When the army spread out over the land, the Greeks realized their inability to cope with it and decided to hazard all on a naval engagement. The famous battle of Salamis followed, in which 1,000 men-of-war belonging to the Persians were destroyed or put to flight by 300 Greek vessels. Xerxes watched the fight from a throne hastily constructed for him on the shore. When at night his naval forces withdrew to Asia, he could scarcely credit the outcome. Byron has immortalized the occasion in a stanza:

> "A king sate on the rocky brow
>   Which looks o'er sea-born Salamis;
> And ships, by thousands, lay below,
>   And men in nations—all were his!
> He counted them at break of day—
>   And when the sun set where were they?"

Leaving a strong land force to conquer the Greeks the next year, Xerxes returned to Persia. By the following spring the Greeks had gathered their forces, and inspired by their glorious victory at Salamis, they defeated the Persian army in the battle of Platæa. Thereupon the Greek cities in Asia Minor asserted their freedom, and Greek independence shone forth triumphantly before the world.

"But this glorious struggle and triumph of the few lifted to superhuman heroism by an ennobling moral principle, as against the merely brutal force of numbers, does not properly belong any more to the history of the East, nor to that of remote antiquity; it is the dawn of a new star in the West, and of times which, from their spirit, actors, and achievements, may almost be called modern. At the bottom of the new departure lies the difference between the ideals—the conceptions of beauty and dignity of the political and social life—set up by the Oriental and Western man: 'A good master!' is the prayer and ideal of the Asiatic. 'No master! Liberty at any price, as the highest good in itself!' is that of the Greek. And the Greek wins the day, for his own time, and for his own race, and for future times and races to come."[1]

The following period, embracing nearly 150 years, was a time of decay and degeneracy. With Xerxes began the corruption of the Persian court—the licentiousness, assassinations, murders, and accompanying crimes which soon undermined the entire social order. Conditions were such that rulers were no longer strong, vigorous men, full of life and ambition—save indeed those usurpers who occasionally appropriated the reins of government. The days of Persian greatness were over, and under guidance of one or another of the

---

[1] Ragozin: Persia.

princes, the state plunged on to ruin. In 336 B. C., Alexander, the young king of Macedonia, embarked upon his world conquests, and the Persian Empire merged into the Empire of Greece.

THE PERSIAN KING
(WITH ATTENDANTS).

CHAPTER XX.

Manners and Customs Among the Persians.

There were wide differences between the civilization of the Persians and of the dwellers in the Tigris-Euphrates valleys. The Persian despised trade. His religion taught him to speak the truth, and he regarded commercial dealings as incompatible with this requirement. No shops made the principal streets in his country the scenes of hot disputes concerning prices and wares. The few shops which existed at all were tucked into obscure places on unfrequented by-ways. It naturally followed that there was an absence of those industrial centers which in Babylonia produced rare stuffs, delicate fabrics and ornaments. Swarms of slaves provided whatever was required by the wealthy, and it was the Persian's boast that his sword brought him the luxury of the world in tribute.

It has been estimated that the total population of Persia did not exceed 2,000,000. A small proportion of these were peasants who tilled the arable soil. Agriculture was held honorable and was encouraged by the national religion. The great majority of men were soldiers.

Since the soldier's life was thought to be worthy of a Persian, we may do well to consider whatever features characterized the service in this empire. Probably because of the mountainous country in which they dwelt, chariots were never popular with these people. Ordinarily they were impractical, being suited to plains and accessible places. Nevertheless a few were used and these were furnished with scythes attached to the axle. Chariots formed the front line of defense. Behind them the foot soldiers were arranged in squares, with cavalry on the wings. One commander—the king, if he were present,—gave commands to all from his position in the center. This was an evident fault, for, were he killed or in any way disabled, the entire army sometimes took fright and fled. When the charge was made, the chariots dashed ahead, hewing right and left. They seldom failed to break the solid line drawn up before them, whereupon the infantry and horse followed, taking advantage of the confusion thus wrought. If the regular line of Persian soldiery was broken or in any way disturbed, since they had no reinforcements in a second division, the battle was almost always lost. To prevent such an occurrence was their aim. It has been said that the Orientals of this time could not be trusted to fight unless they were well supported at the rear—hence the custom of forming one deep line. The native Persians were brave soldiers, but their ranks were generally composed largely of subjects levied throughout the empire. Scantily clothed Nubians fought with clubs and stones in the same army with well-equipped natives. Drawn up by nation, in native custom, it is not surprising that they presented a sight marvellous indeed to the foreigner.

The contrast between Greek and Persian military tactics was marked. The Greeks trusted to their solid, heavily-armed phalanx; the Persians tried to equip themselves as lightly as possible, and trusted to their agility and swiftness of motion. Their leniency toward captives has been mentioned before. They found no delight in mere slaughter.

Literature and learning had little part in the life of the average citizen. The boy was left with his mother until five years of age. Then his education began. He rose before dawn and was trained in running, throwing stones, and shooting with an arrow. At seven he was taught to ride, and in Persia this implied much. He must be able to spring on a horse running at full speed, to shoot accurately when under rapid motion. In course of a few years' practice it was not strange that a Persian was never so at ease as on his horse. Furthermore, he was compelled to endure severe hardships—sleeping under the open sky, eating only one meal in two days, making long marches, and swimming streams burdened with his weapons. At fifteen years of age he was considered a man and was enlisted in the army, where he ordinarily served until fifty.

During the period of the Persian empire, a numerous body of officials made up the king's retinue. Besides the farmers, soldiers and officials, there were many slaves, who completed the social body. They performed all kinds of labor, built the palaces and made fine roads throughout the realm.

The Persian court has probably never been excelled in ceremony and pomp. Ceremony surrounded the monarch during hours of retirement and seclusion as well as when before the public eye.

"The officers in most close attendance on the monarch's person were, in war, his charioteer, his stool-bearer, his bow-bearer, and his quiver-bearer; in peace, his parasol-bearer, and his fan-bearer, who was also privileged to carry what has been termed the 'royal-handkerchief.' Among the officers of the Court, less closely attached to the person of the monarch than these, may be mentioned the steward of the household; the groom or master of the horse; the keeper of the women's department, the king's 'eyes' and 'ears'—persons whose business it was to keep him informed on all matters of importance; his scribes, who wrote his letters, his messengers who went his errands, his ushers, his tasters, who tried the various dishes set before him lest they should be poisoned; his cup-bearers, who handed him wine and tasted of it; his chamberlains who assisted him to bed; and his musicians, who amused him with song and harp. Besides these, the Court comprised various classes of guards, doorkeepers, huntsmen, grooms, cooks, and other domestic servants in abundance, together with a vast multitude of visitors, guests, princes, captives of rank, foreign refugees, ambassadors, and travellers. We are assured that the king fed daily within the precincts of his palace as many as 15,000 persons, and that the cost of each day's food was 400 talents. A thousand beasts were slaughtered for each repast, besides abundance of feathered game and poultry. On all occasions the guests, if they liked, carried away any portion of the food set before them, conveying it to their homes where it served to support their families."[1]

Prescribed etiquette governed everyone, from the king to his meanest subject. The august king must dine alone, or at best have with him the queen and her son. He could be approached only with certain ceremony. Ceremony and form were by no means confined to royalty and the court. Men of different rank met each other with established form and salutation; certain tasks could be performed only by persons who

[1] Rawlinson: Persia.

Copyright by Underwood & Underwood, N. Y.
DAMASCUS SWORD-MAKER

could perform no other tasks. This led to a large body of idlers around the court, ready to take part in any intrigue or conspiracy. They gathered around the homes of the wealthy as well as the palace of the king—water-bearers, adorners, awakers, and each rigidly confined himself to his single duty.

In early times the Persians indulged in a single meal each day. The custom continued later, but now the feast began with the morning and ceased only with night. The amount of wine a man could drink became his boast. In place of the regular habits, frugal fare and constant exercise of early times, were substituted the prolonged feast, all kinds of indulgencies, and idleness.

The royal harem provided apartments for the king's several wives in early years. Towards the close of the empire, provision had to be made for some three hundred and sixty —if we may trust one writer. The jealousies, differences and intrigues which arose from this quarter can scarcely be imagined. Each wished her son to be given preference, and this ambition, together with the restlessness accompanying enforced seclusion, stimulated crime and fostered conspiracies. The favorite of the king might toy with the lives of his subjects—even with the lives of those dear to him, at will. No subject in the land had reason to think his life secure—least of all, he who was today powerful.

For diversions—other than Court intrigues—the king turned to the hunt. Dice throwing was the national game, and the carving of wood was a frequent pastime. Since little was known of books, men were forced to find some means of passing hours unoccupied with national affairs or private concerns.

Dress had been simple in early years. As time went on, it became more complex; even matters of cosmetics and perfumes were later deemed of weighty importance.

There is more to attract us in the Persian state during years of its earlier simplicity, while yet the soldier found his deepest satisfaction in military skill, bodily exercise and great endurance, than in the period of imperial greatness, when the court of Persia exceeded in splendor anything since known.

The Religion of Persia.

Some time between 1000-650 B.C., it is supposed there lived a religious reformer by the name of Zarathushtra, or Zoroaster. Both his birth-place and birth-date are alike unknown, but it is supposed that he lived in Bactria, a country which reached indefinitely along the Caspian Sea.

Little has come down to us concerning the great teacher himself. He early felt called to his religious mission. Retiring from the world, tradition says he lived for some years upon a remote mountain, and here a divine vision came to him. He communed with Ormuzd, the spirit of Good, and knew that his work was to reclaim man, who in blindness had wandered away from truth and light, and to bring him into new relationship with the divine spirit which was ever ready to win mankind to himself.

At the age of thirty, Zoroaster was prepared to preach the new law. For ten years he wandered about, but found few to listen to him. His family and friends were gradually won to the faith he taught, and returning to the Caspian Sea region, he found more willing hearers.

The conceptions from which he had evolved his faith were already accepted to some extent by those among whom he came. He taught that there were two spirits—Ormuzd or Good, embodying all truth, life, beauty, order, light; and Ahriman, or Evil, including all darkness, death, falsity and disorder. Life was a struggle between these two contending forces. "He laid before his people their own thoughts in all the pure transparency of crystal waters cleared from muddiness and unwholesome admixtures in the filter of his own transcendent and searching mind. He guided their groping hands, and made them grasp the truth for which they were blindly reaching. Such is the mission of every true prophet. Had the people not been ripe for his teaching, he could not have secured a hearing, or made himself understood; the people, on the other hand, could never have worked out unaided the ideal to which they were vaguely and only half-consciously drawn. They listened and understood, and were won, because, to use the expression of a great writer, they had in themselves the seed of the thoughts which the prophet expounded to them."[2]

---
[2] Ragozin: Media and Persia.

Seven times divine beings brought messages to Zoroaster. "They inculcate the doctrine of purity of body as well as of soul; they enjoin the care of useful animals, especially the cow and the dog; they emphasize the necessity of keeping the earth, the fire and the water undefiled; and from several of their ordinances we can see that Zoroaster was a civil reformer as well as a spiritual guide. Foremost among the commandments is the abhorrence of falsehood, the universal obligation to speak the truth. This is one of the most fundamental of the ethical tenets which form the basis of the entire ancient Persian religious system."[3]

The writings which contained the teachings of Zoroaster are commonly known as the Zenda-Vesta. The name is misleading however, and should read Avesta-u-Zend, which translated means: "Law and Commentary." Among students the compilation is generally called the Avesta. Even a casual reading of the Old Testament reveals the fact that the various books composing it were written by different writers, writing under radically different circumstances, and at widely distant periods. The same is true of the Avesta. One of its books was probably written either by Zoroaster himself or under his supervision. This is the Gathas, or book of songs, and is the most ancient portion of the entire collection. Sermons, prayers, and sayings are therein contained, some of which possess poetic beauty and rare purity. Other books were added from time to time, until the Avesta is said to have been made up of twenty-one books, and to have covered 1,200 cowhides.

When Alexander the Great conquered Persia in 332 B. C., elated by his victory, and having drunk heavily of wine, he allowed his soldiers to burn the capital, and with it perished much of greatest value. Most of the Persian literature was then destroyed, together with the noblest specimens of Persian architecture and decoration. While cities were few, it seems remarkable that the only copies of the Avesta were burned. For several centuries following, the teachings of this sacred book lived only in the memories of priests. Finally in 325 A. D., a council was called to take measures to have these ancient doctrines committed to writing. Naturally the result

[3] Jackson: Persia, the Land and Its History.

was fragmentary and incomplete. Only those portions of the original text which had been in daily use proved to be well remembered. These were mainly prayers and invocations. The priests in all probability, seized the opportunity to insert whatever forms of worship and modified beliefs they desired to emphasize. Their final effort, while far from satisfactory, embraces all which now remains of the religion of Zoroaster and his followers.

In 636 A.D. the Mohammedan Arabs made a religious crusade and undertook to blot out the old Persian religion. Most of the descendants of the early nation yielded to the fire and sword. A small portion of them took refuge in India, where they were allowed to worship as they chose. Only with them was the Avesta preserved. These Parsis have been called "the ruins of a people, as their sacred books are the ruins of a religion." Of them Justi writes: "There is no religious body in the world whose practice is so completely in harmony with their moral code."

The collection of Zend Fragments, commonly known as the Zend-Avesta, falls into two parts: The Avesta, properly so-called, which contains (1) compilations of religious laws and mythical tales; (2) collections of litanies for the sacrifice; (3) litanies and hymns written in a language older than the rest of the Avesta. Secondly, these writings contain the Small Avesta, made up of short prayers, recited by all the faithful. It was fitting that these collections of fragments be preserved, so far as possible, in their original dialect, but since these were no longer intelligible even to the educated, the Zend, or explanation —commentary—was attached in the prevailing tongue. Otherwise the greater portion of the work could not have been understood. Some of the creation stories were not included in the Avesta, but were gathered together with other myths in the Bundehesh.

All worshippers are classified by the Avesta as followers of Ormuzd—Good,—or Ahriman—Evil. One could either stand for good or against it. "Now shall I proclaim unto you, O ye all that here approach me, what the wise should lay to their hearts; the songs of praise and the sacrificial rites which pious men pay the Lord, and the sacred truths and ordinances, that what was secret until now may appear in the light 'Hear with your ears that which is best, and test it with a clear understanding, before each man decides for himself between the two teachings.'

"The two Spirits, the Twins, skilfully created, in the beginning, Good and Evil, in thought, in speech, in deed. And, between these two, the wise have made the right choice; not so the senseless. If, O men, you lay to your hearts these ordinances which Ormuzd instituted, and the good and evil, and the long torments which await the followers of falsehood, and the bliss that must come to the holders of the true faith, it will go well with you."

Followers of Zoroaster abhorred idolatry. No image of their God corrupted their conceptions. In early times they built no temples, having only altars whereupon sacrifices were made. Darius often mentions Ahuramazda (Hormuzd) in his inscriptions as the highest god of the Persians, and it is highly probable that Cyrus was also a worshipper, a fact which made him sympathetic toward the religion of the Jews and accounts for his willingness that they rebuild a temple in Jerusalem for the worship of Yahweh.

In later years, forms and symbols crept into the service, for abstract teachings did not hold the masses of the people. Fire was conceived to be a symbol of the God of Light, and even today there seems to be a certain charm in the conception that "a pure and undefiled flame is certainly the most sublime natural representation of Him who is in Himself Eternal Light." There must have been a sublimity in the sight of the pure flames, rising to heaven from the mountain-tops, while prayers and hymns of praise were poured out to the one great Spirit, by whatever name known.

As days of degeneracy overtook Persia, the religion was affected by the general lassitude and decay. A modernized form of the early faith is found today among some 100,000 worshippers in Arabia and India.

A Hymn.

"We worship Ahura Mazda (Ormuzd), the pure, the master of purity.
"We praise all good thoughts, all good words, all good deeds which are or shall be; and we likewise keep clean, and pure all that is good.
"O Ormuzd, thou true, happy being! We strive to think, to speak, and to do only such actions as may be best fitted to promote the two lives (the life of the body and of the soul).

"We beseech the spirit of earth for the sake of these our best works to grant us beautiful and fertile fields, to the believer as well as to the unbeliever, to him who has riches as well as to him who has no possessions."

From the Avesta. Part I.

"O Maker of the material world, thou Holy One! Which is the first place where the Earth feels most happy?"

Ahura Mazda, the Good Principle, answered: "It is the place whereon one of the faithful steps forward, O Zoroaster, with the holy wood in his hand,[1] the baresma in his hand,[2] the holy meat in his hand,[3] the holy mortar in his hand,[4] fulfilling the law with love, and beseeching aloud Mithra.[5]

"O Maker of the material world, thou Holy One! Which is the second place where the Earth feels most happy?"

Ahura Mazda answered: "It is the place whereon one of the faithful erects a house with a priest therein, with cattle, with a wife, with children, and good herds within; and wherein afterwards the cattle go on thriving, holiness is thriving, fodder is thriving, the dog is thriving, the wife is thriving, the child is thriving, the fire is thriving, and every blessing of life is thriving."

"O Maker of the material world, thou Holy One! Which is the third place where the Earth feels most happy?"

Ahura Mazda answered: "It is the place where one of the faithful cultivates most corn, grass and fruit, O Zoroaster! where he waters ground that is too dry, and dries ground that is too wet."

"O Maker of the material world, thou Holy One! Which is the fourth place where the Earth feels most happy?"

Ahura Mazda answered: "It is the place where there is most increase of flocks and herds."

"O Maker of the material world, thou Holy One! Which is the first place where the Earth feels sorest grief?"

Ahura Mazda answered: "It is the neck of Arezura,[6] whereon the hosts of fiends rush forth to the burrow of the Drug.[7]"

---

[1] Food for the altar fire. [2] Sacred twigs held by the priest while reciting prayers. [3] Meat for sacrifice. [4] Used for crushing the Haoma, an intoxicating plant, whose juice is used by the faithful. [5] God of good fields and pastures. [6] Mount at the gate of hell whence demons rush forth. [7] Hell.

"O Maker of the material world, thou Holy One! Which is the second place where the Earth feels sorest grief?"

Ahura Mazda answered: "It is the place where most corpses of dogs and of men lie buried."

"O Maker of the material world, thou Holy One! Which is the fifth place where the Earth feels sorest grief?"

Ahura Mazda answered: "It is the place whereon the wife and children of the faithful, O Zoroaster, are driven along the way of captivity, the dry, the dusty way, and lift up a voice of wailing."

"O Maker of the material world, thou Holy One! Who is the first that rejoices the Earth with greatest joy?"

Ahura Mazda answered: "It is he who digs out of it most corpses of dogs and men."

Ancient Hymn from the Avesta.

"I am the Keeper; I am the Creator and the Maintainer; I am the Discerner; I am the most beneficent Spirit.

My name is the bestower of health; my name is the best bestower of health.

My name is the Holy; my name is the most Holy.

My name is the Glorious; my name is the most Glorious.

My name is the far-seeing; my name is the Farthest-seeing.

My name is Holiness; my name is the Great one; my name is the good Sovereign; my name is the best of Sovereigns.

My name is the Wise One; my name is the Wisest of the Wise; my name is He who does good for a long time.

These are my names.

And he who in this material world, O Zoroaster! shall recite and pronounce these names of mine either by day or by night;

He who shall pronounce them when he rises up or when he lays him down; when he lays him down or when he rises up; when he binds on the sacred girdle, or when he unbinds the sacred girdle; when he goes out of his dwelling-place, or when he goes out of his town, or when he goes out of his country and comes into another country;

That man, neither in that day nor in that night shall be wounded by the weapons of the foe.   .; not the knife, not the cross-bow, not the arrow, not the sword, not the club, not the sling-stone shall reach him and wound him.

But these names shall come in to keep him from behind and to keep him in front   from the evil ones, bent on mischief, and from that fiend which is all death—Angra Mainyu.

It will be as if there were a thousand men watching over one man."

—*Trans. Zend-Avesta: Sacred Books of the East.*
Max Muller, ed. V. 4, 23, 31.

PART OF ARCHER'S FRIEZE IN AN
ANCIENT PERSIAN PALACE.

CHAPTER XXI.

CONTRIBUTIONS OF BABYLONIA, ASSYRIA AND PERSIA TO MODERN CIVILIZATION.

It is often difficult to correctly estimate the power exerted by a statesman upon his country. The movements he has espoused, the reforms he may have championed, the institutions he helped to call into being, all stand as monuments to his memory. But the subtle effects of his influence, his personality and character upon his own generation and others still to come, are seldom understood or adequately judged. In the case of a nation the task becomes still more complicated, and we cannot today know how many of our ideas, inventions, and attainments have been shaped by nations whose light went out long centuries ago. Nevertheless, our inability to estimate these various inheritances aright need not deter us from an attempt to classify such bequeathments as are universally acknowledged, and we may be sure that the present world owes much to the earliest nations of Western Asia. Their contributions, however, have not come down to us directly, but have been passed along, like legends, from one people to another, until their present form scarcely suggests their origins.

Let us consider first our indebtedness to Babylonia. In recent years discoveries in the Euphrates valley and the mastery of the cuneiform style of writing have given us masses of material wherefrom to reconstruct the past. Not only has light thus been thrown upon the early history of Babylonia and Assyria, but aid has been rendered biblical study. The tribal life of the Hebrews, and the civilization of other contemporary peoples has been better understood because of these revelations. However, acquisitions of the last century have had no part in molding modern civilization, and we pass on to matters of earlier significance.

No people could have worked as diligently in the field of science as the Babylonians did and failed to leave important results of their investigations. "In *Geometry* the Chaldeans made about the same progress as the Egyptians; in *Arithmetic* more. Their notation combined the decimal and duodecimal systems. Sixty was a favorite unit, used as the hundred is by us. Scientific *Medicine* was hindered by the belief in charms and amulets; and even *Astronomy* was studied chiefly as a means of fortune-telling by the stars,—so that in Europe through the Middle Ages an astrologer was known as a Chaldean. However, the level plains and clear skies, as in Egypt, invited to an early study of the constellations, and some important progress was made. As we get from the Egyptians our year and months, so from the Chaldeans we get the week, with its 'day of rest for the heart,' as they called the seventh day, and the division of day and night into twelve hours each, with the subdivisions into minutes. They also invented the water clock and the sundial. They foretold eclipses, made star maps, and marked out on the heavens the apparent yearly path of the sun. The zodiacal 'signs' of our almanacs commemorate these early astronomers. Every great city had its lofty observatory and its royal astronomer; and in Babylon, in 331 B. C., Alexander the Great found a continuous series of observations running back nineteen hundred and three years.

"To a degree peculiar among the ancients, the men of the Euphrates made practical use of their science. They understood the lever and pulley, and used the arch in vaulted drains and aqueducts. They invented the potter's wheel, and an excellent system of weights and measures. Their treatises on agriculture passed on their knowledge in that subject to the later Greeks and Arabs. They had surpassing skill in cutting gems, and in enameling and inlaying; and their looms produced the finest of muslins and of fleecy woolens, to which the dyer gave the most brilliant colors. In many such industries little advance has been made since, so far as results are concerned."[1]

Certain unfortunate bequests were left by them. Babylonian belief in demons was handed down through the Hebrews, and in the Middle Ages took the form of the devil, with horns and a cloven foot. Their faith in magic and incantations also descended to Mediæval times, and as scientific interest superseded religious fervor, inspired men to search for the "philosopher's stone."

[1] West: Ancient History.

The intensely practical turn of mind in Mesopotamia revealed itself in the literature, which was bare of imagery. Material beauty—artistic carpets, tapestries, and rugs, was developed, but for beauty of conceptions, we must turn to the Greeks.

What did the war-loving, blood-thirsting Assyrians leave for future ages? At first the question seems not to be easily answered. One calls to mind their ravaging raids and unparalleled carnage, and remembering that their palaces and stores of inscribed tablets were recovered only within the last fifty years, their contributions are not so apparent. Yet, having studied the government enforced by Darius upon his empire, we are compelled to admit that he but improved upon the system evolved by the Assyrian kings, unknown before their time in Asia. Again, the very conquests themselves were helpful, in spite of their cruelty, for they brought the best civilization of their day to half-barbarous tribes who otherwise might have passed century after century before reaching the degree of progress so rudely thrust upon them. These conquests opened up routes of commerce, and trade has always exceeded all other factors as a civilizing force.

To science the Assyrians appear to have made no contributions whatever.

Coming to ancient Persia, we find a wholly different culture. The people of this country lacked the practical turn of mind so characteristic of the Babylonian, and his mercenary point of view was quite unknown to them. Persian literature, while scanty, embodied poetical conceptions, and several of the ancient poems possess much art. "The Persians had fancy and imagination, a relish for poetry and art, and they were not without a certain power of political combination. Yet we cannot justly ascribe to them any high degree of intellectual excellence. If the great work of Firdausi represents to us, as it probably does, the true spirit of their ancient poetry, their efforts were but of moderate merit. A tone of exaggeration, an imagination exuberant and unrestrained, a preference for glitter over solid excellence, a love of far-fetched conceits, characterize the Shahnameh; and, though we may ascribe something of this to the individuality of the poet, still the conviction presses upon us that there was a childish and grotesque character in the mass of old Persian poetry, which marked it as the creation of moderate rather than of high intellectual power, and prevents us from regarding it with the respect with which we view the labors of the Greeks and Romans, or again, of the Hebrews, in this department. A want of seriousness, a want of reality, and, again, a want of depth, characterize the poetry of Iran, whose bards do not touch the chords which rouse what is noblest and highest in our nature. They give us sparkle, prettiness, quaint and ingenious fancies, grotesque marvels, an inflated kind of human heroism; but they have none of the higher excellences of the poetic art, none of the divine fire which renders the true poet, and the true prophet, one."[2]

The Persian religion was both noble and sublime, and its teaching concerning the two opposing forces of good and evil, affected the philosophy of the Greeks, and indirectly, the thought of the later Christian world.

By carrying the plan of Assyrian conquest further, the Persians opened districts remote from social centers and helped the course of civilization. Their systematic government improved upon the one developed by Assyria in this particular: each governor was made supreme in his province under Assyrian administration, none other being accountable to the king for conditions in his territory. An opportunity thus offered for the governor to seize any favorable moment to shake off allegiance to the state and attempt to establish his own supremacy. Darius, on the other hand, posted troops in each satrapy, and both the commander of these troops and the governor were required to submit reports, and to act jointly in certain matters. In this way, one served as a check upon the other.

Fine roads were built to allow rapid communication between the capital and distant provinces; these naturally facilitated commerce, and made travel safe—as one has graphically expressed it, "helped set the world a-mixing."

A new day was dawning for humanity, and an age coming when one might look back to the infancy of the world, likening its progress to that of a man who has gained some perceptions, some ideas and experiences in childhood days which unconsciously but surely, influence his later life, illuminated by wider experiences and deeper truths.

[2] Rawlinson: Persia.

THE BOOK-STAMP OF SARDANAPALUS.

Assurbanipal, or, as the Greeks called him, Sardanapalus, is supposed to have stored in his palace at Nineveh not less than 30,000 tablets. Upon every work in his library his ownership was stamped as follows:

> The Palace of Assurbanipal, King of Regions, King of Multitudes, King of Assyria, to whom the God Nebo and the Goddess Tasmeti have granted attentive ears and open eyes to discover the Writings of the Scribes of my Kingdom, whom the Kings my Predecessors have employed. In my respect for Nebo, the God of Intelligence, I have collected these tablets: I have had them copied: I have marked them with my name; and I have deposited them in my Palace.

THE CHALDEAN ACCOUNT OF THE DELUGE.

This account was first translated by George Smith from the eleventh of a series of tablets describing the adventures of the mythical hero, Izdubar (or Gilgamish), supposed to be the same as Nimrod. The whole series of tablets relates his early life and exploits in hunting, his friendship with the faun Iabani, his victory over the tyrant Humbaba, the love of the Goddess Ishtar, his illness, the death of Iabani, his wanderings to find his ancestor, Hasisadra (or Pir-napishtim), who for his piety had been translated to the fellowship of the gods. This ancestor relates to Gilgamish the story of a great flood resembling in general outline the narrative in Genesis, but stamped with the impress of the Chaldean religion. Shamas was the Sun-god.

The early literature of many nations contains stories of a universal flood, from which a favored family or individual alone escapes. None is more striking than the one deciphered from the clay tablets of Chaldea, or more nearly parallel to that of the Hebrew Scriptures.

TABLET XI. OF THE GILGAMISH EPIC.

The following translation is from Professor Craig:

The Babylonian Story of the Deluge.

Pir-napishtim saith to him, even to Gilgamish;
I will relate to thee, Gilgamish, a secret story,
And the decision of the gods I will tell thee.

The city Shurippak, which thou knowest,
Is situated on the shore of the Euphrates.
This city was old when the gods within it
Were moved to produce a flood, even the great gods.
They were Anu, their father,
The warrior Bel, their counsellor,
Their throne-bearer, Ninib,
Their leader, Ennugi,
Ninigiazag (the god Ea) had spoken with them
And their decree he repeated to the reed-house (saying):
"Reed-house! reed-house! house-wall! house-wall![1]
Reed-house, hear! and house-wall, consider!
O man of Shurippak, son of Ubar-Tutu!
Construct a house, build a ship,
Abandon possessions, seek life,
Property despise, and life save,
Put seed of life of every kind into the ship.
The ship which thou shalt build, even thou,
Let be measured her dimensions:
Let her breadth and length be equal,
Upon the ocean launch her."

I understood, and said to Ea, my lord:
"Behold, my lord, what thou hast commanded
I hold in reverence, I shall do.
(But what) shall I answer the city, the people, and the elders?"

Ea opened his mouth and speaketh,
Saith unto his servant, unto me:
"O man! Thus shalt thou say unto them:
Bel has rejected me and cursed me.
I shall dwell no more in your city,
And upon Bel's ground I shall not set my face.
But to the ocean shall I descend; with Ea, my lord, I shall dwell.
Upon you he shall cause to pour out abundance,
Game of birds and game of fishes,
(Animals of all kinds); field-fruits in plenty,
When in the evening the ruler of the darkness (?)
Shall cause to rain upon you a heavy rain."

[1] The house for its inhabitants. Compare Isaiah 1, 2: Hear, O heavens, and give ear, O earth.

As soon as dawn began to appear,
  (Five or six lines wanting)
The weak (?)
The strong brought to (the building-place) what was necessary.
On the fifth day I laid down her form.
Ina Kar-Hi-Sa one hundred and twenty cubits high were her walls,
One hundred and twenty cubits likewise was the extent of her roof.
Its outer frame I constructed, enclosed it.[1]
I   her six times.
I divided   seven times.
Its interior I divided nine times.
Water plugs I beat into it on its inside.
I provided a rudder (?) and what was needed I added.
Six *sars* of bitumen I spread on the outside (?).
Three *sars* of pitch (I spread) on the inside.
Three *sars* of basket-bearers brought oil.
I left one *sar* of oil which the offering consumed,
Two *sars* of oil the shipman stowed away.
For the people I slaughtered oxen,
I killed   every day.
New w(ine, sesame) wine, oil and wine,
Like the waters of the river (I gave the people to drink)
And (held) a religious feast like unto the New-Year's Feast.
I opened (?) . . . of anointing oil, my hand applied (it).
(In the month) of Shamash, the great god, the ship was completed.
Because   were difficult
(Untranslatable) they brought above and below.
         two-thirds of it.

All that I had I put on board of it.
All that I had of silver I put on board of it.
All that I had of gold I put on board of it.
All that I had of seed of life of every kind I put on board of it.
I caused to go up into the ship all my family and relatives.
Cattle of the field, beasts of the field, all the craftsmen, I caused to go up.

[1] The meaning here and in the next four lines is not clear.

A definite time the god Shamash had appointed:
The ruler of the darkness (?) at even-tide shall cause to rain a
    heavy rain,
Enter thou (then) within the ship and close thy door."
That appointed time came.
The ruler of the darkness (?) at eventide rained a heavy rain.
The appearance of that day I (fore)saw.
To behold the day I had fear.
I entered into the ship and closed my door.
For the control of the ship to Puzur-Bel
The great-house I gave over together with its store.
With the first appearing of dawn
There rises from the foundation of the heavens a black cloud,
Ramman within it thunders.
Nebo and Marduk march in front;
Over mountain and plain march the throne-bearers.
The *tar-kul-li* the great Dibbarra tore away.
Ninib advances, ruin he pours out.
The Anunnaki bear aloft torches,
With their brightness they set the land aflame.
The dread of Ramman reaches to heaven.
Everything bright he turneth to darkness.
      the land like   he covered(?)
One day the hurricane (raged),
Violently it blew, the waters (covered?) the mountains.
Like the (onslaught of) battle over mankind (they) came.
Brother sees not (his) brother.
Men are not discerned in heaven (*i. e.*, by the gods).
The gods were terrified by the flood, and
Withdrew and ascended to the heaven of Anu.
The gods dog-like cower, crouch on the wall (of heaven).
Ishtar screams like a woman in travail.
She cries aloud the lady of the gods, the sweet-voiced:
"Verily the former race is turned to clay.
Just as I in the assembly of the gods proclaimed evil,
As I proclaimed in the assembly of the gods evil
For the destruction of my people war I foretold,
So, verily, will I bring forth my people
Tho' like the fry of fishes they fill the sea."
The gods, the highest of the Anunnaki weep with her.

The gods are downcast, sit, and weep,
Covered were their lips
Six days and nights
The wind prevailed, flood and storm overwhelmed the land.
When the seventh day came the storm abated, the flood was overcome,
Which had battled like a warring host;
The sea calmed, the hurricane ceased, the flood was restrained,
I beheld the sea, uttering a lamentation,
Seeing that all mankind was turned to clay.
When the light had fully dawned I prayed.
I opened an airhole and light fell upon my cheeks.
I bowed myself, I sat down, I wept.
Over my cheeks ran my tears.
I looked upon the far-spread waters of the sea.
After twelve double-hours a peak arose,
Towards the mountain of Nitsir the ship took its course.
The mountain of Nitsir held the ship and let it not rise.
One day, a second day, the mountain of Nitsir, *ditto*
A third day, a fourth day the   "   "   "   "
A fifth day, a sixth day   "   "   "   "   "
When the seventh day arrived
I brought forth a *dove* and let it go.
The dove went forth, flew to and fro, but
A resting-place there was not, so it returned.
Then I brought forth a *swallow* and let it go,
The swallow went forth, flew to and fro, but
A resting-place there was not so it returned.
(Then) I brought forth a *raven* and let it go.
The raven went forth, the disappearance of the waters he saw,
He eats, caws, flies to and fro, and returns not.
(Then) I brought forth to the four winds, I offered a sacrifice.
I made an incense-offering on the top-most peak of the mountain.
Seven and seven *adagur*-vessels I placed.
Into them I cast reeds, cedar-wood, and
The gods inhaled the good odour.
The gods like flies swarmed about the offerer.
As soon as the mistress of the gods arrived
She lifted up the great jewels (?) that the god Anu had devised and made for her (and said)

"These gods, by my *lapis lazuli* necklace I shall not forget.
These days, verily I shall reflect upon and never forget.
The gods, let them go to the incense-offering.
(But) let not Bel go to the incense-offering,
Seeing that he did not reflect but caused the flood.
And my people he counted for destruction.
As soon as Bel arrived
He saw the ship and Bel was sore angry,
He waxed wroth against the gods, the Igigi.
"Some soul has escaped" (he said),
"Let no man survive the destruction."
Ninib openeth his mouth and speaketh,
He speaks to the warrior Bel:
"Who but Ea doeth (this) thing?
But Ea is wise in every undertaking."
Ea openeth his mouth and speaketh,
Saith to the warrior Bel:
"Thou sage of the gods, warrior!
Verily, verily, thou didst not reflect, and didst make a flood:
Upon the sinner lay his sins,
Upon the impious his impiety.[1]
Spare, let him not be cut off, have mercy, let him (not be utterly destroyed).
Instead of bringing on a flood,
Let the lion come and reduce mankind.
Instead of bringing on a flood,
Let the hyaena come and reduce mankind.
Instead of bringing on a flood,
Let famine be sent and the land (reduced).
Instead of bringing on a flood,
Let the Pest-god come and destroy the land.
As for me, I have not revealed the secret of the gods.
I caused Atrahasis to see a vision and thus he learned the secret of the gods."
Thereupon his counsel was taken
And Bel ascended within the ship.
Seized me by the hands and brought me up (to a point still higher).

---

[1] This is evidence that the deluge, as in the Old Testament, was a punishment for sin, which some writers (not Assyriologists) have denied in the interest of an outgrown view of the Bible.

He brought up and made to bow beside me my wife,
Turned us face to face, stood between us and blessed us:
"In former times Pir-napishtim was human
But henceforth Pir-napishtim and his wife shall be like us gods
And Pir-napishtim shall dwell afar off at the mouth of the rivers."
Then they took me and afar off at the mouth of the rivers they
    caused me to dwell.

THE DESCENT OF ISHTAR TO HADES.

ISHTAR was the Babylonian Venus or goddess of love. The story of her descent to Hades and return to the world of the living is found on a tablet now in the British Museum, and is perhaps the most poetical legend of the recovered Assyrian literature. It has been suggested that the story is the text of a religious drama, resembling the miracle-plays of mediaeval Europe. The legend shows no reason for Ishtar's desire to enter Hades, but it is easy to suppose that she went thither to rescue some beloved person. This supplies a connection with the familiar story of Venus and Adonis (or Tammuz), which the Greek writers declare to be of Syrian origin. The drama, if such it were, was probably part of the annual celebration of the return of Spring. Ninkigal, the Queen of Hades, corresponds to the Greek Persephone, and Latin Proserpina, the wife of Pluto. In like manner, Ea, the king of the gods, corresponds to Zeus or Jupiter, and the divine messenger to Hermes or Mercury.

A BABYLONIAN EPIC—ISHTAR'S DESCENT TO HADES.

(Translation by Professor Craig.)

On the land without regress, the land (that thou knowest),
Ishtar, Sin's daughter, did fix her attention,
The daughter of Sin did fix her attention,
On the dwelling of darkness, the abode of Irkalla,
On the dwelling whose inhabitant comes no more out,
On the road whose advancing knows no returning,
On the house whose inhabitants removed from the light,
Where they're nourished with dust and clay is their food,
Where they see not the light, but in darkness are dwelling,
And are clad like the birds with a covering of wings;
On door and on bars lies the dust thickly gathered.

Arrived at the door of the land without regress,
To the porter in keeping, this order she giveth:
Thou watcher of waters, throw open thy portal!

Throw open thy portal, within will I enter!
If the door be not opened that I may pass through it,
The door will I shatter, its bolt break in pieces,
Its sills will I burst, its doors tear asunder,
The dead will I raise up, devourers and living,
Even more than the living the dead will I raise up.

The porter then opened his mouth and made answer,
To the great goddess Ishtar, made answer the porter:
"Withhold! O my lady, do not break it away,
I go to Allatu, thy name to announce."
The porter announced to the queen, to Allatu:
"Thy sister, Ishtar, is come over these waters
                                                    "

When Allatu these tidings received (from the porter),
Like a tamarisk cut she (bowed herself down) (?).
Like a reed that is broken she (bent to the ground) (?).
"What bringeth her heart to me, pray? What trouble?
With this one forsooth (shall I share my dwelling?)
As food eat the clay and as wine drink the water,
Weep over men who their wives have abandoned,
O'er maidens who mourn the embrace of their lovers,
Weep o'er the infants destroyed e'er their day?
Go! porter, throw open thy door—open to her!
And treat her according to olden-time law."
The porter departed, threw open his door;
"O enter, my lady, a welcome in Hades!
Palace of the land, that knows no returning,
O let it rejoice in thy presence."

The first door he caused her to enter, and halting,
Removed the great crown from her head.
"Why tak'st thou the great crown from my head, O porter?"
"O enter, my lady, 'tis the law of Allatu."
The next door he caused her to enter, and halting,
The rings were removed from her ears.
"Why tak'st thou the rings from my ears, O porter?"
"O enter, my lady, 'tis the law of Allatu."
The third door he caused her to enter, and halting,

The necklace removed from her neck.
"Why tak'st thou from my neck the necklace, O porter?"
"O enter, my lady, 'tis the law of Allatu."
The fourth door he caused her to enter, and halting,
Her jewels removed from her breast.
"Why tak'st thou from my breast the jewels, O porter?"
"O enter, my lady, 'tis the law of Allatu."
The fifth door he caused her to enter, and halting,
The bearing-stone girdle he took off from her waist.
"Why tak'st thou from my waist my gemmed-girdle, O porter?"
"O enter, my lady, 'tis the law of Allatu."
The sixth door he caused her to enter, and halting,
Took the rings from her hands and her feet.
"Why from hands and from feet take the rings, pray, O porter?"
"O enter, my lady, 'tis the law of Allatu."
The seventh door he caused her to enter, and halting,
From her body her cincture removed.
"Why take from my body my cincture, O porter?"
"O enter, my lady, 'tis the law of Allatu."
To the land without regress when Ishtar descended,
Allatu beheld her and raged in her presence;
Imprudently, boldly, did Ishtar attack her.
Then opened Allatu her mouth and commanded,
To Namtar, her servant, the order was given:
"Go Namtar, confine her
With disease of the eye, and the hip, and the foot,
With disease of the heart, and the scalp, go smite Ishtar,
Afflict her whole person!"

After Ishtar, the goddess, had (been thus afflicted) (?)
The bull no more covered the cow, nor ass gendered;
No more in the street lay the man with the maiden;
The man went asleep in his place,
In her place slept the maiden.

The god's-servant, Pap-su-kal, face down and sad-visaged,
Was clothed in the garb of deep mourning.
Shamash went, sorely wept before Sin, his father,
His tears ran down before the king, Ea,
Saying: "Ishtar's gone down to the land, and returns not.

Since Ishtar's descent to the land without regress
The bull no more covers the cow, nor ass genders;
No more in the street lies the man with the maiden.
The man falls asleep in his place,
In her place sleeps the maiden."

Then Ea created a male in his wisdom,
The god's-servant, Uddushu-namir, created.
"Go! Uddushu-namir, to land without regress,
Seven doors of the land without regress be opened!
Allatu behold thee, rejoice in thy presence!
Her heart when at ease, and her spirit when joyful;
In name of the great gods do thou adjure her:
'Thy head raise, to Hal-skin direct thy attention,
O lady, I pray thee, Halziqu-skin give me;
I desire to drink of the waters within it.'"

This hearing, Allatu her sides smote, her nails bit.
"Of me thou hast asked an impossible favor.
Hence! Uddushu-namir, with curse will I curse thee;
Thy food it shall be the foul mud of the city,
From drains of the city shalt thou drink the water,
The shade of the wall shall be thy dwelling,
Thy place of abiding a stone-block shall build it.
Confinement, privation, thy strength let them shatter."

Allatu then opened her mouth and commanded,
To Namtar, her servant, the order was given:
"Go! Namtar, beat on the palace eternal!
Go! rap on the stone slabs, those made out of *pa*-stone.
Go! lead forth the spirits, on golden thrones set them,
With water-of-life sprinkle Ishtar, the goddess,
Lead her forth from my presence."

Then went Namtar, beat on the palace eternal,
And shook the stone slabs those made out of *pa*-stone;
He led forth the spirits, on golden thrones set them,
With water-of-life sprinkled Ishtar the goddess.
Led her forth from her presence.
Through first door he led her, gave to her her cincture.

ISHTAR'S DESCENT TO HADES.

Through second door he led her, her rings he gave to her.
Through third door he led her, gave back her gemmed-girdle.
Through fourth door he led her, gave back her breast-jewels.
Through fifth door he led her, gave to her her necklace.
Through sixth door he led her, gave to her her ear-rings.
Through seventh door he led her, the great crown gave to her.

Here ends the descent of Ishtar. The priest continues:

"If free she'll not free her, return with her to her
And for Tammuz, her bridegroom in years that were youthful,
Pour water e'en purest, with sweet balm (anoint him)
And clothe him with garments, a flute (give unto him),
Companions of Ishtar, let them wail with loud (wailing),
The goddess, Belili, her treasure completed,
High heaped are the eye-stones, her knees now supporteth,
Her brother's complaint she then understanding,
The great goddess Belili her treasures outpouring,
She fills with the eye-stones the floor round about her (saying)
'My only one, brother mine, do me no evil.'
When Tammuz with flute of fine lapiz discourseth,
Then play with him joyfully flute of fine beryl,
And play with him joyfully men mourners and women,
The dead may arise the sweet incense inhaling."

NOTE.—See Jastoon, "Religion of Babylonia and Assyria," page 563 ff., for a full discussion of this epic.

GYGES AND ASSURBANIPAL.

GYGES, king of Lydia, reigned B.C. 716–678. The Greek historian Herodotus has given an interesting account of him, but still more interesting is the following extract showing how he was regarded by the great king of Assyria, Assurbanipal (Sardanapalus).

Gyges was the king of Lydia, a country beyond the seas, a distant land, of which the kings, my fathers, had never even heard the name. Assur, my divine generator, revealed my name to him in a dream, saying: "Assurbanipal, the king of Assyria; place thyself at his feet, and thou shalt conquer thy enemies in his name." The same day that he dreamed this dream, Gyges sent horsemen to salute me, and related to me the dream which he had had, by the mouth of his messengers. When the latter reached the frontiers of my empire and encountered the people of my empire, they said to him, "Who then art thou, stranger, whose land has never yet been visited by one of our couriers?"

They sent him to Nineveh, the seat of my royalty, and brought him before me. The languages of the East and of the West, which Assur had given into my hand, none of those who spoke them could understand his language, and none of those who surrounded me had ever heard speech like unto it. In the space of my empire at last I found one who understood it, and he told me the dream. The same day that he placed himself at the feet of me, the king Assurbanipal, he defeated the Cimmerians, who oppressed the people of his land, who had not feared the kings, my fathers, and had not placed themselves at my feet. By the grace of Assur and Ishtar, the gods my masters, they took amidst the chiefs of the Cimmerians, whom he had defeated, two chiefs whom he chained heavily with manacles and fetters of iron, and he sent them to me with a rich present.

Nevertheless the horsemen that he at first sent regularly to pay homage to me, he soon ceased to send. He would not obey the commands of Assur, my divine generator, but foolishly trusted in his own strength, and in the wishes of his heart. He sent his troops to the assistance of Psammetichus, king of Egypt, who had contemptuously thrown off my yoke. I heard this, and prayed to Assur and Ishtar: "May his body be thrown down before his enemies, and may his bones be dispersed." The Cimmerians, whom he had crushed in my name, reappeared and subjugated his whole land, and his son succeeded him upon the throne. The punishment which the gods, who are my strength, had drawn upon his father at my request, he told me by his messengers, and he placed himself at my feet, saying: "Thou art a king acknowledged by the gods. Thou cursedst my father, and misfortune fell upon him. Send me thy blessing, for I am thy servant, who fears thee, and will wear thy yoke."

PURITY.

"Purity is the best of all things; purity is the fairest of all things, even as thou hast said, O righteous Zarathustra." With these words the holy Ahura-Mazda rejoiced the holy Zarathustra: "Purity is for man, next to life, the greatest good; that purity which is procured by the law of Mazda to him who cleanses his own self with good thoughts, words and deeds."

O Maker of the material world, thou Holy One! This law, this fiend-destroying law of Zarathustra, by what greatness, goodness, and fairness is it great, good, and fair above all other utterances?

Ahura-Mazda answered: "As much above all other floods as is the sea, so much above all other utterances in greatness, goodness, and fairness is this law, this fiend-destroying law of Zarathustra. As much as a great stream flows swifter than a slender rivulet, so much above all other utterances in greatness, goodness, and fairness is this law, this fiend-destroying law of Zarathustra. As high as the great cypress tree stands above the small plants it overshadows, so high above all other utterances in greatness, goodness, and fairness is this law, this fiend-destroying law of Zarathustra. As high as heaven is above the earth that it compasses around, so high above all other utterances is this law, this fiend-destroying law of Zarathustra.

"Therefore when the high priest has been applied to by a penitent, when any of the Magi has been applied to, whether for draona-service* that has been undertaken or that has not been undertaken, the priest has power to remit one-third of the penalty he had to pay: if he has committed any other evil deed, it is remitted by his repentance; if he has committed no other evil deed, he is absolved by his repentance forever and ever."

---

* A service in honor of spirits or deceased persons in which small cakes (*draona*) are blessed in their name and eaten by those present.

ZOROASTER'S PRAYER.

THIS Gatha or hymn is supposed to be a prayer prescribed by Zoroaster for the teachers of his religion. The first verse is the prelude always used before reciting or chanting any of the Gathas in the Parsi religious service.

A strengthening blessing is the thought, a blessing is the word, a blessing is the deed of the righteous Zarathustra. May the Bountiful Immortals accept and help on the chants. Homage to you, O sacred Gathas!

With venerating desire for this gift of gracious help, O Mazda, and stretching forth my hands to Thee I pray for the first blessing of Thy bountiful Spirit; that is, I beseech of Thee that my actions toward all may be performed in Righteousness; and with this I implore from Thee the understanding of Thy Good Spirit, in order that I may propitiate the Soul of the Kine.

And therefore, O Great Creator, the Living Lord! inspired by Thy Good Spirit, I approach You, and beseech of Thee to grant me as a bountiful gift for both the worlds, that of the body and that of mind, those attainments which are to be derived from the Divine Righteousness, and by means of which those who receive it may enter into beatitude and glory!

O thou Divine Righteousness, and thou Good Spirit of Deity! I will worship you, and Ahura Mazda the first, for all of whom the pious ready mind within us is causing the imperishable Kingdom to advance. And while I thus utter my supplications to You, come Ye to my calls to help!

Yea, I will approach You with my supplications, I who am delivering up my mind and soul to that heavenly Mount whither all the redeemed at last must pass, knowing full well the holy characteristics and rewards of the actions prescribed by Ahura Mazda. And so long as I am able and may have the power, so long will I teach Your people concerning these holy deeds to be done by them with faith toward God, and in the desire for the coming of the Divine Righteousness within their souls.

And, thou Righteousness! when shall I see thee, knowing the Good Mind of God, and above all the Obedience of our lives which constitutes the way to the most beneficent Ahura Mazda? Asking this, I thus beseech thee, for with this holy word of supplication we best keep off with tongue the flesh-devouring fiends, **the very sign and power of all spiritual foulness!**

THE HEBREWS AND THEIR NEIGHBORS.

CHAPTER I.

Syria.

SYRIA is the northern extremity of the Arabian peninsula. The word *Syria* is a shortened form of *Assyria*, and was given by the Greeks, at first to the whole Assyrian empire, and later restricted to the strip of land between the Mediterranean Sea and the Euphrates valley. To-day the name is applied to the region east of Palestine, reaching to the Taurus mountains on the north and on the south and west bounded by deserts.

Its very location determined that this should never become the home of a united, homogeneous people. It has always been a highway connecting Asia and Africa and trade routes have extended through it since the earliest recorded ages. Egyptian armies pressing into Asia in an early day traversed its midst and so did those of somewhat later times pushing westward from Mesopotamia, bound upon foreign conquest.

"Syria lies between two continents—Asia and Africa; between two primeval homes of men—the valleys of the Euphrates and the Nile; between two great centers of empire—Western Asia and Egypt: between all these, representing the Eastern and ancient world, and the Mediterranean, which is the gateway to the Western and modern world. Syria has been likened to a bridge between Asia and Africa—a bridge with the desert on one side and the sea upon the other; and, in truth, all the great invasions of Syria, with two exceptions, have been delivered across her northern and southern ends. . Syria is not only the bridge between Asia and Africa: she is the refuge of the drifting populations of Arabia. She has not only been the highroad of civilizations and the battle-field of empires, but the pasture and the school

SYRIA.

of innumerable little tribes. She has been not merely an open channel of war and commerce for nearly the whole world, but the vantage-ground and opportunity of the world's highest religions. In this strange mingling of bridge and harbour, of highroad and field, of battle-ground and sanctuary, of seclusion and opportunity—rendered possible through the striking division of her surface into mountain and plain—lies all the secret of Syria's history, under the religion which has lifted her fame to glory."[1]

The country falls naturally into many small districts in which petty states have arisen but which never developed into strong kingdoms. These have left but scanty remains of their civilizations.

We know nothing of Syria prior to 3500 B. C. There are evidences that this region, like Chaldea, was occupied first by a primitive people, probably belonging to the Turanian race. When a great Semitic outpouring from Arabia caused the ancient Chaldean nation to be engulfed by a vigorous people, Syria as well suffered an invasion.

During years of Babylonian dominance, Syria fell to the share of Babylonian kings. "The land of the setting sun," as they called it, was named with their possessions.

When Thutmose III. led his armies into Asia to avenge the insult done Egyptian honor when the Hyksos kings ruled the valley of the Nile, he established a certain supremacy over Syria which lasted for perhaps two centuries. He established several royal cities, or "halting places"—so called because his majesty tarried in them and directed the construction of fortifications. Tribute was exacted and was paid with some regularity until the time of Amenhotep IV. He was too occupied with religious reformation and the exaltation of the Solar Disk faith to give attention to his foreign possessions. The Tell-el-Amarna letters in many instances portray the condition of Syria when Egypt's name was no longer a protection and incoming tribes were plundering right and left.[2]

The spirit of unrest was again abroad among the nations and the Hittites now invaded Western Asia. Who they were and from whence they came has never been satisfactorily set-

---

[1] George Adam Smith: Historical Geog. of the Holy Land, 6. [2] Tell-el-Amarna Letters described in The Story of Babylonia and Assyria.

tled. Certain it is they were not Semitic. They belonged to the great white race, but their history is still to be written. Part of the natives sided with them; part remained loyal to Egypt, and the rest attempted to establish their own independence. Commerce was interrupted, caravans were plundered, and civil strife was general throughout the land. In a brief time the Hittites made themselves supreme in Syria, which became known as the Land of the Hittites.

About 1200 B. C. a fresh invasion brought several new tribes, among others, the Philistines. They again were probably not Semitics but of the Aryan race. The Hittite nation was now broken up into several small states, none of which became as powerful as the original nation. With the weakening of Hittite strength, opportunity arose for petty states to develop. The great powers left the country in peace for three or four hundred years, and Syrian states prospered and grew strong.

The era of the Judges in Israel fell into this period, and between the Hebrews and certain Syrian tribes there was intermittent war.

With the reign of Tiglath-Pileser I. Assyria launched forth on her career of conquest. In a westward march made by this conqueror, northern Syria yielded to Assyrian arms and offered tribute. Damascus alone was left undisturbed, for opposition was sure to be strong on the part of this ancient city. With some intervening years during which tribute could not be collected and when allegiance to Nineveh was denied, Assyrian influence dominated Syria, and frequently vigorous rule was enforced. When Assyria fell, the New Babylonian empire kept guard over the west. With the end of Babylonian rule, and the ascendency of Persia, Semitic dominance came to an end. Under Persia, and later under Greece, new states came into existence and Aryan rule began.

In the ages with which we are at present concerned, however, Syria remained to the portion of Semitic tribes. We have found Arabia the original home of this race. Providing at best but a scanty living for her children, when tribes multiplied rapidly Arabia seems to have cast out a portion of her inhabitants to make room for the rest. Chaldea—later Babylonia—was peopled by such an outpouring, while at the same time tribes spread into Syria and settled spots which promised adequate food and pasturage. Later comers were compelled to journey past these occupied lands and seek lands farther west, or to overcome the natives and supplant them. Some one has aptly said that different tribes fitted themselves into the "shelves and corners of Syria," and that is just what they did. It would have been as impossible for Syria, with its irregular surfaces, to have produced one united nation as for Greece or Switzerland to have contained a people whose national concerns outweighed their local interests. Highland and lowland, plateau and plain, mountain range and valley—these at length were occupied by little clans or more numerous tribes, while the more exposed regions were open to the nomads who came like birds for a season, or tarried a few brief years and penetrated farther west, or who perhaps merely loitered on their way to Egypt—the land of water and abundant grain.

"Syria is the northern and most fertile end of the great Semitic home—the peninsula of Arabia. But the Semitic home is distinguished by its central position in geography—between Asia and Africa, and between the Indian Ocean and the Mediterranean, which is Europe; and the *role* in history of the Semitic race has been also intermediary. The Semitics have been the great middlemen of the world. Not second-rate in war, they have risen to the first rank in commerce and religion. They have been the carriers between East and West, they have stood between the great ancient civilizations and those which go to make up the modern world; while by a higher gift, for which their conditions neither in place nor in time fully account, they have been mediary between God and man, and proved the religious teachers of the world, through whom have come its three highest faiths, its only universal religions. Syria's history is her share in this great function of intermedium, which has endured from the earliest times to the present day."[a]

"The head of Syria is Damascus," wrote Isaiah two thousand years ago. So it has since continued to be, with short periods of change. The venerable city, made possible and beautiful by the waters of the Abana, has survived many sacks and slaughters. It is sometimes called the oldest city

[a] Smith: Hist. Geog. of Holy Land, 5.

in the world, meaning of course, the one of greatest age yet standing. Still it has few relics of antiquity. Old material has constantly been utilized in the construction of new buildings and monuments. Its position has often been commented upon. "It is an astonishing site for what is said to be the oldest, and is certainly the most enduring, city of the world. For it is utterly incapable of defence; it is remote from the sea and the great natural lines of commerce. From the coast of Syria it is double barred by those ranges of snow-capped mountains whose populations enjoy more tempting prospects to the north and west. But look east and you understand Damascus.

"You would as soon think of questioning the site of New York or of San Francisco. Damascus is a great harbour of refuge upon the earliest sea man ever learned to navigate. It is because there is nothing but desert beyond, or immediately behind this site; because this river, the Abana, instead of wasting her waters on a slight extension of the fringe of fertile Syria, saves them in her narrow gorge till she can fling them well out upon the desert, and there, instead of slowly expending them on the doubtful possibilities of a province, lavishes all her life at once in the creation of a single great city, and straightway dies in face of the desert—it is because of all this that Damascus, so remote and so defenceless, has endured throughout human history, and must endure. Nineveh, Babylon and Memphis easily conquered her—she probably preceded them, and she has outlived them. She has been twice supplanted—by Antioch, and she has seen Antioch decay, by Baghdad, and Baghdad is forgotten. She has been many times sacked, and twice at least the effective classes of her population have been swept into captivity, but this has not broken the chain of her history. She was once capital of the world from the Atlantic to the Bay of Bengal, but the vast empire went from her and the city continued to flourish as before. Standing on the utmost edge of fertility, on the shore of the much-voyaged desert, Damascus is indispensable alike to civilization and to the nomads. Moreover, she is the city of the Mediterranean world which lies nearest to the far East, and Islam has made her the western port of Mecca."[*]

[*] Smith: Hist. Geog. of Holy Land, 642.

Having traversed the desert wastes, the city of Damascus lies invitingly before the wearied traveller. There is an old tradition that Mohammet once approached the town and viewed it from neighboring hills. Before him lay its grateful shade and restful streets, its tide of busy life, its wealth, its diversions—behind him lay the monotonous sea of sand, its parching heat and treeless plains. The great religious teacher was apparently afraid to trust himself to the enticing influences of the city. He turned away, saying: "Man can enter Paradise but once; if I pass into Damascus I shall be excluded from the other Paradise reserved for the faithful."

Our word *damask* stands today in memory of the age when damask or Damascus silk, embroidered in richest colors, with threads of silver and gold, stood forth unmatched by fabrics of other lands. Today the word is ordinarily applied to round linen thread, woven in fruit, flower, or conventional designs, as was the silk originally.

The swords of Damascus also gained world-renown. They were so thin that they could be tied into knots without injuring them in the least, and so strong that they would cut through iron or wood without being marred. A certain watery steel, more true and resilient than ordinary, made the "trusty sword of Damascus" popular in many lands.

It lies beyond our province to trace the comings and goings of tribes within the land of Syria. At best Syrian history is fragmentary and is suited for the student of the Semitic race rather than the general reader. We shall happen upon facts connected with it as we study the history of the Hebrews, and the empire age of the Mesopotamian states.

CHAPTER II.

The Land of Phoenicia.

Geographically, Phœnicia was a small state. It lay between a spur of the Taurus mountains—Mt. Casius—on the north and Carmel on the south; washed by the Mediterranean Sea on the west, it was protected by a lofty mountain range on the east. These natural boundaries were important, since they shut in the land and sheltered it in a great measure from invasions and plundering raids.

About 200 miles in length, Phœnicia ranged from one to thirty-five miles in width. A narrow sandy coast-belt skirted the western side and was covered with date-palms, which gave the region its name. Greek sailors, coasting along the eastern shore of the sea, saw the luxuriant palms from afar, and called the whole eastern coast Phœnike—Land of Palms. Later, learning more particularly of the various nations which dwelt therein, they restricted the name to the country we are now studying.

East of the palm belt extend the fertile plains of Phœnicia. Here grew gardens, orchards and fields of grain, which made the district a veritable paradise. "'The cultivated tract presents for the most part an unbroken mass of corn, out of which rise here and there slight eminences in the midst of gardens and orchards—the sites of cities.' The gardens are gay with scarlet blossoms of the pomegranate, the orchards famous for the enormous oranges which diversify the green foliage of their shady groves."[1] Here was grown the food supply which supported the whole population of the country, generally speaking, while on the low hills which bounded the plain on the east, the vine, olive and mulberry were cultivated. At last, the high mountains arose, bare in spots and elsewhere covered with forest trees—oaks, chestnuts and the mighty cedars.

Several streams, mountain-born, rushed down steep sides, furnished moisture and added fertility to the plains, then found

---

[1] Rawlinson: Phoenicia, 3.

their way to the sea. Chief of these in early times, as today, was the Litany. This river rises 10,000 feet above the sea, and " forces its way through Lebanon by a deep and narrow gorge, in which it frets and chafes many hundred feet below the eye of the spectator, descending precipitously, and at last debouching upon the plain by a ravine, about five miles northeast of Tyre. It has been compared to a 'monster serpent chained in the yawning gulf, where she writhes and struggles evermore to escape from her dark and narrow prison, but always in vain, save only near the sea-shore, where her windings reach a close.' "[2]

Irregularities of the coast supplied harbors which would be quite inadequate for modern ships, but sufficed for the vessels of antiquity. Fringes of islets, near the shore, made refuge for sailors in time of storm in an age when no boats drew deep water, and when even the largest might be drawn up on the beach if necessary.

The climate of Phœnicia varied according to the locality. That of the plain was mild and pleasant, while snow lay most of the year upon the mountain peaks rising easterly. The scenery of the narrow strip changes constantly as one journeys east or west. Islands of the Mediterranean invited the sailor to venture far out from his native shore, and at an early period the sea was dotted over by the merchant-ships of the Phœnicians. East, north and south high mountains offer a varied aspect to the traveller. The Lebanon range has always been notably beautiful. " The elevation rises gradually as we proceed north-ward, until the range culminates in the peaks above the cedars, which are estimated to attain a height of from nine thousand to ten thousand feet. Garden cultivation carpets the base of the mountain; above this is, for the most part, a broad fringe of olive groves; higher up, the hill sides are carefully terraced, not an inch of ground being wasted; and among sharp cliffs and pointed rocks of a grey-white hue are strips of cornfields, long rows of dwarf mulberries, figs, apricots, apples, walnuts, and other fruit trees. Gorges, ravines, charming glens, deep valleys, diversify the mountain sides; here and there are tremendous chasms, with precipices that go sheer down for a thousand feet; tiny rivulets bound

[2] Rawlinson: Phoenicia, 11.

and leap from rock to rock and from terrace to terrace, forming chains of cascades, refreshing and fertilizing all around. In the deep gorges flow copious streams, shaded by overhanging woods of pines or cedars; and towards the summit are in several places magnificent cedar groves, remnants of the primeval forest which once clothed the greater part of the mountain. Above all towers the bare limestone of the dorsal ridge, always white enough to justify the name Lebanon (White Mountain), and for eight months of the year clothed with a mantle of snow." [3]

Semitic tribes, journeying out of Arabia at a remote period, crossed into Chaldea, and after a sojourn which cannot now be estimated, worked their way westward to the region just described. In all probability Turanians held the territory. With these they intermingled and inter-married, while kinsmen coming later from the old Arabian home, kept the stock nearly pure Semitic.

One of the oldest settlements was made at Sidon, the name of the town commemorating the earliest occupation of its people. *Sidon* signifies *fishery,* and it is supposed that the first comers were fishermen. In later years when Sidon was the wealthiest city in Western Asia, and when her proud merchantmen had left nets to the portion of the humblest born, the early name stood in memory of primitive days.

Sidon was built on the shore, while her natural harbor consisted of a little circlet of islands which afforded shelter for sailing crafts. An excellent harbor was constructed with this breakwater, but it is significant to note that Sidon's strongholds were on the shore.

Some of her inhabitants at length departed from the mother-city and settled at Tyre, near the southern part of the Phœnician coast. The word *Tyre* means *rock,* and while settlements were made on the shore as well, the famous city of antiquity was built on an island, half a mile from the mainland. This island was about two and one-half miles in width and was completely surrounded by a wall, one hundred feet high. With water around her and mighty walls as well, Tyre was wellnigh impregnable in times of siege.

The little town of Dora grew up where shell-fish abounded

---
[3] Rawlinson: Phoenicia, 17.

These were valued for a secretion they yielded which was made up into a dye of royal purple, world-renowned in ancient times. Gebal became famous for its shipyards. Tripolis gained celebrity as head of a league of cities made up of Tyre, Aradus and Tripolis.

The Phœnicians left no history of their country. No other ancient people came in contact with so many nations and none had more material at hand from which to formulate a record of their time, but they were a nation of traders and appear to have been quite lacking in literature of their own and in chroniclers of any sort. Not only is there utter dearth of writings, but ruins and remains of Phœnician civilization are comparatively few. The Phœnicians built well, but their structures were either torn down by ruthless conquerors, or, like those of Carthage, became quarries for other nations. We are consequently forced to reconstruct their history from other sources—from writings of men of other lands, often hostile to them and so prejudiced in their point of view. The characteristic life of the Phœnicians led into the busy marts of men—not to the library or cloister, and a study of their history involves a study of the commerce of their time.

It is doubtful whether the future can produce material for any complete history of Phœnicia. We know practically nothing of the prehistoric period in the country, and when reports of the nation begin, the people had already reached a high proficiency on the sea and possessed wealthy cities. The commercial spirit, so strong in the Semitic race seems to have reached its extreme expression in the people of this little state. If they possessed any aptitude for pursuits other than trading, we know little of them. In the periods known to us there was no national life nor government. Each city developed independently and appears to have had only commercial ambitions.

The natural contour of the land allowed the people to build up a mighty system of trade which penetrated into every country known to antiquity, while their sea-ports remained long protected from aggressive rulers of Egypt and Mesopotamia.

The Phœnician cities were mentioned as early as 1475 B. C., when Thutmose III. made his strength felt in Western Asia. They united with the Hittite nation against him, but were defeated and made gifts of submission.

Sidon was the older city, and tradition has it that about 1200 B. C. the Philistines—earlier inhabitants of the country—fought a battle with Sidon and defeated her, whereupon some of her citizens escaped and founded Tyre. Quite as probable is a more recent supposition that Sidon, wealthy and given over to ease and pleasure, gradually weakened, while the younger and more vigorous town of Tyre became the leader.

Hiram seems to have been the most renowned king of Tyre. He enlarged the island upon which the city stood. Filling in the lagoon between two islands, he joined them together, forming thus one large island. Being a prolific builder, he erected huge structures of stone, which together with wood, made up the building material of Phœnicia.

For some time previous to his reign, Judah had been growing in strength. She had held out against the Philistines, and was being welded into a well organized state. Hiram considered it good policy to seek the friendship of Judah's king, and he and King David remained good friends. This same friendship was offered to Solomon when he succeeded his father as ruler of the Hebrews, and aid was given the Hebrews in the construction of their temple, Phœnician timber and skilled workmen being supplied. An account of the matter has come to us from the Hebrews: "And Hiram, king of Tyre, sent his servants unto Solomon; for he had heard that they had anointed him king in the room of his father: for Hiram was ever a lover of David. And Solomon sent to Hiram saying: 'Thou knowest how that David my father could not build an house unto the name of the Lord his God for the wars which were about him on every side, until the Lord put them under the soles of his feet. But now the Lord my God hath given me rest on every side, so that there is neither adversary nor evil occurrent. And behold, I purpose to build an house unto the name of the Lord my God, as the Lord spake unto David, my father, saying: 'Thy son whom I will set upon thy throne in thy room, he shall build an house unto my name. Now therefore command thou that they hew me cedar trees out of Lebanon; and my servants shall be with thy servants; and unto thee will I give hire for thy servants according to all that thou shalt appoint: for thou knowest that there is not among us any that can skill to hew timber like unto the Sidonians.'

"And it came to pass, when Hiram heard the words of Solomon, that he rejoiced greatly, and said: 'Blessed be the Lord this day, which hath given unto David a wise son over this great people.' And Hiram sent to Solomon, saying: 'I have considered the things which thou sentest to me for; and I will do all thy desire concerning timber of cedar and concerning timber of fir. My servants shall bring them down from Lebanon unto the sea: and I will convey them by sea in floats unto the place that thou shalt appoint me, and I will cause them to be discharged there, and thou shalt receive them: and thou shalt accomplish my desire, in giving food for my household.'

"So Hiram gave Solomon cedar trees and fir trees according to all his desire. And Solomon gave Hiram twenty thousand measures of wheat for food to his household, and twenty measures of pure oil: thus gave Solomon to Hiram year by year. And there was peace between Hiram and Solomon; and they two made a league together. And the king commanded and they brought great stones, costly stones, and hewed stones, to lay the foundation of the house. And Solomon's builders and Hiram's builders did hew them, and the stonequarriers: so they prepared timber and stones to build the house." [4]

The temple stood at last a memorial to the skillful workmanship of Phœnicia as well as a tribute of honor to Jehovah, God of Israel.

After the death of Hiram, during whose reign the country had prospered, the government soon passed from his family. A class of wealthy merchants had arisen in Tyre and they demanded official positions for themselves. The king they crowned became king of Sidon as well. Before 1000 B. C. exiles from Tyre, driven out for political reasons, founded Carthage, best known of all Phœnicia's colonies.

As early as 880 B. C. danger threatened Phœnicia from Assyria. Protected by the efficient barrier of a mountain range, the commercial ports had been free to develop their trade without serious interruption. They immediately offered to pay tribute rather than fight, and Assyrian tablets recount products sent by them.

[4] I Kings, 5, 1-18.

By 727 B. C. the yoke of Assyria had become oppressive and Tyre revolted. A siege of five years followed and was at length raised with no result, for Tyre could not be cut off from the sea. About 680 B. C. Baal was crowned king of Tyre with the consent of the Assyrian ruler. Nevertheless, he shortly announced his independence and became a sturdy opponent of Assyrian aggression. In 668 B. C. Asshurbanipal led an army against the sea-coast cities, especially against the most powerful, Tyre.

"Against Baal, King of Tyre, dwelling in the midst of the sea, I went, because my royal will he disregarded, and did not harken unto the words of my mouth. Towers round about him I raised, and over his people I strengthened the watch. On land and sea his forts I took; his going out I stopped. Brackish water and sea water their mouths drank to preserve their lives. With a strong blockade, which removed not, I besieged them; their spirits I humbled and caused to melt away; to my yoke I made them submissive." When Assyria was threatened by Median power, the cities on the coast again shook themselves free from the hated tribute and at this juncture Tyre rose to her greatest influence. About 600 B. C. Egypt tried to bring Western Asia under her dominance and under her direction Phœnician sailors circumnavigated Africa.

Nebuchadnezzar determined to end rebellions in the west for all time and to bring the coast under Babylonian rule. Tyre held out against him and a siege of thirteen years ensued. The Hebrew prophet Ezekiel foretold the result:

"Behold I am against thee, O Tyre, and will cause many nations to come up against thee, as the sea causeth his waves to come up. And they shall destroy the walls of Tyre, and break down her towers: I will also scrape her dust from her, and make her like the top of a rock. . .

"Behold I will bring upon Tyre Nebuchadnezzar, king of Babylon, a king of kings, from the north with horses, and with chariots and with horsemen, and companies, and much people. He shall slay with the sword thy daughters in the field: and he shall make a fort against thee, and cast a mount against thee, and lift up the buckler against thee. And he shall set engines of war against thy walls, and with his axes he shall break down thy towers. By reason of the abundance of his horses their dust shall cover thee: thy walls shall shake at the noise of the horsemen, and of the wheels and of the chariots, when he shall enter into thy gates, as men enter into a city wherein is made a breach. With the hoofs of his horses shall he tread down all thy streets: he shall slay thy people by the sword, and thy strong garrisons shall go down to the ground. And they shall make a spoil of thy riches, and make a prey of thy merchandise: and they shall break down thy walls, and destroy thy pleasant houses: and they shall lay thy stones and thy timber and thy dust in the midst of the water.

"And I will cause the noise of thy songs to cease; and the sound of thy harps shall be no more heard. And I will make thee like the top of a rock: thou shalt be a place to spread nets upon."[5]

These prophecies were fulfilled, and having rallied again, and once more sent forth their merchant vessels, these cities fell shortly to the share of Persia. Cambyses depended wholly upon their navy, so that when Phœnician sailors refused to sweep down upon Carthage, he was obliged to abandon his idea of subduing that colony.[6]

In 362 B. C. Sidon revolted against Persian oppression. When at last the fall of their city was at hand, 40,000 Sidonians shut themselves in their houses and set fire to them rather than become spoils for the conqueror.

Some years later, when the young Macedonia conqueror, Alexander the Great, reached this district in course of his brief conquest, the Phœnician cities, wearied of Persian taxes, hailed his coming with joy. One after another, the towns sent presents until it was left for Tyre alone to do homage to the young monarch. Her citizens sent an embassy to meet him with a crown of gold and announced their willingness to do his bidding. Alexander replied that he was pleased by their action and would visit their city to offer sacrifices in their temple—for the Greeks identified the god of the Phœnicians with their Hercules. The reply being made known in the city, the people feared that some hidden purpose prompted the Greek to seek their island home, and they sent to him again saying that they would pay whatever tribute he exacted, but

[5] Ezekiel 26, 3-14. [6] See The Story of the Persians.

that they did not wish the Greek army to march through their streets. This angered Alexander and he announced that if the gates of Tyre did not open to him, he would open them by force. Tyre had withstood many a siege and she did not hesitate to take a firm stand. Carthaginians who chanced to be within her walls advised that help would be forthcoming were it needed, and it was supposed furthermore, that Persia would never see her empire turned over to the Greeks without a struggle. Above all, Tyre had faith in the strength of her walls and in her fleet.

Sieges in the past had often failed because Tyre could not be approached by battering rams and engines of war. As has already been said, the island upon which the city stood lay one-half mile from the shore. Her harbors were the best on the Phœnician coast. One lay on the north side and was called the Sidonian harbor because it looked towards Sidon; the other was on the south side, and was called the Egyptian harbor since it faced the land of the pyramids. Stone piers ran out some considerable distance in the sea and made safe refuge for vessels in stormy weather. Rough winds might have made entrance to the port impossible had the harbor extended on one side only, hence the two harbors were early constructed and were connected by a canal, extending through the city, making it thus possible for a ship to enter by one harbor and clear port from the other.

Now Alexander conceived the bold design of building a broad bridge or mole from the continent to the island, that he might bring his war engines up to the city walls. Forthwith, operations were started on the shore, in shallow water. Two rows of piles were driven 200 feet from each other and the intervening distance was filled in with earth and stone. When the mole reached out where the force of the current was felt, however, the earthwork was carried away as rapidly as it was built. Moreover, the Tyrians grasped his plan and harried the laborers continually. They brought their boats near enough to attack them and compel them to abandon their undertaking. The Greeks met this obstacle by preparing a curtain of hides to cover the workmen, and raised two lofty wooden towers wherein soldiers were stationed to charge upon ships interfering with the work. The citizens of Tyre thereupon equipped one of their largest transports as a fire-ship, and filling it with all sorts of combustible material, sent it floating against the Greek towers, a mass of fire. · This was effectual, and Alexander returned from a temporary absence to find the work of weeks obliterated. This general never allowed confronting obstacles to baffle him, and under his personal supervision the labor began anew. The struggle had come to mean more than the subjection of an independent city —it signified Greek capacity and ingenuity against Asiatic opposition on the very threshold of a coveted continent.

Earth, trees and stones were hurled rapidly into the sea, but Tyrian divers with grappling hooks dragged out whole trees and brush, destroying the solidity of the mass. Then Alexander realized that he could accomplish nothing without a navy. Without aid of a fleet he might be detained indefinitely with one obstinate city. He immediately levied vessels and crews from those towns which had already surrendered to him. As fate would have it, the Persian fleet came voluntarily into his hands and shortly 224 vessels were ready to move against Tyre. Under their protection the construction of the mole went on rapidly. Tyre soon understood that her only hope lay in chancing a sea battle. The number of ships against her was overwhelming, and after a gallant start, she was defeated.

"The last chance was over—the last effort had failed—but the Tyrians would not give in any the more. They still met every attack upon the walls with a determined resistance, and with a fertility of resource that was admirable. To deaden the blows of the battering-ram, and the force of the stones hurled from the catapults, leather bags filled with sea-weed were let down from the walls at the point assailed. Wheels set in rapid motion intercepted the darts and javelins thrown into the town, turning them aside, or blunting, or sometimes breaking them. When the towers erected upon the mole were brought close up to the defences, and an attempt was made to throw bridges from them to the battlements, and thus to pass soldiers into the city, the Tyrians flung grappling-hooks among the soldiers on the bridges, which caught in the bodies of some, mangling them terribly, dragging their shields from others, and hauled some bodily into the air, dashing them against the wall or upon the ground. Masses of red-hot metal were prepared and hurled against the towers and against the scaling parties. Sand was heated to a glow and showered upon all who approached the foot of the walls: it penetrated through the joints of the armour, and caused such intolerable pain, that the coats of mail were torn off and flung aside, whereupon the sufferers were soon put *hors de combat* by lance thrusts and missiles. The battering-rams were attacked by engines constructed for the purpose, which brought sharp scythes, attached to long poles, into contact with the ropes and thongs used in working them, and cut them through. Further, wherever the wall showed signs of giving way, the defenders began to construct an inner wall, to take the place of the outer one, when it should be demolished."[7]

When the walls at length gave way and soldiers made an entrance into the town, they had to fight a battle in every house and win their ground in street and building, foot by foot. Ten thousand were massacred and thirty thousand women and children were sold into slavery. The city was left in 332 B. C. in a half-ruined condition with few inhabitants. In a few years Tyre rose again but the days of her greatness were gone.

We have seen that during the first part of her history Phœnicia was left practically alone and during the later portion suffered repeated attacks. How can we account for the frequent despoiling of her proud cities during her later years? Owing to their position and consequent trade, the Phœnician cities became wealthy rapidly. They naturally attracted the notice of kings who were trying to carry on extensive projects at home. Those who conquered them, or who sought to do so, coveted their riches for the adornment of their own capitals or for some personal enterprise at home. So advantageous was the situation of these cities that, left crippled and in ruins by the enemy, or under less severe circumstances, forced to pay a heavy tribute, losses were quickly made good, and the stricken towns would soon again be amassing wealth. Having control of the greater portion of the commerce of their day, they were able to exchange commodities of slight value with nations who possessed gold or other precious wares

---

[7] Rawlinson; Phoenicia, 231.

and knew nothing of their value, save that they were thereby enabled to procure articles they desired. "Gold for brass, the worth of a hundred oxen for the value of nine,"—it was this opportunity, recognized and seized upon, which made it possible for this little strip of land to become the store-house of riches coveted by nations on all sides.

Concerning the political history of Phœnicia we know little, as has already been said. When her wealthy cities were attacked by foreigners, these strangers have sometimes told the story from their own point of view, but so far as government in times of peace, local administration and kindred matters, material has not survived to allow its course of progress to be reconstructed.

PHOENICIAN	OLD GREEK	OLD ROMAN	ENGLISH
∀	A	A	A
ꟼ	B	B	B
⟩	C	⟨C	C
△	▷D	D	D
⊒	E	E	E
Y	⟨	F	F
		C	G
⊟H	⊏H	H	H
ᴢ	I	I	I
			J
⅄	K	K	K
	⌐	⌐L	L
﹀	M	M	M
Y	N	N	N
O	O	O	O
⊃	⌐	⌐P	P
ϙ	ϙ	ϙQ	Q
ꟼ	PR	R	R
⌇	⌇S	⌇S	S
⊁	T	T	T

GROWTH OF THE ALPHABET.

CHAPTER III.

Phoenician Colonies and Commerce.

It is natural to consider Phœnicia's colonies in connection with her commerce, for while many nations have colonized regions remote for the purpose of extending their territory or perpetuating a faith, her outposts were opened solely for the benefit of trade. Phœnicia's colonies may be said to have been the outgrowth of her mercantile concerns, although in some instances, dissatisfaction with political conditions in the home city proved an additional incentive.

Probably the first foreign settlement was made in Egypt. Desiring to control routes of trade in the valley of the Nile, Tyrians obtained permission to settle in Memphis. This settlement could hardly be called a colony in the ordinary sense of the word, for the home city exercised no political control over those of its subjects dwelling in Egypt—nor did it seek to do so. Phœnicia excelled in trade—not government. With this station at Memphis, Tyre was able to obtain not only products of the valley but those also which were brought into Egypt from the south. Ivory, ebony, skins, ostrich feathers, grain, pottery, glass—these and other commodities here available were shipped away for consumption in Italy, Greece and Asia Minor. The Egyptians, so resentful of foreigners ordinarily, appear to have found the Phœnicians unobjectionable and of actual service to them. The little colony was allowed to maintain its own customs, and it is supposed that a temple sacred to Astoreth was erected here as early as 1250 B. C.

The islands west of Tyre were early peopled by Phoenicians, or, at least, contained Phœnician settlements. Timber suitable for ship-building was obtained in Cilicia, copper and precious stones in Cyprus, pine lumber and figs in Rhodes.

Utica, on the Gulf of Tunis, was an early colony on the African side of the Mediterranean. Coasting alone this shore, the sea-farers came to Spain, where they established important trading points. They penetrated as far west as the Cornwall mines, which supplied an inexhaustible amount of tin.

The islands off the Cornish coast they called the "Cassiterides" or Tin Islands.

"Phœnician colonization—or colonization from Phœnicia Proper—was in all probability limited within the extremes of the Dardanelles to the north, Memphis to the south, and Gadeira and the Cassiterides to the west. It was less widely diffused than the Greek, and less generally spread over the coasts accessible to it. With a few exceptions, the colonies fall into three groups—first, those of the Eastern Mediterranean and Aegean, beginning with Cyprus and terminating with Cythera; secondly those of the Central Mediterranean, in North Africa, Sicily, and the adjacent islands; and thirdly, those of the Western Mediterranean, chiefly on the south coast of Spain, with perhaps a few on the opposite (African) shore. The other settlements, commonly called Phœnician on the eastern coast of Spain, in the Balearic Islands, in Corsica and Elba; and again those on the Western Africa coast, between the Straits of Gibraltar and the Cape de Verde, were Punic or Carthaginian, rather than Phœnician."[1]

Finally something must be said of Carthage, for while her palmy days as well as her decline, were closely related to Roman history, her beginnings were inseparable with the mother-country.

The word Carthage signifies *New City,* and the settlement was so named in all probability to distinguish it from Utica, founded 300 years before. 850 B. C. has been considered the latest possible date for the founding of the town, while many hold that it was settled as early as 1000 B. C. It matters little which is accepted, since the place was neither strong nor influential for many years after either date. Its citizens came originally from Tyre. The "New City" was built on what is now the Bay of Tunis, a little to the north-west of the present town of Tunis. Nothing, practically, is known of its early history. Kings ruled at first, but were later abolished. Polybius, a Greek historian, stated that he had seen a treaty made betwen Rome and Carthage as early as 509 B. C., by which the Carthaginians bound themselves not to injure any Latin city while the Romans were pledged not to interfere with Carthaginian markets in the western Mediterranean. Because of its fortunate position the city became very pros-

[1] Rawlinson: Phoenicia, 71.

perous. The Greeks tried to divert some of its trade into their own channels, and later, Rome was its hated rival and continued to struggle with the city until she effected its downfall.

"From the time when the first adventurers from the Syrian coast entered the sheltered inlets of the African shore—a remote period, even before Saul was made king of Israel and while Priam sat on the throne of Troy—down to the seventh century of the Christian era, when the Arabs passed over it like a whirlwind, this land has been the battlefield where destinies of nations have been sealed, and where heroes and warriors have sought their last resting place. The myths that surround its earliest development and shed a halo of romance over the career of its primitive races are somewhat obscured by the sterner facts of later times—by wars innumerable, wars of invasion and local disturbances, succeeded by a long period of piracy and power insured, and finally by neglect, abandonment, and decay. The legend of Dido still hangs over Carthage hill. The spirit of Hannibal haunts the fateful Zanca, and the banks of the Midjerda hold in everlasting memory the story of Regulus and his affrighted array. The air is full of myths and old-world stories which faithfully represent the traditions of the country in its varying fortunes; and slight as may be their connection with events in prehistoric times, yet they serve as foundations for a historic superstructure of never-failing interest. The earliest records are fragmentary, but we learn that the library of the Carthaginians, written in Phœnician characters, was presented by the Romans, after the fall of Carthage, to one of the kings of Numidia; and that Sallust, as pro-consul of that province in the time of Julius Cæsar, borrowed largely from it while writing his history of the Jugarthine war. There is little doubt, however, that most of the earliest records passed to Alexandria, which became the rival of Athens as a seat of learning. With the burning of its library by the fanatical Arabs in the seventh century many a link betwen the old world and the new was severed, and reliable information concerning the laws and traditions, and the manners and customs of a people, who were the fathers of navigation and the founders of commerce, was swept away."[a]

[a] Graham: Roman Africa, preface.

THE RIVER JORDAN.

Phœnician commerce was facilitated by the establishment of many out-posts, and while none other reached such size and importance as Carthage, several controlled routes which were almost as valuable. No modern account of that vast commerce approaches the one written long ago by the prophet Ezekiel, when Tyre was, or had just been, at the zenith of her power.

"O thou that dwellest at the entry of the sea, which art the merchant of the people unto many isles, O Tyre, thou hast said: 'I am of perfect beauty.'

"Thy borders are in the midst of the seas, thy builders have perfected thy beauty. They have made all thy ship boards of fir trees of Senir: they have taken cedars from Lebanon to make masts for thee. Of the oaks of Bashan have they made thine oars; the company of the Ashurites have made thy benches of ivory, brought out of the isles of Chittim. Fine linen with broidered work from Egypt was that which thou spreadest forth to be thy sail; blue and purple from the isles of Elishah was that which covered thee.

"The inhabitants of Sidon and Arvad were thy mariners: thy wise men, O Tyre, that were in thee, were thy pilots.

"The ancients of Gabal and the wise men thereof were in thee thy calkers: all the ships of the sea with their mariners were in thee to occupy thy merchandise. They of Persia and of Lud and of Phut were in thine army, thy men of war: they hanged the shield and helmet in thee; they set forth thy comeliness. . . .

"Tarshish was thy merchant by reason of all kinds of riches; with silver, iron, tin and lead, they traded in thy fairs.

"Javan, Tubal, and Meshech, they were thy merchants: they traded the persons of men and vessels of brass in thy market. They of the house of Togarmah traded in thy fairs with horses and horsemen and mules. The men of Dedan were thy merchants; many isles were the merchandise of thine hand: they brought thee for a present horns of ivory and ebony. Syria was thy merchant by reason of the multitude of the wares of thy making: they occupied in thy fairs with emeralds, purple, and broidered work, and fine linen, and coral, and agate.

"Judah, and the land of Israel, they were thy merchants:

they traded in thy market wheat of Minnith, and Pannag, and honey, and oil, and balm. Damascus was thy merchant in the multitude of the wares of thy making, for the multitude of all riches; in the wine of Helbon, and white wool. Dan also and Javan going to and fro occupied in thy fairs; bright iron, cassia, and calamus, were in thy market. Dedan was thy merchant in precious cloths for chariots. Arabia, and all the princes of Kedar, they occupied with thee in lambs, and rams, and goats: in these were they thy merchants. The merchants of Sheba and Raamah . occupied in thy fairs with chief of all spices, and with all precious stones, and gold.

"Haran, and Canneh, and Eden, the merchants of Sheba, Asshur, and Chilmad, were thy merchants. These were thy merchants in all sorts of things, in blue clothes, and broidered work, and in chests of rich apparel, bound with cords, and made of cedar, among thy merchandise. The ships of Tarshish did sing of thee in thy market: and thou wast made very glorious in the midst of the seas.

"When thy wares went forth out of the seas, thou filledst many people; thou didst enrich the kings of the earth with the multitude of thy riches and of thy merchandise."[3]

The produce of the ancient world passed through routes controlled by Phœnicia, and she acted as middleman in its distribution. Commerce was of two kinds, overland, and by sea. Traffic by water greatly exceeded that by land, yet both were necessary and were mutually dependent upon one another.

The products of interior Asia were brought, then as now, by caravans. Even today it is possible to see trains of caravans similar to those in the service of ancient Tyre, laden with costly wares, crossing the desert. Not only were spices and wares of Western Asia taken to Phœnician sea-ports for distribution, but Mesopotamia was supplied with articles from Europe and Africa by the same overland travel.

"Imagine the arrival of a Tyrian caravan at Babylon. The travellers have been on the march for three or four months. They have arrived weary, dusty, travel-stained. Their tents are pitched outside the town, not far from the banks of the river, or of a water-course derived from it, under

[3] Ezekiel, 27.

the pleasant shadow of a grove of palms, near the northern gate of the great city. The tall necks of their camels are seen from a distance by the keen-eyed watchers of the gate-towers, and reported by them to the civic authorities, whence the secret soon oozes out and creates a bustle in the town. All are anxious to obtain some object of their desire from the long expected traders; but especially anxious are the great storekeepers and shopkeepers, who look to the occasion for the replenishing of their stock-in-trade for the next six months, or, it may be, even for the next year. But the weary travellers must have a night's rest ere they can be ready to open their market, must unload their camels and their mules, dispose their bales of goods as seems most convenient, and prepare themselves for the fatigues of commercial dealing by a light supper and a sound sleep ensuing thereupon. How glad are the camels to have the loads removed from their galled backs, to repose their weary limbs upon the green grass of the yellow sand, and to lay their tired necks along the ground! Not a moan is heard, scarcely a grunt, unless it be one of satisfaction. The mules, and the camels, and the horses of the wealthier sort, enjoy themselves equally. We hear the tinkling of their bells, as they shake themselves, freed from all their trappings but the head stall. Some are picketed about where the turf is richest, others contentedly munch the barley that has been placed before them in portable mangers, to reward them for the toils that they have gone through. Many prefer sleeping to eating, and, leaving their food untouched, stretch themselves upon the sward. Night falls—the stars come out—the traders sleep in their tents, with a stone or a bale of goods for their pillow—a profound hush sinks upon the camp, except for the occasional squeal of a skittish pair of mules, which have exchanged bites under cover of the darkness.

"The camp, however, wakes up with the first gleam of dawn in the eastern sky. Each man busily sets about his proper work. Mules and horses are groomed and are arranged in rows, with their mangers in front, and their pack-saddles and trappings near at hand. Bales of goods are opened, and a display made of a portion of their contents. Meantime, the town gates have been unclosed, and in holiday apparel a gay crowd streams forth from them. Foremost come the loafers, hoping to make an honest penny by 'lending a hand,' or to make a dishonest one by filching some unguarded article. Then follow the ordinary customers and the petty traders whose arrangements have not been made beforehand. The last to appear are the agents of the great merchants, whose correspondents at Tyre have made them consignments of goods and sent the goods by the caravan to their destination; these clamor for invoices and bills of lading. But the noisiest and most pressing are the petty traders and the mere chance customers, who have a special need to supply, or covet a good bargain. With them what a chaffering there is! What a screaming and apparent quarrelling! One buyer wants a purple robe for half its value, another a Damascene blade for next to nothing, a third, a Greek statuette for half a shekel of silver. The seller asks at least four times the sum that he intends to take; the buyer exclaims, swears perhaps by the beard of his grandfather that he will not give a farthing more than he has offered; then relents, and doubtless doubles his bid; the seller comes down a little, but they are still 'miles apart,' so to speak; it takes an hour of talking, swearing, screaming, raving, before the *juste milieu* is hit off, an agreement come to, and buyer and seller alike made happy by a conviction on the part of each that he has over-reached the other."[*]

The companion picture to the caravan would be the merchant vessel on the seas, together with the eager anticipation that attended its arrival in port. The earliest portrayal of Phœnician boats show them to have been provided with oars and sails. From small crafts, partially cabined, built of unseasoned timber and poorly caulked, were gradually evolved the stately biremes, perfect in construction and equipment. The testimony of an eye-witness is vastly preferable to descriptions of moderns, however scholarly. The following description of Xenophon, a Greek general who often saw Phœnician vessels, contains valuable information regarding the degree of skill reached by these sea-farers in the equipment of their ships:

"I think that the best and most perfect arrangement of things which I ever saw was when I went to look at the great Phœnician sailing vessel: for I saw the largest amount of naval

[*] Rawlinson: Phoenicia, 157. ff.

tackling separately disposed in the smallest stowage possible. For a ship, as you well know, is brought to anchor, and again got under way, by a vast number of wooden implements, and of ropes, and sails the sea by means of a quantity of rigging, and is armed with a number of contrivances against hostile vessels, and carries about with it a large supply of weapons for the crew, and, besides, has all the utensils that a man keeps in his dwelling-house, for each of the messes. In addition, it is loaded with a quantity of merchandise, which the owner carries with him for his own profit. Now all the things which I have mentioned lay in a space not much bigger than a room that would conveniently hold ten beds. And I remarked that they severally lay in such a way that they did not obstruct one another, and did not require any one to look for them, and yet they were neither placed at random, nor entangled one with another, so as to consume time when they were suddenly wanted for use. Also I found the captain's assistant, who is called the 'look-out-man,' so well acquainted with the position of all the articles, and with the number of them, that even when at a distance he would tell where everything lay, and how many there were of each sort. Moreover, I saw this man, in his leisure moments, examining and testing everything that a vessel needs when at sea; so, as I was surprised, I asked him what he was about, whereupon he replied, 'Stranger, I am looking to see, in case anything should happen, how everything is arranged in the ship, and whether anything is wanting or is inconveniently situated; for when a storm arises at sea, it is not possible either to look for what is wanting, or to put to rights what is arranged awkwardly.'"[5]

One mast and one sail seem to have been commonly used. The biremes and triremes were so-called because of their two or three banks of oars. The oarsmen sat in the hold, their oars passing through the vessel's side.

Phœnician traffic was always most extensive by sea. Products of Egypt, Greece, Cyprus, Carthage, Spain, Britain, besides those of countless islands, were transported constantly by water.

[5] Xenophon: Aeconom., VIII., 11

The Approach of a Caravan.

"When spring-time flushes the desert grass,
  Our kafilas wind through the Khyber Pass.
  Lean are the camels, but fat the frails,
  Light are the purses but heavy the bales,
  As the snow-bound trade of the North comes down
  To the market-square of Peshawur town.

  In a turquoise twilight, crisp and chill,
  A kafila camped at the foot of the hill.
  Then blue smoke-haze of the cooking rose,
  And tent-peg answered to hammer-nose.
  And the picketed ponies shag and wild,
  Strained at their ropes as the feed was piled;
  And the bubbling camels beside the load
  Sprawled for a furlong adown the road;
  And Persian pussy-cats, brought for sale,
  Spat at the dogs from the camel-bale;
  And the tribesmen bellowed to hasten the food;
  And the camp-fires twinkled by Fort Junrood;
  And there fled on the wings of the gathering dusk
  A savour of camels and carpets and musk,
  A murmur of voices, a reek of smoke,
  To tell us the trade of the Khyber woke."

         —*Kipling: Ballad of the King's Jest.*

CHAPTER IV.

Occupations and Industries.

Of first concern among the industries of Phœnicia were her maritime activities. While many Phœnician voyages led from island to island, and from one port to another almost in sight, nevertheless the sailors frequently made trips that necessitated their steering away from the shore, and venturing out into the open sea. They probably made charts of the sea and acquired some elementary knowledge of nautical affairs. Their greatest undertaking was the circumnavigation of Africa. This was attempted when Neccho was pharaoh of Egypt and held Western Asia in temporary tribute. Hoping to find a water communication between the Red Sea and the Mediterranean, he engaged Phœnician seamen to sail around Africa. Three years were consumed in the journey, since they had to land each year and grow food sufficient for the continuance of their voyage. When they returned, through the Straits of Gibraltar, they reported that the sun had been upon their right hand throughout the trip, which, Herodotus said: "others may perhaps believe, though I certainly do not." Little attention was given the matter until scholars began to investigate the possibility of the earth's rotundity, whereupon the information so long cast aside was once more noted.

For the most part it is probably true that the art of navigation was but crudely developed, compared with the progress reached later by the Greeks. Yet the Greeks themselves were indebted to some extent to the earliest seamen of unquestioned courage and venturesome spirit.

Of most vital importance were Phœnicia's activities in commerce and trade, to quite a degree dependent upon her control of the sea.

"Gather now an idea of Phœnicia in the days of her greatest power. Station yourself upon the rocky island of Tyre, and turn your eyes toward the west. Were your vision powerful enough, you might see the towers of Phœnician settlements dotting the Grecian seas and lining the coast of Africa. Meeting for a moment at the Strait of Gibraltar, again the two lines would diverge to the north and to the south, encompassing the known seas. Turn now to the east, and you behold the caravans extending in long dark lines to the north and to the south. At the extremities of the Lebanon mountains, crossing the ridge, the lines divide and subdivide, like streams toward their sources, until they penetrate and permeate the jungles of India and the valleys of the Himalayas. Such was Phœnicia in her palmy days, garnering and distributing the produce and riches of the world."[1]

Farming was also important. Products raised within Phœnicia were used chiefly for home consumption. Orchards, gardens, and grain-fields yielded abundant returns and provided the food supply of the population, save for fish, and such articles of luxury as were demanded by the citizens of the wealthy ports. The country was too small and its arable acreage too limited to admit of extensive agricultural pursuits.

While the manufactories of the country were less important, they had an important place. Phœnicia was widely famed for the production of four distinct articles, in the making of which her people excelled. First of these was a purple dye. Other nations attempted to provide the same commodity but never equalled the perfection of the Tyrian dye. Large quantities of shell-fish yielding the precious fluid from which it was made, were found off the Tyrian coast. They were of two species. A little *sac* containing a creamy secretion was opened in one, and the fluid carefully extracted. The other was ground up, shell and all. Both were necessary to produce the beautiful tints peculiar to Phœnician cloths.

Their special processes of dyeing, exposing the materials to the different degrees of light while drying, as well as the chemical employed to make the colors fast, were secrets well guarded, so that no imitation could deceive when compared to the splendid purples of Tyre. Since dress fabrics and material for covering furniture were most desired in rich and costly hues, raw wool was extensively imported and woven to meet the ever increasing demand. Dress stuffs from Phœnicia were prized as booty or as tribute by the several countries which at different periods exacted homage from Tyre and Sidon.

Sidon was famous for her glassware. Pliny the Elder, a Roman who wrote on History and Science during the first

[1] Boughton: History of Ancient Peoples.

century of the Christian era, gave the tradition current in his day concerning the so-called "discovery of glass."

"It is said that some Phœnician merchants, having landed on the shores of the river Belus, were preparing their meal, and not finding suitable stones for raising their saucepans, they used lumps of natrum contained in their cargo for the purpose. When the natrum was exposed to the action of the fire, it melted into the sand lying on the banks of the river, and they saw transparent streams of some unknown liquid trickling over the ground; this was the origin of glass." At least the tale is reasonable, and might have been the experience of people at different times. At all events, the art becoming known to the Phœnicians, they attained notable skill in imitating precious stones in colored glass. It was their experience that trinkets, such as beads, were in great favor among half-civilized tribes with whom they traded, and the satisfaction was mutual when a few strings of glass beads had been exchanged for skins, ivory and even gold. It is now believed that some of the rare glass-ware, treasured as Grecian in museums today, was really produced in Sidon.

Articles fashioned of gold, silver and other metals were especially attractive. Such bits of jewelry as have been discovered—necklaces, bracelets, and rings, give evidence of a high degree of workmanship. Bowls, goblets, and dishes were elaborately wrought from metals, and while the decorative designs upon them were often borrowed from the Greeks or the Egyptians, the original was frequently improved upon. The following lines from the Iliad show how bits of Phœnician work were treasured among the Hellenes:

> "And then the son of Peleus placed in sight
> Prizes of swiftness,—a wrought silver cup
> That held six measures, and in beauty far
> Excelled all others known; the cunning hands
> Of the Sidonian artisans have given
> Its graceful shape, and over the dark sea
> Men of Phœnicia brought it, with their wares,
> To the Greek harbors; Achilles now
> Brought it before the assembly as a prize,
> For which, in honor of the friend he loved,
> The swiftest runners of the host should strive."

Hebrew chroniclers have described the decoration of Solomon's temple—all wrought by Phœnician skill:

"And King Solomon sent and fetched Hiram out of Tyre. He was a widow's son, and his father was a man of Tyre, a worker in brass: and he was filled with wisdom and understanding, and cunning to work all works in brass. And he came to King Solomon, and wrought all his work.

"For he cast two pillars of brass, of eighteen cubits high apiece: and a line of twelve cubits did compass either of them about. And he made two capitals of molten brass, to set upon the tops of the pillars: the height of the one capital was five cubits, and the height of the other capital was five cubits. And nets of checker work, and wreaths of chain work, for the capitals which were upon the top of the pillars, seven for one capital and seven for the other capital. And he made the pillars, and two rows round about upon the one network, to cover the capitals that were upon the top, with pomegranates: and so did he for the other capital. And the capitals that were upon the top of the pillars were of lily work in the porch, four cubits. And he set up the pillars in the porch of the temple: and he set up the right pillar and called the name thereof Jachin: and he sat up the left pillar and called the name thereof Boaz. And upon the top of the pillars was lily work: so was the work of the pillars finished.

"And he made a molten sea, ten cubits from one brim to the other: it was round all about, and its height was five cubits: and a line of thirty cubits did compass it round about. And under the brim of it round about there were knobs compassing it. It stood upon twelve oxen, three looking toward the north, and three looking toward west, and three looking toward the south, and three looking toward the east: and the sea was set above them, and all their hinder parts were inward. And it was an hand breadth thick, and the brim thereof was wrought like the brim of a cup, with flowers of lilies: it contained two thousand baths. So Hiram made an end of doing all the work that he made King Solomon for the house of the Lord."[2]

The Phœnicians never developed an imposing architecture. Timber was abundant on the mountain slopes, and was the

[2] I. Kings, 7.

principal building material. The great lack of architectural ruins in the country today may be largely accounted for by its perishability. Stone was also available, and appears to have been used chiefly for foundations, which were laid deep and skillfully constructed. City walls were built of stone, and a few remnants of these may yet be found. Gigantic stones of prodigious size were piled one upon another and often held in place by their own tremendous weight. In places where the solid blocks were joined together, they were united so evenly that the blade of a knife may not now be placed in the seam.

Tyre and Sidon were both beautiful cities, as abundant evidence goes to testify. Carthage with her great structures of stone, became a quarry for Italy, but the Phœnicians were imitators and never developed a distinctive style of building.

Their sculpture survives only in tombs. A few of these have been recovered. Some of the figures adorning the interiors of tombs are said to possess richness and beauty. Their artists made use of huge blocks, and for this reason their carving was in low relief, or gave such appearance. The Greeks, on the other hand, found gigantic blocks unwieldy, and took smaller stones for their embellishment. Consequently the grace and delicacy of Greek sculpture was not reached in Phœnicia.

"It seems strange that these Canaanites or Phœnicians, the scorn of Israel, and the people against whom Joshua bent all his powers, should have enjoyed such an uncheckered career, making themselves sole navigators of every sea, and finally founding a city which stod unrivalled for more than 700 years. Through their hands . passed grain, ivory, and skins from Libya; slaves from the Soudan, purple and cedar from Tyre, frankincense from Arabia, copper from Cyprus, iron from Elba, tin from Cornwall, wine from Greece, silver from Spain, and gold and precious stones from Malabar. As a nation of traders and navigators they established themselves on the coast, and wherever they settled, depots and factories of various kinds were erected. We do not find them in the interior of a country. Neither do we hear of alliances with the people with whom they came in contact, nor of their impressing barbarian tribes with any notions of the advantages of civilization. In the field of intellectual acquirements the Carthaginian, as the descendant of the Phœnician, has no place, and his skill in the gentler arts of life has no recognition. We find no native architecture, nor do we hear of any industrial art worth recording. Carthage, it is true, became the metropolis of their widespread kingdom, and one of the wealthiest cities of the world. Temples and stately edifices adorned its streets, and the remains of great constructional works still attest the solid grandeur of the city. But the architecture was the work of Greek, not of Punic, artists; and the few sculptures of note, which may be assigned to a period anterior to the last Punic war, have nothing in common with the rude carvings which bear the impress of Carthaginian origin. On the other hand the art of navigation, the science of agriculture, the principles of trading, and a system of water supply combined with the construction of gigantic cisterns, which may still be seen at Carthage, and in the outskirts of many towns in North Africa, became Rome's heritage from Phœnicia."[3]

Literature and Learning.

Among the bequests of Phœnicia to mankind, first will always stand the giving of an alphabet to the world. It is true that other nations possessed a written language, but their symbols were generally so complicated and so numerous that they could hardly have become of general service. It was earlier assumed that the Phœnicians invented the alphabet which they spread among the nations around them, but now it is believed that they simply shortened and simplified symbols already in existence. Their alphabet was widely adopted, to be sure, not because it was most convenient, but because it was the only one known to many nations, who never came in direct contact with dwellers on the Nile or Mesopotamians.

In Phœnicia's palmy days literature and learning were neglected—at least so far as can now be ascertained. It is not unlikely that scholars lived sometimes in the larger cities, and schools were probably maintained to some extent, but at all events, no remains of a Phœnician literature has come down to us, and it has been commonly surmised that no extensive

[3] Graham: Roman Africa, 1, 2.

literature ever existed. The nation was bent upon its commercial life, and only such knowledge as would be essential to traders was regarded as necessary. In later times, in the last century before Christ and in the first century of the new era, literary activity was more marked. We are told that there was a school of philosophy at Sidon, and the city became a literary center, but this had little to do with the period of Phœnician ascendency which practically ended with Greek dominance.

Religion.

Somewhat more is known of the religion of Phœnicia, but here again we are not able to trace its development in any complete sense, and most that has been recorded concerning it was written by foreigners whose attitude was uniformly hostile.

It is now supposed by some scholars that the Phœnician religion was at first monotheistic, and that later the worship of many gods was common. The third stage in its progress would be the greater portion of the period known to us, when the gods of other peoples were allowed, by the side of those native to the country. In Carthaginian tombs images of Egyptian deities have been found side by side with those of ancient Tyre and Sidon. In the beginning, the Phœnician worship was probably one manifestation of the Sun-worship, common to Semitic peoples. The religion of any people is a matter of growth, invariably undergoing change, until it finally resembles but slightly what it was in the beginning. Thus the faith of Phœnicia underwent many changes during her 1500 years. It is agreed that the Phœnicians worshipped curiously shaped stones at an early period, believing that deities had their abode within them; plants also were importuned, to appease the spirit that dwelt within them and cause each to yield food. Finally the heavenly bodies became objects of worship, the sun being considered most important. There must always be something appealing in the adoration felt by primitive minds toward the sun. Most ancient people worshipped it in one form or another, and the planet was surrounded by unfathomable mystery in the infancy of the world.

Baal was god of the sun, Astoreth, goddess of the moon.

Baal symbolized the life-giving power of the sun as well as its destructive forces.

Maleck or Molock was the god of fire. He was a god of cruelty and thirsted for blood. It was to satisfy some of his supposed cravings that the human sacrifices took place. The first-born child, pure maidens, favorite sons, were fed to the flames to appease his wrath. These sacrifices seem strange to us today, and nations of antiquity, immuned to cruelty and bloodshed, turned from these Phœnician customs in horror.

An annual spring festival of great antiquity was celebrated. Probably in early times it lacked the feature of the human sacrifice which made it most objectionable later. Great forest trees were brought into the temple court and planted. From their branches were suspended animals, birds and all else intended for the sacrifice. After the images of the gods were marched around these trees, all was set on fire and consumed in a mighty conflagration. To make the celebration more impressive, human sacrifices were added, especially before some great undertaking, or upon the occasion of some national calamity.

Astoreth was the great virgin goddess. In the beginning she was worshipped with simple rites.

> "Astoreth, whom the Phœnicians called
> Astarte, queen of heaven, with crescent horns;
> To whose bright image nightly by the moon
> Sidonian virgins paid their vows and songs."

In course of time the character of the goddess changed, and she was worshipped by most licentious practices.

In addition to their own gods, the Phœnicians readily incorporated into their pantheon deities of those tribes and nations with whom they opened trade. Some years after Phœnicia ceased to be a power, a Carthaginian general made a treaty with the Emperor of Greece. The two are reported to have sworn by numerous deities that they would preserve it. "They swore by Zeus, Hera, and Apollo, by the tutelary deities of the Carthaginians, by Hercules, by the moon, and the earth, by rivers, meadows, and waters, by the gods of the allied armies, and the sun, by all the gods who ruled over Carthage, by all the gods who ruled over Macedon and the rest of Greece, and by all the gods of those who were present to ratify the treaty."

At first the Phœnicians worshipped in the open air, with merely an altar of stone. Later they built elaborate and costly temples, but they still celebrated certain ceremonies out of doors, in groves or under the shade of trees.

The religion of the Phœnicians was most innocent and attractive in its earliest stages. As it developed, with its numerous priesthood performing their bloody rites, and its necessary sacrifices, teaching cruelty and blunting the sensibilities of its adherents, it became very repulsive. Far from inculcating noble ideals, it made a virtue of renouncing dear ones to agony and death; and a people who from infancy grew accustomed to such scenes and such conceptions could never develop finest qualities of character. Wherever Phœnician vessels landed with their wares, there Phœnician gods and practices went also. The good done in spreading the habits of civilization to regions remote was mitigated by the harm done in spreading this abhorrent faith.

Several Greek myths tell of maidens being sacrificed to some monster, such, for example, as Theseus and The Minotaur. These are believed to have had their origin in rumors of Phœnician sacrifices. The stories reached the shores of Greece in various forms and with the aid of Greek imaginations were woven into the tales as we know them.

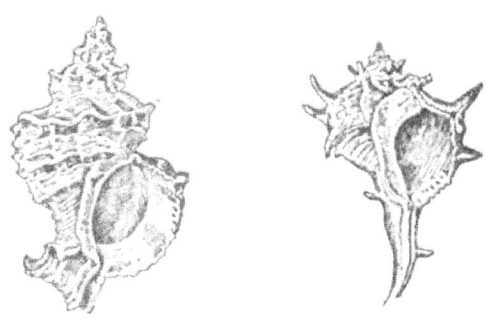

SHELLS OF THE SEA SNAIL FROM WHICH THE PURPLE DYE WAS MADE.

CHAPTER V.

THE PHYSICAL GEOGRAPHY OF PALESTINE.

It is essential that the student of Hebrew history understand the topography of Palestine, wherein the nation developed. Names of rivers, mountains, cities, in this historic land grow familiar from frequent repetition in the Bible, but where each was located, and what was its position relative to other oft-mentioned spots, are queries left unsettled by the average reader. Still more necessary is a general idea of the country as a whole, because the very formation of the land determined in a large measure the destiny of those who dwelt within it.

Palestine is bounded on the north by the base of the Lebanons, on the east by the Arabian desert, on the south by the Wilderness of Judah—an extension of this desert—, and on the west by the Mediterranean Sea below Mount Carmel, while north of this mighty mountain the Phœnicians held the coast, although the Hebrews occupied the province of Galilee, east of the Phœnician shore.

This celebrated land is scarcely more than 150 miles in length, and approximates 100 miles in breadth, yet every known variety of climate may be found within its confines. From regions lying 1300 feet below sea-level, with heat of the tropics, mountains rise to 9000 feet above the sea, with Alpine snows and cold.

Palestine, like Greece or Switzerland, falls naturally into many small divisions, each shut off in a measure from the rest. This explains how it was possible for the Hebrews to occupy a considerable portion of the land while the Canaanites, earlier inhabitants of the country, remained undisturbed in other localities. It also explains the fact that for many years some of the Hebrews dwelt in tents and clung to their nomadic customs while no great distance away others of their kinsmen cultivated the vine and tilled the soil.

While the shore of the Mediterranean was broken by several harbors along the Phœnician coast, south of Mount Carmel the shore reaches in a nearly straight line to Egypt.

No havens invite ships to safety; no islands dot the rocky shore. To the Hebrew the sea was a frontier rather than a means for outside communication. So inhospitable was this coast that invasions of Palestine were made by land rather than sea. A rocky line of cliffs varying from thirty to one hundred feet makes landing impossible save at two or three artificially constructed modern ports.

Six distinct land features are to be found in Palestine and deeply affected the people who dwelt there in antiquity. First of these is the Coast Plain, varying in width from two hundred yards to thirty miles. The northern portion of it was known as the Plain of Sharon; the southern portion, as the Plain of Philistia. The word *Sharon* signifies "forest," and in an early day a dense wood of oaks covered the region and gave it this name. Only in the north has the forest been perpetuated to our day. The plain was formerly, and is still, productive. It contains gardens, orchards, and grain fields. Lacking the inspiring beauty of the high tablelands, it possesses a quiet charm of its own. Farther south, the Plain of Philistia stretches off in the direction of Egypt.

This Coast Plain, falling for the most part into these two smaller plains, has been a continuation of the great highway between Egypt and Syria, and a famous war-path. For Egypt particularly, it was a simple matter to dispatch troops along the shore, to strike terror to less inaccessible inland districts. Today it lies in peaceful cultivation or in woodlands of low undergrowth.

"The whole Maritime Plain possesses a quiet but rich beauty. If the contours are gentle the colors are strong and varied. Along almost the whole seaboard runs a strip of links and downs, sometimes of pure drifting sand, sometimes of grass and sand together. Outside this border of broken gold there is the blue sea, with its fringe of foam. Landward the soil is a chocolate brown, with breaks and gullies, now bare to their dirty white shingle and stagnant puddles, and now full of rich green reeds and rushes that tell of ample water beneath. Over corn and moorland a million flowers are scattered—poppies, pimpernels, anemones, the convolvulus and the mallow, the narcissus and blue iris—*roses of Sharon and lilies of the valley.* Lizards haunt all the sunny banks.

The shimmering air is filled with bees and butterflies, and with the twittering of small birds, hushed now and then as the shadow of a great hawk blots the haze. The soft night is sprinkled thick with glittering fireflies."[1]

Passing the sea and the Coast Plain, the Central Range rises high and extends throughout the entire length of Palestine, with some variations. In this great tableland lay the famous kingdom of the Hebrews—Judaea and Samaria. Judaea lay farther to the south and was separated from the Coast Plain by the Shephelah—a series of low foot-hills. The Hebrews built their western cities on these low hills rather than along the shore. In fact the frequent attacks of the Philistines left the Coast Plain only now and then in the hands of the Hebrews.

The word *Shephelah* has been thought to signify *lowlands*, and may have been applied in contrast to the highlands farther east. Ranging from five to fifteen miles in width, this elevated strip was the scene of constant warfare between the Hebrews and Philistines. Numerous valleys led across it, Ajalon being perhaps most famous.

"The prevailing scenery of the region is of short, steep hillsides and narrow glens, with a very few great trees, and thickly covered by brushwood and oak-scrub—crags and scalps of limestone breaking through, and a rough grey torrent-bed at the bottom of each glen. Caves, of course, abound —near the villages, gaping black dens for men and cattle, but up the unfrequented glens they are hidden by hanging bush, behind which you disturb only the wild pigeon. Bees murmur everywhere, larks are singing; and although in the maze of hills you may wander for hours without meeting a man, or seeing a house, you are seldom out of sound of the human voice, shepherds and ploughmen calling to their cattle and to each other across the glens. Higher up you rise to moorlands, with rich grass if there is a spring, but otherwise, heath, thorns, and rough herbs that scent the wind. Bees abound here, too, and dragon-flies, kites and crows; sometimes an eagle floats over the cliffs of Judaea. The sun beats strong, but you see and feel the sea; the high mountains are

[1] George Adam Smith: Historical Geography of the Holy Land, 148.

behind, at night they breathe upon these ridges gentle breezes, and the dews are very heavy.

"Altogether it is a rough, happy land, with its glens and moors, its mingled brushwood and barley-fields; frequently under cultivation, but for the most part broken and thirsty, with few wells and many hiding places; just the home for strong border-men, like Samson, and just the theatre for that guerilla warfare, varied occasionally by pitched battles, which Israel and Philistia, the Maccabees and the Syrians, waged with each other."[a]

At last the foot-hills merge into lofty mountains and series of plateaus, or table-lands, surrounded by high peaks, appear. Here was Judaea, the true home of the Hebrews. Farther north, and rising directly from the Coast Plain, without the intervening foot-hills, was Samaria. The physical outlines of this long, narrow range determined in advance that it would not permanently be politically united.

Judaea was quite secure in her mountain heights. On the east her mountains descend abruptly to the lower Jordan and the Dead Sea; on the south lies the desert; on the east the low foot-hills, and on the north the table-land ends in ten miles of wild, waste land. "A desolate, fatiguing extent of rocky platforms and ridges, or moorland strewn with boulders, and fields of shallow soil thickly mixed with stone, they are a true border—more fit for the building of barriers than for the cultivation of food."

Some parts of this stony plateau were fit for cultivation, but for the most part, Judaea was a pastoral land—a country of shepherds and herdsmen. Flocks of sheep fed on the moorlands in ancient times, as they do today. Water has always been scanty and is preserved in wells and cisterns for the cattle during months of drouth.

Samaria possesses softer outlines and is a land beautified by nature. As Judaea was isolated and secure in her natural boundaries, so was Samaria open to approach. The "openness" of the land is constantly dwelt upon by those who picture its location. It was difficult to resist invasion and Samaria was attacked much more often than her sister to the south. Samaria was a fruitful land, yielding to cultivation;

[a] George Adam Smith: Historical Geography of the Holy Land, 208.

she lay open to influences on every hand, and was the first to receive fresh impulses and ideas. " Today, amid the peaceful beauty of the scene—the secluded vale covered with corn fields, through which the winding streams flash and glisten into the hazy distance, and the gentle hill rises without a scarp to the olives waving on its summit—it is possible to appreciate Isaiah's name for Samaria, *the crown of pride of Ephraim, the flower of his glorious beauty which is on the head of the fat valley.*"[a]

East of both countries and the Central Range which contained them, flows the Jordan. Geological ages ago it is supposed that a great sea occupied the valley of the Jordan and the regions on either side. Beneath its deep waters, layers of limestone accumulated. In course of time, mighty convulsions within the earth hurled these layers of rock in twain and threw them up on both sides, until the present mountain ranges were formed. At the same time a series of rocks were cast up diagonally across this region to the south, thus enclosing a portion of the salt waters within the basin so formed. Ages of rain and of glaciers followed and when these abated, the new surface was left to develop its system of drainage. The situation at present is almost identical with that in early Bible times. In the northern part of Palestine, at the base of the Lebanons, a series of streams, mountain-born, take a southerly direction and empty into a marshy pool known as Lake Huleh; from the southern part of this lake the river Jordan flows on to the Lake of Galilee, whence the stream once again issues forth, this time down a steep incline, giving it rapid impetus of motion, from whence comes its name: Jordan— the *Down-comer*. At last its valley widens and by several estuaries the river finally empties into the Dead Sea.

The beauty attending many rivers of the earth is lacking in the Jordan. Cutting down its channels in a rift left already deep by eruption, this valley lies deep below the sea-level and is exceedingly hot. Malaria lurks in the jungles that border the river-sides, and at no time has the region been thickly populated. The river is not suited to irrigation, but certain portions of the valley are watered by its tributaries sufficiently to make gardens possible.

[a] George Adam Smith: Historical Geography of the Holy Land, 349.

The Dead Sea occupies the lowest portion of the valley. Soundings have shown it to be very deep. Not only are its waters heavily charged with salt, but other chemicals make yet more uninhabitable its basin. No fish or other form of life lives in its waters, which possess remarkable clearness and are intensely blue. Having no outlets save evaporation, and lying where heat is great, the sea is like a mighty caldron, above which a column of steam rises constantly. 6,000,000 tons of water are estimated to rise from it daily in the form of vapor.

From its very nature, the Jordan was not a river to which a nation might become devoted—as, for example, the Egyptians were to their Nile. Nevertheless, no other stream has become so embodied into literature, or so endeared to a great religious world. The Hebrews regarded the Jordan as a boundary—a frontier. Significant is the fact that when it is mentioned in the Bible it is generally accompanied by some word meaning *over* or *across*. *Over* Jordan, *beyond* the stream which because of its fever-breeding, lion-populated jungles and its strange sea, signified death, destruction, calamity, rather than life. *Beyond* the Jordan, then, lay the Promised Land, flowing with milk and honey.

East of the Jordan valley, the Eastern Range rises similarly to the Central Range on the west side. The plateaus of Moab and Gilead seem higher than the others, for whereas the Central Range rises gradually from a series of foothills to its exalted height, the Eastern Range rises abruptly from the extremely low river-valley.

The Eastern Range is blessed with a temperate climate. Heat is always moderated by breezes which bring health and prosperity with them. The soil is fertile, sufficiently watered and very productive. It is a region where agriculture and grazing are followed, and natural conditions are favorable to both occupations. In spite of these advantages, the region lies exposed to the south and east. Desert tribes make life and fortune uncertain for the inhabitants. Even today, when conditions have been somewhat improved, those who grow crops in this region must pay tribute to wandering tribes who demand it, or lose their all. How much more precarious must life have been in those days when even among the most enlightened nations the hand of the plunderer was scarcely restrained at all. The Hebrew tribes which settled this plateau were in the beginning as strong as those that located farther east, but they could not maintain their individuality against the conditions that beset them. Sooner or later, they drifted with the restless hordes and lost their identity.

One more natural division remains to be considered—the Plain of Esdraelon. Triangular in shape, one point lies north of Mt. Carmel, while the two long lines extend south-easterly, and meet the third near the river Jordan. It was this famous plain that gave access to the Central Range from the west— from the Coast Plain, approach to Samaria was not difficult by this means.

The region is rather made up of a series of plains, broken by scattered mountains, yet permitting free passage from the sea to the river Jordan. An ancient route lay along this way. It has been called the key to Palestine, and over it came the enemies of Israel. Especially interesting is the following description, with the added explanation of a bit of ancient Hebrew poetry characterizing the region:

" As you stand upon that last headland of Gilboa, 200 feet above the plain, the great triangle is spread before you. Along the north of it the steep brown wall of the Galilean hills, about 1000 feet high, runs almost due west, till it breaks out and down to the feet of Carmel, in the forest slopes just high enough to hide the Plain of Acre and sea. But over and past these slopes Carmel's steady ridge, deepening in blue the while, carries the eye out to its dark promontory above the Mediterranean. From this end of Carmel the lower Samarian hills, green with bush and dotted by white villages, run southeast to the main Samarian range, and on their edge, due south, seven miles across the bay, Jenin stands out with its minarets and palms. But the rest of the plain is before you—a great expanse of loam, red and black, which in a more peaceful land would be one sea of waving wheat with island villages; but here is what its modern name implies, a free, wild prairie, upon which but one or two hamlets have ventured forth from the cover of the hills and a timid and tardy cultivation is only now seeking to overtake the waste of coarse grass and the thistly herbs that camels love. There is no water visible. The Kishon itself flows in a muddy trench, unseen five yards away. But here and there a clump of trees shows where a deep well is worked to keep a little orchard green through summer. The roads have no limit to their breadth, but sprawl, as if at most seasons one caravan could not follow for mud on the path of another. But these details sink in a great sense of space, and of a level made almost absolute by the rise of hills on every side of it. It is a vast inland basin, and from it there breaks just at your feet, between Jezreel and Shunem, the valley Jordanwards,—breaks as visibly as river from lake, with a slope and almost the look of a current upon it. From Jezreel you can appreciate everything in the literature and in the history of Esdraelon.

"To begin with, you can enjoy that happiest sketch of a landscape and its history that was ever drawn in half a dozen lines, *Issachar*—to which the most of Esdraelon fell—

"Issachar is a large-limbed ass,
Stretching himself between the sheepfolds:
For he saw a resting-place that it was good,
And the land that it was pleasant.'

"Such exactly is Esdraelon—a land relaxed and sprawling up among the hills to north, south and east, as you will see a loosened ass roll and stretch his limbs any day in the sunshine of a Syrian village yard. To the highlander looking down upon it, Esdraelon is room to stretch in and lie happy. Yet the figure of the ass goes further—the room must be paid for—

'So he bowed his shoulder to bear
And became a servant under task-work.'

"The inheritors of this plain never enjoyed the highland independent of Manasseh or Naphtali. Open to east and west, Esdraelon was at distant intervals the war-path or battle-field of great empires. . . . Even when there has been no invasion to fear, Esdraelon has still suffered: when she has not been the camp of the foreigner she has served as the estate of her neighbors."[4]

[4] George Adam Smith: Historical Geography of the Holy Land, 381.

Climate and Productivity of Palestine.

As we might expect in a land possessing such a varied topography, nearly every known climate is represented in Palestine. Along the seashore the salt breezes of ocean blow; the climate of the Coast Plain is mild and pleasant, and favorable to the growth of gardens and orchards; within the Central Range itself several varieties of climate prevail, and in the low valley of the Jordan and in the region of the Dead Sea, the heat of the tropics obtains. The plateaus of the Eastern Range are visited by health-giving breezes, which moderate the atmosphere. Farther east and south extends the desert, with its parched sands and sultry air, yet in the very sight of these desert wastes rise snowy mountain peaks.

"There are palms in Jericho and pine forests in Lebanon. In the Ghor, in summer, you are under a temperature of more than 100 degrees Fahrenheit, and yet you see glistening the snow-fields of Hermon. All the intermediate steps between these extremes the eye can see at one sweep from Carmel— the sands and palms of the coast; the wheat-fields of Esdraelon, the oaks and sycamores of Galilee; the pines, the peaks, the snows of Anti-Lebanon. How closely these differences lie to each other! Take a section of the country across Judaea. With its palms and shadoofs the Philistine Plain might be a part of the Egyptian Delta; but on the hills of the Shephelah which overlook it, you are in the scenery of Southern Europe; the Judaean moors which overlook them are like the barer uplands of Central Germany; the shepherds wear sheepskin cloaks and live under stone roofs—sometimes the snow lies deep; a few miles farther east and you are down on the desert among the Bedouin, with their tents of hair and their cotton clothing; a few miles farther still, and you drop to torrid heat in the Jordan Valley; a few miles beyond that and you rise to the plateau of the Belka, where the Arabs say 'the cold is always at home.' Yet from Philistia to the Belka is scarcely seventy miles."[5]

The year is divided into a wet and a dry season. The rains begin the last of October and are over by the last of March. These are called the "early" rains in the Old Testa-

[5] George Adam Smith: Historical Geography of the Holy Land, 56.

ment. Showers which fall in the late spring are called the "latter" rains. From May until October the summer is dry. The vegetation is sustained in many places by the heavy dews. Water is not abundant and the rain-water which falls during the winter months is stored in wells and cisterns for use in the dry months.

Flowers of many varieties are found through the land and range from those common to tropical and desert lands to those native to high altitudes. As in Egypt the fertile land borders upon the shifting desert sands, so in Palestine the strong contrasts between the productive and waste lands is the more marked because of their proximity.

Palestine is not a land of heavy forests. To be sure, ages upon ages of habitation have divested many slopes of native timber, but evidences go to show that at no time since records began has the country been heavily forested. Today the woodlands are frequently mere undergrowth. Orchards are plentiful. The olive is most widely cultivated; apricots, figs, oranges, almond and walnut trees are grown, and the vine is grown extensively. Grain fields wave on the plains, in the valleys and lowlands, wheat, barley and millet being most abundant. Vegetables of many varieties are commonly raised. Beans, tomatoes, onions and melons are produced in large quantities. Grass is grown only on small areas, pasturage being for the most part found on the public land. During the summer months pasturage exists only near the large fountains or the carefully built cisterns. These are jealously guarded by their owners. In earlier times and now, to some extent, wells and pools are provided to preserve water falling during the winter, and these are for the use of all who come to them with their flocks and herds.

We find no such condition here as in Egypt, where crops grow abundantly if the seeds be but once dropped into the ground. On the contrary, while grains, fruits and garden produce are generally grown, care and constant industry are required to bring forth good yields. Certain portions of the country are adapted to the art of husbandry, while others have always been better suited to cattle and sheep raising. So much of the tablelands is rocky and stony and unsuited for cultivation that no arable spots are allowed to go untended.

CHAPTER VI.

Effects of Geographical Conditions Upon the Hebrews.

Certain natural effects of the physical conditions upon the people in Palestine have been apparent as we traced the general land formation. It is evident that in an age when easy communication was essential to union, there could be no political unity among a people dwelling in a country so divided by mountains, plains, and valleys. Again, we would expect tribes settling the plateaus of the Central Range to develop differently from those peopling the fertile plain of Sharon. Indeed, within this range itself we have found that the inhabitants of austere Judaea led a life unlike that of more accessible Samaria. Other effects of natural conditions upon the Hebrews are evident, as we shall see.

The very climate of Palestine seems to have had its influence in molding the religious thought of Israel. "The climate of Palestine is regular enough to provoke men to methodical labour for its fruits, but the regularity is often interrupted. The early rains or the latter rains fail, drought comes occasionally for two years in succession, and that means famine and pestilence. There are too, the visitations of the locust, which are said to be bad every fifth or sixth year, and there are earthquakes, also periodical in Syria. Thus a purely mechanical conception of nature as something certain and inevitable, whose processes are more or less under man's control, is impossible; and the imagination is roused to feel the presence of a will behind nature, in face of whose interruptions of the fruitfulness or stability of the land man is absolutely helpless. To such a climate, then, is partly due Israel's doctrine of Providence."[1] In Deuteronomy the contrast between Egypt, the land just left, and Palestine, to which Israel was then passing, is drawn, and the price of prosperity definitely given.

" But the land, whither thou goest in to possess it, is not as the land of Egypt, from whence ye came out, where thou

[1] Smith: Historical Geography of Holy Land, 73.

sowedst thy seed, and wateredst it with thy foot, as a garden of herbs: but the land, whither ye go to possess it, is a land of hills and valleys, and drinketh water of the rain of heaven. A land which Jehovah thy God careth for: the eyes of Jehovah thy God are always upon it, from the beginning of the year even unto the end of the year.

"And it shall come to pass, if ye shall harken diligently unto my commandments which I command you this day, to love Jehovah your God, and to serve him with all your heart and with all your soul, that I will give you the rain of your land in his due season, the first rain and the latter rain, that thou mayest gather in thy corn, and thy wine, and thine oil. And I will send grass in thy fields for thy cattle, that thou mayst eat and be full. Take heed to yourselves, that your heart be not deceived, and ye turn aside, and serve other gods, and worship them; and *then* Jehovah's wrath be kindled against you and he shut up the heaven, that the land yield not her fruit; and lest ye perish quickly from off the good land which Jehovah giveth you." [2]

The productivity of the soil had two important results in the development of the Hebrews. The first affected the very nature of their being, for it changed them from desert nomads into herders and small farmers. In place of the tent, they adopted the house, the *fixed* habitation. Instead of wandering from pasture to pasture with their cattle and families, as they had done for generation upon generation before their sojourn in Egypt, they cultivated the land and found it overflowing with "milk and honey." In the Song of Moses this great transformation is pictured with vividness and beauty:

"Remember the days of old,
   Consider the years of generation on generation.
  Ask thy father and he will show thee,
   Thine elders and they will tell thee.
  When the highest gave nations their heritage,
   When he sundered the children of men.
  He set the border of the tribes,
   By the number of the children of Israel.
  For the portion of Jehovah is his people,

---

[2] Deuteronomy 11, 10.

Jacob the measure of his heritage.
He found him in a land of the desert,
   In a waste, in a howling wilderness.
He encompassed him, He distinguished him,
   He watched him as the apple of His eye.
As an eagle stirreth his nest,
   Fluttereth over his young,
Spreadeth abroad his wings, taketh them,
   Beareth them up on his pinions,
Jehovah alone led him
   And no strange god was with him.
He made him to ride on the Land's high places,
   And to eat of the growth of the field.
He gave him to suck honey from the cliff,
   And oil from the flinty rock.
Cream of kine and milk of sheep,
   With lambs' fat and rams'
Breed of Bashan and he-goats,
   With fat of the kidneys of wheat;
And the blood of the grape thou drankest in foam!"

While settlement in Palestine produced an advancement in civilization, it brought at the same time a lower plane of religious life and thought. With sudden plenty and no longer enforced abstinence of the desert, came a certain confusion and riot. The desert tends to inspire monotheistic ideas and conceptions; lands of varied aspect, such as Greece or Palestine, inspire polytheistic conceptions—divided power rather than unity.

"The creed of the desert nomad is simple and austere—for nature about him is monotonous, silent, and illiberal. But Syria is a land of lavish gifts and oracles—where woods are full of mysterious speech, and rivers burst suddenly from the ground, where the freedom of nature excites, and seems to sanction, the passions of the human body, where food is rich, and men drink wine. The spirit and the senses are equally taken by surprise. *No one can tell how many voices a tree has who has not come up to it from the silence of the great desert.*

"But with the awe comes the sense of indulgence, and

the starved instincts of the body break riotously forth. . . .
All this is said to have happened to Israel from almost their
first encampment in Canaan."

> "They moved him to jealousy with strange gods,
>   With abominations provoked him to anger.
> They sacrificed to monsters undivine,
>   Gods they had known not,
> New things, lately come in,
>   Their fathers never had them in awe."

One more effect of physical conditions may be noted here, leaving the rest to appear in connection with Israel's story—namely, the effect of the picturesqueness of the land upon these former desert nomads. For one who has made himself familiar with the beautiful places of earth, Palestine has its charm, but to people journeying thither from the wastes of desert, the land possesses matchless beauty. Before calling attention to the reflection of scenery to be found in ancient Hebrew writings, let us read the description of certain aspects of the country, as given by one who knows every foot of the land and has watched it in and out of season.

"There is the coast-line from the headland of Carmel—northwards the Gulf of Haifa, with its yellow sands and palms,   southwards Sharon with her scattered forest, her coast of sand and grass: westwards the green sea and the wonderful shadows of the clouds upon it—grey when you look at them with your face to the sun, but, with the sun behind you, purple, and more like Homer's 'wine-colored' water than anything I have seen on the Mediterranean. There is the *excellency of Carmel* itself: wheat-fields climbing from Esdraelon to the first bare rocks, then thick bush and scrub, young ilex, wild olives and pines, with undergrowth of large purple thistles, mallows with blossoms like pelargoniums, stocks of hollyhocks, golden broom, honeysuckle, and convolvulus—then, between the shoulders of the mountain, olive-groves, their dull green mass banked by the lighter forest trees, and on the flanks the broad lawns, where in the shadow of great oaks you look far out to sea. There is the Lake of Galilee as you see it from Gadara, with the hills of Naphtali above it, and Hermon filling all the north. There is the prospective of the Jordan Valley as you look up from over Jericho, between the bare ranges of Gilead and Ephraim, with the winding ribbon of the river's jungle, and the top of Hermon like a white cloud in the infinite distance. There is the forest of Gilead, where you ride, two thousand feet high, under the boughs of great trees creaking and rustling in the wind, with all Western Palestine before you. There is the moonlight view out of the bush on the northern flank of Tabor, the leap of the sun over the edge of Bashan, summer morning in the Shephelah, and sunset over the Mediterranean, when you see it from the gateway of the ruins on Samaria down the glistening Vale of Barley. Even in the barest provinces you get many a little picture that lives with you for life—a chocolate-coloured bank with red poppies against the green of the prickly pear hedge above it, and a yellow lizard darting across; a river-bed of pink oleanders flush with the plain; a gorge in Judaea, where you look up between limestone walls picked out with tufts of grass and black-and-tan goats cropping at them, the deep blue sky over all, and, on the edge of the only shadow, a well, a trough, and a solitary herdsman.

"And then there are those prospects in which no other country can match Palestine, for no other has a valley like the Ghor, or a desert like that which falls from Judaea to the Dead Sea. There is the view from the Mount of Olives, down twenty miles of desert hill-tops to the deep blue waters, with the wall of Moab glowing on the further side like burnished copper, and staining the blue sea red with its light. There is the view of the Dead Sea through the hazy afternoon, when across the yellow foreground of Jeshimon the white Lisan rises like a pack of Greenland ice from the blue waters, and beyond it the Moab range, misty, silent and weird. There are the precipices of Masada and Engedi sheer from the salt coast. And, above all, there is the view from Engedi under the full moon, when the sea is bridged with gold, and the eastern mountains are black with a border of opal."[3]

The literature of no other people has more vividly reflected a landscape than has that of the ancient Hebrews. Without some understanding of Palestine, one would fail to appreciate much that is beautiful in Hebrew poetry. While we shall

[3] Smith: Historical Geography, 94.

touch upon this again in the consideration of Hebrew literature, some examples will sufficiently illustrate this point. Take, for example, a portion of the Hundred and Fourth Psalm:

> He sendeth forth springs into the valleys;
> They run among the mountains:
> They give drink to every beast of the field;
> The wild asses quench their thirst.
> By them the fowl of the heaven have their habitation,
> They sing around the branches.
> He watereth the mountains from his chambers:
> The earth is satisfied with the fruits of thy work.
> He causeth the grass to grow for the cattle,
> And herb for the service of man:
> That he may bring forth food out of the earth,
> And wine that maketh glad the heart of man,
> And oil to make his face to shine,
> And bread that strengtheneth man's heart.
> The trees of Jehovah are satisfied;
> The cedars of Lebanon, which he hath planted;
> Where the birds make their nests:
> As for the stork, the fir trees are her house;
> The high mountains are for the wild goats;
> The rocks are a refuge for the conies.
>
> O Jehovah, how manifold are thy works!
> In wisdom hast thou made them all:
> The earth is full of thy riches.
> Yonder is the sea, great and wide,
> Wherein are things creeping innumerable,
> Both small and great beasts.
> There go the ships;
> There is leviathan, whom thou hast formed to take his pastime therein.
> These wait all upon thee,
> That thou mayest give them their meat in due season.

This poem reflects general characteristics of the land. The next is a pastoral poem which could have been written only in Judaea. Its figures are pastoral throughout, and lack of acquaintance with the land wherein it was produced often causes one to miss the successive pictures it portrays. Reference is made to the Twenty-third Psalm, wherein the comparison of the shepherd with his sheep is maintained.

"The Lord is my shepherd,
I shall not want."

Only a good faithful shepherd could lead his sheep in Judaea so that at no time would they want for care or food.

"He maketh me to lie down in green pastures:"

Pasturage was often scanty, and to lie always in *green* pastures was the greatest boon that could befall the sheep.

"He leadeth me beside the still waters."

Not lakes, but cisterns or pools, constructed to hold the rains of winter for use in the dry months of summer. Unless these were carefully sought out in each new pasture, the sheep would suffer from thirst.

"Yea, though I walk through the valley of the shadow of death,
I will fear no evil;
For thou art with me:
Thy rod and thy staff they comfort me."

When one pasture was exhausted, it was necessary to journey to another. Danger lurked on every side. Did the sheep wander away, they were sure to be attacked by fierce animals, or stolen by other herders. The shepherd led the way amid all dangers, and his rod and staff gave assurance to the sheep some distance from him.

"Thou preparest a table before me
In the presence of mine enemies:
Thou anointest my head with oil;
My cup runneth over."

The figure is not changed here, as some have supposed, and a banquet introduced. Quite on the contrary. In that land grew many poisonous herbs, likely to be unnoticed by the sheep. The shepherd watched to see that his flock found food free from these enemies. Then at last, when the night fell, and the flock was gathered into the fold, the shepherd stood by the door with a cup of oil in his hand ready to pour on the heads of weary, exhausted lambs, thus to refresh and revive them. Only a little could be spared for each one. To have a cup filled to overflowing was a wonderful blessing. So is the figure carried on to the end of the beautiful song, and only goodness and mercy could possibly attend one so protected.

CHAPTER VII.

Sources of Hebrew History.

We may divide the sources of early Hebrew history into (1) Hebrew sources, and (2) sources supplied by contemporaneous nations and by archæology. The Hebrew sources are principally three: the historical books of the Old Testament, the Talmud, the writings of Josephus. The sources derived elsewhere are records and inscriptions throwing light upon the events of this ancient nation as chronicled by the Egyptians, Babylonians, and Assyrians, and statements of Greek travellers and writers bearing upon their later development. Moreover, in late years the spade of the excavator has unearthed ruins and remains which have added materially to previous knowledge of the subject and have established beyond any doubt facts previously unsettled.

Before taking up a discussion of the historical books of the Old Testament—the first of the Hebrew sources,—it is necessary that we consider the compilation of the Bible, and understand how the many books which compose it were made up, and gathered into the one volume with which we are now familiar.

Only in late years have people generally been ready to approach the study of the Bible in the spirit of modern investigation long applied to other fields of learning. While the reasons for this reluctance may not be at once apparent, they are not difficult to discover.

During the Middle Ages religious teaching was guarded and kept alive by monks in the monasteries of Europe. Only with them was learning of any sort fostered and saved from extinction during the period known as the Dark Ages. The books which these monks studied, and the records and productions they committed to paper or parchment, were invariably written in Latin—a tongue unknown to the people at large. Since the Bible existed only in Latin, Hebrew or Greek, it was a sealed book to the masses, who knew it only through brief portions read and explained to them by the priests.

After a time, translations were made, first of portions only, then the entire work was rendered in modern languages. Still it was not considered fitting to allow its contents to be generally known. Copies were chained to pulpits in the cathedrals and were opened by the priest alone. Those who might have been able to procure the costly copies were not permitted to do so. In the story of England we shall find that only a few centuries ago, to possess a Bible and read it aloud in the family was made an offense and was punishable if discovered. Thus a mystery attached to the Scriptures, instilled into the masses by those who guarded the ancient volume. The awe and reverence so aroused, clung to the Bible generations after its contents had become familiar to the Christian world. One scholar calls the Bible "literature smothered in reverence."

Again, no other event can be cited throughout history which has had so great an effect upon the world as had the ministry of Christ, recorded at length in the New Testament. The doctrines he taught have been held sacred by his followers in all subsequent ages.

The prophetic literature of the Old Testament had foretold the coming of some one who should restore Israel, and the ancient Hebrew nation looked with expectancy to the birth of one who should raise their kingdom to the rank of powerful nations of the earth. By some, Christ was identified with the one whose coming the prophets had proclaimed, and thus a continuity was found throughout the Bible—from the epic of creation in the beginning, to the birth and teaching of Christ, and the added records of his apostles. For many years the entire work was spoken of as the "Word of God," and equal reverence given the sixty-four books which compose it. A verse would be quoted from one chapter with no regard to its context quite as freely as from another. Sentences would be extracted from primitive Hebrew law and put side by side with portions of Christ's Sermon on the Mount, or Paul's letters to mission churches. Finally scholars began to exclaim against such crude and literal interpretation of the Scriptures. "Here," they exclaimed, "is a book embodying legends current among a Semitic people twenty-five hundred years before the birth of Christ; there are prayers and hymns of praise composed at varying periods and finally brought together into one collection; and once again, here is a series of letters written by early preachers of the gospel to their outlying churches, and you are culling a stanza here, a verse there, and a sentence in a third place, as though they were of equal value and had been written under similar circumstances!" Far from welcoming new light upon the subject of deep importance, a cry of indignation arose, from the clergy as well as laymen. It was argued that a scientific study of the Bible would be sure to detract from the force and influence of its teachings, and was in itself irreverent. But the spark of Promethean fire was not destined to go out—the spirit of investigation was abroad. The more scholars searched and studied, the more they were persuaded that a scientific exposition of the Bible would enhance rather than lessen its value. They saw that changing ideas in the book itself existed and had been passed over by those who did not understand them and who thought it their duty to blindly accept what they did not comprehend; while a broader conception was destined to lead to the establishment of profound religious truths, far more satisfying than the earlier blind belief.

At last the facts these scholars derived, the methods they applied, the conclusions they reached, largely overcame prejudices of long standing, and it may safely be said that to-day only those people oppose a scientific study of the Bible who are themselves unfamiliar with scientific study in other fields of knowledge.

With this explanation, the results of careful investigation of the Old Testament will henceforth be cited and used freely with no further comment, since by such study alone can we come into a true understanding of a wonderful literature and a remarkable people.

The word *Bible* means *books,* or *a library.* A considerable portion of Hebrew literature has herein been preserved to us. Originally these productions were written in the ancient Hebrew tongue, and had no connection with one another save that they treated of the same people at different stages of their development, and further, treated in some form —most of them, at least—of their faith. When these writings were first collected and bound together, more books were included than at present. Since then the collection has been edited and re-edited. Compilers have introduced notes in the text and assigned authorship of certain writings to those who were themselves mere compilers. Later still, it became customary to write books in verses; into this form the contents of the Scriptures were thrown. Instead of a narrative being given at length it was divided into verses, as in our Bibles at present used. Instead of a poem being reproduced in its original form, or a drama being divided by the speeches of its participants, both were cast into verses and numbered. Thus prose and poetry came to have the same appearance.

"More than fifty books, the production of a large number of different authors representing periods of time extending over many centuries, are all comprehended between the covers of a single volume. There is no greater monument of the power of printing to diffuse thought than this fact, that the whole classic literature of one of the world's greatest peoples can be carried about in the hand or pocket.

"But there is another side to the matter. A high price has been paid for this feat of manufacturing a portable literature: no less a price than the effacement from the books of the Bible of their whole literary structure. Where the literature is dramatic there are no names of speakers nor divisions of speeches; there are no titles to essays or poems, nor anything to mark where one poem or discourse ends and another begins. It is as if the whole were printed 'solid,' like a newspaper without newspaper headings. The most familiar English literature treated in this fashion would lose a great part of its literary interest; the writings of the Hebrews suffer still more through our unfamiliarity with many of the literary forms in which they were cast. Even this statement does not fully represent the injury done to this literature of the Bible by the traditional shape in which it is presented to us. Between the Biblical writers and our own times have intervened ages in which all interest in literary beauty was lost, and philosophic activity took the form of protracted discussions of brief sayings or 'texts.' Accordingly this solidified matter of Hebrew literature has been divided up into single sentences or 'verses,' numbered mechanically one, two, three, etc., and thus the original literary form has been further obscured. It is not surprising that to most readers the Bible has become, not a literature, but simply a store-house of pious 'texts.'"[1]

We call certain books of the Old Testament *historical,* but this does not mean, in this case, that they were written with the sole object of chronicling the events of Hebrew progress. They were at the same time books of devotion, showing God's dealing with them, His chosen people.

Before the ninth or eighth century B. C., records of Israel's past existed only in snatches of song and in traditions handed down by word of mouth from one generation to another. The Song of Deborah, preserved in the Book of Judges, belongs to a remote period; the legends of creation, common to the Semitic race, as related in Genesis were current from time immemorial. In the eighth century before Christ an effort was made in the " Schools of the Prophets " to compile the history of Israel, but the leading motive was rather to illustrate God's favor to them in the past by citing instances familiar to them all, and to prove that divine protection had been withdrawn from them when they had gone astray—as exemplified in their past, rather than to leave for future ages records of their heroic deeds and victories and civil administration. The result was that the historical writings prepared were based on ancient traditions, to be sure, but reflected the religious beliefs and the normal ideas of the age in which they were produced.

The historical books include Genesis, Exodus, Leviticus, Numbers, Joshua, Judges, I. and II. Samuel, I. and II. Kings, Chronicles, Ezra, and Nehemiah. Other books, such as Isaiah, for example, include historical matter.

" The first portion of the history, the biblical *Genesis,* gives us what that word implies—the Gradual Formation of the Chosen Nation. The next section on the Exodus (the biblical *Exodus, Leviticus, Numbers*), the Emigration of the Chosen People to the Land of Promise; with migration goes the gradual evolution into an organized nation, and the massing at this point of legal documents makes the Constitutional History of Israel. Under the name of The Judges (the biblical *Joshua, Judges,* part of *Samuel*) we next distinguish the Grand Transition: a people starting with theocracy, the government

---

[1] Biblical Masterpieces, Moulton, Intro.

of an invisible God, comes to accept the rule of visible kings copied from nations around. But precisely at the time these kings begin there is established a regular order of 'prophets,' or interpreters for God, representing the old idea of theocracy: the fourth period of the history may be named as The Kings and The Prophets, a regular Government of Kings tempered by an Opposition of Prophets. Then comes the Exile: the witnessing of Israel for Jehovah has to be carried on in the land of strangers. There return from exile, not the whole people, but only those who are devoted to the service of God; not the Hebrew Nation, but the Jewish Church: and the final section is thus the Ecclesiastical History of *The Chronicles.* The spirit of the history is throughout made emphatic by story, or at times by fable or song. But in addition to the formal historic books we have to note two others:

"*Deuteronomy* gives us the Orations and Songs of Moses, emphasizing the crisis of the leader's Farewell to Israel. And in Isaiah we find a certain dramatic work, which, in connection with the deliverance from exile, reads a meaning into events such as strikes a unity through the whole career of the chosen people: it is an Epilogue to the History of Israel."

The *Talmud* has been mentioned as a second source of Hebrew history. The word itself means literally "learning," or "teaching." It is the name given a collection of Hebrew writings which were written primarily to explain and exemplify Jewish law. Two Talmuds were prepared, one in Babylon—known as the Babylonian Talmud, or the Talmud of the Eastern land; the other written in Jerusalem, known as the Talmud of the Western land. They were kept in the temples and added to and continued by rabbis through the first five centuries after the Christian era. The interest in them for the historian today centers around the traditions and legends introduced, these having been current among the Hebrews generations earlier. The Talmud is rich in folklore, and so possesses relative value from a historical standpoint.

Third among Hebrew sources we have noted the Writings of Josephus. Josephus was a Jewish priest who lived in the first century after Christ. Not only was he himself a priest but for twenty-four generations before him his forefathers had presided in the temple. During his life, Palestine was held by the Romans, and he wrote the "Antiquities of the Jews," and a history of the Jewish War, to acquaint the people of his day with the story of his people. He claims to have found his material in the sacred books of the temple and frequently explains at length events merely mentioned in the Old Testament. His writings have been valued both in early and recent times.

Among the sources elsewhere obtained, the records of contemporaneous nations are of first importance. The oppression of the Israelites under the Egyptian pharaoh, for example, is believed to find confirmation in scenes and inscriptions recently discovered in the valley of the Nile. In our study of Assyrian conquest, we have noted tribute lists and memorials celebrating victories over the Hebrew kingdoms, recovered among other ruins in Mesopotamia. The king of Babylonia finally left Jerusalem, the beautiful city of Palestine, demolished and well nigh abandoned. Thousands of her noblest citizens were taken captives to Babylon. This incident was naturally chronicled in Babylonian annals. Similar instances might be cited, but these serve to show ways in which material for Hebrew history may be gleaned from the records of nations that flourished by her side.

Lastly we may note the results of archæological research as supplying material for the reconstruction of Israel's past. In 1883 M. Naville opened a mound wherein was discovered a portion of what is supposed to have been Pithom—one of the two "store-cities," built by the Children of Israel while in bondage. The bricks still remaining verified the story as it has come down to us from the Hebrews themselves, in the Book of Exodus. The lower rows of bricks were mixed with straw; those laid in later were kneaded with stubble, and those last placed were formed simply of sun-dried mud.

Explorations have been carried on recently in Jerusalem and elsewhere in Palestine, and some important discoveries have already been made.

In spite of these various means, we have scanty material at best for the reconstruction of Hebrew history. The Hebrews were unhistorical and did not appreciate, nor apparently care to preserve, their secular history. Records of priceless value were allowed to perish and we have today only ex-

HARBOR OF JAFFA.

tracts from them, or some simple phrase concerning them. It was the portion of Israel to tell the world of her religion and to leave to others the extolling of earthly successes and failures. The comments of alien nations are unsatisfactory, for their attitude was generally hostile, or at least, unsympathetic. Nevertheless, while questions remain unanswered and certain points disputed by authorities, we are able to follow with some degree of certainty the formation of the Hebrew nation and its political development.

HIGH PRIEST.

CHAPTER VIII.

THE HEBREWS PRIOR TO THEIR OCCUPATION OF CANAAN.

Regarding the earliest period of Israel's existence there has been wide difference of opinion. Until recently there have been many who have accepted literally the early books of the Old Testament, composed hundreds of years after the events recorded took place, and the product of several writers, all of whom were filled with a desire to show the favor of God exemplified in every detail of Hebrew progress. If one takes the position that the history of the Hebrews is different from that of every other people in the world's history, if it be held that their development cannot be traced as the unfolding of all other peoples has been traced, then there is nothing more to be said—one can merely chronicle the wonders and marvel. If, on the other hand, one accepts the absolutely established historical fact that these people began as other nations began, in a very crude and primitive state, and came slowly into enlightenment as did nations contemporaneous with them, then the progress of the early Hebrews can be similarly followed. The conclusions which seem to be best substantiated are the ones we shall consider, noting at the same time that among authorities and scholars many differences of opinion still exist.

It is generally conceded that about 1500 B. C. a company of Semitics, originally inhabiting Arabia, but for some years settlers in Mesopotamia, set out from the Euphrates valley—probably from Ur—and journeyed westward. The name Abraham is the one tradition gives as the leader of this company, which after the fashion of nomads, sought new pastures in districts less crowded than those of Chaldea. Among those who attached themselves to this migration appear to have been the ancestors of the tribes later known as the Moabites, Ammonites and Edomites. By slow stages this band of emigrants passed into Syria and reached at length the country we know as Palestine. At that time it was known as Canaan, and was the home of Semitics more or less closely related to the people we know as Phœnicians. The Canaanites and Phœnicians are often identified. As a matter of fact, the Canaanites were Phœnicians who occupied the country districts and, save for a common heritage, had little in common with those merchantmen who filled the great sea-ports of Phœnicia.

The Moabites and Ammonites immediately settled the most fertile places in the plateaus of the Eastern Range, and continued the sheep-raising and cattle grazing to which they had long been accustomed. The Edomites also found homes for themselves. The few followers of Abraham appear to have continued their life as tent-dwellers in the southern part of Canaan.

There is no reason to doubt the existence of this ancient hero of the Jewish people, whose name is preserved in the two forms of Abram and Abraham. It was natural that various stories from later periods should be attached to his name, but in himself and his fellow wanderers we have the beginnings of the Hebrews. The story of their wanderings along the Euphrates and thence on to Palestine is typical of the manner in which nomadic bands skirted the borders of Babylonian culture to make settlements of their own.

In the course of a few generations this Abrahamic settlement in Palestine became several tribes, named after successive leaders, all represented in Genesis as immediate descendants of Abraham. Later tradition of these early days condensed the time and the characters to the life of a single family. Thus the stories surrounding the lives of the patriarchal heroes Abraham, Isaac and Jacob are the visualization of the characteristics of the heroic age of the Hebrews.

The descendants of the tribes represented by these names finally journeyed further south, settling in a fertile district northeast of the delta of the Nile and known by the name of Goshen. Famine was responsible for this migration and the closer alliance of the tribes under the general term of "the children of Israel."

When these Israelites first came into Egypt, a great Semitic upheaval had taken place in the ancient world, and there seem to be reasons for thinking that the welcome given them was due to the fact that a Semitic pharaoh ruled in

[1] History of the People of Israel; Cornill, 30.

Egypt. In any event, they lived peaceably for two or three generations—how much longer we do not know—when the aspect of matters changed. The native rulers were restored and because Egypt was having difficulty with tribes in Western Asia, foreigners within her immediate borders were looked upon with suspicion. A large number of laborers were needed to carry on gigantic building projects, and the Israelites were suddenly impressed as public slaves, and set to work under armed guards.

It was against all nature that desert nomads, accustomed to the freedom of the wide world, would long endure this servitude. The instincts of their ancestors would live on for many generations, although temporarily overpowered. After being ground down by the heel of the oppressor for a considerable number of years, they were at length incited by Moses to depart for the land still known to them by stories handed down from father to son—the land of Canaan.

Moses, by birth a Hebrew, had been educated in the family of an Egyptian, but became an outlaw upon killing an Egyptian while defending one of his own kinsmen. Escaping to the land of the Midianites, he had drunk in the air of freedom and the instincts of his forefathers were stimulated into activity. Learning from his priest father-in-law in Midian he accepted Jahweh as his God. He grieved over the condition to which his people had fallen, and brooding over it, experienced a divine commission to restore them to freedom. Rallying them in the name of Jahweh, he led them out of the land of bondage. According to the Hebrew account, Egypt was at that particular time stricken by plagues, and the people, naturally superstitious, attributed their afflictions to the foreigners within their land. So incensed against them did they become that the ruler, in a moment of weakness, consented to their exodus. No sooner had they departed, however, than he bethought him of the laborers he had lost, and dispatched the flower of his cavalry to compel their return.

A wind, blowing fiercely, made a fording of the Sea possible for the Israelites, but the cavalry, sent in pursuit, was engulfed and lost. This incident was seized upon as a mark of divine favor by these disheartened people, who saw direct intervention of Jahweh in their behalf. Thus the power of a supreme God was impressed upon their minds as long years of religious instruction could never have impressed it.

For forty years the Children of Israel wandered in the desert, loitering here and there, finding their way between hostile tribes. During these years the figure of Moses stands forth with unfailing strength and courage. The people he had led thither were mere children, rendered dependent and unsteadfast by their long period of servitude. When difficulties beset them, they did not hestiate to turn upon their deliverer and reproach him, and to wish often to return to the land they had recently left, where food was always forthcoming, even though at the expense of liberty and self-respect. But Moses, with staunch heart and great patience, slowly organized them into a religious body, finding unity for them in the one God, Jahweh. Meanwhile a new generation was growing up among them; sons and daughters who were born in the air of freedom, assimilated new ideas more readily, were more steadfast in their purpose, and grew into greater self-reliance than their fathers knew. With this new spirit manifest, we see the possibilities of a dawning nation, and a more promising future.

Not long before the exodus, incoming Philistines pressed the Canaanites farther east, and they in turn displaced the Moabites and Ammonites from their fertile homes in the Eastern Range. These Semitics remembered their old allies, now in the desert, and besought them for aid. The Israelites helped them defeat the Canaanites and then appropriated the fertile places for themselves. Soon, however, increasing numbers made it necessary to seek wider room, and the tribe of Judah crossed the Jordan and settled the tableland which afterwards bore its name. This settlement was not made without great effort, for the earlier inhabitants held tenaciously to the land. The tribes of Simeon and Levi tried to do likewise, but their treachery made them victims to the revenge of the Canaanites. The Levites disappeared as a tribe, but were perpetuated as a priestly order. The Simeonites became absorbed with the tribe of Judah. Reuben and Gad remained east of the Jordan, and the remaining tribes united under Joshua and made an attack upon the central part of Canaan. Jericho fell into their hands, also Ai and Bethel. When these most exposed places fell to their portion, the inhabitants of

Gibeon, a Canaanite stronghold, grew alarmed for their own safety and craftily sought a treaty with the invaders. This becoming known among the league of Canaanite cities, banded together to drive out the Israelites, the members of the league were so incensed that they marched against the walls of Gibeon for thus deserting their common cause. The citizens of Gibeon appealed to the Hebrews for aid, and according to their treaty, Joshua led his army out to meet the forces of the besiegers.

The Hebrews were accustomed to hand-to-hand conflicts, and to the heights; the Canaanites fought wherever possible with chariots, and naturally preferred the plains. At first it seemed as though the advantage belonged to the Canaanites, for they carried the battle into the plain, and had strong cities behind them. Nevertheless, a sudden rain made the earth so soft that their chariots availed them little, and when the rain changed to hail, their ranks were thrown into confusion.

The book of Jashar, an ancient Hebrew work, has not been preserved but was apparently made up of old ballads and war songs. A fragment repeated in the book of Joshua recounts that Joshua, the famous Hebrew warrior, commanded the sun and moon to stand still until the battle ended. Some infer that he wished daylight to remain until the battle could be fought out; others hold that he wanted the darkness of the storm to continue, to further discomfit the Canaanites.

"Sun, stand thou still upon Gibeon;
  And thou, Moon, in the valley of Ajalon.
  And the sun stood still, and the moon stayed,
  Until the nation had avenged themselves of their enemies."[1]

Victory belonged to the Israelites, and the seven tribes took possession of trans-Jordan regions.

"But this does not mean that Israel was in full possession of the land: by far the best and most fertile portions of it, and especially the majority of the cities, whose strong fortifications made them impregnable to the primitive military skill of the Israelites, remained in possession of the Canaanites; it was chiefly the woody mountain chains of northern and middle Palestine that had come into the power of Israel, and the

[2] Joshua, 10. 12.

Canaanites had partly to be subdued by force and partly to be peacefully absorbed—a long and difficult task."[a]

"'Then sang Moses and the Children of Israel this song unto the Lord:

"I will sing unto the Lord, for he hath triumphed gloriously:
 The horse and his rider hath he thrown into the sea.
 The Lord is my strength and song,
  And he is become my salvation:
 This is my God, and I will praise him;
  My father's God, and I will exalt him.

(1) *Sung by Men.*

"The Lord is a man of war:
 The Lord is his name.
 Pharaoh's chariots and his host hath he cast into the sea:
  And his chosen captains are sunk in the Red Sea.
 The deeps cover them:
  They went down into the depths like a stone.

Sung by Women.

"Sing ye to the Lord, for he hath triumphed gloriously:
 The horse and his rider hath he thrown into the sea.

(2) *Men.*

"Thy right hand, O Lord, is glorious in power,
 Thy right hand, O Lord, dasheth in pieces the enemy.
 And in the greatness of thine excellency thou overthrowest
  Them that rise up against thee:
 Thou sendest forth thy wrath, it consumeth them as stubble
 And with the blast of thy nostrils the waters were piled up,
  The floods stood upright as an heap;
  The deeps were congealed in the heart of the sea.
 The enemy said, I will pursue, I will overtake, I will divide
  the spoil:
  My lust shall be satisfied upon them;
  I will draw my sword, my hand shall destroy them
 Thou didst blow with thy wind, the sea covered them:
  They sank as lead in the mighty waters.

[a] History of People of Israel, 47.

Women.

"Sing ye to the Lord, for he hath triumphed gloriously:
    The horse and his rider hath he thrown into the sea.

(3)   *Men.*

"Who is like unto thee, O Lord, among the Gods?
    Who is like thee, glorious in holiness,
    Fearful in praises, doing wonders?
Thou stretchest out thy right hand,
    The earth swallowed them.
Thou in thy mercy hast led the people which thou hast redeemed:
    Thou hast guided them in thy strength to thy holy habitation.
The peoples have heard, they tremble:
    Till thy people pass over, O Lord,
    Till the people pass over which thou hast purchased.
Thou shalt bring them in, and plant them in the mountain of thine inheritance,
    The place, O Lord, which thou hast made for thee to dwell in,
    The sanctuary, O Lord, which thy hands have established.
The Lord shall reign forever and ever.

Women.

"Sing ye to the Lord, for he hath triumphed gloriously:
    The horse and his rider hath he thrown into the sea."
               —*Modern Reader's Bible.*

CHAPTER IX.

The Era of the Judges.

As we have seen, Joshua's victory left the conquest of Canaan but begun. It so happened that the great powers were too absorbed with their own affairs to expand by conquest, so the earlier inhabitants of Palestine and the Hebrews were left to fight out their difficulties as best they might. For some generations after the entrance of the Israelites into Canaan, confusion and disorder ruled. The invaders would win the heights in a given region, while around them in the plains and valleys, flourished hostile clans, often harassing and threatening their settlements. Years of peace would settle over the land, and the two peoples—Israelites and Canaanites—would intermarry, when again the old hatred would break out anew.

The period following the death of Joshua has been called the "Era of the Judges." The simple statement of the ancient Hebrew chronicler makes clear the situation: "And there was no king in Israel; each man did that which was right in his own eyes." Our knowledge of this age is derived chiefly from the Book of Judges, which contains some of the earliest records of the Israelites. However, the material herein contained has not come down to us first hand. A prophet of later times selected such material as suited his purpose from records which were accessible to him. The writer or writers of the Book of Judges desired to inculcate religious truths—not to recount historical events. Such pictures of the life during those years which followed Hebrew occupation of Canaan as seemed best were fitted into phrases like these: "And the people of Israel did that which was evil in the sight of Jahweh, and Jahweh delivered them into the hands of their enemies." "The people of Israel cried unto Jahweh and He raised up to them a deliverer, and the land had rest." It seems to have been fortunately the case that the older material was incorporated into the phrases with little change, and from it one is able to get a very fair idea of the stage of progress to which the Hebrews had then arrived.

Thirteen *Judges* are mentioned in the Old Testament, and there were surely many more whose names were not recorded. In times of emergency, danger, attack or oppression, a clan, or several clans, one tribe or possibly two or three tribes, would voluntarily unite under some chosen chieftain, whose duties and powers were indefinite. If he were able to deliver them in their distress, they acknowledged him as their leader so long as he lived. When a similar occasion arose, it was met in a similar way. Since differences between clans, disputes between individuals, and various questions were referred to this chief for settlement, later writers named these men from this duty of referees, *Judges*. Their earliest title of "deliverer" was more expressive. The story of the several recorded judges may be read in the biblical book bearing that name. We shall consider the work of three—not necessarily the most important in Israel's history.

Matters had become most threatening in Canaan. The Canaanites had united for a final reduction of Israel and were led by Sisera. This chief was victorious and seemed about to overcome the Hebrew tribes. The very existence of Israel was in gravest danger. The highways were unsafe, for these were held by the Canaanites who were preparing for a final stand. At this juncture Deborah, an inspired prophetess, called upon Barak, a chieftain of the north, to deliver the people. Intermarriage between the Israelites and Canaanites had become so common that it was useless to attempt to rally the early tribes—early distinctions were no longer closely drawn. So Deborah called on all who worshipped Jahweh to rally in His cause. The old enthusiasm was rekindled, and the Canaanites suffered a great defeat. Their king Sisera escaped and took refuge in the tent of a peasant woman. Trusting to her hospitality, he partook of refreshment she offered him. Asking simply for water, she gave him milk. When he fell asleep for a brief rest, she drove a tent-pin through his head, thus killing him. It has been fully observed that "only in an age of tents could such a deed have been thus extolled." The Canaanites never recovered the loss of that day's defeat, and their strength was permanently broken.

The Song of Deborah, recorded in the Book of Judges, is one of the earliest writings in the Old Testament. It has recently been thrown again into its original verse form, and rings clear of an early age, echoing the spirit of a crude but vigorous race.

Deborah's Song.

Men.   For that the leaders took the lead in Israel—
Women. For that the people offered themselves willingly—
All.   Bless ye the Lord!

Prelude.

Men.   Hear, O ye kings—
Women.   Give ear, O ye princes—
Men.   I, even I, will sing unto the Lord—
Women.   I will sing praises to the Lord, the God of Israel.
All.   Lord, when thou wentest forth out of Seir,
        When thou marchedst out of the field of Edom,
     The earth trembled, the heavens also dropped,
        Yea, the clouds dropped water.
     The mountain flowed down at the presence of the Lord.
        Even yon Sinai at the presence of the Lord, the God of Israel.

I. The Desolation.

Men.   In the days of Shamgar, the son of Anath,
        In the days of Jael,
     The highways were unoccupied,
        And the travellers walked through byways;
     The rulers ceased in Israel,
        They ceased—
Women. Until that I, Deborah, arose,
        That I arose a mother in Israel.
     They chose new gods;
        Then was war in the gates:
     Was there a shield or spear seen
        Among forty thousand in Israel?
Men.   My heart is toward the governors of Israel—
Women. Ye that offered yourselves willingly among the people—
All.   Bless ye the Lord!

Men.	Tell of it, ye that ride on white asses,
	Ye that sit on rich carpets,
	And ye that walk by the way:—
Women.	Far from the noise of archers,
	In the places of drawing water:—
All.	There shall they rehearse the righteous acts of the Lord,
	Even the righteous acts of his rule in Israel.

II. The Muster.

All.	The people of the Lord went down to the gates—
Men.	Awake, awake, Deborah,
	Awake, awake, utter a song:—
Women.	Arise, Barak,
	And lead thy captivity captive, thou son of Abinoan.
All.	Then came down a remnant of the nobles,
	The people of the Lord came down for me against the Mighty.
Women.	Out of Ephraim came down they whose root is in Amalek—
Men.	After thee, Benjamin, among thy peoples —
Women.	Out of Machir came down the governors—
Men.	And out of Zubulum they that handle the marshal's staff—
Women.	And the princes of Issachar were with Deborah—
Men.	So was Issachar, so was Barak:
All.	Into the valley they rushed forth at his feet.
Men.	By the water courses of Reuben
	There were great resolves of heart.
Women.	Why satest thou among the sheepfolds,
	To hear the pipings for the flocks?
Men.	At the watercourses of Reuben
	There were great searchings of heart!
Women.	Gilead abode beyond Jordan—
Men.	And Dan, why did he remain in ships?
Women.	Ashur sat still at the haven of the sea,
	And abode by his creeks.
Men.	Zebulum was a people that jeoparded their lives unto the death,
	And Naphtali upon the high places of the field.

III. The Battle and the Rout.

Men.   The kings came and fought;
        Then fought the kings of Canaan,
    In Taanach by the waters of Megiddo:—
        They took no gain of money.

Women. They fought from heaven,
        The stars in their courses fought against Sisera.
    The river Kishon swept them away,—
        That ancient river, the river Kishon!

Men.   O my soul, march on with strength!
        Then did the horsehoofs stamp
    By reason of the prancings,
        The prancings of their strong ones.

Women. Curse ye, Meroz, said the angel of the Lord,
        Curse ye bitterly the inhabitants thereof;
    Because they came not to the help of the Lord,
        To the help of the Lord against the mighty!

IV. The Retribution.

Men.   Blessed above women shall Jael be the wife of Heber
        the Kenite,
        Blessed shall she be above women in the tent!
    He asked water, and she gave him milk;
        She brought him butter in a lordly dish.
    She put her hand to the nail,
        And her right hand to the workman's hammer;
    And with the hammer she smote Sisera.
        She smote through his head,
    Yea, she pierced and struck through his temples.
        At her feet he bowed, he fell, he lay:
        At her feet he bowed, he fell:
    When he bowed, there he fell down dead!

Women. Through the window she looked forth, and cried,
        The mother of Sisera, through the lattice,
    "Why is his chariot so long coming?
        Why tarry the wheels of his chariots?"
    Her wise ladies answered her,
        Yea, she returned answer to herself,
    "Have they not found,
        Have they not divided the spoils?

>   A damsel, two damsels to every man;
>   To Sisera a spoil of divers colors,
>   A spoil of divers colors of embroidery,
>   Of divers colors of embroidery on both sides, on
>   the necks of the spoil!"
>
> *All.* So let all thine enemies perish, O Lord:
>   But let them that love him be as the sun when he
>   goeth forth in his might!

Having overcome the Canaanites, the Israelites were not destined to long enjoy peace. Their own kinsmen, the Ammonites and Moabites looked with envy upon their good fortune in winning such desirable land and tried now to rob them of it. Notwithstanding the fact that the Israelites, Moabites and Ammonites had all a common ancestry, they were never on that account restrained from plundering one another's territories. Forced to take a definite stand against them, the Hebrews cast about for a leader. Jephthah was named. He was an outlaw, a bold border man, who belonged to the Hebrew race, and his bravery was unquestioned. When besought, he agreed to drive out the Ammonites on one condition only: that he be acknowledged chieftain after the battle. This being conceded, he led the Hebrew forces. It was in keeping with his rough, reckless nature that he should vow to sacrifice the first living thing he met upon his return were he victorious. The Ammonites were defeated and to Jephthah's utter consternation, his daughter, his only child, rushed forth to meet him. We are told that his vow was kept, and thus we know that human sacrifices were sometimes offered to Jahweh.

During the era of the Judges, the Philistines on the southwest began to expand, upon land already settled by the Israelites. They overran the Plain of Sharon, and the Hebrews who had peopled the plain were driven into the hills. This crisis brought forth Samson, one of the chiefs who essayed to stay the power of these new enemies. He was a simple child of nature—a giant in strength, a weakling in steadfast purpose. He lacked the capacity to plan a campaign and execute it. The stories of his prodigious power, his feats of physical endurance, are too well known to require repetition. They were lauded by his admirers and delighted in by the Israelites when directed against their enemies, but his blows were invariably given to avenge personal wrongs, and he left his people no farther on their way against the Philistines than he found them.

The great difficulty during this period was that there was no tendency to hold long together. "Israel had within itself the worst of enemies and a germ of destruction. This was the proud sense of independence and the strongly-developed family feeling of the nomad, which did not immediately vanish from the national character with the surrender of the nomadic fashion of life. After the united effort under Joshua had but barely laid the foundation, the people again broke up into tribes and clans, which now aimlessly sought new places of settlement, each on its own account and unmindful of its neighbors."[1]

This tendency to fall apart was the most dangerous sign of Israel's progress, and we shall see how it lasted through her history. Nevertheless, for the time being the lesson was learned that only by uniting against the enemy could victory be won. The era of the Judges so far impressed this truth upon the minds of the Hebrews that we note the beginnings of Hebrew unity.

[1] Hist. of People of Israel, 47.

CHAPTER X.

THE MORALITY OF THE HEBREWS PRIOR TO THE KINGDOM.

It is a mistake to suppose that the lofty conceptions of Israel's later seers and prophets were manifest among the people from the earliest times. Quite the reverse was true. Like all primitive people, the Hebrews passed through the usual stages of development, religiously and morally. Sufficient evidence goes to show that they worshipped many gods in the beginning, as did other Semitics. Joshua once reminded them of their earlier faith:

"Your fathers dwelt on the other side of the flood in old time, even Terah, the father of Abraham, and the father of Nachor: and they served other gods."[1]

"In many respects doubtless their religion was closely akin to that of neighboring Semitic people. They had their sacred pillars, trees, and other emblems of the divine power and presence; they carried with them *teraphim*, which were apparently images venerated as household gods. In many of their beliefs and practices they did not rise above the general level of their age."[2]

During their long sojourn in Egypt, as might have been expected, they grew to worship Egyptian gods. "Cast ye away every man the abominations of his eyes, and defile not yourselves with the idols of Egypt."[3]

The explanation which has seemed to make clear the unique development of the Hebrew above other Semitics, is this one —only recently offered. It is well-known that the Israelites were originally henotheists—that is, they believed in many gods—believed that many divinities were powerful, but they gave allegiance to one, the god of their tribe. This god belonged to their tribe, and shared its successes and failures. Now when Moses accepted Jahweh, probably in Midian, he persuaded the Israelites to forsake the gods they were worshipping and give their homage to Jahweh. At the foot of

[1] Joshua, 24, 2. [2] Short Hist. of the Hebrews: Ottley, 26. [3] Ezekiel, 20, 7.

Sinai he caused them to make a covenant with Jahweh: the God was to give them protection, and they were to worship him alone. Because he was an adopted God and not a member of their tribe, he was bound to protect them only when they served him faithfully. The adopted God could cast off his adopted people if they failed to fulfill their part of the contract. The Hebrews always said that they were a peculiar people. They repeatedly referred to the fact that God could cast them off if they were unloyal to him. Such a thing is unknown among other nations. No other God could cast off his people; he was one of them. This explains also why the Hebrews were always so ready to abandon their God and take on the gods of their neighbors.

" In any case it is clear that Jahweh was not originally the god of Israel, but only became such in consequence of the work of Moses and of the events of the exodus.

" Israel's relation to Jahweh was unique. He was not an ancestral god who stood in a natural and necessary relation to his people, like the gods of other Semitic tribes; but he was the god of Sinai and of Midian, who had come into connection with Israel only through his own free, moral choice. Israel belonged to him, not by birth, but by election. Its existence and its continuance were dependent upon his sovereign good pleasure, and he might cast it off as easily as he had adopted it. Under these circumstances he had the right to make conditions upon which his favour should depend such as other gods could not make. This fact does not explain the ethical character of the Mosaic religion; it explains only why an ethical religion was promulgated at this particular time." [4]

It is the custom of all primitive people to ascribe their early laws and government to divine origin. This rule is seldom varied, and was adhered to by the ancient Hebrews. Instead of conceiving the God-Spirit as having endowed Moses with true insight, wise judgments, and high ideals, the Israelites believed that their Covenant had been dictated, word by word, by Jahweh, while it was further claimed that tablets with words inscribed upon them were given Moses by God himself. As a matter of fact, the earliest decalogue differed

[4] Early Hist. of Syria and Palestine: Paton, 139, 141.

widely from the one best known. The commandments first given the people after they were led forth from Egypt were probably the ones recorded in the thirty-fourth chapter of Exodus, and were something like these:

1. Thou shalt worship no other god.
2. Thou shalt make thee no molten gods.
3. The feast of unleaven bread shalt thou keep.
4. Every firstling is mine.
5. Thou shalt keep the feast of the weeks.
6. Thou shalt keep the feast of the ingathering at the end of the year.
7. Thou shalt not offer the blood of my sacrifice with leaven.
8. The fat of my feast shall not be left over until the morning.
9. Thou shalt bring the best of the first fruits of thy land to the house of Jehovah thy God.
10. Thou shalt not seethe a kid in his mother's milk.

Because Moses was known to the Israelites as a law-giver, laws passed long after his death were attributed to him, quite as laws which came into being years after the death of Hammurabit in Babylon were probably attributed to this great national law-giver.

A company of slaves, escaping from servitude after serving for two or three generations, and having possessed but a crude civilization previous to that experience, would require only the simplest laws, and any one reading the various rules and regulations attributed to this period will easily see how crude was the stage of development which made such instruction necessary. As time went on, and the people advanced and became more enlightened, new laws were possible. These continued to be known as the "Laws of Moses," as laws in all early countries have been attributed to some renowned personage, to give them added force.

In these early periods which we have been studying, the religion of the Hebrews possessed many features in common with those of surrounding nations. We read that the "Children of Israel walked through the fire," which means that they sacrificed their first-born in flames as offerings to their God. Jahweh was believed to be a jealous God, vindictive, demanding cruel treatment of captives, and fierce and relentless in battle. A man cannot get a higher ideal of God than that of a perfect human being, and this was an age when all ideas and ideals were crude.

When the Hebrews settled Canaan, they learned much from the earlier inhabitants of the land. Becoming farmers, they quite naturally fell into the way of worshipping the god of harvests, and other agricultural deities of the Canaanites. The "high places" are repeatedly spoken of, these being places where other gods were worshipped. When roused by danger, they renewed their covenant with Jahweh and returned to more careful performance of their part of the early agreement.

The system of polygamy was well established. Several of the patriarchs took two or more wives. If a man died childless, it was not only customary but a duty that the next in line should marry the widow and raise up seed to his memory. This is expressly shown by the story of Ruth, most attractive in its early simplicity. We learn more of the every day life of the Israelites in the period following Hebrew occupancy of Canaan from this little idyl than from any other source, or from all other sources combined.

So far as germs of government and judicial administration of the people thus far discernible are concerned, they had seemingly not progressed farther than the instruction of Moses led them. The years spent in the wilderness after the exodus were very essential to the future welfare of the Hebrew nation. Their government—to whatever extent they possessed one—was closely allied to their religion. There were many experiences met with in these forty years which seemed to prove Jahweh's care and protection over them, and Moses was regarded as his representative on earth, who received his instructions from Jahweh and delivered them to his people.

"His words were Jehovah's message to them. As he led them in their wilderness wandering, they felt themselves under the direct guidance of their God; he attended to the simple ritual of the desert sanctuary at Kadesh; to him, as the representative of Jehovah, were referred the more difficult cases of dispute which arose; his decisions had all the weight of Jehovah's authority. *In this way he laid down by practical illustration the principles of that civil and religious law which bears his name.* As these cases multiplied, he was led to constitute a rude patriarchal tribunal composed of the elders of the tribes. In this simple organization is found the germ of the Hebrew judicial and executive system.

"Thus Moses was the man who under divine direction 'hewed Israel from the rock.' Subsequent prophets and circumstances chiselled the rough boulder into symmetrical form, but the glory of the creative act is rightly attributed to the first great Hebrew prophet. As a leader, he not only created a nation, but guided them through infinite vicissitudes to a land where they might have a settled abode and develop into a stable power; in so doing, he left upon his race the imprint of his own personality. As a judge, he set in motion forces which ultimately led to the incorporation of the principles of right in objective laws. As a priest, he first gave form to the worship of Jehovah. As a prophet, *he gathered together all that was best in the faith of his age and race,* and, fusing them, gave to his people a living religion."[5]

Before the time of the monarchy, their darkest years were those wherein the Israelites departed from this Mosaic teaching; their best periods, those in which they assimilated it and attempted to carry it out. To whatever extent they developed strength and stability for their future nation before the birth of their kingdom, such strength came as a result of the Mosaic religious and moral teaching.

[5] Hist. of the Hebrew People: Kent Vol. I 44.

CHAPTER XI.

Causes Leading to the Kingdom.

1250 B. C. has been taken as an approximate date for the exodus of the Israelites from Egypt, some placing the event still earlier. After the wandering in the desert, considerable time was spent winning Canaan from its earlier possessors before any settlement was possible. The twelfth century and first part of the eleventh before Christ were years of re-adjustment, the Israelites losing the habits of desert nomads and becoming tillers of the soil.

In rocky districts they still raised sheep and cattle but acquired fixed homes. Warfare had been constant, but in later years had been carried on wholly by individual tribes, there being no concerted action. The tendency to divide and seek each its own peculiar interests had been apparent from the first, and the beginning of the eleventh century B. C. found the tribes prostrated as a result. The Canaanites no longer threatened them but the Philistines constantly grew bolder. When they pressed into the plain of Jezreel, the Israelites were forced to fight them, but lacking an able leader and sufficient numbers, they lost the day. Surviving instincts of earlier superstitious practices led them to bring the ark containing their covenant with Jehovah from its sanctuary at Shiloh, thinking this might aid them in a second struggle. "Let us fetch the ark of the covenant of Jehovah out of Shiloh unto us, that it may come among us, and save us out of the hand of our enemies." But instead of leading to victory, 30,000 Israelites fell upon the battle field and the sacred ark itself fell into the hands of the Philistines.

"The Philistines burned and destroyed the temple at Shiloh, carried the captured sacred ark to the temple of their chief god, Dagon, and subjected the land, even to the Jordan; the people were disarmed and held in check by Philistine prefects and strongholds. And from all evidence this Philistine domination must have lasted a considerable time. Israel seemed paralyzed and submitted, though with gnashing of teeth."[1]

---

[1] Hist. of the People of Israel: Cornill, 75.

When Israel lay stricken and at the mercy of her enemies on the west, the Ammonites thought the time favorable to lead a new attack for the purpose of recovering their earlier territories on the east. The town of Jabesh was first afflicted, and when its inhabitants offered to surrender, feeling helpless to overpower their ancient foes, the king of the Ammonites insolently replied that he would cause the right eye of each citizen of the town to be cast out, as a reproach to Israel. In the quaint expression of Josephus: "The king of the Ammonites sent ambassadors to them, commanding them either to deliver themselves up, on condition to have their right eyes plucked out, or to undergo a siege, and have their cities overthrown. He gave them their choice, whether they would cut off a small number of their body, or universally perish." Implored to grant them a few days respite, the king of the Ammonites scornfully conceded it, sure of his ultimate triumph.

In Ephraim dwelt a seer, Samuel by name. He was a godly man, having rare purity of character and intense religious fervor. Dedicated when a child to the service of Jehovah, the course of his life had led him to catch the spirit of the great founder of the Hebrew nation and beyond him, to gain a broader conception of the great God-Spirit. He understood why his people were a prey to every neighbor, and knew better than most how much a firm leadership was needed by them. With eyes that saw far into the future, Samuel realized that the crying need was unity and concerted action. Now in these ancient days, unity meant kingship. Under strong kings, contemporary nations flourished, and a king was apparently necessary in Canaan.

Saul, of the tribe of Benjamin, seeking his father's asses, approached the seer, whose prophetic powers were well known in his vicinity. The youth thought simply to invoke his aid in his private interests, but Samuel recognized in the broad-shouldered, well-proportioned Benjaminite one who might come to the rescue of stricken Israel. With prophetic vision, Samuel foretold coming events and anointed Saul as one chosen of Jehovah to rule the nation of His special care. Since he was not called immediately to action, Saul returned to his father's house, where he went about his ordinary duties. But the words of the seer had sunk deep into his heart. Indications of Israel's stricken condition were not wanting on every hand, and Saul brooded over her helplessness and his call to save his people. At length, when the citizens from mourning Jabesh visited his vicinity, vainly trying to rouse their kinsmen to action, Saul saw that his opportunity had come. Sympathy had been everywhere expressed by the Israelites, but they had suffered too many recent defeats to feel confidence in their ability to win.

Saul hastily cut up a yoke of oxen, and sending these bloody tokens to the various tribes, he notified them that such treatment would be meted out to their flocks and herds unless they came to the relief of the trans-Jordan cities. Recognizing a leader at last, men quickly gathered. The desert tribe was surprised, defeated and pursued into its desert strongholds. Thereupon Saul was popularly proclaimed king, as it was now believed that he alone could save the Hebrews from the Philistines, who were heavily oppressing them.

A king is ordinarily one who rules a kingdom, but in the case of Saul, a kingdom had first to be won. His encounters with the Philistines were successful, but his reign proved to be a continual campaign against them. Gradually Saul became estranged from Samuel, who represented the best element in Israel. Priests of a later period assigned the difference between them as having arisen over Saul's leniency toward his captives, but it is believed that instead it came naturally between two men whose ideals were wide apart. Saul was incapable of taking an exalted view of his people's mission, as did his priest and prophet.

Beset on all sides by the enemy, estranged from Samuel and in general from the priesthood, Saul became moody and subject to fits of melancholia. To dispel these, David, son of Jesse, was brought from his father's flocks on the mountainside, to gladden the king's idle hours. David was accomplished upon the harp, and his music had power to quiet the restless king, who heaped favors and honors upon him—after the nature of his impulsive disposition. As armour-bearer to the king, David had frequent opportunities to distinguish himself, while he and the king's son Jonathan became fast friends. However, as David grew in favor with the people, Saul became intensely jealous of him. Where the kingship was but an experiment, popularity was important to a ruler. In his disordered brain, Saul conceived that a plot was being laid by his son and David, and as a result, David was obliged to flee for his life. He raised his standard as an outlaw chief, and all the dissatisfied element of the land flocked to his side. Yet even here David favored the people of Israel whenever he could; for protection he went into the service of the Philistine king of Gath, but we are told that when he was supposed to be fighting against the Hebrews, he was in reality fighting off their desert enemies.

The division within the ranks of Israel once more gave opportunity to the watchful Philistines. They made ready for a final assault, and the moody and disheartened Saul prepared to fight them back. He was no longer able to rouse his kinsmen as at first. Many were discontented with his rule, and many favored David. Before the battle, Saul, grown more superstitious with the pressure of circumstance, visited the witch of Endor to learn by her art the issue of the battle. Never does the king, tall in stature and once confident, but now broken in spirit, appear more tragic. When she predicted defeat—and small art was needed to foretell such an apparent outcome—Saul felt that all was lost. One feels as when the voice of Cæsar spake unto Brutus in the great play: "Thou shalt see me at Philippi"—the battle is lost before it is begun.

When all was lost, Saul gave his sword to his armourbearer to stab him lest he fall into the hands of the enemy. When he lacked courage, he plunged it into his own breast. Both he and his noble son Jonathan went down on that fateful field, and so ended the first reign in Israel. David is believed to have composed his beautiful elegy "How are the Mighty Fallen" upon this occasion.

David's Lament.

>Thy glory, O Israel,
>Is slain upon thy high places!
>>How are the mighty—
>>Fallen!

Tell it not in Gath,
Publish it not in the streets of Ashkelon;
>Lest the daughters of the Philistines rejoice,
>Lest the daughters of the uncircumcised triumph.

Ye mountains of Gilboa, let there be no dew nor rain upon you,
Neither fields of offerings:
>For the shield of the mighty was vilely cast away,
>The shield of Saul, as of one not anointed with oil.

From the blood of the slain,
From the fat of the mighty,
>The bow of Jonathan turned not back,
>And the sword of Saul returned not empty.

Saul and Jonathan were lovely and pleasant in their lives,
And in their death they were not divided;
>They were swifter than eagles,
>They were stronger than lions.

Ye daughters of Israel,
Weep over Saul,
>Who clothed you in scarlet,
>Who put ornaments of gold upon your apparel.

>>How are the mighty—
>>Fallen in the midst of the battle!
>>>O Jonathan,
>>>Slain upon thy high places.

I am distressed for thee, my brother Jonathan:
Very pleasant hast thou been unto me:
>Thy love to me was wonderful,
>Passing the love of women.

How are the mighty—
   Fallen!
And the weapons of war—
   Perished!

—*Modern Reader's Bible.*

In the Old Testament itself are two contradictory estimates of the character of Saul. One was written by those who favored and cared for him; the other, by the faction which favored David. Later compilers have thrown the two together, and the result is that we must once more disentangle the two narratives and then judge between them. The following characterizations of him differ considerably, and yet have certain ideas in common:

"Saul is one of the most tragic figures in history. A great and nobly endowed nature, heroic and chivalrous, inspired with fiery zeal, he finally accomplished nothing.
He lacked appreciation of the true character of Israel; in this regard tradition has given a wholly correct picture of him. He was exclusively a soldier, and was in a fair way to exchange Israel into a secular military state and thus divert it from its religious function in universal history. Saul may claim our deepest compassion and our heartiest sympathy, but the fall of his power was a blessing for Israel."[2]

The second criticism upon the fallen king seems more fair and sympathetic:

"Saul was a simple-minded, impulsive, courageous warrior; he was a loyal patriot who loved his people and was ready to give his life for them; his physical pre-eminence, combined with energy and enthusiasm, fitted him to lead a sudden attack and to awaken loyal support, while his intrepid courage kindled the same in others. But Saul was a son of that rude age whose roots were found in the period of the Judges. In a sense he was a child grown big. The position which he occupied demanded executive ability, tact, the power of organization, and, above all, patience and persistency. In these maturer qualities he was deficient; they are rarely the possession of fiery, impetuous natures. In addition, Saul was unable to understand and appreciate the higher religious ex-

[2] Hist. of the People of Israel: Cornill, 83.

periences and ideals which were already becoming the possession of the more enlightened souls of seers like Samuel. As is frequently true with such a nature, Saul was superstitious. Circumstances tended to develop the darker rather than the brighter side of his character. The constant trials and cares of the court and battle-field daunted his enthusiasm, and induced those attacks of melancholia which obscured the nobler Saul and led him to commit acts which constantly increased the density of the clouds that gathered about his latter days.

"When he fell at Gilboa, and the Philistines again became masters of northern and central Canaan, Saul's work seemed to be completely undone; *but its foundations were laid too deeply to be undermined by political changes.* Saul found the Hebrews ground down under Philistine dominance, broken in spirit, undisciplined, and little more than cowards. He united and aroused them to strike for independence. By his successes he inspired in them confidence and courage. In the severe training-school of Philistine warfare, he developed out of the cowards who had fled before the Philistine army to hide themselves in caves and cisterns, the hardy, brave warriors with whom David made his conquests. Above all, he taught the Hebrews by practical illustration, more clearly than ever before, that by union and union alone they could be free, and enjoy peace and prosperity. As is often the case, *the pioneer perished amidst seeming failure before he saw the ripe fruits of his labors; but his work was absolutely necessary.* David reaped the fruits of Saul's sowing, but the harvest would never have been so glorious without the pioneer's toils."[1]

Reign of David.

Saul is supposed to have ruled not longer than eight or ten years. His youngest son, Eshbaal, was recognized as his natural successor. Abner, Saul's commander-in-chief, gave Eshbaal the support of whatever army survived, and he was established on the east side of the Jordan, while all the territory west of the river receded to the Philistines.

David realized that he was in no position to assume con-

[1] Hist. of the Hebrew People: Kent, Vol. I, 180.

trol of the Hebrews at this juncture, for he had but a few hundred followers and he was sure to be welcomed by all the tribes only when his services were required for the common safety. Judah was deeply attached to him at this time, and he allowed himself to be made king of the tribe of Judah, and established himself at Hebron.

As soon as Eshbaal felt sufficiently secure on the east of Jordan Abner was sent to overcome David and his followers, who had thus failed to recognize the kingship of Eshbaal. They suffered defeat and had to retreat across the river. The times were troublous and before eight years had passed, both Eshbaal and Abner were murdered. This left the way open for David, to whom the subjects of Eshbaal sent homage.

The Philistines had considered the little kingdom of Saul's son unworthy of attention, but a kingdom on the west side of the river might prove a menace to their power, so they hastened to attack the newly crowned king. David marched against them and broke forever their strength. They retired into their earlier possessions and harassed Israel no more.

One by one the old enemies of the Hebrews had to be reckoned with. The Moabites attacked the territory of David and were overcome and made vassals. On the north the Ammonites made a raid and were so completely defeated that we hear of them no more. On the south the Edomites made war, and their lands also became a Hebrew province. In all these wars, David was the defender of his people—never the aggressor, yet he left each tribe with no further desire to make war upon Israel.

David was a statesman, and he saw at once that as king of the Hebrews, he must no longer remain isolated with his native tribe, in the vicinity to him most familiar. He saw that the site of Jerusalem was capable of excellent defense, and this he made his capital.

"Jerusalem is situated pretty near the central part of the entire country, and belonging to none of the tribes it stood on neutral ground above them and their rivalries. When it is called the City of David this is no mere phrase, for Jerusalem is altogether the creation of David; and when we consider what Jerusalem was to the people of Israel, and through the people of Israel to all mankind, we shall recognize in the foundation of this City of David an event of world-wide importance."

Israel had reached the highest pinnacle of its political power. David's kingdom was the most powerful one between the valley of the Euphrates and the Nile. While disturbances extended throughout the reign until within the last ten of David's forty years, yet the nation was saved from impending danger and was placed on a sure basis. Now it was that David allowed his personal desires to lead him into difficulties which followed him many years and which darkened the reign which had promised so much. An infatuation for Bath-sheba, wife of one of his officers, took possession of him, and caused him to make way with her husband who stood in his way. Like other Semitic and Oriental nations, the Hebrews were accustomed to take more than one wife, but the religion of Jehovah had been from the beginning a moral religion, and the more earnest among Israel's people could but be shocked by this action on the part of the king. Much has been made of David's remorse, but it was not so great but that he allowed the unscrupulous woman who had aided him in his wrongdoing to exercise a strong influence over him throughout his life. His sons seemed to feel no restraint upon them and added crimes to their house. Absalom, David's favorite son, took advantage of his father's loss of popularity to raise a revolt against him. This was easily put down, but the death of Absalom quite unnerved the king. Bath-sheba rested not until she had settled the succession upon her son, Solomon. Shortly after this decision was made known, David died, having reigned forty years. In realizing what all these years meant for Israel, we can never lose sight of the pioneer work of Saul which alone made possible the more brilliant one of his successor.

"It is not possible to overestimate what David did for Israel: Israel as a people, as a representative of political life, as a concrete quantity in the development of universal history, as a nation in the fullest sense of the word, is exclusively his work. With this he completed what Moses had begun in quiet and inconspicuous labors on Sinai and at Kadesh. And all of this David created as it were out of nothing, under the most difficult conditions conceivable, with no other means than his own all-inspiring and all-compelling personality. . .

"David created Israel and at the same time raised it to

its highest eminence; what Israel was under and through David it never again became. And so we can easily understand how the eyes of Israel rested in grateful reverence upon this figure, and how a second David became the dream of Israel's future.

"True, the picture of David does not lack the traits of human frailty, which Israelitish tradition, with a truly admirable sincerity has neither suppressed nor palliated; but the charm which this personality exercised over all contemporaries without exception has not yet faded for us of later day; whoever devoted himself without prejudice to the contemplation of David's history and character cannot fail to like him. A saint and psalm-singer, as later tradition has represented him, he certainly was not; but we find in him a truly noble human figure, which, in spite of all, preserved the tenderest and most fragrant bloom of its nature, perfect directness and simplicity; nowhere any posing, nothing theatrical, such as is always found in sham greatness; he always acts out what he is, but his unspoiled nature, noble at heart, generally comes very near to the right and good. At the same time the whole personality is touched with a breath of genuine piety and childlike trust in God, so that we can wholly comprehend how he appears to tradition as the ideal ruler, the king after God's own heart.

"This king, who did more for the worldly greatness and earthly power of Israel than any one else, was a genuine Israelite in that he appreciated also Israel's religious destiny: he was no soldier-king, no conqueror and warrior of common stamp, no ruler like any one of a hundred others, but he is the truest incorporation of the unique character of Israel, a unique personality in the history of the world, and we understand how he could become the impersonation of an idea— how the highest and holiest that Israel hoped for and longed for appears at the Son of David."[*]

We are shocked as we read of David's cruelty to captives, but in his ferocious treatment he was but following an instinct common to the Semitic race. It is to be remembered that he was but a brief time removed from the era of the Judges, when even Samuel, the far-seeing seer, and God-fearing man, hacked an enemy to pieces before the altar of Jehovah, to the supposed

[*] Cornill: Hist. of People of Israel, 83.

gratification of his God. David's faults were common to his age, and they were not looked upon by his contemporaries as we look upon them today, but his virtues and redeeming characteristics raised him far above the majority of Israel's people, and his reign was harked back to as most worthy in Hebrew annals.

Solomon.

Solomon was the son of David's fourth wife—Bathsheba. Selfish, devoid of principle and fond of intrigue, she influenced David to recognize her son as his successor, setting aside the right of an older son. It is not unlikely that David believed Solomon the more capable of serving Israel.

Solomon had inherited his mother's selfishness and love of display. He soon caused the death of his brother, in order to make his crown secure. Having neither aptitude nor ability for war, fortifications took the place of active armies. The vassal-kingdoms which David had won were soon lost. Forts were erected at important border places, and the city of Jerusalem was strongly fortified.

Oriental display and absolutism were emulated by the young king. He desired to set his kingdom on a footing with other kingdoms of his time, and, ignoring the early aims and mission of the Israelites, he made everything else subordinate to the exaltation of the court and king. Commercial alliances were made with neighboring peoples; wives were taken from many states—petty and great. Most flattering was thought to be the marriage alliance between the Hebrew king and a daughter of the pharaoh of Egypt, and elaborate apartments were provided her. In early times a king added materially to his property and prestige by making numerous alliances of this sort. David had deemed it best to do so and Solomon followed the principle on a much wider scale.

Naturally ample funds were now required to meet the expenses of the court, and various means were provided to secure the necessary income. The whole kingdom was divided into twelve districts and each was required to defray the court's expenses for one month. Moreover, commercial enterprises were entered upon; toll was collected from the overland trade, and the king himself dealt heavily in horses, which he imported from Egypt and sold to the neighboring peoples at a good profit. Suddenly the little nation of Israelites, so long isolated and remote from the influences of wealth, was thrown open to outside contact on every hand.

"Hitherto struggles within and hostility without had rendered the Hebrew peasants almost impervious to foreign influences; now, all at once, the bars were thrown down, and these came rushing in like a tidal wave. The horse took the place of the ass; metal weapons and tools supplanted the rude ones of flint and wood; walled cities arose on the sites of the primitive towns with their mud and stone hovels; the rude barracks of David grew into a palace; the simple gathering of followers about Saul, as he sat under his tamarisk-tree in Ramah, developed into a great Oriental court; luxuries undreamed of before came to be regarded as necessities; foreign spices, apes, peacocks, ivory, precious stones and woods aroused the curiosity and delighted the senses of the inhabitants of the gay capital."[3]

Nations entering into commercial relations with Solomon expected as a matter of course that their gods would be welcomed in the land of the Hebrews. Many of the commercial treaties were cemented by marriage alliances, and the princesses who came into the king's harem brought their own forms of worship with them. Places of worship had to be provided for them, and the idolatry of later years may be traced back in a large measure to the laxity of this period.

The adornment of Jerusalem demanded much of the king's attention. In place of the simple quarters which had sufficed for David, a noble palace arose. Apartments for the queens were needed. It has recently been insisted that instead of the three hundred and sixty wives credited to Solomon, he had but seventy, but a few more or less seem of little moment. The harem rivaled that of Persia, and the cost of maintaining so elaborate a court was out of all proportion to the resources of the kingdom. The people were taxed to the utmost. The Canaanites, who had long been permitted to live in peace by the side of the Hebrews, were now reduced to slavery and put at forced labor, quite as the Hebrews had been in Egypt.

Notwithstanding, many ties bound the people to their king. They took great pride in the splendor of their capital,

---

[3]Kent: Hist. of Hebrew People, 180.

& Underwood, N. Y.
ROSES OF SHARON.

and especially were they gratified by the erection of the temple in Jerusalem. Hither David had brought the ark of the covenant, which had been recovered from the Philistines, and here with due ceremony the center of the kingdom had already been made the religious center as well. It seems probable that to Solomon the temple was but a necessary adjunct to his court buildings. Among most ancient peoples temples were erected in connection with the king's palace. It gave added dignity and inspired wonder. To the masses it probably meant much more. Certainly it grew later to be the center for their religious enthusiasm and spirit.

Nor was Solomon's popularity based alone upon his achievements. He had a way of awakening personal popularity. He attained a wide reputation for his so-called "wisdom." As we follow his reckless policy of plunging his country on to ruin, this far-famed wisdom is not at once apparent. It consisted in subtlety, quick wit, ready answers and apt sayings, so much in favor among all oriental peoples. His wisdom is well exemplified by the stories told of the visit of the Queen of Sheba to his court, and her tests as to the truth of his famed gift. It is probable that this Arabian queen came to negotiate commercial advantages for her subjects, but we are told only the ostensible reason for her coming: to test the wisdom of Solomon, whose fame had reached her kingdom. The dusky queen of renowned beauty brought costly presents to the Hebrew king, and received high honor and attention at his court. Stories have survived of questions put to his majesty by this queen. Two bouquets were held out before him, apparently alike, yet one was just gathered from his garden, and the other had been fashioned by the maidens of the queen. The simple tale is told in a little poem entitled "King Solomon and the Bees," and we leave the verses to complete it.

King Solomon and the Bees.

A Tale of the Talmud.

When Solomon was reigning in his glory,
   Unto his throne the Queen of Sheba came,
(So in the Talmud you may read the story)
   Drawn by the magic of the monarch's fame,

To see the splendors of his court, and bring
Some fitting tribute to the mighty king.

Nor this alone; much had her Highness heard
    What flowers of learning graced the royal speech;
What gems of wisdom dropped with every word;
    What wholesome lessons he was wont to teach
In pleasing proverbs, and she wished, in sooth,
To know if Rumor spoke the simple truth.

Besides, the queen had heard (which piqued her most)
    How through the deepest riddles he could spy;
How all the curious arts that women boast
    Were quite transparent to his piercing eye;
And so the queen had come—a royal guest—
To put the sage's cunning to the test.

And straight she held before the monarch's view,
    In either hand, a radiant wreath of flowers;
The one, bedecked with every charming hue,
    Was newly culled from Nature's choicest bowers;
The other, no less fair in every part,
Was the rare product of divinest art.

"Which is the true, and which the false?" she said.
    Great Solomon was silent. All-amazed,
Each wondering courtier shook his puzzled head,
    While at the garlands long the monarch gazed,
As one who sees a miracle, and fain,
For very rapture, ne'er would speak again.

"Which is the true?" once more the woman asked,
    Pleased at the fond amazement of the king,
"So wise a head should not be hardly tasked,
    Most learned liege, with such a trivial thing!"
But still the sage was silent; it was plain
A deepening doubt perplexed the royal brain.

While thus he pondered, presently he sees,
    Hard by the casement,—so the story goes,—

A little band of busy, bustling bees,
   Hunting for honey in a withered rose.
The monarch smiled, and raised his royal head;
' Open the window!"—that was all he said.

The window opened, at the king's command;
   Within the room the eager insects flew,
And sought the flowers in Sheba's dexter hand!
   And so the king and all the courtiers knew
That wreath was Nature's; and the baffled queen
Returned to tell the wonders she had seen.

My story teaches (every tale should bear
   A fitting moral) that the wise may find
In trifles light as atoms in the air,
   Some useful lesson to enrich the mind,
Some truth designed to profit or to please,—
As Israel's king learned wisdom from the bees!

                                      —*Saxe.*

Six little boys and six little girls, all dressed alike, with cropped heads, were led into the king's presence, and he was asked to tell which were girls and which boys. "Bring in basins of water," he commanded, "and bid them wash their hands." Now in that land the girls wore short sleeves and the boys long ones. Unthinking, the girls washed their arms as well, but the boys washed their hands alone. So were the spectators silently told which were which.

Such ingenious answers as these established for Solomon his reputation for wisdom, and many of the wise sayings imputed to him are known now to have been the sayings of others.

Before the king's death, murmurings were not uncommon because of the oppressive administration, and the high-minded of the religious body looked with grave misgivings upon the influx of foreign gods. Even to them the whole danger was not apparent. That was left for a period more remote to understand.

When Solomon died, his son came forward as his successor. The usual custom among Semitics was for the crown to descend to the eldest son, but the kingship was a new institution in Israel and the people had held to the right of electing their king. They now gathered around Rehoboam, clamoring for promises. They recalled that his father had taxed them heavily and asked that he deal with them more leniently. Instead of answering such reasonable demands at once, the king told them he would make reply three days later. Meanwhile he counselled with his ministers—how should he meet the popular demand. The older men immediately pointed out the safer policy, but the younger ones held that he should resent the liberty the people had taken in making any demands whatever, and should assure them that his demands would be even greater than those of his father. Their folly prevailed. When the people heard his reply, they were momentarily grieved. Then all the tribes save two—Judah and Benjamin—withdrew and vowed they would no longer support the house of David. Solomon's son received the support of two tribes, and his kingdom was henceforth known by the name of Judaea, while the northern kingdom was called by the name of Israel.

Having seen the dangers assailing the united kingdom, we realize at once the recklessness of the policy that divided it and set two kingdoms with lessened strength to hold their own among their neighbors.

CHAPTER XII.

After the Division of the Kingdom.

While the arrogance of Rehoboam and the extravagances of Solomon were the direct causes of the disunion, yet other agencies had long been at work to bring it about. In the first place, natural land features divided the ridge on the west side of the Jordan into two distinct parts. Any permanent union was not probable. Again, the northern tribes inhabited the more prosperous district. Their resources were greater; and with the jealousies that always manifested themselves among the tribes, it was hardly to have been expected that they would indefinitely consent to be ruled by Judean kings. Moreover, during the reign of Solomon, Judah had been exempt from taxation. Into a Judean city had poured the wealth of the kingdom, while the hand of oppression, so heavy elsewhere, was unfelt alone in this province. Indignation had apparently reached a high pitch before Solomon's death, yet spokesmen for the northern tribes met with the new king and made a simple and reasonable demand for reduced taxes in turn for allegiance. A statesman might have held the kingdom intact, yet it is scarcely probable that union would have indefinitely endured. The royal messenger sent to reconcile the northern tribes after their withdrawal was so speedily stoned to death that the king fled for safety to Jerusalem. Jeroboam, an experienced general, was elected king of Israel—the northern kingdom, and hostilities between the two kingdoms were inevitable.

Judah was somewhat protected—on the north by the newformed state, on the east by the river and Dead Sea, on the south by the desert. On the other hand, Israel, with her traversable plains, lay open to approach from every side, and she it was who had to bear the brunt of outside attack for the next two centuries.

A comparison of the two states at the outset shows Israel to have been first in natural resources, size and population; to have been second in unity and centralized government. Judah, with her limited area, scarcity of water, absence of fertile soil and scanty population, had marked advantage in her unity and hereditary kingship. There were ten tribes to be pacified in the north—only two in the south. In Israel the jealousies were so strong that it was the work of a moment for an influential prince to assassinate the reigning king and usurp the crown.

Judah was crippled shortly after the division by an invasion of Egyptian forces. They penetrated into Israel as well, but treasure was greatest in Jerusalem. Three hundred golden shields, made by Solomon for his guards, were taken, together with the rich decoration of the temple. Rehoboam soon after had the ornaments of gold replaced by others of bronze, so the splendor of the temple was not greatly changed.

For some time hostilities continued between the Hebrew kingdoms. Then danger from Syria, a rising state with Damascus at its head, made an alliance desirable to both kings.

After the disunion, Jeroboam felt that it would be manifestly unsafe to allow the people of Israel to go to Jerusalem to celebrate their national festivals, lest they might be led to return to Judah's king. Consequently he established two sanctuaries, one at Bethel and one at Dan, instructing people to worship at the one nearest them. He caused a golden bull to be placed before the altar of each, thus violating the commandment forbidding graven images. Perhaps in so doing the king was merely symbolizing the strength of Jehovah. At an earlier period this would have been less objectionable, but the people had grown somewhat accustomed to worship without symbols, and this was plainly a retrogression. The imageless worship of Jehovah was one of its distinctive features, lifting it above that of surrounding peoples.

While prophets of a later day denounced the act of Jeroboam, the priests of his own day were too near the change to discern its grave dangers.

The kingdoms which centered at Damascus began to reach out for territory, and harassed Israel until the imperial growth of Assyria caused the withdrawal of Syrian troops to protect their own land. Left alone, the northern kingdom developed her own resources and attained a prosperity rivaling the time of Solomon. Meanwhile, Judah had been sheltered from outside wars and less affected by religious orders.

The period intervening between the fall of Damascus and the wars of Tiglath-Pileser III. has been aptly called "Israel's Indian Summer." The outlying territories of David came once more under Hebrew rule, divided between the kingdoms of the north and south. Commerce, long abandoned, sprang up and rivaled its tide in Solomon's reign. Unfortunately, the social life of the people lacked its earlier simplicity, and there were tendencies within the kingdom itself which pointed to the disintegration of the state as surely as did the forces that were soon to approach its walled cities.

First, recent wars had fallen most heavily upon the middle class. Small farmers, returning from campaigns of defense of Hebrew borders, found their estates run down, sometimes dismantled. Having no means of building them up again, they frequently sank into the peasantry. In periods of reaction, when property and commercial activity returned, it was the wealthy who were benefited, while the poor became poorer yet. In this way the middle class had practically disappeared. Such a loss would be serious enough to a state, but this was by no means all. The simplicity of living which had characterized the early years of the Hebrew nation had given way to extravagance and reckless waste on the part of the rich, throwing into powerful contrast the condition of the poor. The humbler classes were oppressed—not by foreign foes, but by the wealthy of their own state, and abandonment of any sympathy between social classes was one of the most alarming tendencies.

The religious life of the country was at a low ebb. By the masses Jehovah was still regarded as God of the Hebrews —a tribal God, quite as Baal was god of the Phœnicians, or Asshur of the Assyrians. It was taught by the priests that Jehovah would cause the Hebrews to win against their enemies, since only by their triumphs was he honored. He was worshipped much as were the gods of other nations. Licentious customs borrowed from neighboring peoples, profaned the very temples, and undermined earlier religious simplicity.

It was such a state of affairs that called forth the utterances of Amos and Hosea, from whose addresses we learn of social conditions in their day. In some hearts the religious mission of the Hebrews still remained the most sacred of all trusts. When evils of their age threatened to engulf them, certain clearsighted ones were moved to rouse the people—to bring home to them the consequences sure to overtake their kingdom unless these glaring wrongs were corrected.

Such a spirit was Amos, a simple, clear-minded shepherd, dwelling on the borderland between Israel and Judah, and closely observant of affairs in both states. Inspired to voice his protest against the corruption of his people, he left his flocks and journeyed to Bethel, the religious center of Israel. Reaching the temple on a feast day, he was confronted by riotous music and unseemly merriment, desecrating the temple itself. It was then he created a sensation by his passionate address, fragments of which are preserved to us in the biblical book which bears his name. Instead of offending at once by quick reproof, and thus losing a chance to he heard, he began by predicting misfortunes certain to overtake neighboring peoples because of their misdoings. In this way he won the attention and approval of an audience who liked to be told that they were the Chosen People, and Jehovah was with them, and that—apparently no matter what they did—he would not permit them to fail. Then Amos launched into the iniquity of Israel, and prophesied disasters sure to befall her. He uttered a new truth when he said that since the Hebrews had received special blessings from Jehovah, even more strictly would they be held to account for their shortcomings; that as their light had been greater than that bestowed upon their neighbors, so would the requirements be greater for them than for others.

"Hear ye this word which I take up against you, even a lamentation, O house of Israel.

"The virgin of Israel is fallen; she shall no more rise up; she is forsaken upon her land; there is none to raise her up. For thus saith the Lord God: The city that went out by a thousand shall leave an hundred, and that which went forth by an hundred shall leave ten, to the house of Israel.

"For thus saith the Lord unto the house of Israel: Seek ye me, and ye shall live; but seek not Bethel nor enter into Gilgal; for Gilgal shall surely go into captivity, and Bethel shall come to nought.

"Seek the Lord and ye shall live; lest he break out like

fire in the house of Joseph, and devour it, and there be none to quench it. Ye who turn judgment to wormwood, and leave off righteousness in the earth, seek him that maketh the seven stars and Orion, and turneth the shadow of death into morning and maketh the day dark with night; that calleth for the waters of the sea, and poureth them out upon the face of the earth: The Lord is his name. . . .

"Forasmuch therefore as your treading is upon the poor, and ye take from him burdens of wheat: ye have built houses of hewn stone, but ye shall not dwell in them; ye have planted pleasant vineyards, but ye shall not drink wine of them.

"For I know your manifold transgressions and your mighty sins; they afflict the just, they take a bribe, and they turn aside the poor in the gate from their right.

"Woe to them that are at ease in Zion, and trust in the mountains of Samaria, which are named chief of the nations, to whom the house of Israel came!

"Ye that put far away the evil day, and cause the seat of violence to come near; that lie upon beds of ivory, and stretch themselves upon their couches, and eat the lambs out of the flock, and the calves out of the midst of the stall; that chant to the sound of the viol, and invent to themselves instruments of music like David; that drink wine in bowls, and anoint themselves with the chief ointments; but they are not grieved for the affliction of Joseph.

"Therefore now shall they go captive with the first that go captive, and the banquet of them that stretched themselves shall be removed."—*Amos 5 and 6.*

Not long after, Hosea came forward with the startling and altogether unpleasant message that Jehovah was not the God of the Hebrews alone, but of the whole world. That he was a God of righteousness, and rewarded it wherever found, and punished evil doing, regardless of the doer. He touched a new chord when he taught that God was love, full of compassion and plenteous in mercy. Heretofore *law* had been the pivot around which religion centered, and the ritual was observed and the sacrifice provided. These attended to, Jehovah was supposed to be appeased. Hosea taught that the sacrifice of burnt offerings availed nothing—that the sacrifice demanded was " an humble and a contrite heart."

A new era was dawning for the Hebrew faith, and truth-divining men grasped at fundamental principles, applicable alike to the whole world. It is not surprising that long years elapsed before such broad conceptions sank deep into the hearts of the Hebrew race. One of their kingdoms was scattered to the winds before these were comprehended, save, indeed, by a few, far-sighted minds; the other kingdom passed through the humiliation of captivity and exile and through these vicissitudes learned the truths from actual experience.

"Hear ye this, O priests; and harken, ye house of Israel; and give ear, O house of the king; for judgment is toward you, because ye have been a snare on Mizpah, and a net spread upon Tabor.

"The pride of Israel doth testify to his face: therefore shall Israel and Ephraim fall in their iniquity; Judah also shall fall with them. They shall go with their flocks and with their herds to seek the Lord but they shall not find him; he hath withdrawn himself from them. They have dealt treacherously against the Lord: for they have begotten strange children: now shall a mouth devour them with their portions.

"O Ephraim, what shall I do unto thee? O Judah, what shall I do unto thee? for your goodness is as a morning cloud, and as the early dew it goeth away.

"For I desired mercy, and not sacrifice; and the knowledge of God more than burnt offerings. But they like men have transgressed the covenant: there have they dealt treacherously against me.

"Israel hath cast off the thing that is good: the enemy shall pursue him. They have set up kings, but not by me: they have made princes, and I knew it not: of their silver and their gold have they made them idols, that they may be cut off. For they have sown the wind, and they shall reap the whirlwind: it hath no stalk: the bud shall yield no meal: if so be it yield, the strangers shall swallow it up.

"They sacrifice flesh for the sacrifices of mine offerings, and eat it; but the Lord accepteth them not; now will he remember their iniquity and visit their sins: they shall return to Egypt. For Israel hath forgotten his Maker, and buildeth temples; and Judah hath multiplied fenced cities: but I will send a fire upon his cities, and it shall devour the palaces thereof.

"Ye have plowed wickedness, ye have reaped iniquity; ye have eaten the fruit of lies: because thou didst trust in thy way, in the multitude of thy mighty men.

"When Israel was a child, then I loved him, and called my son out of Egypt. As they called them, so they went from them: they sacrificed unto Baalim, and burned incense to graven images. I taught Ephraim also to go, taking them by the arms; but they knew not that I healed them. I drew them with cords of a man, with bands of love: and I was to them as they that take off the yoke on their jaws, and I laid meat unto them.

"O Israel, thou hast destroyed thyself; but in me is thine help.

"O Israel, return unto the Lord thy God, for thou hast fallen by thine iniquity."—*Hosea, 5-14 chapters.*

End of Israel.

About 745 B. C. Tiglath-Pileser III. began his westward conquest, incorporating great areas into his already spacious empire. Heavy tribute was exacted from provinces so annexed. The amount required of the northern kingdom—now known by the name of its new capital, Samaria—was so great that the state soon drooped under the load. Egypt, desiring also a foothold in western Asia, employed agents to stir the conquered countries against Assyria, promising aid in case they would revolt, but meaning only to appropriate territory for the Nile kingdom should confusion make it possible.

Because the tribute was grievous in Samaria, the party opposed to paying it desired an alliance with Egypt. Statesmen saw that such a movement was ill-timed, but their voices were drowned in the multitude. In 735 B. C. a coalition was formed by the sea-coast states against Assyria, and the revolting states refused the yearly tribute. Before the allies could rally, Tiglath-Pileser III. reached the west by forced marches, and defeated each state separately. Much land was laid waste, captives were taken, and Hosea, deemed loyal to the Assyrian government, was made king of Samaria. For ten years the annual levy was paid, but upon the death of the great Assyrian conqueror, Hosea yielded to the popular clamor for a revolt. He himself was soon taken prisoner, but Samaria prepared for a siege. It lasted nearly three years, during which time intense suffering afflicted the city. At last the capital fell to Sargon, who destroyed it, taking 27,290 of its noblest citizens captives, deporting them to distant points. An Assyrian governor was placed over the desolate land and Israel ceased to exist longer as a state.

The Hebrew chronicler tells us that those taken into captivity took on the religions of the people among whom they settled. Generally speaking this was no doubt true. On the other hand, traditions have come down from other sources concerning families who continued to worship Jehovah as before. However, after a few generations, their descendants no doubt drifted away from the faith of the Hebrews.

Thus ends the story of the ten tribes who broke away from the kingdom of Solomon's son and organized their own northern kingdom. While enduring prophecies and messages have been contributed by members of these tribes, their kingdom presented no such example as did the smaller state of Judah during the closing years of her national life. More accessible to outside influences, more ready to compromise, Israel's early religious fervor gradually abated. Some explanation for her inglorious end is to be found in the physical geography of her country.

Before the fall of Samaria, Judah enjoyed years of material prosperity, with varying fortune. Shortly before the siege of the northern capital, Ahaz, a mere boy, succeeded to the Judah throne. Inexperienced in the affairs of state, he was nevertheless reluctant to heed the counsels of older advisers. Assyria was threatening like a huge monster on the eastern horizon and the only possible way to check her approach lay in organizing a strong coalition of the sea-coast states. Syria, instead of taking the initiative, joined with Israel for the purpose of invading Judea, and dividing the spoils between them. This fatal mistake led ultimately to the destruction of both aggressive countries. King Ahaz of Judaea, against the wise and urgent advice of Isaiah, offered allegiance to the Assyrian emperor in turn for protection against his neighbors, selling his countrymen into tribute slavery and despoiling the temple of its treasure for gifts of submission. Thus it happened that while Damascus and Samaria fell before the armies of Assyria, Jerusalem was not approached, nor Judaea invaded, although her king became a vassal of Tiglath-Pileser III.

Under such trying conditions as these Isaiah came into national view and evinced qualities which have given him rank with the great statesmen of the world. Denouncing social wrongs, he was soon drawn into the affairs of the state. Taking no part in the politics of his day, he stood steadfastly for fidelity to the ideals of his race and faith. He appreciated the position that his country ought to occupy, knowing well that as a political power she could not hope to cope with even the secondary nations around her. Only by holding herself aloof from material considerations, and clinging tenaciously to the religious principles earlier evolved, could she come safely through the critical times encompassing her. Isaiah taught that it was for Judah to purge her worship of idolatrous practices which had drifted into it and to go forward with unfaltering faith in the ultimate dominance of right over wrong, justice over injustice. However he spoke to deaf ears, for the ideals for which he stood, the moderate measures for which he pleaded, were unpopular with the people at this time.

For some years Judaea paid her tribute, thankful to be left undisturbed. Gradually a party sprang up which opposed the tribute payment, and during the reign of Hezekiah its adherents became numerous enough to control the policy of their nation. Babylonia was secretly planning a revolt which she desired to make general; accordingly ambassadors were dispatched to the court of Hezekiah—ostensibly to congratulate him on his recent recovery, but really to win him to this revolt, and to estimate the resources of his kingdom. About 702 B. C. all was ripe for the planned revolt, and Assyrian officials were refused the tribute. Sargon was dead and it was not expected that his son would prove so successful a warrior as he had been. But no sooner had news of the revolt reached Sennacherib than he pushed west, and reached the coast before the allies were prepared. Meeting them separately, they quickly melted away before his disciplined troops. Cities of Phœnicia and the Philistines surrendered, and armies spread into the valleys of Judaea, surrounding Jerusalem itself. Hezekiah was terrified into offering heavy tribute, stripping the temple of its remaining ornaments to provide the sum exacted by the emperor as the price of peace. Cities around about were being laid waste and their inhabitants carried into captivity.

In spite of the booty sent him, Sennacherib felt that his victory over Jerusalem was incomplete, and turning to meet an Egyptian relief force approaching Judaea from the south, Sennacherib sent word to Hezekiah that, unless the city gates swung open to him on his return, he would storm its walls.

It had been a grievous matter to provide the treasure already required by the Assyrian, and consternation filled Jerusalem, where little hope of holding out against the veteran troops could longer be entertained. With characteristic calm, Isaiah declared that deliverance for Zion would be forth-coming, and he took occasion to bring home to the people their deep corruption and idolatrous wanderings, while safety for them lay in devotion to Jehovah. For once the terrified Hebrews were ready to harken to any counsel that carried with it a promise of hope.

The fate of Sennacherib's army is well known: how encamped in a fever-breeding swamp, it was stricken in a night. The few who escaped the plague, set out at once on a homeward march, and Jerusalem was left unmolested. As was their custom, the Hebrews attributed their escape to direct intervention of Jehovah in their behalf. The beautiful poem of Byron touching the incident, expresses well their convictions:

Destruction of Sennacherib.

The Assyrian came down like the wolf on the fold,
And his cohorts were gleaming in purple and gold;
And the sheen of their spears was like stars on the sea,
When the blue waves roll nightly on deep Galilee.

Like the leaves of the forest when summer is green,
That host with their banners at sun-set was seen;
Like the leaves of the forest when autumn hath blown,
That host on the morrow lay withered and strewn.

For the angel of death spread his wings on the blast,
And breathed in the face of the foe as he passed;
And the eyes of the sleepers waxed deadly and chill,
And their hearts but once heaved—and forever grew still.

And there lay the steed with his nostril all wide,
But through it there rolled not the breath of his pride;
And the foam of his gasping lay white on the turf,
And cold as the spray of the rock beating surf.

And there lay the rider, distorted and pale,
With the dew on his brow and the rust on his mail;
And the tents were all silent, the banners alone,
The lances unlifted, the trumpet unblown.

And the widows of Asshur are loud in their wail,
And the idols are broke in the temple of Baal;
And the might of the Gentile, unsmote by the sword,
Hath melted like snow in the glance of the Lord!

—Byron.

Hezekiah was so affected by his marvellous deliverance, that he listened to the voice of Isaiah throughout the remainder of his days, and instigated both social and religious reforms. These were so radical that ere long a reaction set in. All religious practices were again tolerated and Isaiah and his followers were forbidden to preach to the people. This forced the prophet to give permanency to his messages by writing them down for future generations. It was now that the book of Deuteronomy was produced, known later as the Book of Law. Many of the rules therein laid down had cause for being in the conditions of the times. For example, every locality had possessed its own peculiar form of sacrifice and its own priesthood. To insure regularity of worship it was now provided that religious festivals should be solemnized only at the temple of Jerusalem, which city should be the religious center of the land. When in the time of Josiah another period of religious reform set in, this Book of Law, or Deuteronomy, was discovered in the temple where it had lain unnoticed. This gave occasion for a complete overturning of social and religious customs. As in previous periods of prosperity, the Hebrews had sunk into reckless extravagances and hopeless poverty; into idolatrous worship and gross immorality. The reforms instituted by Josiah were designed to recall the masses to paths outlined for them by their greatest teachers and prophets.

"The full significance of this sweeping innovation can be appreciated only by a comparison with the practices which it supplanted. Hitherto sacrifices appear to have been offered anywhere and by any one; in fact, every animal slain was regarded as shared with the deity. At every town there was a *high place* to which the people went, not only on feast days, but whenever they wished, through the priest, to have a disputed case settled, or to ascertain the divine will respecting their private matter. Religion entered into all their life. The enactments of Deuteronomy swept away the high places, placed a ban upon private sacrifice, and restricted all offerings to the Temple. A sharp distinction was thereby drawn between the laity and the priests, between secular and holy things. Religion henceforth became something formal, above and apart, rather than in all which concerned the nation or individual. Conventionality took the place of the old freedom and joyousness which had so often degenerated into laxness. The end desired by the reformers was attained. The narrowing of religion saved it from the shallowness of heathenism. The Jehovah who was worshipped in the Temple with jealously guarded forms was not in danger of being degraded to a level with the surrounding deities. That which henceforth constituted the Jewish church was divorced from the state, and so survived the downfall of the nation. Unfortunately the narrowing process did not cease after the crisis was past, so that its later effects were deplorable; but, measured in the light of existing circumstances, the reformation of Josiah marks the beginning of that movement which ultimately resulted in the complete elimination of the practical heathenism which had long threatened the extinction of the pure worship of Jehovah."[1]

After the fall of Nineveh, Egyptian forces attempted to cross Palestine on their way to the east. Their progress was forbidden by the Judean king. In the battle which ensued Josiah was slain. This has been called the "most tragic event

[1] Hist. of the Hebrew People: Vol. II, 180.

in Hebrew history." In the crude judgment of his day, the masses regarded his death as punishment for the destruction of the high places throughout the land. These were re-established, and for the moment it seemed that all the results of the late reformation were swept away.

Egypt held Judah in tribute for three or four years. Then Babylonia defeated the Egyptian army and appropriated its conquests for the new Chaldean empire.

About 597 B. C., tribute having been refused Nebuchadnezzar, he marched against Jerusalem and took the flower of her people into captivity. Those who were left foolishly planned a second revolt. Jeremiah filled the place once occupied by Isaiah, and he denounced the folly of the popular party with great force, vividly picturing the ruin a revolt would cause. His very life was in danger because of the boldness of his counsel, and at times he was held prisoner. Shortly again the armies of Babylonia stood before the walls of Jerusalem. The great king remembered the history of centuries wherein the resources of Assyria and Babylonia had been squandered in holding the western states. He resolved to settle the matter for all time, and the city of Jerusalem was utterly laid waste, while its inhabitants were for the most part deported to Babylonia. Jeremiah was left free to go wherever he chose, and he remained with the poor peasants who were left to till the soil. Shortly after the stricken band migrated to Egypt where they soon lost their identity.

After the fall of Jerusalem in 586 B. C., the perpetuation of the Hebrew faith was left solely to those thousands of captives who had been sent to Babylon. Of all who had peopled the fair land of Israel and the hills of Judah, they alone remained to hold fast the inheritances of their fathers and to preserve the ancient faith. During the seventy years of their captivity it was the remembrance of their once proud nation and beloved Jerusalem, together with the hope of again returning to its hills, that sustained those stricken hearts and gave them courage. Living as much as possible to themselves, they held to their peculiar customs and in some ways were not materially changed by the enforced exile. However their religious conceptions underwent a marked change, and the experiences of the exile itself brought them finally into a fuller realization of the faith they had long followed blindly.

DESCRIPTION OF ILLUSTRATIONS

IN PART L

Distant View of the Pyramids.

This road leading from Cairo to the Pyramids is often spoken of as the "high road." Were it not built up in this way, communication would be cut off during the period of the inundation.

Camels, "ships of the desert," are commonly used in Egypt. Arabs populate the land and are clamorous in their demands for coins from travelers.

Great Pyramid, Sphinx and Temple of Armachis.

The great Pyramids had stood approximately 800 years when Abraham first came into the Delta; they had existed approximately 1500 years when Moses led the Israelites out of the land of bondage. The largest of the three is indeed stupendous, its base covering thirteen acres. In the foreground of the picture is seen the ruins of the Temple of Armachis.

Like the Pyramids, the Sphinx has stood wrapped in mysterious silence these thousand years. The form of the Sphinx was very common in ancient Egypt, it being a symbolic representation of the king. The body of the lion symbolized his strength, or power; the human face was a portrait of the monarch. Shifting sands have accumulated to the breast of the body—said to be 140 feet long. Of the huge proportions one may judge from the fact that should a man stand upon the ear of the Sphinx his hand could not reach the top of the head. A little chapel of comparatively recent date has been placed between the paws of the lion.

Tourists Scaling the Great Pyramid.

The Great Pyramid was originally covered with blocks of the hardest granite. This casing was removed by the Mohammedans for use in building the mosque of Cairo. Thus removed, the blocks of building stone of which the huge pile is for the most part composed, were left exposed. Laid down in the form of steps, tourists today are able to climb to the very top. To be sure, some of these steps are shoulder high, but with much pulling by guides in front and some pushing from those behind, one may ascend in about half an hour. The splendid view over the valley and neighboring desert amply repay one for the discomforts of the climb.

Dromos (Columns) and Second Pylon (Gateway) Temple of Karnak.

The great temple of Karnak was begun by Seti I., and was enlarged by many succeeding Pharaohs. An avenue of rams led to the gateway, which was the last portion to be completed. Crossing a court, one came at length to the temple itself.

The figures and letters carved on the stone may be plainly seen in this picture.

Beautiful Island of Philae and the Nile.

This templed island of Philae, known sometimes as "the pearl of Egypt," lies uppermost of a group of islands forming the first cataract. Isis was the local deity and to her a temple was built in remote times. Recently a great dam has been constructed near Philae to insure a larger supply of water for the valley. It has been estimated that $13,000,000 will accrue to Egypt annually by this means, but the island of Philae, with its beautiful temple, is thereby doomed. Indignant protests have been made from lovers of the beautiful in many lands, but the English government has shown itself more determined to insure the prompt payment of interest upon its bonds than to preserve monuments of antiquity.

Harem Window and Court.

As is well known, in all Mohammedan countries, women pass their lives in closest seclusion. Their quarters are provided in the upper story of the house, the windows being small indeed. Seldom going out, living their years in idleness, it is small wonder that these unfortunate creatures often resort to intrigues to absorb their interest.

Winged Lion.

These symbolic animals in stone were stationed at the portals of the royal palace and sometimes guarded the palaces of the wealthy in Assyria. The lion's body symbolized strength, the wings of the eagle, swiftness; the human head, human intelligence. It was believed that evil spirits would pause before such emblems of majesty, nor dare to enter.

Musicians and Attendants in the Garden of Asshurbanipal.

After the war was over, the king, satiated with booty and slaughter, sought the quieter pleasures of the banquet. This was frequently served in the royal garden, while musicians dispensed sweet strains of music. To make more animated the joyous occasion, the head of the defeated king or general was sometimes suspended from a nearby tree, so that the Assyrian ruler might exult over his own triumph as he drank his wine.

Damascus Sword-maker.

The swords of Damascus have always been famous. The ancient sword-makers understood a secret process of tempering steel which rendered it very pliable and at the same time imparted to it astonishing strength.

The River Jordan.

The word *Jordan* means "the down-comer," and truly a river which drops 3,000 feet in a course of 150 miles is indeed a "descender." In the spring the stream is brown and muddy, heavily charged as it is with debris from the mountains. Ships never journey far up or down the river. Below the level of the sea, the climate is hot and sultry and the region full of malaria.

Harbor of Jappa.

Jappa is the old Joppa of Bible times. It is almost the only approach to a seaport that Palestine can claim, yet even here large boats must remain out in deep waters, and travelers for the Holy Land who enter in this way must climb down the side of the steamer and be rowed to shore in small boats. The sea is usually very rough at this point, adding to the general discomfort of the situation for travelers.

Roses of Sharon.

Palestine is beautiful with flowers in the spring. Narcissus, the "roses of Sharon," and Iris, "the lilies of the valley," grow in profusion over the foothills.

STUDY GUIDE

THE LAND OF THE PYRAMIDS

"The plainest row of books that cloth or paper ever covered is more significant of refinement than the most elaborately carved sideboard."

H.W. Beecher

LIFE AND LITERATURE OF EGYPT

Each year the number of travelers to the old world grows larger. It was once unusual for the tourist to make his way to Egypt—the Nile valley lay outside the regular beaten track. Those who undertook the journey, however, returned with so much to tell that others were induced to follow and today the majority of those who travel extensively include the Land of the Pyramids as a matter of course.

The amount of benefit we derive from travel depends very largely upon the amount of general knowledge and information we have gathered concerning the country visited. Those who are unfamiliar with the wonderful civilization that developed in Egypt before the first book of the Old Testament was written, see huge piles of stone still retaining the form of pyramids and heaps of ruined temples; they see wide reaches of desert and a river; Arabs inhabit the land and the idle extort money from the visitor. These are the main features of the story. The one who knows something of this ancient country sees much more. His fancy repeoples the valley with its former inhabitants. Ruins rise again and he reconstructs in his imagination temples and tombs. The intruding Arabs disappear together with English officials, and for a brief while he lives in the past.

Busied with cares and responsibilities or with manifold interests, the moments are few wherein the average person can review and extend his knowledge of history, literature and art. For this reason the following outlined reading is offered with the hope of meeting present-day conditions. It is not expected that the whole subject shall be covered at once; rather, for years one may find it a basis for continued study and profit.

It is suggested that study clubs and circles will find this a convenient foundation for satisfactory work, and beyond all question High School students will be greatly aided by the matter contained in the text books and by suggestive questions in the outlines.

Introductory: Prehistoric Man
1. What is the meaning of the term *prehistoric,* and how have people found out about conditions existing in *prehistoric times*? Part I, xvii.
2. Note the slow stages of progress made in the three general prehistoric *ages.* I, xiv.
3. For what reasons has it nearly always been true that civilization has developed in the first place along streams and sea-coasts? I, xiv.
4. To what extend did the discovery of fire contribute to the welfare of man? I, xvi.
5. Note how the resources of countries have controlled the kinds of dwellings of mankind in different ages. I, xviii.
6. What conditions first led to the cultivation of plants? I, 1.
7. What have been the motives leading to a development of primitive art? I, 5.
8. *Hide pictures* were made in what way? I, 8.
9. How were primitive men led to conceive of a future existence? I, 8.
10. What heritage did prehistoric ages leave for future generations? I, 111.

I. Political Life in Egypt
1. Compare the antiquity of Egypt with that of other lands. Part I, 20-22.
2. Consult the map to see the location of Egypt and its position relative to other lands.
3. What is the significance of the saying: "Egypt is the gift of the Nile?" I, 24-26.
4. Is it true that the temperament of nations is influenced by geographical conditions? Did this apply in the case of the Egyptians? I, 27.
5. What is the most valuable source of present-day knowledge concerning ancient Egypt? I, 31.

6. To what extent can we depend upon the writings of Herodotus? I, 31.
7. How many acres of ground are covered by the base of the Great Pyramid? Note how many problems are left still unsettled in regard to these huge piles. I, 39.
8. Why was Thebes better adapted than Memphis would have been for the capital of the later kingdom? I, 43-45.
9. Read Herodotus' description of the Labyrinth. I, 48.
10. What conditions within Egypt made it possible for foreign chiefs to invade during the Fourteenth Dynasty? I, 51.
11. Note that by the expulsion of the Hyksos, Egypt became a military power. I, 55.
12. Read of the interesting expedition undertaken by Queen Hatasu's subjects to the land of Punt. I, chapter VI.
13. Why did the religious crusade attempted by Amenhotep IV. fail? I, 68.
14. Who were the great pharaohs of the later kingdom? I, 72-77.
15. How were the priests of Amon finally able to seize the throne of Egypt? I, 81.
16. What about the later fortunes of the country? I, 83.

II. Social Life

1. What similarities can one find between modern life and conditions prevailing in ancient Egypt, as described in Part I, 85?
2. What were the popular sports among the Egyptians? I, 96.
3. What light is shed upon the life of the Egyptian farmer by tomb pictures? I, 100.
4. For an account of an old-time market, read I, 106, and following.
5. What practical view of education was held by the Nile-dwellers? I, 113.
6. Did these people worship the sun? I, 120.
7. What was their theory about the Apis bull? I, 120.
8. How was the spirit of the Nile appeased? I, 123.
9. For what reason was food placed in tombs? I, 124.
10. Did the people have any part in temple worship? I, 128.

11. Note that a religion that became degraded was nevertheless capable of being given an exalted interpretation. I, 131.
12. For an account of embalming see I, 138.
13. What part did magic play in the care of the dead? I, 139.
14. There were three essential parts to an Egyptian tomb. Note the uses of each. I, 140.
15. What was the original significance of the scarab? I, 141.
16. Why were cemeteries in the Nile valley always infested with robbers? I, 143.
17. When were excavations systematically begun in Egypt? I, 144.
18. Read the accounts of two important discoveries in recent years. I, 146-148.

III. Art and Architecture

1. What materials were used for the construction of private dwellings? Part I, 87.
2. What substitutes were used in boat-building, etc., for wood, in a land where wood was scarce? I, 103.
3. How can we reconstruct the general plan of the Egyptian temple today? I, 126.
4. Read the description of the wonderful temple of Karnak. I, 69.
5. For its appearance today, see description on page 159.
6. The grotto temple of Abou Simbel is very famous. Note what is said of it on page 78, I.
7. For what purpose was the great Sphinx probably constructed? I, 130.
8. Why did Egyptian drawing remain so rigid? I, 133.
9. Distinguish between the conventional and realistic schools of art. I, 133.
10. Did the Egyptians understand proportion? I, 134.
11. What uses did sculpture serve? I, 135.
12. What special designs were characteristic of decorative work in the Nile valley? I, 135-137.

IV. Literature

1. Were the Egyptians as a whole a literary people? Part I, 115.

2. For what reason are ancient folk-songs interesting and valuable to us today? I, 116.
3. What is the oldest book in the world? I, 17.
4. Read selections from it as rendered in English, I, 164, and following.
5. The Book of the Dead was important to the living and indispensable to the dead. A portion of it is given in I, 168, and following.
6. Read the Negative Confession made by the soul, I, 169.
7. Magic was firmly believed in by the ancient Egyptian. This is borne out by the Tales of the Magicians, popular with the Nile-dwellers. I, 171.
8. The Song of the Harper gives us an example of the song frequently sung for the entertainment of pharaohs and nobles. I, 179.

V. Education in Antiquity

1. What very practical view did the Egyptian hold as to education and its value? Part I, 113.
2. Are there people today who seem to have the same attitude toward the subject? Are they few or many?
3. Read *The Praise of Learning*, I, 112.
4. Were the majority of Egyptian children given more than the most elementary training?
5. What vocations lay open to the youth who was proficient? I, 113.
6. What made the acquiring of an education tedious work? I, 114.
7. What peculiarity in the matter of computing by fractions has been noted?

VI. Religion

1. In general, what was the religion of Egypt? I, 119.
2. What was the most degrading feature of this religion? I, 120
3. What motives led the Egyptians to worship the Nile? I, 123
4. Was this religion capable of an exalted interpretation? I, 131. Compare the hymn quoted in I, 132, with similar Hebrew hymns. Do you think that the average congregation would distinguish it from those frequently read during service?

5. Amenhotep IV attempted a religious reform. What was the nature of it? The result? I, 68.

VII. Home-Life

1. Were the years of the Egyptian mother busily filled? I, 91.
2. What evidences have we that children in ancient Egypt were much like those of today? I, 92.
3. Why were children particularly desired? Was this true also of the ancient Hebrews? I, 93.
4. What is said of the clothing worn by women in ancient Egypt? I, 94
5. What fabrics were used and by whom were they made?
6. Were Egyptian women fond of jewelry?

IX. Books for Further Reading

- A History of Egypt, Breasted. Best political work. 1 volume.
- A History of Egypt, Petrie. Compiled from evidences of tombs. Not useful for general reader. 6 volumes.
- Ancient Egypt, Rawlinson. Useful; not complete. Story of the Nation series. 1 volume.
- Life in Ancient Egypt, Erman. Excellent social history. 1 volume.

GUIDE BOOKS

- A Thousand Miles up the Nile, Edwards. Popular book written some time ago.
- Pyramids and Progress, Ward. Good for present conditions.
- Manual of Egyptian Archaeology, Maspero. Authoritative. Author long curator at Cairo Museum.

EGYPTIAN STORIES

- Uarda, Ebers.
- The Egyptian Princess, Ebers. Ebers made a thorough study of Egyptian life and wrote several good stories of Ancient Egypt.

OTHER BOOKS

There are several works of great merit for those who wish to make an extended study of Egyptian life. Maspero has written a work of several volumes well illustrated from finds at present in the Egyptian museums.

Petrie has spent many years in the Nile valley and has written several books. Ward was a well-illustrated volume on the Scarab.

Within the last few years several novels have been given a setting in ancient Egypt. Seldom are they true to facts as revealed by scientific study.

BABYLONIA AND HER NEIGHBORS

"Books are the first and the last, the most home-felt, the most heart-felt of all our enjoyments." --Hazlitt.

BABYLONIA AND HER NEIGHBORS: ASSYRIANS, MEDES, PERSIANS, PHOENICIANS

The civilizations of Mesopotamia flourished four thousand years ago and have long since disappeared. Shifting sand and desert wastes characterize the very sites of ancient Babylon and Nineveh; even in the days of Greek ascendancy, travelers passed over the region, and did not know that they were treating over heaps of buried cities. In comparatively recent times excavators have set to work to recover whatever the earth held secret concerning the past and their discoveries have astonished the world. Royal palaces have been unearthed; colossal winged-bulls, alabaster friezes and tiled floors. More interesting still, the library of Asshur-banipal was found, with its priceless tablets.

In view of such evidences of a culture so remote in point of time, the minds of men have been stimulated to find out who were the people thus early enlightened, what did they achieve and especially, what did they bequeath the posterity. Americans have been generous in making contributions to carry on this work of excavation and students of one of our leading universities have gone eagerly into the field and dug for hidden remains. Those of us whose lives fall in different ways can at least keep abreast with the revelations of our age and by making the most of brief periods of leisure, may become familiar with the results of these undertakings.

I. Political Life
1. Compare the antiquity of Egyptian and Babylonian civilizations. Part I, 202.
2. What American university has carried on extensive excavations recently in the Tigris-Euphrates valleys? I, 210.
3. How has the Old Testament stimulated efforts made for the recovery of forgotten cities? I, 211.

4. To which one of our states may ancient Babylonia be likened in the matter of soil, climate, etc.? Assyria? I, 215-216.
5. The first great king of Babylonia was Hammurabi. For an understanding of his achievements, see Chapter V, I, 232; also Chapter XI, 276.
6. Under what circumstances were nations placed under tribute in antiquity? I, 241.
7. The Assyrians were great warriors. For accounts of their relentless conquests see I, 238-242.
8. What measures did Assyrian kings take to make their conquests lasting? I, 246.
9. Compare the Hebrew and Assyrian versions of Sennacherib's famous retreat. I, 250-255.
10. What Assyrian king was a great book-collector? I, 259.
11. What people finally dealt out to the Assyrians the same destruction that they had so often meted out to others? I, 262.
12. What reasons prompted the Babylonians to destroy Jerusalem and take thousands of Hebrews into captivity? I, 266.
13. What king permitted them to return and rebuild their city? I, 268.
14. Who were the Medes and where did they live? I, 328.
15. What training did the Persians value? I, 334.
16. Compare the treatment of captives by Persians and Assyrians. I, 338.
17. What inheritances did the Greeks receive from Babylonians, Assyrians and Persians? I, 357.
18. How did the very nature of Syria determine that it should never become the home of a united people? I, 372.
19. Phoenicia—Land of Palms—lay north of Palestine. Note its appearance, size, climate, etc. I, 378.
20. How did the city of Sidon receive its name? I, 380.
21. Is it probable that any satisfactory history of the Phoenicians will ever be written? I, 381.
22. How successfully did the people of Tyre resist the attacks of Alexander the Great? I, 385-388.

II. Social Life

1. Compare the Babylonian and Assyrian in appearance and character. Part I, 270.
2. What position was accorded to women in Babylonia? I, 274.
3. Compare the clothing in vogue in Mesopotamia with that commonly seen today. I, 293.
4. For what reason did men wear tiny cylinders attached to their wrists? From what were these made? I, 294.
5. The chief articles of food were what? I, 295.
6. What were the favorite recreations of Assyrian nobles? I, 295.
7. In what particulars were the religions of early Hebrews and Assyrians similar? I, 310.
8. Aside from religious considerations, what role did the temple fill in Babylonia? I, 313.
9. The Chaldeans were firm believers in magic. Note some of their charms. I, 314-316.
10. What was the condition of slavery in Mesopotamia? I, 317.
11. What rates of interest were charged here? I, 322.
12. What prevented the progress of medical science? I, 323.
13. How did the standards of living held by Persians differ from those of this age? I, 346.
14. From what does our word *damask* come, and what was its original significance? I, 377.
15. How is it supposed that the Phoenicians happened upon the discovery of glass-making? I, 401.

III. Literature

1. Of what general subjects did the Babylonian literature treat? Part I, 283-287.
2. In what manner were written communications prepared and transmitted in Mesopotamia? I, 290.
3. Note that the Flood legend was common to all Semitic peoples. I, 209.
4. Read the Chaldean version of this well-known story. I, 361.
5. Zoroaster was a great religious teacher. Read the prayer always included in the Parsi service. I, 371d.

6. Did literature flourish in Phoenicia? I, 404.
7. What part did these people have in the early diffusion of learning? I, 404.

IV. Art and Architecture
1. What building materials were available in Mesopotamia? Part I, 272.
2. After what fashion were houses built? I, 273.
3. What purpose did the ziggurat serve? I, 300.
4. In what ways were palaces made beautiful? I, 301.
5. What was the significance of the winged bulls and lions so often found in Assyria? I, 303-304.
6. The walls of Babylon were among the wonders of the ancient world. How were they constructed according to Herodotus? I, 304.
7. What were the so-called Hanging Gardens? I, 305.
8. Enameled tiles were used for what purpose in Babylonian buildings? I, 320.

V. Education in Antiquity
1. To what extent was education general in Babylonia? Part I, 288.
2. What evidences have we that a knowledge of writing was common in this country?
3. Read the two old letters translated from Assyrian tablets. I, 289.
4. How were these letters conveyed? I, 290.
5. Was education given prominence by the Phoenicians? I, 404.
6. What kind of training was considered essential for Persian youths? I, 347.

VI. Religion
1. Note that the early inhabitants of Babylonia were nature worshippers—as were all primitive peoples. I, 307
2. Did the Babylonians worship the sun? Can you understand why all early people have worshipped the great illuminating body? The American Indians greeted the rising sun with a hymn.
3. Contrast the religion of Assyria with that of Babylonia and account for the differences. I, 310

4. The Assyrian religion was similar to that of what other ancient people? I, 310.
5. Was the worship of Mesopotamia conducive to high morality and noble ideals? I, 314.
6. Note that little is known of Zoroaster and probably in the first instance he was simply a man who went about doing and teaching good. It is natural for mankind to exalt the personalities of its seers until sometimes they cease to be regarded as human. I, 350.
7. What two spirits were recognized by Zoroaster's followers? I, 352. Remember these two conflicting forces have been fundamental in all religions.
8. Note that while several contemporary peoples looked with abhorrence upon the human sacrifices offered by Phoenecians, each had passed through the same stage of development itself. I, 406. The study of comparative religions makes clear the truth that men living in remote lands and in ages widely separated have felt the same needs and have met them in similar ways in their upward strivings.

VII. Home-Life
1. What degree of freedom was enjoyed by Babylonian women? Was this true of all classes? I, 274.
2. What is said of child life in Mesopotamia? I, 275.
3.

Books for Further Reading

HISTORICAL

- History of Babylonia and Assyria, Robt. W. Rogers; Eaton & Mains. 2 volumes.
- Babylonian and Assyrian Laws, Contracts, etc., C.H.W. Johns; Scribner.
- History, Prophecy, and the Monuments, McCurdy.
- History of Ancient Peoples, Boughton.
- History of Babylonians and Assyrians, Goodspeed; Scribner.

SOCIAL HISTORY

- Life in Ancient Egypt and Assyria, Maspero; Appleton.
- Babylonians and Assyrians—Life and Custons, Sayce; Scribner.
- Assyria, its Princes, Priests and People, Sayce.
- Stories of Ancient Peoples, Emma Arnold; American Book.

HEBREW LIFE AND LITERATURE

"It is nearly an axiom that people will never be better than the books they read."
                                                                Dr. Alonzo Potter

THE ANCIENT HEBREWS: THEIR LIFE AND LITERATURE

So long as records of the past remain and people read them, the wanderings of the early Hebrews, their triumphs and back-slidings, their beautiful songs and poems, their prophecies, their wisdom, literature and their mysticism will fascinate the intelligent. Other ancient peoples were more successful in matters of conquest, government, industry and the fine arts, but none equaled them in evolving a religion of purity and in setting forth religious truths in a literature of great variety. It is a fact to be lamented that while the literatures of several nations are frequently studied, the literature of the Hebrews is seldom in comparison appreciated. Even when rendered into English, wherein much of their beauty is lost, these writings of the Old Testament have a wonderful imagery and forcefulness.

Aside from all religious considerations, in these days when travelers of all Christian nations find Palestine accessible to them, every well-informed reader should have some familiarity with this celebrated land and some knowledge concerning the peculiar people who once inhabited it. The following outlined reading is offered with the hope of aiding and stimulating such a desire.

I. Physical Geography of Palestine
   1. Refer to the map and get the location of Palestine clearly in your mind.
   2. How large is this celebrated land? Part I, 408.
   3. What six distinct land features are found there? I, 409.
   4. What was the meaning of the word *Sharon*? I, 409.
   5. The "roses of Sharon" and the "lilies of the valley" are often mentioned in the Bible. What flowers are meant? I, 409.
   6. What striking contrasts of climate are comprised in this limited area? I, 416.

7. Is the soil productive or not? What is its nature? I, 417.
8. What does the word *Jordan* mean? I, 412.
9. What place does it hold in Hebrew history? I, 413.
10. What facts are peculiar about the Dead Sea? I, 413.
11. Read the contrast drawn in Deuteronomy between Egypt and Canaan. I, 419.
12. What changes were wrought in the Hebrews by their occupation of such a land? I, 420.
13. Is Palestine beautiful or not, today? I, 421.

II. Political History

1. What sources have we for a study of Hebrew history, aside from biblical books? Part I, 426, 433.
2. The Hebrews found the Promised Land occupied by people whom they called Canaanites; the country they called Canaan. I, 434.
3. What part did Moses take in guiding the Children of Israel thither? I, 436.
4. What biblical book gives earliest pictures of these people? I, 441.
5. Three stories from this book are retold here. I, 443-447. Turn to the Old Testament and read the others.
6. How far had the Hebrews progressed before the close of the Era of Judges? I, 448-453.
7. What motives led them to choose kings to rule over them? I, 453.
8. Read the story of Saul. I, 454-459. This story has been the theme for great poems and musical compositions.
9. In what sense was Jerusalem truly the *City of David*? I, 460.
10. How much was accomplished by David in welding the nation together? I, 461.
11. Compare Solomon with Israel's earlier kings. I, 463.
12. To understand the peculiar wisdom for which Solomon was famed, read the little poem entitled *King Solomon and the Bees*. I, 465.
13. What caused the division of the kingdom? I, 469.
14. Compare the resources of the two divisions. I, 470.
15. Read concerning the fall of Samaria and Judaea. I, 475.

III. Manners and Customs

1. What were the teraphim? Part I, 448.
2. Compare the earliest commandments given to the Hebrews with those commonly known. I, 450.
3. What is meant by the expression: "And the Children of Israel walked through the fire"? I, 450.

IV. Literature

1. How was Hebrew literature affected by the physical nature of Palestine? Part I, 423.
2. What well-known psalms plainly illustrate this? I, 423-425.
3. What is the meaning of the word *Bible*? I, 428.
4. When was the Talmud written and what does it contain? I, 431.

V. Religion

1. Did the Hebrews once worship many gods? I, 448.
2. What made the Hebrews a peculiar people, in the opinion of certain modern scholars? I, 449.
3. Compare the earliest Roman commandments of the Hebrews with the ten commonly known. I, 450. This comparison enables one to somewhat appreciate the great changes through which this people, like others, passed.
4. What is the significance of the phrase frequently found in the Old Testament: "And the Children of Israel passed through the fire"? I, 450.
5. What message did Amos bring his people? I, 472.
6. Who taught that Jehovah was God of the whole world—not merely of the Hebrews? I, 473.

NOTE: It should be remembered that the Hebrews, starting with the same primitive beginnings in the matter of worship, gradually evolved a pure and exalted faith which far transcended the religious beliefs of their contemporaries.

Books for Further Reading

HISTORICAL

- Historical Geography of the Holy Land, Geo. Adams Smith; Amstrong.
- History of the People of Israel, Cornill; Open Court Pub.
- Short History of the Hebrews, Ottley; Macmillan.
- History of the Hebrew People, Kent; Scribner. 2 volumes.

SOCIAL

- Social Life of the Hebrews, Edward Day; Scribner.

HEBREW LITERATURE

- Modern Reader's Bible, including all biblical books, Ed. Moulton.
- Life and Literature of the Ancient Hebrews, Lyman Abbott Houghton, Mifflin.
- Short Intro. to Literature of the Bible, Richard Moulton; Heath.
- Literary Study of the Bible, Richard Moulton; Heath.

OTHER BOOKS

- What is Christianity? Adolph Harnack; Putnam.
- History of Apostolic Church, Oliver Thatcher; Houghton, Mifflin.
- Out-of-Doors in the Holy Land, Henry Van Dyke.

Made in the USA
Middletown, DE
31 August 2025